LISP

SECOND EDITION

Patrick Henry Winston
Massachusetts Institute of Technology

Berthold Klaus Paul Horn
Massachusetts Institute of Technology

ADDISON-WESLEY PUBLISHING COMPANY
Reading, Massachusetts • Menlo Park, California
London • Amsterdam • Don Mills, Ontario • Sydney

Library of Congress Cataloging in Publication Data

Winston, Patrick Henry.
   LISP.

   Includes bibliographical references and index.
   1. LISP (Computer programming language). I. Horn, Berthold. II. Title.
QA76.L23W56   1984   001.64'24   84-9328
ISBN 0-201-08372-8

Reproduced by Addison-Wesley from camera-ready copy supplied and approved
by the authors.

ABCDEFGHIJ-AL-8987654

Preface

This book is about LISP, a programming language that takes its name from List Programming.

Until recently, the LISP programming language appeared to be breaking up into many dialects, with no single dialect dominating the others. Fortunately, however, a powerful group of world-class programming-language experts, representing many key institutions, have designed COMMON LISP, a happy amalgam of the features in previous LISPs. We believe COMMON LISP has the beauty to be a worthy standard, and perhaps more importantly, we believe COMMON LISP has the necessary documentation and commercial support to be a real standard, widely available.

Consequently, COMMON LISP is the dialect of LISP used in this second edition. People who have access to MACLISP or INTERLISP, but not to COMMON LISP, should have little trouble adapting.

By switching to COMMON LISP, we have simultaneously made the material useful to a much larger audience, and we have improved on the first edition, taking advantage of certain LISP features we dared not use before. For the cognoscenti, here are the most conspicuous of those improvements:

- We introduce the backquote mechanism, greatly increasing the transparency of macro definition and of PRINT arguments.

- We introduce structures via DEFSTRUCT.

- We introduce the generalized assignment function, SETF, for properties, structures, and arrays.

- We use lexical scoping as the default, with dynamic scoping in reserve.

- We eliminate PROG constructions, replacing them with DO, LET, and ordinary recursion, as appropriate.

- We eliminate FEXPRs, replacing them with optional-argument constructions and macros, as appropriate.

Of course, we have taken advantage of the opportunity to improve the book in other ways.

- We have introduced discussions of procedure abstraction and data abstraction.
- We have added an introduction to message passing and flavors in the chapter on object-centered programming.
- We have completely redone the chapters on mathematical examples, natural-language interfaces, symbolic pattern matching, and rule-based expert systems.

Moreover, the book is better matched to the companion book, *Artificial Intelligence* (*Second Edition*):

- The block-movement system, introduced here in chapter 13, is described in chapter 2 of *Artificial Intelligence*.
- Search, introduced here in chapter 11, is covered in chapter 4 of *Artificial Intelligence*.
- Fancy control ideas, introduced here in chapter 16, are covered in chapter 5 of *Artificial Intelligence*.
- Rule-based expert systems, introduced in chapter 14, are covered in chapter 6 of *Artificial Intelligence*.
- The frames idea, introduced in chapter 22, is treated in chapter 8 of *Artificial Intelligence*.
- Transition trees for natural language analysis, described here in chapters 19, 20, and 21, are covered in chapter 9 of *Artificial Intelligence*.
- Feature-space oriented pattern recognition, in chapter 10, is treated lightly in chapter 10 of *Artificial Intelligence*.

P.H.W.
B.K.P.H.

Acknowledgments

The cover painting and the drawings are by Karen A. Prendergast. The cover design is by Daniel J. Dawson. The book design is by Marie McAdam. Margaret Pinette handled production.

The fonts are Almost Computer Modern. The text was set using TEX, Donald E. Knuth's typesetting system, with help from Daniel C. Brotsky. Boris Katz prepared the index. Priscilla Cobb and Blythe Heepe conquered all the page-layout problems. Dikran Karagueuzian also helped enormously.

Boris Katz and David A. Moon read drafts of this book with great care. In addition, Kent M. Pitman and Gerald R. Barber helped considerably.

Most of our program testing was done using NIL, a superset of COMMON LISP developed at MIT and supplied to us by Glen S. Burke, one of NIL's principal developers. We also used VAX LISP, an implementation of COMMON LISP, developed by Digital Equipment Corporation, and GOLDEN COMMON LISP, a subset of COMMON LISP developed for the IBM Personal Computer and other small machines by Gold Hill Computers, of Cambridge, Massachusetts.

The COMMON LISP standard, on which this book is based, was made possible by the active encouragement of the Defense Advanced Research Projects Agency. In addition, most of the research work described in the examples in the second part of this book was sponsored by the Defense Advanced Research Projects Agency.

Contents

Networks of memory cells represent lists ● CONS builds new list structure by depositing pointers in free cells ● APPEND builds new list structure by copying ● NCONC, RPLACA, RPLACD, and DELETE dangerously alter memory-cell contents ● EQUAL is not the same as EQL ● A keyword alters member to use EQUAL instead of EQL ● Single quote marks are a shorthand form for QUOTE expressions ● Garbage collection reclaims memory cells for the free storage list ●

AREF and SETF are used with arrays ● Binary images are easy to process ● An object can be found using binary image analysis ● Features found in binary images can be used for classification ● Components of a binary image can be labeled in two passes ●

Breadth-first and depth-first searches are basic strategies ● A node queue facilitates depth-first search and breadth-first search ● Best-first search and hill-climbing require sorting ●

It is easy to translate infix notation to prefix ● It is useful to represent sparse matrices as lists of lists ● Roots of numbers can be found using tail recursion ● Representing complex numbers is straightforward ● Roots of algebraic equations can be found easily ●

Part I

Basic LISP

1

Understanding
Symbol
Manipulation

This book is about LISP, a programming language that takes its name from List Programming. The book has two parts, each written to accomplish a particular purpose:

- The purpose of Part One of this book is to introduce the ideas of symbol manipulation and to teach the basics of LISP programming.

- The purpose of Part Two is to demonstrate LISP's muscle and to excite people about what LISP can do.

This brief chapter defines symbol manipulation, explains why LISP is the right symbol-manipulation language to learn, and previews the ideas that will be covered.

Symbol Manipulation Is Like Working with Words and Sentences

Everything in a computer is a string of binary digits, ones and zeros, that everyone calls bits. From one perspective, these binary digits are interpreted as a code for objects called decimal digits. But from another perspective, groups of those same bits can be interpreted as a code for wordlike objects and sentencelike objects.

- In LISP, the fundamental objects formed from bits are wordlike objects called *atoms*.

- Groups of atoms form sentencelike objects called *lists*. Lists themselves can be grouped together to form higher-level lists. Indeed, the ability to form hierarchical groups is of fundamental importance.

- Atoms and lists collectively are called *symbolic expressions*, or more succinctly, *expressions*. Working with symbolic expressions is what symbol manipulation using LISP is about.

A symbol-manipulation program uses symbolic expressions to remember and work with data and procedures, just as people use pencil, paper, and human language to remember and work with data and procedures. A symbol-manipulation program typically has procedures that recognize particular symbolic expressions, tear old ones apart, and assemble new ones.

Here are two examples of symbolic expressions. The parentheses mark where lists begin and end. The first is a description of a structure built out of children's blocks. The second is a description of a certain university.

```
(ARCH (PARTS LINTEL POST1 POST2)
      (LINTEL MUST-BE-SUPPORTED-BY POST1)
      (LINTEL MUST-BE-SUPPORTED-BY POST2)
      (LINTEL A-KIND-OF WEDGE)
      (POST1 A-KIND-OF BRICK)
      (POST2 A-KIND-OF BRICK)
      (POST1 MUST-NOT-TOUCH POST2)
      (POST2 MUST-NOT-TOUCH POST1))

(MIT (A-KIND-OF UNIVERSITY)
     (LOCATION (CAMBRIDGE MASSACHUSETTS))
     (PHONE 253-1000)
     (SCHOOLS (ARCHITECTURE
               BUSINESS
               ENGINEERING
               HUMANITIES
               SCIENCE))
     (FOUNDER (WILLIAM BARTON ROGERS)))
```

Certainly these are not very scary. Both just describe something according to some conventions about how to arrange symbols. Here is another example, this time expressing a rule for determining whether some animal is a carnivore:

```
(RULE IDENTIFY6
      (IF (ANIMAL HAS POINTED TEETH)
          (ANIMAL HAS CLAWS)
          (ANIMAL HAS FORWARD EYES))
      (THEN (ANIMAL IS CARNIVORE)))
```

What we see is just another way of expressing the idea that an animal with pointed teeth, claws, and forward-pointing eyes is probably a carnivore. To use such a rule, a program must take it apart, find the antecedent conditions following the IF, check to see if those antecedents are on a list of believed assertions, and add the consequent conclusion following the THEN to the same list of believed assertions. Using such a rule is an example of symbol manipulation.

Symbol Manipulation Is Needed To Make Computers Intelligent

These days, there is a growing armamentarium of programs that exhibit what most people consider intelligent behavior. Nearly all of these intelligent, or seemingly intelligent, programs are written in LISP. Many have the potential of great practical importance. Here are some examples:

- Expert problem solvers. One of the first LISP programs did calculus problems at the level of university freshmen. Another early program did geometric analogy problems of the sort found in intelligence tests. Since then, newer programs have configured computers, diagnosed infections of the blood, understood electronic circuits, evaluated geological evidence for mineral prospecting, and invented interesting mathematics. All are written in LISP.

- Commonsense reasoning. Much of human thinking seems to involve a small amount of reasoning using a large amount of knowledge. Representing knowledge means choosing a vocabulary of symbols and fixing some conventions for arranging them. Good representations make just the right things explicit. LISP is the language in which most research on representation is done.

- Learning. Much work has been done on the learning of concepts by computer, and certainly most of what has been done also rests on progress in representation. LISP again dominates.

- Natural-language interfaces. There is a growing need for programs that interact with people in English and other natural languages. Full understanding of natural languages by computer is probably a long time off, but practical systems have been built for asking questions about constrained domains ranging from moon rocks, to the ships at sea, to the inventory of a carpet company.

- Education and intelligent support systems. To interact comfortably with computers, people must have computers that know what people know and how to tell them more. No one wants a long-winded explanation once they know a lot. Nor does anyone want a telegramlike explanation when just beginning. LISP-based programs are beginning to make user models by analyzing what the user does. These programs use the models to trim or elaborate explanations.

- Speech and vision. Understanding how people hear and see has proved fantastically difficult. It seems that we do not know enough about how the physical world constrains what ends up on our ear drums and retinas. Nevertheless, progress is being made and much of it is made in LISP, even though a great deal of straight arithmetic-oriented programming is necessary. To be sure, LISP has no special advantages for arithmetic-oriented programming. But at the same time, LISP has no debilitating disadvantages for arithmetic either. This is surprising to some people, because LISP was once molasses slow at such work.

Consequently, people who want to know about computer intelligence at some point need to understand LISP, if their understanding is to be complete. And there are certainly other applications, some of which are again surprising. At least the following deserve mention:

- Computer science education. LISP facilitates procedure abstraction and data abstraction, thereby emphasizing two important points of programming style. Also, LISP is a superb implementation language. Consequently, LISP is a good language with which to build miniature interpreters and compilers for a variety of languages, including LISP itself. These interpreters and compilers help explain important concepts like lexical scoping, dynamic scoping, call by value, and call by reference.

- Systems programming. LISP Machines are modern personal computers programmed from top to bottom in LISP. The operating system, the user utility programs, the compilers, and the interpreters are all written in LISP, with a saving in cost of one or two orders of magnitude.

- Word processing. EMACS is a powerful text editor. Several versions have been written entirely in LISP. Similarly, some text justifiers, programs that arrange text for output on pages, have been written in LISP.

- Symbolic mathematics. The MACSYMA system is a program that enables scientists and engineers to handle mathematical expressions that would defy pencil and paper efforts.

Given all these examples, it is no surprise that the following is accepted by nearly everyone:

- Symbol manipulation is an essential tool. Computer scientists and engineers must know about it.

LISP Is the Right Symbol-Manipulation Language To Learn

There are too many programming languages. Fortunately, however, only a few are for symbol manipulation, and of these LISP is the most used. After LISP is understood, most of the other symbol-manipulation languages are easy to learn.

Why has LISP become the most used language for symbol manipulation, and lately, much more? There is some disagreement. All of the following arguments have adherents:

- The interaction argument. LISP is oriented toward programming at a terminal with rapid response. All procedures and all data can be displayed or altered at will.

- The environment argument. LISP has been used by a community that needed and got the best in editing and debugging tools. For more than two decades, people at the world's largest artificial intelligence centers have created sophisticated computing environments around LISP, making a combination that is unbeatable for writing big, complicated programs.

- The features argument. LISP was designed for symbol manipulation and has been developed for even better symbol manipulation. Consequently, LISP has just the right features.

- The uniformity argument. LISP procedures and LISP data have the same form. One LISP program can use another as data. One LISP program even can create another and use it.

Happily, LISP is an easy language to learn. A few hours of study is enough to understand some amazing programs. Previous exposure to some other programming language is not necessary. Indeed, such experience can be something of a handicap, for there can be a serious danger of developing a bad accent: other languages do things differently, and procedure-by-procedure translation leads to awkward constructions and poor programming practice.

One reason LISP is easy to learn is that its syntax is extremely simple. Curiously, LISP's present syntax has strange roots. John McCarthy, LISP's inventor, originally used a sort of old LISP, that is about as hard to read as old English. At one point, however, he wished to use LISP to do a piece of mathematics that required both procedures and data to have the same syntactic form. The resulting form of LISP quickly caught on and became the standard.

**The First Part of the
Book Introduces LISP**

We now outline what is to come:

- **Chapter 2, Basic LISP Primitives.** About twenty LISP primitives constitute a minimal symbol-manipulation vocabulary. This chapter introduces half of them, along with primitives for doing arithmetic.

- **Chapter 3, Definitions, Predicates, Conditionals, and Binding.** This chapter shows how to make new procedures using DEFUN and how to bind variables using LET. It also introduces testing primitives called predicates and branching primitives called conditionals.

- **Chapter 4, Recursion and Iteration.** Sometimes the best way for a procedure to solve a problem is to break the problem up into simpler problems and to hand these off to copies of itself. In such a copy, the processes of breakup and handoff may be repeated. This is called recursion. On the other hand, sometimes it is best to use DO, a primitive that enables explicit test-compute-test sequences. Something is repeated until a condition is met. This is called iteration.

- **Chapter 5, Association Lists, Properties, and Data Abstraction.** There are a number of ways to attach information to a symbol. This chapter describes three of the most popular: using association lists, using properties, and using structures. Simultaneously, we introduce the notion of data abstraction.

- **Chapter 6, Definition Using LAMBDA.** Many times it is useful to define procedures that appear only once and hardly deserve a name. This chapter shows how to define such procedures.

- **Chapter 7, Printing and Reading.** LISP comes with PRINT and READ, two simple primitives for getting results out of procedures and getting data in. This chapter explains them and mentions certain others, for people who prefer fancy input and output.

- **Chapter 8, Optional Parameters, Macros, and Backquote.** Some procedures in LISP are idiomatic in that they take optional parameters. Others translate their arguments into new forms before doing evaluation. This chapter explains how to define such procedures.

- **Chapter 9, List Storage, Surgery, and Reclamation.** At times it is useful to know how lists are actually represented. This chapter explains box-and-arrow notation and describes certain dangerous, structure-altering primitives.

- **Chapter 10, Examples Involving Arrays and Binary Images.** LISP is not limited to symbolic computation. This chapter uncovers LISP's ecumenical spirit, showing that it is possible to use LISP in a style that is like that of other programming languages, if one so chooses. The chapter also demonstrates the use of arrays and shows how simple objects can be identified using binary image processing techniques.

- **Chapter 11, Examples Involving Search.** Many problem-solving jobs require searching through a network of places and connections. This chapter shows how to implement the most popular techniques. Sorting is also touched upon.

- **Chapter 12, Examples from Mathematics.** There are some numeric calculations for which LISP is well suited, such as those involving the manipulation of sparse arrays. This chapter presents some examples, including matrix multiplication and finding roots of algebraic equations.

The Second Part of the Book Demonstrates LISP's Power

- **Chapter 13, The Blocks World.** Eventually, the time comes to get a feeling for larger programs that do things that are beyond what one or two procedures can do. The blocks-world system is such a collection. Its purpose is to move toy blocks from place to place, moving obstacles as necessary. This chapter introduces the system, shows how it works, and establishes it as an example to be exploited in the following three chapters.

- **Chapter 14, Rules for Good Programming and Tools for Debugging.** It is wrong to expect all procedures to work the first time. The job of getting things right is a proper thing for LISP itself to help with. This chapter uses the blocks-world system to introduce break points, tracing, and some rules of good programming practice.

- **Chapter 15, Answering Questions about Goals.** Complex systems should be able to explain how they reached any decision that they have made. Fortunately, it is easy to add machinery to the blocks-world system that enables it to answer questions about its past behavior. This chapter shows how to arrange for answering questions like "How did you ...," "Why did you ...," and "When did you ...."

- **Chapter 16, Object-centered Programming, Message Passing, and Flavors.** The proper action for a procedure is often determined by the type of data it is working with. The standard way to ensure that things are handled properly is to start off by determining what the type of the argument is and then to call upon that part of the procedure that handles the given type. The nonstandard way is to attach procedures to the names of the types and to fetch them automatically as needed. The standard way is said to be action centered. The nonstandard way is object centered. The chapter concludes with discussions of message passing and flavors.

- **Chapter 17, Symbolic Pattern Matching.** The purpose of a matcher is to compare two symbolic expressions to determine if they are enough alike to say that one is an instance of another. The chapter develops a simple pattern matcher in preparation for understanding well-known classic programs like DOCTOR and STUDENT and for building the rule-based expert system in the following chapter.

- **Chapter 18, Expert Problem Solving with Rules and Streams.** Problem solvers have reached the point where they do all sorts of expert work, including some forms of medical diagnosis and some forms of engineering design. Many of these problem solvers are based on the use of if-then rules, also known as situation-action rules or productions. This chapter shows how to implement a simple version of such a system, focusing on an animal-identification illustration. The implementation is done in a way that introduces the powerful idea of streams.

- **Chapter 19, Interpreting Augmented Transition Trees.** One prominent feature of LISP is that procedures and the data they work on are both represented by symbolic expressions. This means that one procedure can treat another as data or even build up a procedure from scratch. This chapter introduces the idea by describing a LISP program that accepts procedures given in a nonLISP, user-convenient way, and follows the nonLISP procedure statement by statement, doing whatever the nonLISP procedure asks for. This is an instance of the process called interpretation. The particular procedures that are interpreted are called augmented transition trees. They have the purpose of analyzing English sentences in preparation for answering questions or following commands.

- **Chapter 20, Compiling Augmented Transition Trees.** When a procedure is described in nonLISP, another option is to translate the procedure into LISP once and for all. This is an instance of the process called compilation. This chapter illuminates the difference between interpreting a procedure and compiling a procedure by introducing a compiler for augmented transition trees to compare with the interpreter of the previous chapter.

- **Chapter 21, Procedure Writing Programs and English Interfaces.** Translating English into formal data-base queries is an exciting use for LISP's procedure-writing ability. It is at the heart of many interesting natural language interfaces, including a system that answers questions using a data base of Moon rocks, a system that eases access to a large data base of information about ships, and a system that has been attached to a variety of commercial management information systems, providing English access to them. This chapter illustrates how such systems work, using a toy data base containing information about the tools in a workshop.

- **Chapter 22, Implementing Frames.** Research has shown that there is great utility in building better tools for representing information. Representing information in packets called frames is one result of this work. In a frame system, the notion of property value is generalized, so that a property can be associated with an ordinary value, a default value, or even a procedure that can compute a value when one is requested. A frame system also allows values to be inherited, as when we know that a particular person breathes air, because all people do.

- **Chapter 23, LISP in LISP.** Often the best way to describe how to do something is to exhibit a program that does it. English can be a poor second. This means that one good way to describe in detail how a LISP system can interpret a user's LISP procedures is to exhibit the LISP interpreter as a program. Curiously, this program itself can be written in LISP, as this chapter shows.

Our LISP Is COMMON LISP

The LISP used throughout this book is COMMON LISP. We use COMMON LISP, because it is modern, powerful, and widely available.

The footnotes sprinkled here and there deal mainly with esoteric, advanced features of COMMON LISP or with other dialects of LISP. Consequently, the footnotes can be ignored safely on first reading.[1]

There Are Some Myths about LISP

There is no perfect computer language, and to be sure, LISP has defects. Many of the original defects have been fixed, even though some people mistakenly cite them even today. Among the most pervasive and unfortunate are the following:

- Myth: LISP is slow at doing arithmetic.

In fact this was true at one time. This historical problem has been corrected by the development of good LISP compilers. (Programming-language compilers are programs that translate the stuff programmers produce into the primitive operations that a computer can do directly, without further decomposition.)

---

[1] Footnotes *should* be ignored on first reading, because many are for the benefit of readers who already know lisp. Beginners are more likely to be confused by the footnotes than helped.

- Myth: LISP is slow.

In fact this also was true at one time. LISP has been used traditionally in research, where interaction is at a premium and high speed for fully debugged production programs is less important. Making a language fast is generally more a matter of effort, than it is a matter of inherent limitations.[2]

- Myth: LISP programs are big.

Actually, this is not a myth. Some are. But that is only because LISP makes it possible to create programs that are big enough to know a lot.

- Myth: LISP is hard to read and debug because of all the parentheses.

In fact the parentheses problem goes away as soon as a person learns to put things down on the page properly or to invoke an editing program that does this. No one finds the following to be particularly clear:

```
(DEFUN FIBONACCI (N) (COND ((= N 0)
1) ((= N 1) 1) (T (+ (FIBONACCI (-
N 1)) (FIBONACCI (- N 2)))))))
```

But the equivalent, formatted version is fine after a little experience:

```
(DEFUN FIBONACCI (N)
  (COND ((= N 0) 1)
        ((= N 1) 1)
        (T (+ (FIBONACCI (- N 1))
              (FIBONACCI (- N 2)))))))
```

LISP-oriented editors quickly convert the ugly version into the pretty one. The process is called prettyprinting.

- Myth: LISP is hard to learn.

LISP earned its bad reputation by being in the company of some hard-to-read books in its youth.

Summary

- Symbol manipulation is like working with words and sentences.
- Symbol manipulation is needed to make computers intelligent.
- LISP is the right symbol-manipulation language to learn.
- The first part of the book introduces LISP.
- The second part of the book demonstrates LISP's power.
- There are some myths about LISP.

---

[2] These days, there are excellent LISP compilers. Strangely, some people still think LISP is only used interpretively.

References

For general information on Artificial Intelligence, see *Artificial Intelligence* (*Second Edition*), by Patrick H. Winston [1984], and its bibliographic material. For information on the commercial applications of Artificial Intelligence, see *The AI Business. The Commercial Uses of Artificial Intelligence*, edited by Patrick H. Winston and Karen A. Prendergast [1984].

For looking at the history of LISP, McCarthy [1960], and McCarthy *et al.* [1962] are musts. White [1979] gives a good account of the development of MACLISP and the relation to other dialects. MACLISP itself is documented in Samson [1966], White [1967, 1970], Moon [1974], Greenberg [1976], and Pitman [1983]. Other, older LISP implementations are described in Blair [1970], Bobrow [1966], Deutsch and Berkeley [1964], Deutsch and Lampson [1965], Hart and Evans [1964], Hearn [1969], Kameny [1965], Martin and Hart [1963], McCarthy *et al.* [1960], Moses and Fenichel [1966], Saunders [1964], and Smith [1970]. A few implementations are covered by Chaitin [1976], Griss and Swanson [1977], LeFaivre [1978], Reboh and Sacerdoti [1973], Urmi [1976a], and White [1978].

Other symbol manipulation languages, some embedded in LISP, are covered in Bobrow [1963, 1974], Burstall [1971], Galley and Pfister [1975], Goldberg and Robson [1984], Johnson and Rosin [1965], McDermott and Sussman [1974], Pratt [1976], Roberts and Goldstein [1977a, 1977b], Rulifson, Derken, and Waldinger [1972], Sussman, Winograd, and Charniak [1971], Sussman and McDermott [1972], Warren and Pereira [1977], and Weizenbaum [1963]. For information on IPL see Newell [1961]. Other discussions of list processing may be found in Bobrow [1964], and Foster [1967].

There are a number of useful books and papers on LISP and its theoretical foundations including these: Berkeley and Bobrow [1964], Church [1941], Kleene [1950], Landin [1964], McCarthy [1978], Moore [1976], Moses [1970], Sandewall [1978], Steele and Sussman [1978], and White [1977a, 1977b]. Some of the important implementation issues are covered in Baker and Hewitt [1977], Baker [1978a, 1978b, 1979], Bawden *et al.* [1977], Bobrow and Murphy [1967], Bobrow and Wegbreit [1973], Bobrow and Clark [1979], Burke *et al.* [1984], Cheney [1970], Fenichel and Yochelson [1969], Fenichel [1970], Greenblatt [1974], Greenblatt *et al.* [1979], Greussay [1976], Hart [1963], Knight *et al.* [1979], Kung and Song [1977], Pitman [1983], Steele [1977a, 1977b, 1977c], and Urmi [1976b].

For arguments in favor of LISP as a programming language, see the papers by Pratt [1979] and Allen [1979]. Henderson [1980] and Morris [1981] propagandize functional programming, for which LISP is admirably suited. Boley [1983] reviews languages and machines for Artificial Intelligence. For details about real time editors written in LISP, see Greenberg [1979, 1980] and Weinreb [1979].

There are definitive manuals for the principal LISP dialects. The most important, now that COMMON LISP has been defined is Steele's [1984].

Among the others, the following are particularly noteworthy: Stanford LISP, Quam and Diffie [1972]; early MACLISP, Moon [1974]; INTERLISP, Teitelman [1975]; INTERLISP/370, Urmi [1976a]; LISPMACHINE LISP, Weinreb and Moon [1978]; FRANZ LISP, Foderaro, Skowler and Layer [1983]; Univac 1108 LISP, Norman [1978]; Dilos INTERLISP, Briabrin [1978]; UCI LISP, Meehan [1979]; LISP/370, Blair [1979]; MODLISP, Davenport and Jenks [1980]; SPICE LISP, Steele [1981]; UTI LISP, Chikayama, [1981]; GLISP, Novak [1982]; S-1B COMMON LISP, Gabriel, Brooks and Steele [1982]; LE LISP de l'INRIA, Chailloux [1983]; recent MACLISP, Pitman [1983]; SCHEME, Abelson and Sussman [1984].

Work on some of the older dialects of LISP have helped in the formulation of COMMON LISP as documented in Steele [1984]. These include MACLISP described by Moon [1974] and Pitman [1983], and STANDARD LISP, described by Hearn [1966, 1969], Marti, Hearn, Griss and Griss [1979], as well as Griss and Morrison [1981]. The newer dialects which have had a strong influence are LISPMACHINE LISP described by Weinreb and Moon [1978]; T described by Rees and Adams [1982], and Rees, Adams and Meehan [1984], NIL described by White [1979] and Burke *et al* [1984], and SCHEME, Abelson and Sussman [1984].

Recently there have been conferences on LISP every second year. See Stanford [1980], Association for Computing Machinery [1982], and University of Texas [1984].

A number of reports discuss existing and proposed LISP Machines. These include Boley [1983]; Greenblatt [1974]; Greenblatt *et al.* [1979]; Guzman [1981]; Hayashi, Hattori and Akimoto [1983]; Holloway *et al.* [1980]; Moon [1981]; Moon, Stallman and Weinreb [1983]; Weinreb and Moon [1978].

There are a number of LISP textbooks. Abelson and Sussman's [1984] is conspicuous for using LISP to teach programming principles and concepts. It uses a dialect of LISP called SCHEME.

Allen's book [1978] is an advanced book, good for its use of LISP as a context for a discussion of certain theoretical issues in modern computer science. It is a must for anyone who wants to thoroughly understand a LISP implementation or to create one. Also, the book by Charniak, Riesbeck, and McDermott [1980] has many good points, particularly for advanced programmers.

Greenberg's notes [1976] provide a brief, well thought out, data structure oriented introduction. Other books include Friedman [1974], Maurer [1973], Ribbens [1970], Shapiro [1979], Siklóssy [1976], Touretzky [1984], and Weissman [1975]. Still other books on related topics, include Organick, Forsythe, and Plummer [1978], and Pratt [1975].

2

Basic
Lisp
Primitives

The purpose of this chapter is to introduce LISP's basic symbol-manipulation primitives. To do this, some primitives are introduced that work on numbers and others are introduced that work on lists. The list-oriented primitives extract parts of lists and build new lists.

LISP Means Symbol Manipulation

As with other computer languages, the best way to learn LISP is bravely, by jumping right into interesting programs. We therefore look occasionally at things that you will not understand completely, with a view toward moving as quickly as possible into exciting applications.

To get started, imagine being seated in front of a computer terminal. You begin, as if engaging in a conversation, with LISP tossing back results in response to typed input. Suppose, for example, that you would like some help adding numbers. The proper incantation would be this:

`(+ 3.14 2.71)`

LISP would agreeably respond:

`5.85`

This is a simple example of LISP's ability to handle arithmetic. Elementary examples of symbol manipulation are equally straightforward. Suppose, for

example, that we are interested in keeping track of some facts needed in
connection with understanding a children's story about, say, a robot. It
might be important to remember that certain children are friends of the
robot. Typically a name is required to identify such a group, and the name
FRIENDS will do as well as any other. If Dick and Jane and Sally are friends
of the robot, this fact could be remembered by typing this line:

```
(SETQ FRIENDS '(DICK JANE SALLY))
```

SETQ associates (DICK JANE SALLY) with FRIENDS. Do not worry about the
quote mark that appears. It will be explained later.

Typing FRIENDS now causes the list of friends to be typed in response.
Note that LISP's responses are indented by two spaces, in this book, to
distinguish them from the user's typed input:

```
FRIENDS
  (DICK JANE SALLY)
```

A list similar to the list of friends can be established for enemies:

```
(SETQ ENEMIES '(TROLL GRINCH GHOST))
```

Because friends and enemies tend to be dynamic categories in children's
worlds, it is often necessary to change the category that a particular individual belongs to. The ghost ceases to be an enemy and becomes a friend
after typing two lines like this:

```
(SETQ ENEMIES (REMOVE 'GHOST ENEMIES))
(SETQ FRIENDS (CONS 'GHOST FRIENDS))
```

The first line changes the remembered list of enemies to what it was
minus the entry GHOST. The second line would be simpler to read if CONS
were replaced by something more mnemonic like ADD, but we are stuck with
historical convention. In any event, FRIENDS and ENEMIES have been changed
such that we now get properly altered responses:

```
ENEMIES
  (TROLL GRINCH)
FRIENDS
  (GHOST DICK JANE SALLY)
```

Later we will see how to write a procedure that does the same job.
In particular we will understand how the following creates a procedure,
named NEWFRIEND, for changing a person from an enemy into a friend:

```
(DEFUN NEWFRIEND (NAME)
  (SETQ ENEMIES (REMOVE NAME ENEMIES))
  (SETQ FRIENDS (CONS NAME FRIENDS)))
```

With NEWFRIEND, the previous elevation of the status of GHOST can be done more simply by typing only this:

```
(NEWFRIEND 'GHOST)
```

LISP Procedures and Data Are Constructed out of Symbolic Expressions

Now is a good time to get some terms straight. First, when left and right parentheses surround something, we call the result a *list* and speak of its *elements*. In our very first example, the list (+ 3.14 2.71) has three elements, +, 3.14, and 2.71.

Note the peculiar location of the +, standing strangely before the two things to be added, rather than between them, as in ordinary arithmetic notation. In LISP the thing to do, the *procedure*, is always specified first, followed then by the things that the procedure is to work with, the *arguments*. Thus 3.14 and 2.71 are the arguments given to the procedure named +.

This so-called *prefix notation* facilitates uniformity, because the procedure name is always in the same place, no matter how many arguments are involved.

We are now prepared to gather together some definitions for important terms, some of which we have used informally already:

- A *procedure* is the basic entity in LISP that specifies how something is to be done. A procedure may be defined by the user or provided directly by the LISP system.

- A procedure, like +, supplied by LISP itself, is called a *primitive*.

- A collection of procedures intended to work together is called a *program*.

There is another term, which we will not use as much, but which it is also good to know about:

- An abstract description of a procedure or program, one not expressed in a programming language, is called an *algorithm*. Such a description may, for example, be given in English or as a block diagram.

A procedure or a program may be considered an implementation of an algorithm in a particular programming language.

Now let us look at more examples. We will stick to arithmetic for the moment, because most people are initially more familiar with arithmetic than with symbol manipulation:

```
(+ 3.14 2.71)
  5.85
```

```
(* 9 3)
  27

(/ 27 3)
  9
```

Note that the names of the primitives can be single characters, rather special ones at that, like +, *, and /.[1] This is just a convenience reserved for often-used primitives. We will see that most primitives have longer names, like MAX and MIN:[2]

```
(MAX 2 4 3)
  4

(MIN 2 4 3)
  2
```

MAX selects the largest of the numbers given as arguments. Note that MAX and MIN can work with any number of arguments, not just two. So can the primitives +, *, -, and /. Just as + keeps on adding, so - will keep on subtracting and / will keep on dividing, when given more than two arguments. There is never any confusion, because the end of the argument sequence is signaled clearly by the right parenthesis.

```
(EXPT 2 3)
  8

(EXPT 3 2)
  9
```

EXPT calculates powers; it raises its first argument to its second.

```
(SQRT 4.0)
  2.0

(ABS 5)
  5
(ABS -5)
  5
```

SQRT, of course, takes the square root, and ABS computes the absolute value.

---

[1] In some LISP dialects the slash, /, signals an unusual treatment for the next character: the slash prevents a space from being interpreted as a separator, for example. In such LISPs, it is necessary to use // to get the equivalent of a single / in COMMON LISP.

[2] In some dialects of LISP, the common arithmetic primitives have mnemonic names like PLUS and TIMES. In COMMON LISP, the symbols used to represent the arithmetic primitives are those used commonly in arithmetic expressions.

SQRT and ABS deal with a single argument.[3] Some primitives that are usually employed with multiple arguments also do useful things when given a single argument:

```
(- 8)
 -8

(- -8)
  8
```

If - is given a single argument, it computes the negative of that argument. Similarly, / computes the reciprocal when given a single argument. Thus, (/ 2.0) is equivalent to (/ 1.0 2.0).[4]

Now consider the following expression, in which + is followed by something other than raw numbers:

```
(+ (* 2 2) (/ 2 2))
```

If we think of this expression as directions for something to do, it is easy to see that (* 2 2) produces 4, (/ 2 2) produces 1, and these results, fed in turn to +, give 5 as the result. But if, instead, we think of this expression as data, then we see that we have a three-element list: + is the first element, the entire expression (* 2 2) is the second element, and (/ 2 2) is the third. Thus lists themselves can be elements of other lists. Said another way, we permit lists in which individual elements are lists themselves. In part, the representational power of LISP derives from this ability to build nested structures out of lists.

Now that we understand what lists are, at least informally, we are equipped to note the following:

- Indivisible things like 27, 3.14 and +, which have obvious meaning, as well as things like FOO, B27, and HYPHENATED-SYMBOL are called *atoms*.

- Atoms like 27 and 3.14 are called *numeric atoms*, or more succinctly, *numbers*.

- Atoms like FOO, B27, HYPHENATED-SYMBOL, FIRST and + are called *symbolic atoms*, or more succinctly, *symbols*.

- A *list* consists of a left parenthesis, followed by zero or more atoms or lists, followed by a right parenthesis.

---

[3] In COMMON LISP, SQRT may produce a complex number when presented with a negative argument. We will not discuss complex numbers at this point, because most dialects of LISP do not support them, so make sure SQRT is fed only nonnegative arguments.

[4] In some dialects of LISP the unary forms of - and / simply return the value of their single argument.

- Both atoms and lists are called *symbolic expressions*, or more succinctly, *expressions*.[5]

We will also use the following frequently:

- An expression is called a *form* if it is meant to be evaluated. If it is a list, the first element generally is the name of a procedure that can be used in the evaluation process.

- The process of computing the value of a form is called *evaluation*. The result often will be referred to as the value *returned* by the procedure specified in the form.

Note that the terms *expression* and *form* may be applied to the same entity. It all depends on the context. Considered as data, a list may be called an expression; considered as a piece of a procedure, the same list may be called a form.

Problems

Problem 2-1:   Each of the following things may be an atom, a list, or neither. Identify each accordingly.

```
ATOM

(THIS IS AN ATOM)

(THIS IS AN EXPRESSION)

((A B) (C D)) 3 (3)

(LIST 3)

(/ (+ 3 1) (- 3 1))

)(

((()))

(() ())

((())

())(

((ABC
```

---

[5] Symbolic expressions used to be called s-expressions, *s* being short for *symbolic*, to distinguish them from m-expressions, *m* being short for *meta*. M-expressions are used to represent s-expressions only by John McCarthy, as far as we know.

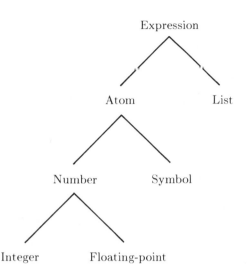

Figure 2-1. The relationships between various types of objects in LISP. An expression can be a list or an atom; an atom can be a symbol or a number; a number can be a floating-point number or an integer.

Problem 2-2:　Evaluate the following forms:

```
(/ (+ 3 1) (- 3 1))

(* (MAX 3 4 5) (MIN 3 4 5))

(MIN (MAX 3 1 4) (MAX 2 7 1))
```

LISP Handles Both Integers and Floating-point Numbers

We summarize the relationships among the various types of objects manipulated by LISP in figure 2-1.[6] The purpose of this section is to discuss the two types that constitute the numeric atoms and some minutiae concerning their use. The discussion is too long for a footnote, but you should treat it like a footnote, especially on first reading, because it is a bit of a diversion, except for those who need to compute with numbers.

We discuss briefly the difference between *integers* and *floating-point* numbers. Like many other programming languages, LISP can handle both. Let it suffice to say that LISP integers are used to represent whole numbers, while floating-point numbers are used to represent reals. Integers usually

---

[6] COMMON LISP also has other types of objects, not shown in the figure. These will not be discussed at great length in this book.

are written without a decimal point,[7] but if one is included, there should not be any digits after it. This is because a number with digits after the decimal point is interpreted as a floating-point quantity. We will not worry too much about the difference, except to point out possible sources of programming errors.

The result of division depends on the numbers involved. First of all, with two floating-point arguments, a floating-point number is produced by /, as expected.

Consider this example:

```
(/ 1.234321 1.111)
 1.111
```

Next, we note that with two integer arguments that happen to divide evenly, / produces an integer:

```
(/ 27 9)
 3
```

However, with two integer arguments that do *not* divide evenly, the result may not be what we expect.[8] What we want can be accomplished in one of two ways, depending on whether the result is to be an integer or a floating-point number. To obtain a floating-point result when dividing two integers, we use FLOAT to convert the integers into floating-point numbers and then use /:

```
(/ (FLOAT 14) (FLOAT 4))
 3.5
```

If, instead, we want an integer answer, we use TRUNCATE:[9]

```
(TRUNCATE 14 4)
 3
```

A related primitive computes the remainder of an integer division:

```
(REM 14 4)
 2
```

---

[7] In COMMON LISP the radix is 10, unless the user asks LISP to change it.

[8] In COMMON LISP, / computes a *ratio* when given two integers that do not divide evenly. We do not discuss ratios, a representation for rational numbers, in this book, because many dialects of LISP do not support them.

[9] TRUNCATE does the same thing as integer division in some other programming languages. To be precise, TRUNCATE takes the true ratio and *truncates* it toward zero; that is, it finds the integer of the same sign that has the greatest integral magnitude not greater than that of the ratio.

Note that there is an inverse relationship between ∗, on the one hand, and TRUNCATE and REM, on the other. This is illustrated as follows, assuming that X and Y are integers (and Y is not zero):

```
(+ (* (TRUNCATE X Y) Y) (REM X Y))   ≡   X
```

Here we use the convention that forms separated by the equivalence symbol, ≡, evaluate to the same thing. If you type one at LISP, LISP will print out the same result as if you had typed the other.

Incidentally, ROUND is a kind of inverse to FLOAT. It produces the integer that is closest to its argument.[10] Thus when the value of X is an integer, the following holds:

```
(ROUND (FLOAT X))   ≡   X
```

The arithmetic primitives like +, -, ∗, and / are called *generic* primitives, because they can deal with all types of numbers.[11]

Something else worth knowing about is the notion of *floating contagion*. If a generic arithmetic primitive is given arguments of mixed types, an integer and a floating-point number, the integer is converted into a floating-point number before the primitive is applied. This conversion avoids possible loss of precision.[12] Consequently, all the following are completely equivalent:

```
(/ (FLOAT 14) (FLOAT 4))
  3.5

(/ 14 (FLOAT 4))
  3.5

(/ (FLOAT 14) 4)
  3.5
```

CAR and CDR Take Lists Apart

Examples from arithmetic are simple, but arithmetic does not expose the talent of LISP for manipulating expressions. Suppose we have an expression like (FAST COMPUTERS ARE NICE). We might like to chip off the first

---

[10] If ROUND gets a floating-point number that happens to lie exactly between two whole numbers, it picks the even one.

[11] Some LISP dialects provide specialized versions of the common arithmetic primitives that operate *only* on integers and others that operate *only* on floating-point numbers.

[12] In COMMON LISP, contagion affects arithmetic operations involving ratios and complex numbers, as well as arithmetic operations involving integers and floating-point numbers.

element leaving (COMPUTERS ARE NICE), or we might like to glue on a new
first element producing something like (SMALL FAST COMPUTERS ARE NICE).
It is time to look at such manipulations starting with basic techniques for
dissecting and constructing lists. In particular we must understand the
primitives CAR, CDR, APPEND, LIST, and CONS. A regrettable historical convention has left three of these five key primitives terribly nonmnemonic—their
meaning simply has to be memorized.

Some examples will help explain how the basic primitives CAR and CDR
work. The value returned by CAR is the first element of the list given as its
argument:

```
(CAR '(FAST COMPUTERS ARE NICE))
  FAST

(CAR '(A B C))
  A
```

Again, do not worry about the quote marks that appear. They will be
explained soon.

In the next example, the argument given to CAR is the two-element list
((A B) C). The first element is itself a list, (A B). Consequently, (A B) is
returned by CAR.

```
(CAR '((A B) C))
  (A B)
```

CDR does the complementary thing. It returns a list containing all but the
first element.

```
(CDR '(FAST COMPUTERS ARE NICE))
  (COMPUTERS ARE NICE)

(CDR '(A B C))
  (B C)

(CDR '((A B) C))
  (C)
```

Note that CDR, unlike CAR, always returns a list. Remembering the following
diagram may help keep the asymmetry of CAR and CDR straight:

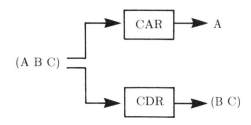

Also note that when CDR is applied to a list with only one element, it returns the *empty list*, sometimes denoted by ( ).

Evaluation Is Often Purposely Inhibited by Quoting

Now it is time to understand those quote marks that have been appearing. We will use the fact that the CAR and CDR primitives can be nested together, just like the arithmetic primitives. To pick out the second element of some list, the first primitive to use is CDR and the second is CAR. Thus if we want the second element of (A B C), it might seem reasonable to write this:

(CAR (CDR (A B C)))

There is a problem, however. We want CDR to take the list (A B C) and give back (B C). Then CAR would certainly return B, the second element in the original list. But how is LISP to know where the specification of what to do leaves off and the data to be manipulated begins? Look at the embedded list:

(A B C)

LISP might legitimately think that A is some sort of procedure, perhaps one defined by the user. Similarly, the following expression is certainly a list:

(CDR (A B C))

And its first element is surely CDR! Thus the following expression could well result in an answer of CDR:

(CAR (CDR (A B C)))

How far should the evaluation process go into an expression? LISP needs help in making this decision. The user specifies where to stop evaluation by supplying an evaluation-inhibiting signal in the form of a single-quote character, '. Thus the following expression returns B:

(CAR (CDR '(A B C)))

B is returned because the quote mark prevents LISP from wading in and thinking of (A B C) as a form in which A is the name of a procedure to be applied to B and C. Instead, (A B C) is given to CDR, which then hands (B C) to CAR, resulting finally in just plain B. Moving the quote mark changes the result:

(CAR '(CDR (A B C)))

Here LISP does not try to take the CDR of anything but simply gives the expression (CDR (A B C)) to CAR as a list to work on, resulting in CDR because CDR is the first element.

Leaving out the quote mark altogether would result in an attempt to use A as a procedure. There is no procedure supplied by LISP, and if none had been defined by you, the user, LISP would report that there has been an undefined procedure error.

Sometimes it is useful to know about an equivalent way to stop evaluation. The expression to be protected against evaluation is simply bracketed on the left by a left parenthesis, followed by the symbol QUOTE, and on the right by a matching right parenthesis. Thus the following stops evaluation of the list (A B C):

(QUOTE (A B C))
   (A B C)

(CAR (CDR (QUOTE (A B C))))
   B

Note this then:

'(A B C)   ≡   (QUOTE (A B C))

Providing the single quote mark as an equivalent for the longer version is considered a form of *syntactic sugaring*. Nothing new is added to the power of the language, but programs become more readable.

Problems

Problem 2-3:   Evaluate the following forms:

(CAR '(P H W))

(CDR '(B K P H))

(CAR '((A B) (C D)))

(CDR '((A B) (C D)))

(CAR (CDR '((A B) (C D))))

(CDR (CAR '((A B) (C D))))

```
(CDR (CAR (CDR '((A B) (C D)))))

(CAR (CDR (CAR '((A B) (C D)))))
```

Problem 2-4: Evaluate the following forms:

```
(CAR (CDR (CAR (CDR '((A B) (C D) (E F))))))

(CAR (CAR (CDR (CDR '((A B) (C D) (E F))))))

(CAR (CAR (CDR '(CDR ((A B) (C D) (E F))))))

(CAR (CAR '(CDR (CDR ((A B) (C D) (E F))))))

(CAR '(CAR (CDR (CDR ((A B) (C D) (E F))))))

'(CAR (CAR (CDR (CDR ((A B) (C D) (E F))))))
```

Problem 2-5: Write sequences of CARs and CDRs that will pick the symbol PEAR out of the following expressions:

```
(APPLE ORANGE PEAR GRAPEFRUIT)

((APPLE ORANGE) (PEAR GRAPEFRUIT))

(((APPLE) (ORANGE) (PEAR) (GRAPEFRUIT)))

(APPLE (ORANGE) ((PEAR)) (((GRAPEFRUIT))))

((((APPLE))) ((ORANGE)) (PEAR) GRAPEFRUIT)

((((APPLE) ORANGE) PEAR) GRAPEFRUIT)
```

Composing CARs and CDRs Makes Programming Easier

When many CARs and CDRs are needed to dig out some item from deep inside an expression, it is usually convenient to substitute a composite primitive of the form CXXR, CXXXR, or CXXXXR. Each X here is either an A, signifying CAR, or a D, signifying CDR. Thus

```
(CADR '(A B C))   ≡   (CAR (CDR '(A B C)))
```

One thing to look out for is the order of the As and Ds in the composite primitives. The order of appearance is the *inverse* of the order of application.

We have already seen lists that have other lists as elements. These sublists, in turn, may have elements that are lists, and so on. A love of precision inspires the following recursive definition:

- The *top-level* elements of a list are the CAR of the list and the top-level elements of the CDR of the list. So the first few top-level elements can be retrieved using CAR, CADR, CADDR, and CADDDR.

- A *nested expression* is a list at least one element of which is also a list. The *depth of nesting* is the maximum number of layers of nesting you can go through before getting to atoms.

Some procedures work only on the top-level elements of a list, while others dive deep into an expression. It will be important later to note the distinction.

Symbolic Atoms Have Values

So far we have seen how symbolic expressions can be taken apart by evaluating forms that begin with CAR or CDR. We have also seen how arithmetic can be done by evaluating forms that begin with +, -, and other related primitives. It seems as if LISP's goal is always to evaluate something and return a value. This is true for symbols as well as lists. Suppose we type a symbol, followed by a space, and wait for LISP to respond:

L

On seeing L, LISP tries to return a value for it, just as it would if some form like (+ 3 4) were typed. But for a symbol, the *value* is something looked up somewhere, rather than the result of some computation, as when dealing with lists.

The process of establishing a value for a symbol is called *assignment*. One way to do assignment is to use SETQ. This primitive causes the value of its second argument to become the value of the first argument, which must be a symbol. Consider this:

(SETQ L '(A B))

The value a procedure gives back when used is the *value returned*. Anything a procedure has done that persists after it returns its value is called a *side effect*.

Thus typing (SETQ L '(A B)) results in a value of (A B) for the expression. But, more importantly, there is a side effect, because (A B) becomes the value of L. We say that L has had a value assigned to it. If we now type L, we see that (A B) comes back:

L

    (A B)

Thus the expression (SETQ L '(A B)) is evaluated mainly for the side effect of assigning the value (A B) to the symbol L.

- A procedure that computes a value based only on its arguments is called a *function*.[13] Procedures are not functions if they have side effects. Thus SETQ is certainly a procedure, but it is not a function.

Now that the value of L is (A B), L can be used in working through some examples of the basic list manipulating primitives. These illustrate that LISP seeks out the value of symbols not only when they are typed in by themselves, but also when the symbols appear as arguments to procedures:

```
L
   (A B)

'L
   L

(CAR L)
   A

(CAR 'L)
   ERROR

(CDR L)
   (B)

(CDR 'L)
   ERROR
```

Note that both CAR and CDR announce an error if asked to work on an atom. Both expect a list as their argument, and both work only when they get one.

APPEND, LIST, and CONS Construct Lists

While CAR and CDR take things apart, APPEND, LIST, and CONS put them together. APPEND strings together the elements of all lists supplied as arguments:

```
(SETQ L '(A B))
   (A B)

(APPEND L L)
   (A B A B)
```

---

[13] A mathematical function defines a correspondence between one variable (the result) and some others (the arguments).

```
(APPEND L L L)
  (A B A B A B)

(APPEND '(A) '() '(B) '())
  (A B)

(APPEND 'L L)
  ERROR
```

Be sure to understand that APPEND runs the elements of its arguments together, but does nothing to those elements themselves. Note that the value returned in the following example is ((A) (B) (C) (D)), not (A B C D):

```
(APPEND '((A) (B)) '((C) (D)))
  ((A) (B) (C) (D))
```

LIST does not run things together like APPEND does. Instead, it makes a list out of its arguments. Each argument becomes an element of the new list.

```
(LIST L L)
  ((A B) (A B))

(LIST L L L)
  ((A B) (A B) (A B))

(LIST 'L L)
  (L (A B))

(LIST '((A) (B)) '((C) (D)))
  (((A) (B)) ((C) (D)))
```

CONS takes a list and inserts a new first element. CONS is a mnemonic for list <u>cons</u>tructor.

Let us now adopt a convention by which the words between angle brackets are taken as descriptions of what should appear in the position occupied. Then the CONS primitive can be described as follows:

```
(CONS <new first element> <some list>)
```

Thus we have these:

```
(CAR (CONS 'A '(B C)))
  A

(CDR (CONS 'A '(B C)))
  (B C)
```

Note then that the following holds, provided that L is a list, as it is at this point:

```
(CONS (CAR L) (CDR L))   ≡   L
```

Representing this inverse relationship between CONS and the pair CAR and CDR in a diagram, we have this:[14]

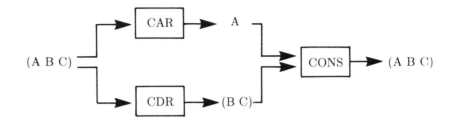

Note that (CONS L '(C D)) yields the result ((A B) C D), in which the list (A B) has become the first element of a list that was just (C D) before. Study how APPEND, LIST, and CONS differ:

```
(APPEND '(A B) '(C D))
  (A B C D)

(LIST '(A B) '(C D))
  ((A B) (C D))

(CONS '(A B) '(C D))
  ((A B) C D)

(APPEND L L)
  (A B A B)

(LIST L L)
  ((A B) (A B))

(CONS L L)
  ((A B) A B)

(APPEND 'L L)
  ERROR

(LIST 'L L)
  (L (A B))

(CONS 'L L)
  (L A B)
```

---

[14] The inverse relationship between CONS on the one hand, and CAR and CDR on the other, may be reminiscent of the inverse relationship between * on the one hand, and TRUNCATE and REM on the other.

Problems

Problem 2-6:   Evaluate the following slightly tricky forms:

```
(APPEND '(A B C) '( ))
```

```
(LIST '(A B C) '( ))
```

```
(CONS '(A B C) '( ))
```

Problem 2-7:   Evaluate the following forms in the order given:

```
(SETQ TOOLS (LIST 'HAMMER 'SCREWDRIVER))
```

```
(CONS 'PLIERS TOOLS)
```

```
TOOLS
```

```
(SETQ TOOLS (CONS 'PLIERS TOOLS))
```

```
TOOLS
```

```
(APPEND '(SAW WRENCH) TOOLS)
```

```
TOOLS
```

```
(SETQ TOOLS (APPEND '(SAW WRENCH) TOOLS))
```

```
TOOLS
```

LENGTH, REVERSE, SUBST, and LAST Round Out a Basic Repertoire

LENGTH counts the number of top-level elements in a list. REVERSE turns the top level of a list around. Both consider the argument they get to be a list of elements, not caring whether the elements themselves are lists or just atoms. Often they are used on lists that have lists as elements, but they do nothing with the insides of those sublists. Assume, in the following examples, that the value of L is still (A B):

```
(LENGTH '(A B))
   2
```

```
(LENGTH '((A B) (C D)))
   2
```

```
(LENGTH L)
   2
```

```
(LENGTH (APPEND L L))
   4
```

```
(REVERSE '(A B))
  (B A)

(REVERSE '((A B) (C D)))
  ((C D) (A B))

(REVERSE L)
  (B A)

(REVERSE (APPEND L L))
  (B A B A)
```

SUBST takes three arguments, the last of which is an expression in which occurrences of a specified atom are to be replaced.

The first argument of SUBST is the new expression to be plugged in; the second is the atom to be replaced; and the third is the expression to work on:[15]

```
(SUBST <new expression> <old atom> <expression to substitute in>)
```

Study the following:

```
(SUBST 'A 'B '(A B C))
  (A A C)

(SUBST 'B 'A '(A B C))
  (B B C)

(SUBST 'A 'X (SUBST 'B 'Y '(SQRT (+ (* X X) (* Y Y)))))
  (SQRT (+ (* A A) (* B B)))
```

Note that SUBST is a primitive that can dive deeply into a list structure. It works on more than just the top level of a list.

LAST returns a list that contains only the last element of the list given as the argument:

```
(LAST '(A B C))
  (C)

(LAST '((A B) (C D)))
  ((C D))

(LAST 'A)
  ERROR
```

---

[15] The second argument of SUBST actually need not be an atom, it can be any expression. It usually does not make sense for the second argument to be other than an atom, however, unless a test-changing keyword is supplied.

Problems   **Problem 2-8:**   Evaluate the following forms:

(LENGTH '(PLATO SOCRATES ARISTOTLE))

(LENGTH '((PLATO) (SOCRATES) (ARISTOTLE)))

(LENGTH '((PLATO SOCRATES ARISTOTLE)))

(REVERSE '(PLATO SOCRATES ARISTOTLE))

(REVERSE '((PLATO) (SOCRATES) (ARISTOTLE)))

(REVERSE '((PLATO SOCRATES ARISTOTLE)))

Problem 2-9:   Evaluate the following forms:

(LENGTH '((CAR CHEVROLET) (DRINK COKE) (CEREAL WHEATIES)))

(REVERSE '((CAR CHEVROLET) (DRINK COKE) (CEREAL WHEATIES)))

(APPEND '((CAR CHEVROLET) (DRINK COKE)))

(REVERSE '((CAR CHEVROLET) (DRINK COKE))))

Problem 2-10:   Evaluate the following forms:

(SUBST 'OUT 'IN '(SHORT SKIRTS ARE IN))

(SUBST 'IN 'OUT '(SHORT SKIRTS ARE IN))

(LAST '(SHORT SKIRTS ARE IN))

The Interpreter Evaluates Forms

When a form is typed by a LISP user, it is automatically handed to the primitive EVAL. The diagram in figure 2-2 describes how this primitive works.

Note that EVAL normally evaluates all of the arguments before feeding them to the specified procedure. Numeric atoms, however, are treated specially, in that they are not evaluated.

Also, a form whose first element is the name of one of certain special primitives is *not* treated in the standard way. Instead, EVAL may evaluate the arguments strangely or not evaluate them at all. Forms in which these special primitives occur are called *special forms*. SETQ is one of the exceptional primitives, because it handles its arguments in a special way: it does not evaluate the first one. This is a great convenience, for otherwise we would have to quote the first argument every time.

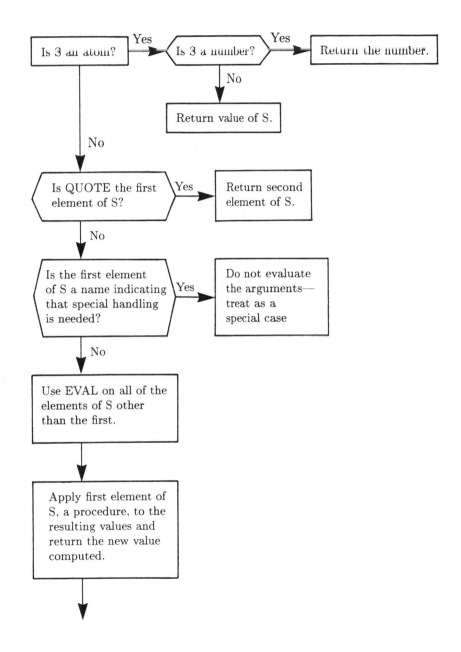

Figure 2-2. Definition of **EVAL**. Note that this version assumes quoting is done with **(QUOTE <EXPRESSION>)** rather than '**<EXPRESSION>**.

Later, we will meet several other special forms that are vital to the effective use of LISP. Note that the term, special form, will actually be used in two ways: to refer to the whole form, and to refer to the special primitive, like SETQ. Context makes the intended use apparent.

Sometimes the pairs of arguments to several SETQs are run together and given to a single SETQ. The odd-numbered arguments are not evaluated but the even ones are, as would be expected. Thus one SETQ can do the work that would otherwise require many:

```
(SETQ ZERO 0 ONE 1 TWO 2 THREE 3 FOUR 4
      FIVE 5 SIX 6 SEVEN 7 EIGHT 8 NINE 9)
   9
```

Now ZERO through NINE have values.

```
ZERO
   0

NINE
   9
```

EVAL Causes Extra Evaluation

Note that one can use the primitive EVAL *explicitly* to call for another round of evaluation beyond the one already employed to evaluate the arguments of a procedure. The following example illustrates:

```
(SETQ A 'B)
   B

(SETQ B 'C)
   C

A
   B

B
   C

(EVAL A)
   C
```

The symbol A is first evaluated because it is the unquoted argument to a procedure. The result is then evaluated because the procedure happens to be EVAL. This EVAL causes whatever the value is to be evaluated.

In chapter 21, we shall see EVAL in use by a procedure-writing program that needs to evaluate a procedure that it has written.

Problems

Problem 2-11:   Evaluate the following forms in the order given:

```
(SETQ METHOD1 '+)
```

```
(SETQ METHOD2 '-)
```

```
(SETQ METHOD METHOD1)
```

```
METHOD
```

```
(EVAL METHOD)
```

```
(SETQ METHOD 'METHOD1)
```

```
METHOD
```

```
(EVAL METHOD)
```

```
(EVAL (EVAL '(QUOTE METHOD)))
```

Summary

- LISP means symbol manipulation.
- LISP procedures and data are constructed out of symbolic expressions.
- LISP handles both integers and floating-point numbers.
- CAR and CDR take lists apart.
- Evaluation is often purposely inhibited by quoting.
- Composing CARs and CDRs makes programming easier.
- Symbolic atoms have values.
- APPEND, LIST, and CONS construct lists.
- LENGTH, REVERSE, SUBST, and LAST round out a basic repertoire.
- The interpreter evaluates forms.
- EVAL causes extra evaluation.

3

Definitions
Predicates
Conditionals
And Binding

The principal purpose of this chapter is to explain how you can create your own procedures, introducing the notion of *procedure abstraction*. Another purpose is to show how tests make it possible to do things conditionally.

Remember that the terms *program*, *primitive*, and *procedure* have slightly different meanings. A program is a collection of procedures. A procedure specifies how something is to be computed. And a primitive is a built-in procedure.

DEFUN Enables Users To Do Procedure Abstraction

One reason LISP is so successful is that hierarchical program layering is encouraged. This layering reflects a powerful idea:

- *Procedure abstraction* is the process of constructing new procedures by combining existing ones.

Procedure abstraction isolates programmers from diverting details by placing existing lower-level procedures underneath a layer of new higher-level procedures. Generally, the higher-level procedures are more mnemonic, transparent, and purpose specific. Each may involve complicated combinations of lower-level procedures.

In LISP, procedure abstraction is done by using DEFUN to combine ingredients, where DEFUN is from define function. The syntax is as follows:

```
(DEFUN <procedure name>
  (<parameter 1>  <parameter 2> ...  <parameter n>)
  <procedure body>)
```

As before, the angle brackets delineate descriptions of things. The descriptions may denote atoms, lists, or even list fragments, as appropriate.

DEFUN does not evaluate its arguments. It just looks at them and establishes a procedure definition, which can later be referred to by having the procedure name appear as the first element of a form to be evaluated. The procedure name must be a symbol. When DEFUN is used it gives back a value. The value DEFUN gives back is the procedure name, but this is of little consequence, because the main purpose of DEFUN is to establish a definition, not to return some useful value.

Recall that anything a procedure has done that persists after it returns its value is called a *side effect*. The side effect of DEFUN is to set up a procedure definition.

The list following the procedure name is called the procedure's *parameter list*. Each parameter is a symbol that may appear in the procedure body. When the procedure name appears later in a form, together with arguments, the value of each parameter in the procedure's body is determined by the value of the corresponding argument in the form.

Let us consider an example immediately. Using DEFUN, it is easy to define a procedure that converts temperatures given in degrees Fahrenheit to degrees Celsius:

```
(DEFUN F-TO-C (TEMP)
  (/ (- TEMP 32) 1.8))
  F-TO-C
```

When F-TO-C is used, it appears as the first element in a two-element list. The second element is F-TO-C's argument. After the argument is evaluated, it becomes the temporary value of the procedure's parameter. In this case, TEMP is the parameter, and TEMP is given the value of the argument while F-TO-C is being evaluated. It is as if the operations shown in figure 3-1 were carried out.

Suppose, for example, that the value of SUPER-HOT is 100. Then consider this:

```
(F-TO-C SUPER-HOT)
```

To evaluate this form, SUPER-HOT is evaluated, handing 100 to the procedure F-TO-C.

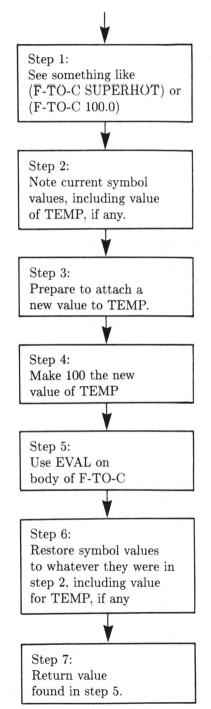

Step 1:
See something like
(F-TO-C SUPERHOT) or
(F-TO-C 100.0)

Step 2:
Note current symbol
values, including value
of TEMP, if any.

Step 3:
Prepare to attach a
new value to TEMP.

Step 4:
Make 100 the new
value of TEMP

Step 5:
Use EVAL on
body of F-TO-C

Step 6:
Restore symbol values
to whatever they were in
step 2, including value
for TEMP, if any

Step 7:
Return value
found in step 5.

Figure 3-1. When entering a procedure, all the parameters are bound and values
are assigned. The parameter values are used in the evaluation of the body.

On entry to `F-TO-C`, 100 becomes the temporary value of `TEMP`. Consequently, when the body of the procedure is evaluated, it is as if the following form were evaluated:

```
(/ (- 100 32) 1.8)
```

The value returned is 37.77.... If `TEMP` had a value before `F-TO-C` was evaluated, that value is restored. If `TEMP` had no value before `F-TO-C` was evaluated, it has no value afterward either.

Now suppose `A` and `B` are procedures. We say that procedure `A` *calls* procedure `B` if the body of `A` contains a form involving `B` that is evaluated in the course of evaluating `A`.

Sometimes several procedures use the same parameter. Because one such procedure may call another, which calls another, and so on, it is necessary for LISP to be able to keep track of several values of the common parameter. Otherwise it would not be possible to restore the parameter's values correctly as the procedure evaluations are completed.

- The process of preparing memory space for parameter values is called *binding*. Parameters are bound when procedures are called.

- The process of establishing a value is called *assignment*. LISP always assigns values to parameters immediately after binding.

Now consider another example, this time involving a procedure that does a symbolic computation, rather than a numerical one. This new procedure exchanges the first and second elements of a two-element list:

```
(DEFUN EXCHANGE (PAIR)
  (LIST (CADR PAIR) (CAR PAIR)))          ;Reverse elements.
  EXCHANGE
```

Note the *comment*. LISP totally ignores semicolons and anything that appears after them on the same line. Consequently, semicolons make it possible to annotate programs without interfering with their operation. Liberal use of comments is good programming practice.

To see how `EXCHANGE` works, suppose the value of `SINNERS` is `(ADAM EVE)`. Then to evaluate `(EXCHANGE SINNERS)`, the first thing LISP does is evaluate the argument, `SINNERS`. The value of `SINNERS` then becomes the temporary value of `PAIR` while `EXCHANGE` is doing its job. Consequently, `(CADR PAIR)` is `EVE`, `(CAR PAIR)` is `ADAM`, and the following is evident:

```
(EXCHANGE SINNERS)
  (EVE ADAM)
```

The next example introduces a procedure with two parameters, rather than just one. Its purpose is to compute percentage.

More specifically, the value returned is to be the percentage by which the second argument is greater than the first:

```
(DEFUN PERCENTAGE-INCREASE (X Y)
  (/ (* 100 (- Y X)) X))          ;Nested forms.
  PERCENTAGE-INCREASE

(PERCENTAGE-INCREASE 10.0 15.0)
  50.0
```

In this example, the temporary value of X becomes 10.0 on entry, and the temporary value of Y becomes 15.0. Note that there is never any confusion about how to match X and Y with 10.0 and 15.0—LISP knows the correct way to match them up, because DEFUN's parameter list specifies the order in which parameters are to be paired with incoming arguments.

Finally, note that the procedure body can consist of any number of forms. The last one always determines the value returned. The others are useful only if they cause some side effect, as in this altered definition of F-TO-C:

```
(DEFUN F-TO-C (TEMP)              ;Second version—awkward but correct.
  (SETQ TEMP (- TEMP 32))         ;Subtract.
  (/ TEMP 1.8))                   ;Divide.
  F-TO-C
```

In this second version, TEMP is used as an input parameter and also as a temporary anchor for the difference between the input and 32. The DEFUN creates a program that specifies two sequential steps.

Note that you can build up a set of procedures incrementally. Each can be entered and tested in turn. If a procedure is found to be faulty, it can be replaced right away simply by using DEFUN again.

Problems

Problem 3-1:   Some people are annoyed by the names of the critical primitives CAR, CDR, and CONS. Define new procedures OUR-FIRST,[1] OUR-REST, and CONSTRUCT that do the same things. Note that OUR-SECOND, OUR-THIRD, and similar procedures are equally easy to create.[2]

---

[1] When COMMON LISP has a primitive that does the same thing as one of our procedures, then we use the prefix OUR-. In most cases our version does exactly what the built-in version does. Occasionally, our version is not as general, or takes slightly different arguments.

[2] COMMON LISP has FIRST, REST, SECOND, and similar primitives.

Problem 3-2:   Define `ROTATE-LEFT`, a procedure that takes a list as its argument and returns a new list in which the former first element becomes the last. The following illustrates:

```
(ROTATE-LEFT '(A B C))
  (B C A)

(ROTATE-LEFT (ROTATE-LEFT '(A B C)))
  (C A B)
```

Problem 3-3:   Define `ROTATE-RIGHT`. It is to be like `ROTATE-LEFT` except that it is to rotate in the other direction.

Problem 3-4:   A palindrome is a list that has the same sequence of elements when read from right to left that it does when read from left to right. Define `PALINDROMIZE` such that it takes a list as its argument and returns a palindrome that is twice as long.

Problem 3-5:   When converting between degrees Fahrenheit and degrees Celsius, it is useful to note that $-40°$ Fahrenheit equals $-40°$ Celsius. This observation makes for the following symmetric conversion formulas:

$$C = (F + 40)/1.8 - 40,$$
$$F = (C + 40) \times 1.8 - 40.$$

Define conversion procedures, `F-TO-C` and `C-TO-F`, using these formulas.

Problem 3-6:   Define `QUADRATIC`, a procedure with three parameters, `A`, `B`, and `C`. `QUADRATIC` is to return a list of the two roots of the polynomial $ax^2 + bx + c$, using this formula:

$$x = \frac{-b \pm \sqrt{b^2 - 4ac}}{2a}.$$

Assume that the roots are real and that a, b, and c are the values of `A`, `B`, and `C`, respectively.

A Predicate Is a Procedure That Returns True or False

More complicated definitions require the use of procedures called predicates. A *predicate* is a procedure that returns a value that signals *true* or *false*.

False is always signaled by `NIL`. True is often signaled by the special symbol `T`, but actually, anything other than `NIL` is considered to signal true.

- Note that T and NIL are special symbols, in that their values are preset to T and NIL. That is, the value of T is T and the value of NIL is NIL.

Consider ATOM and LISTP, for example. ATOM is a predicate that tests its argument to see if it is an atom, while LISTP tests its argument to see if it is a list. To facilitate showing how ATOM, LISTP, and other important predicates behave, let us make the value of the symbol DIGITS be a list of the names of the numbers from zero to nine:

```
(SETQ DIGITS '(ZERO ONE TWO THREE FOUR FIVE SIX SEVEN EIGHT NINE))
  (ZERO ONE TWO THREE FOUR FIVE SIX SEVEN EIGHT NINE)
```

Now ATOM and LISTP can be demonstrated:

```
(ATOM 'DIGITS)
  T

(ATOM 'FIVE)
  T

(ATOM DIGITS)
  NIL

(ATOM '(ZERO ONE TWO THREE FOUR FIVE SIX SEVEN EIGHT NINE))
  NIL

(LISTP 'DIGITS)
  NIL

(LISTP 'FIVE)
  NIL

(LISTP DIGITS)
  T

(LISTP '(ZERO ONE TWO THREE FOUR FIVE SIX SEVEN EIGHT NINE))
  T
```

EQUAL is another fundamental predicate. It takes two arguments and returns T if they are the same.[3] Otherwise it returns NIL:

```
(EQUAL DIGITS DIGITS)
  T

(EQUAL 'DIGITS 'DIGITS)
  T
```

---

[3] What EQUAL thinks is the *same* is clarified in chapter 9. For now, expressions that print out the same way can be considered to be the same, as far as EQUAL is concerned.

```
(EQUAL DIGITS '(ZERO ONE TWO THREE FOUR FIVE SIX SEVEN EIGHT NINE))
  T

(EQUAL DIGITS 'DIGITS)
  NIL
```

The predicate = checks to see whether two numbers are equal. If two numbers are of the same type one can, of course, use EQUAL to compare them. Using =, however, makes the intent of the test more apparent.[4]

```
(= 3.141592653 2.718281828)
  NIL

(= (* 5 5) (+ (* 3 3) (* 4 4)))
  T
```

Now it is time to consider an important peculiarity:

- NIL and the empty list, ( ) are completely equivalent: NIL ≡ ( ). NIL and ( ) satisfy the EQUAL predicate, for example:[5]

```
(EQUAL NIL '( ))
  T
```

Note that:

- By convention, the empty list is printed out as NIL.

- Occasional bugs derive from the fact that (ATOM '( )) is T. This happens because NIL is considered an atom.

It helps to remember that the empty list is the only expression that is both an atom and a list. Thus, both (ATOM NIL) and (LISTP NIL) return T.

NULL checks to see if its argument is an empty list:

```
(NULL '( ))
  T

(NULL T)
  NIL

(NULL DIGITS)
  NIL
```

---

[4] Using = may in some cases be more efficient than using EQUAL, because = assumes that its arguments are numbers.

[5] Some say the reason that the equivalence of NIL and ( ) was originally arranged has to do with the instruction set of the ancient 709 computer. Others believe the identity was always known to be a programming convenience. No one seems to know for sure.

```
(NULL 'DIGITS)
  NIL
```

MEMBER tests to see if an atom is an element of a list.[6] It would be natural for MEMBER to return T if the first argument is an element of the following list and NIL otherwise. Actually MEMBER returns the fragment of the list that begins with the first argument, if the first argument is indeed an element of the list. This is a special case of a common programming convenience. The general idea is that a procedure can return either NIL or something that is both nonNIL *and* useful for feeding further computation.

```
(MEMBER 'FIVE DIGITS)
  (FIVE SIX SEVEN EIGHT NINE)

(MEMBER 'TEN DIGITS)
  NIL
```

The first argument must be a top-level element of the second argument. It is not enough for the first argument to be buried somewhere in the second argument, as in this example:

```
(MEMBER 'FIVE '((ZERO TWO FOUR SIX EIGHT) (ONE TWO THREE FOUR FIVE)))
  NIL
```

The following use of MEMBER exploits the fact that MEMBER returns something other than T when an element is present. It determines the number of digits after the first instance of the symbol FIVE in the list DIGITS.

```
(LENGTH (CDR (MEMBER 'FIVE DIGITS)))
  4
```

For some further examples, let us establish values for the elements of DIGITS:

```
(SETQ ZERO 0 ONE 1 TWO 2 THREE 3 FOUR 4
      FIVE 5 SIX 6 SEVEN 7 EIGHT 8 NINE 9)
  9
```

Using these values, we can look at some predicates that work on numbers. NUMBERP tests its argument to see if it is a number:

```
(NUMBERP 3.141592653)
  T

(NUMBERP FIVE)
  T
```

---

[6] The first argument given to MEMBER need not be an atom, it can be an expression. It usually does not make sense for the first argument to be other than an atom, however, unless there a test-changing keyword is supplied.

```
(NUMBERP 'FIVE)
  NIL

(NUMBERP DIGITS)
  NIL

(NUMBERP 'DIGITS)
  NIL
```

The > and < predicates expect their arguments to be numbers. The predicate > tests them to see that they are in strictly descending order, while < checks to see that they are in strictly ascending order. Both may be given one, two, or more arguments.

```
(> FIVE 2)
  T

(> 2 FIVE)
  NIL

(< 2 FIVE)
  T

(< FIVE 2)
  NIL

(< 2 2)
  NIL

(> FIVE FOUR THREE TWO ONE)
  T

(> THREE ONE FOUR)
  NIL

(> 3 1 4)
  NIL
```

ZEROP expects a number. It tests its argument to see if it is zero:

```
(ZEROP ZERO)
  T

(ZEROP 'ZERO)
  ERROR

(ZEROP FIVE)
  NIL
```

MINUSP tests whether a number is negative:

```
(MINUSP ONE)
  NIL

(MINUSP (- ONE))
  T

(MINUSP ZERO)
  NIL
```

EVENP checks whether a number is even:

```
(EVENP (* 9 7 5 3 1))
  NIL
```

Note that several predicates end in P, a mnemonic for predicate. The predicate ATOM is an unfortunate exception that tends to suggest, wrongly, that LIST should be a predicate too.

Problems

Problem 3-7:   Define your own version of the predicate EVENP for checking whether an integer is divisible by 2. Call it OUR-EVENP. You may want to use REM, a primitive that takes two integer arguments and returns the remainder left over when the first argument is divided by the second.

Problem 3-8:   Define PALINDROMEP, a predicate that tests its argument to see if it is a list that has the same sequence of elements when read from right to left as when it is read from left to right.

Problem 3-9:   Define RIGHTP, a predicate that takes three arguments. The arguments are the lengths of the sides of a triangle that may or may not be a right angle triangle. RIGHTP is to return T if the sum of the squares of the two shorter sides is within 2% of the square of the longest side. Because the floating-point representation of real numbers has limited precision, it would be unreasonable to test for exact equality here. Otherwise RIGHTP is to return NIL. You may assume the longest side is given as the first argument.

Problem 3-10:   Define NOT-REALP, a predicate with three parameters that returns T if $b^2 - 4ac < 0$.

AND, OR, and NOT Are Used To Do Logic

NOT returns T only if its argument is NIL.

```
(NOT NIL)
  T

(NOT T)
  NIL

(NOT 'DOG)
  NIL

(SETQ PETS '(DOG CAT))
  (DOG CAT)

(NOT (MEMBER 'DOG PETS))
  NIL

(NOT (MEMBER 'TIGER PETS))
  T
```

AND and OR make composite tests possible. AND returns nonNIL only if all arguments are nonNIL. OR returns nonNIL if any argument is nonNIL. Both take any number of arguments.

```
(AND T T NIL)
  NIL

(OR T T NIL)
  T

(AND (MEMBER 'DOG PETS) (MEMBER 'TIGER PETS))
  NIL

(OR (MEMBER 'DINGO PETS) (MEMBER 'TIGER PETS))
  NIL
```

The arguments of AND and OR are not treated in the standard way. Consequently, AND and OR are considered to be special forms:

- AND evaluates its arguments from left to right. If a NIL is encountered, NIL is returned immediately. Any remaining arguments are not even evaluated. Otherwise AND returns the value of its last argument.

In other words, anything other than NIL behaves like T as far as AND is concerned. This is a great feature. OR behaves similarly:

- OR evaluates its arguments from left to right. If something other than NIL is encountered, it is returned immediately. Any remaining arguments are not even evaluated. Otherwise OR returns NIL.

Note that both AND and OR return the last value computed, when successful, rather than just plain T. Often the computed values are useful in further computation. Consider the following examples, recalling that MEMBER also returns something more useful, namely the remainder of its second argument, if it finds its first argument in that second argument:

```
(AND (MEMBER 'DOG PETS) (MEMBER 'CAT PETS))
  (CAT)
```

```
(OR (MEMBER 'DOG PETS) (MEMBER 'TIGER PETS))
  (DOG CAT)
```

Predicates Help COND Select a Value among Alternatives

Predicates are most often used to determine which of several forms should be evaluated. The choice is usually determined by predicates in conjunction with COND, an extremely common special form. Regrettably, it has a somewhat peculiar syntax. In a *conditional* form, the symbol COND is followed by a number of lists, each of which contains a test, as well as something to evaluate and return if the test succeeds.

Thus the syntax of COND is as follows:

```
(COND (<test 1> ...  <result 1>)
      (<test 2> ...  <result 2>)
        .
        .
        .
      (<test n> ...  <result n>))
```

Each list is called a *clause*. The idea is to search through the clauses, evaluating only the test form of each, until one is found whose value is nonNIL. Then the other forms in the successful clause are evaluated and the value of the *last* form is returned as the value of the conditional form. All forms standing between the first and the last in a clause must be there only for accomplishing side effects. There are two special cases:

• If no successful clause is found, COND returns NIL.

• If the successful clause consists of only one form, then the value of that form itself is returned. Said another way, the test and result forms may be the same.

The following is a simple example. Assuming L is a list, the result is the symbol EMPTY if L is empty, and NOT-EMPTY, otherwise:

```
(COND ((NULL L) 'EMPTY)
      (T 'NOT-EMPTY))
```

The following will also work, because L is nonNIL whenever there is something in L:

```
(COND (L 'NOT-EMPTY)
      (T 'EMPTY))
```

As shown in this example, the first form in a COND clause may be a symbol whose value is a list that may or may not be empty. If the list *is not* empty, it triggers the COND clause, because it is not NIL; if the list *is* empty, it does not trigger the clause, because it is the same as NIL. Note, however, that most programmers consider this use of an unsurrounded list to be a parlor trick to be avoided.

Note that NULL and NOT are actually equivalent primitives, because NULL returns T only if its argument is an empty list and NOT returns T only if its argument is NIL:

```
(NOT X)   ≡   (NULL X)
```

Also, while on the subject of the empty list, it is important to know what happens when CAR or CDR gets one:

- CAR and CDR both return NIL when given an empty list.

Both CAR and CDR return NIL if given an empty list by reason of programming convenience. If they were to complain instead, it would be necessary to test lists before working on them.

Problems

Problem 3-11:   Express (ABS X), (MIN A B), and (MAX A B) in terms of COND.

Problem 3-12:   Express (NOT U), (OR X Y Z), and (AND A B C) in terms of COND.

Problem 3-13:   What is the value of the following:

```
(CONS (CAR NIL) (CDR NIL))
```

COND Enables DEFUN To Do More

Now we are ready to use conditional forms when defining new procedures using DEFUN. Suppose we want to have a procedure whose arguments are an atom and a list. The procedure is to return the list with the atom added to the front, if that atom is not already in the list. Otherwise the procedure is to return the unaltered list. Clearly the desired procedure must do a test and act according to the result. This will do:[7]

---

[7]   COMMON LISP has the primitive ADJOIN, which is similar to OUR-ADJOIN.

```
(DEFUN OUR-ADJOIN (ITEM BAG)
  (COND ((MEMBER ITEM BAG) BAG)          ; Already in?
        (T (CONS ITEM BAG))))            ; Add ITEM to front.
  OUR-ADJOIN
```

Note that the T in the conditional expression ensures that the last clause will be triggered if the others are not. A T is often seen in the last clause of a conditional form, where it clearly establishes that the evaluation will not run off the end. The T is not really necessary, however, because the same values would result were it left out.[8]

Problems

Problem 3-14: Define CHECK-TEMPERATURE, a procedure that is to take one argument, such that it returns RIDICULOUSLY-HOT if the argument is greater than 100, it returns RIDICULOUSLY-COLD if the argument is less than 0, and it returns OK otherwise.

Problem 3-15: Write MEDIAN-OF-THREE, a procedure of three numeric arguments that determines which is in the middle, that is, neither the smallest nor the largest. It may be helpful to think of sorting the three numbers and picking the middle one. Alternatively, consider the six possible permutations of three numbers. Use a conditional form to determine which of the six you are given.

Variables May Be Free or Bound

In LISP, relating arguments to parameters on entering a procedure is called *lambda binding*. Consider the following slightly peculiar procedure:

```
(DEFUN SCREWY-INCREMENT (PARAMETER)       ; PARAMETER is bound.
  (SETQ PARAMETER (+ PARAMETER 10))
  (SETQ FREE PARAMETER))                   ; FREE is free.
  SCREWY-INCREMENT
```

Evidently SCREWY-INCREMENT is to add 10 to its argument, returning the result after arranging for the result to be the value of FREE. Now let us try something:

```
(SETQ PARAMETER 15)
  15

(SETQ FREE 10)
  10

(SETQ ARGUMENT 10)
  10
```

---

[8] Curiously, using T to trigger the final clause does matter if the value form returns multiple values.

```
(SCREWY-INCREMENT ARGUMENT)
  20

FREE
  20

PARAMETER
  15

ARGUMENT
  10
```

The value of ARGUMENT never changes, not even inside of SCREWY-INCREMENT. The value of FREE is permanently altered while that of PARAMETER is not. PARAMETER is temporarily changed—its value becomes 10 on entry to SCREWY-INCREMENT and then becomes 20 by virtue of the SETQ. The value of PARAMETER is restored on exit, because PARAMETER appears in the procedure's parameter list. We say that PARAMETER is bound with respect to SCREWY-INCREMENT while FREE is free in the same context.

So far we have talked about parameters, which appear in procedure definitions, and arguments, which appear when procedures are used. It is also common to refer to a symbol as a *variable* whenever we are thinking about the symbol's value.

- A *bound variable*, with respect to a procedure, is a symbol that appears in the procedure's parameter list.

- A *free variable*, with respect to a procedure, is a symbol that does not appear in the procedure's parameter list.

Note that changing the value of PARAMETER using SETQ did not change the value of ARGUMENT, even though PARAMETER inherited its original value from ARGUMENT. In some programming languages ARGUMENT and PARAMETER would get tied together, and as a result, the value of ARGUMENT would change as well.

Free-variable Values Are Determined Lexically, Not Dynamically

A collection of bindings is called an *environment*. A symbol's value is found by looking in the appropriate environment.[9] If a language uses *dynamic scoping*, as did some older dialects of LISP, the values of free variables are determined by the *activation environment*, the environment in force when the procedure requiring the free-variable values is called. If a language uses *lexical scoping*, as COMMON LISP normally does, then the values of free variables are determined by the *definition environment*, the environment in force when the procedure requiring the free-variable values was defined.

---

[9] An environment can be represented by an association list, to be discussed later.

- A *global free variable*, with respect to a procedure, is a symbol that does not appear in the procedure's parameter list and also does not appear in its definition or activation environment (depending on whether lexical or dynamic scoping are in force).

Programming beginners can ignore the subtleties involved for now by simply avoiding free variables.

Problems

Problem 3-16: Define CIRCLE such that it returns a list of the circumference and area of a circle whose radius is given. Assume PI is a global free variable whose value is π.[10]

LISP Does Call-by-value Rather Than Call-by-reference

In the world of programming languages, there are two commonly employed options for handling procedure arguments. They are referred to as *call by reference* and *call by value*. To understand the difference, consider the following definition:

```
(DEFUN DEMONSTRATE-CALL (PARAMETER)        ;PARAMETER is bound.
  (SETQ PARAMETER (+ PARAMETER 10))
  (+ PARAMETER FREE))                       ;FREE is free.
DEMONSTRATE-CALL
```

Now suppose we use FREE as an argument to DEMONSTRATE-CALL:

```
FREE
  20

(DEMONSTRATE-CALL FREE)
  50
```

The result is 40 because the initial value of PARAMETER is 20, the incremented value of PARAMETER is 30, and the value of FREE is 20, just as it was before entering DEMONSTRATE-CALL.

The important point is that the value of FREE is *not* changed when the value of PARAMETER is changed, even though the initial value of PARAMETER is determined by FREE's value. Only FREE's value is handed over, not control of FREE's value. We say that LISP obeys the conventions of *call by value*.[11]

---

[10] In COMMON LISP, there actually *is* a built-in global free variable called PI.

[11] Although LISP is a call-by-value language, the value of an argument can be changed by a change to a parameter if that change is done by certain surgical primitives that alter lists like those described in chapter 9. Only pointers to lists are copied, not lists themselves.

Suppose, by contrast, that the parameter, PARAMETER, and the argument, FREE, were tied together on entry to DEMONSTRATE-CALL such that a change to one would change the other automatically. Then the initial value of PARAMETER would be 20, as before, and the incremented value of PARAMETER would be 30, the value of FREE would be 30 too, and the result returned by DEMONSTRATE-CALL would be 60. If LISP were to work this way, we would say that it would obey the conventions of *call by reference.*

Procedure Names Can Be Used as Arguments

Sometimes it is useful for the value of a symbol to be a procedure name. Then the procedure FUNCALL makes it possible to retrieve the value and use the procedure.

Let the value of BANKING-PROCEDURE be the symbol CALCULATE-INTEREST, let the value of INTEREST-RATE be 0.1, and let the definition of CALCULATE-INTEREST use INTEREST-RATE:

```
(SETQ BANKING-PROCEDURE 'CALCULATE-INTEREST)
   CALCULATE-INTEREST

(SETQ INTEREST-RATE 0.1)
   0.1

(DEFUN CALCULATE-INTEREST (BALANCE)
  (* BALANCE INTEREST-RATE))
```

Note that INTEREST-RATE is a free variable with respect to the procedure CALCULATE-INTEREST. Now BANKING-PROCEDURE can be used as the first argument to FUNCALL. FUNCALL finds its value, namely CALCULATE-INTEREST, and uses the remaining argument to feed CALCULATE-INTEREST:

```
(FUNCALL BANKING-PROCEDURE 100.0)
   10.0
```

Evidently all of the following produce exactly the same result:

```
(CALCULATE-INTEREST 100.0)

(FUNCALL 'CALCULATE-INTEREST 100.0)

(FUNCALL BANKING-PROCEDURE 100.0)
```

Actually, because the first argument to FUNCALL is evaluated, any form can be there, including a conditional form.

Thus the following determines which of three interest procedures, and consequently which of three interest rates, is to be used by testing the type of the account:

```
(SETQ ACCOUNT-TYPE 'NORMAL)
  NORMAL

(FUNCALL (COND ((EQUAL ACCOUNT-TYPE 'NORMAL) 'CALCULATE-INTEREST)
               ((EQUAL ACCOUNT-TYPE '90DAY) 'CALCULATE-HIGH-INTEREST)
               (T 'CALCULATE-NO-INTEREST))
         100.0)
  10.0
```

Certainly the same effect could be obtained in another way, but there are many situations in which the use of FUNCALL is appropriate, rather than contrived, as we shall see later, when talking about data-driven programming.

With two banking procedures, CALCULATE-INTEREST and CALCULATE-NEW-BALANCE, it is possible to define TRANSACT, a procedure whose first argument is intended to be the name of a procedure:

```
(DEFUN TRANSACT (PROCEDURE-NAME BALANCE)
  (FUNCALL PROCEDURE-NAME BALANCE))
```

This leads to the following examples:

```
(TRANSACT 'CALCULATE-INTEREST 100.0)
  10.0

(TRANSACT 'CALCULATE-NEW-BALANCE 100.0)
  110.0
```

LET Binds Parameters, Too

Finally it is time to learn about LET, a popular procedure that binds parameters and assigns values to them. Along the way we will consider many alternative ways of writing the OUR-ADJOIN procedure previously defined this way:

```
(DEFUN OUR-ADJOIN (ITEM BAG)
  (COND ((MEMBER ITEM BAG) BAG)          ; Already in?
        (T (CONS ITEM BAG))))            ; Add ITEM to front.
```

Suppose you are not good at remembering argument order. You might elect to write a new version, called AUGMENT, that will take its arguments in either order, testing to see which is the item and which is the bag by determining which is the list:

```
(DEFUN AUGMENT (FIRST SECOND)
  (COND ((LISTP FIRST) (COND ((MEMBER SECOND FIRST) FIRST)
                             (T (CONS SECOND FIRST))))
        (T (COND ((MEMBER FIRST SECOND) SECOND)
                 (T (CONS FIRST SECOND))))))
```

Unfortunately, flexibility along one dimension has brought complexity in others. We now have a longer procedure, with two nearly identical COND forms, and because the argument order is unknown, the nice mnemonic parameter names have been dropped in favor of the neutral names FIRST and SECOND. Here is a misguided way out:

```
(DEFUN AUGMENT (FIRST SECOND)
  (COND ((LISTP FIRST)                    ;Determine which is which.
         (SETQ ITEM SECOND BAG FIRST))
        (T (SETQ ITEM FIRST BAG SECOND)))
  (COND ((MEMBER ITEM BAG) BAG)           ;Already in?
        (T (CONS ITEM BAG))))             ;Add ITEM to front.
```

The problem with this definition is that ITEM and BAG are free variables, with values that persist even after AUGMENT is finished. Other uses of ITEM and BAG can be influenced mysteriously, making debugging a nightmare. Consequently, the following is better:

```
(DEFUN AUGMENT (FIRST SECOND)
  (COND ((LISTP FIRST)                    ;Determine which is which.
         (AUGMENT1 SECOND FIRST))         ;Call AUGMENT1 with arguments
        (T (AUGMENT1 FIRST SECOND))))     ; the right way around.

(DEFUN AUGMENT1 (ITEM BAG)                ;Like the old AUGMENT.
  (COND ((MEMBER ITEM BAG) BAG)           ;Already in?
        (T (CONS ITEM BAG))))             ;Add ITEM to front.
```

The auxiliary procedure, AUGMENT1, introduces the new parameters we need, making ITEM and BAG bound variables instead of free variables.

There is still another, and usually better way out, because parameters can be bound using LET.

Here is an example:

```
(DEFUN AUGMENT (FIRST SECOND)
  (LET ((ITEM FIRST)                      ;Bind ITEM and assign initial value.
        (BAG SECOND))                     ;Bind BAG and assign initial value.
    (COND ((LISTP FIRST)                  ;Determine which is which.
           (SETQ ITEM SECOND BAG FIRST)))  ;Reverse if necessary.
    (COND ((MEMBER ITEM BAG) BAG)          ;Action.
          (T (CONS ITEM BAG)))))
```

Evidently, LET arranges for parameters to be bound and assigned. Here is the syntax:

```
(LET ((<parameter 1> <initial value 1>)
      (<parameter 2> <initial value 2>)
      ...
      (<parameter n> <initial value n>))
  <let body>)
```

Thus LETs generally begin with a parameter list consisting of two-element lists, each of which has a symbol and an initial value form. In our previous AUGMENT example, the parameter list is ((ITEM FIRST) (BAG SECOND)). Sometimes you will see parameters alone, with no initial value forms. Such parameters have NIL assigned as initial values.

Here is another version of AUGMENT, this time with initial-value forms containing CONDs:

```
(DEFUN AUGMENT (FIRST SECOND)
  (LET ((ITEM (COND ((LISTP FIRST) SECOND)     ;Compute correct value for ITEM.
                    (T FIRST)))
        (BAG (COND ((LISTP SECOND) SECOND)     ;Compute correct value for BAG.
                   (T FIRST))))
    (COND ((MEMBER ITEM BAG) BAG)              ;Action.
          (T (CONS ITEM BAG)))))
```

Now note an important detail about LET in general:

- The initial values for the bound variables are all computed before any values are assigned.

Thus the initial values are said to be assigned *in parallel*, rather than *sequentially*. Here, for example, sequential thinking with parallel assignment produces a bug:

```
(DEFUN AUGMENT (FIRST SECOND)                  ;BUGGED!
  (LET ((ITEM (COND ((LISTP FIRST) SECOND)     ;Compute correct value for ITEM.
                    (T FIRST)))
        (BAG (COND ((EQUAL ITEM SECOND)        ;User foolishly expects ITEM to
                     FIRST)                     ; have a value and tests
                   (T SECOND))))                ; accordingly.
    (COND ((MEMBER ITEM BAG) BAG)              ;Action.
          (T (CONS ITEM BAG)))))
```

Because all initial values are computed *before* assignments are made, ITEM does not yet have a value when (EQUAL ITEM SECOND) is evaluated, causing an unbound-variable error.

Happily, however, there is a related procedure, LET*, that does assign initial values sequentially. Thus this version of AUGMENT works:

```
(DEFUN AUGMENT (FIRST SECOND)
  (LET* ((ITEM (COND ((LISTP FIRST) SECOND)   ;Compute correct value for ITEM.
                     (T FIRST)))
         (BAG (COND ((EQUAL ITEM SECOND)      ;User correctly expects ITEM to
                     FIRST)                    ;  have a value and tests
                    (T SECOND))))             ;  accordingly.
    (COND ((MEMBER ITEM BAG) BAG)             ;Action.
          (T (CONS ITEM BAG)))))
```

Incidentally, PSETQ is to SETQ, as LET is to LET*: whereas SETQ assigns all variable values sequentially, as they are computed, PSETQ postpones assignment until after all values are computed. Consequently, it is easy to reverse the values of two variables using PSETQ:

```
(SETQ A 'X B 'Y)

(PSETQ A B B A)

A
  Y

B
  X
```

Trying to reverse values using SETQ fails, of course:

```
(SETQ A 'X B 'Y)

(SETQ A B B A)

A
  Y

B
  Y
```

Interestingly, with PSETQ, we can avoid all the commotion concerning AUG-MENT by way of the following definition:

```
(DEFUN AUGMENT (ITEM BAG)
  (COND ((LISTP ITEM)                 ;ITEM wrongly assigned?
         (PSETQ ITEM BAG              ;Reset parameters in parallel.
                BAG ITEM)))
  (COND ((MEMBER ITEM BAG) BAG)
        (T (CONS ITEM BAG))))
```

Summary

- DEFUN enables users to do procedure abstraction.
- A predicate is a procedure that returns true or false.
- AND, OR, and NOT are used to do logic.
- Predicates help COND select a value among alternatives.
- COND enables DEFUN to do more.
- Variables may be free or bound.
- Free-variable values are determined lexically, not dynamically.
- LISP does call-by-value rather than call-by-reference.
- Procedure names can be used as arguments.
- LET binds parameters, too.

References

For an excellent treatment of procedure abstraction, see Abelson and Sussman [1984].

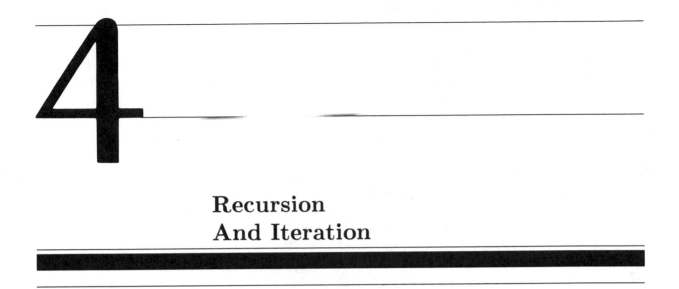

Recursion
And Iteration

The first purpose of this chapter is to understand how a procedure can use itself in its own definition. This proves useful, because it enables a procedure to solve a problem by simplifying it slightly and handing the simplified problem off to one or more exact copies of the procedure itself. So far, you have seen nesting of procedures, where one calls upon others to do part of the work, like people do when working in a mature bureaucracy. Here, however, the procedure calls upon *itself*, either directly or through an intermediary, to tackle a subtask. This is called *recursion*.

The second purpose is to see how to make a procedure do something over and over until an explicit stopping criterion is satisfied. This is called *iteration*.

Programming Requires Control Structure Selection

A *control structure* is a general scheme by which a procedure can go about getting things done. Recursion and iteration are examples of control structures. In general, the choice of a control structure should be determined by the problem under consideration. Sometimes a mathematical function is specified in a way that suggests how it should be computed. Sometimes the way a problem is represented determines the proper thing to do. Sometimes either recursion or iteration will do equally well.

Recursion Allows
Procedures To Use
Themselves

To calculate the nth power of some number, m, it is sufficient to do the job for the $(n-1)^{\text{th}}$ power, because this result, multiplied by m, is the desired result for the nth power:

$$m^n = \begin{cases} m \times m^{n-1}, & \text{for } n > 0; \\ 1, & \text{for } n = 0. \end{cases}$$

Definitions that describe a procedure partly in terms of fresh starts on simpler arguments are said to be *recursive*. The procedure for computing powers of a number, as just specified, suggests a recursive definition. Let us look at a recursive definition for OUR-EXPT expressed in LISP (because it handles only nonnegative integer exponents, it is somewhat weaker than the primitive EXPT supplied by LISP itself):

```
(DEFUN OUR-EXPT (M N)
  (COND ((ZEROP N) 1)                        ;n = 0?
        (T (* M (OUR-EXPT M (- N 1)))))))     ;Recurse.
```

Using figure 4-1, we can easily follow the history of M and N as LISP evaluates (OUR-EXPT 2 3). The conventional device used to show how the recursion works is an inverted tree in which nodes represent fresh entries to the procedure as required by the computation. Each entry is listed with its order in the sequence of entries to the procedure. Downward portions of the flow of control show the argument or arguments carried down while upward portions indicate the values returned.

In the OUR-EXPT example, each place in the inverted tree sprouts only one new branch, because each copy of OUR-EXPT can invoked only one new copy. A procedure that does this is said to be *singly recursive*. Such procedures are particularly easy to convert into procedures that do *not* call themselves, and therefore are not recursive.

The Fibonacci function provides a different example. Leonardo of Pisa, also known as Fibonacci, was curious about the rate of reproduction of rabbits. To be able to apply formal mathematical methods to the problem, he made some simplifying assumptions:

- We start with one immature female rabbit at time zero.

- Reproduction is synchronized. That is, there are distinct generations at fixed time intervals. All rabbits in a particular generation are exactly the same age.

- Only mature rabbits reproduce. It takes one time step, that is, one generation, to become mature.

- Each mature female rabbit produces exactly one female offspring during each time step.

- Rabbits live forever.

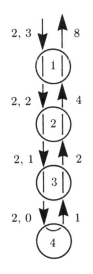

Figure 4-1. A simulation often helps illuminate the strategy of a recursive procedure. Here each copy of the OUR-EXPT procedure reduces the value of N by one and passes it on until N is reduced to zero. The arrows show how control moves from one numbered application of OUR-EXPT to another. Arguments are shown on the downward pointing arrows; values returned, on the upward.

Thus the number of female rabbits added during a particular time step equals the number of mature female rabbits. This in turn is the total number of rabbits, mature or immature, at the previous time step. Accordingly, the Fibonacci function, $f(n)$, is defined as follows:

$$f(n) = \begin{cases} f(n-1) + f(n-2), & \text{for } n > 1; \\ 1, & \text{for } n = 1; \\ 1, & \text{for } n = 0. \end{cases}$$

Putting this function into LISP, we have the following:

```
(DEFUN FIBONACCI (N)
  (COND ((= N 0) 1)                    ;n = 0 ?
        ((= N 1) 1)                    ;n = 1 ?
        (T (+ (FIBONACCI (- N 1))      ;Recurse.
              (FIBONACCI (- N 2)))))))  ;Recurse.
```

Figure 4-2 shows FIBONACCI computing a result when given 4 as its argument.

Computing Fibonacci numbers this way is more interesting than computing powers of numbers, because each copy of FIBONACCI can create *two* new copies, not just one. FIBONACCI is said to be *doubly recursive*. The

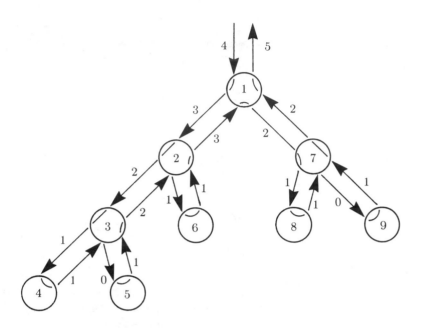

Figure 4-2. A simulation of FIBONACCI. Note that recursion activates two copies each time the argument proves to be hard to handle.

definition of Fibonacci's function directly suggests such a doubly recursive procedure. But as you can see in figure 4-2, the doubly recursive procedure inefficiently works identical subproblems over and over. We will look at other ways to compute Fibonacci numbers later.

Having seen recursion at work on two simple numerical problems, we next pretend that LISP did not come equipped with the primitive MEMBER. We define OUR-MEMBER to be a predicate that tests to see if its first argument is a top-level element of its second.[1]

```
(DEFUN OUR-MEMBER (ITEM L)
   (COND ((NULL L) NIL)                          ; List empty?
         ((EQUAL ITEM (CAR L)) L)                 ; First element wins?
         (T (OUR-MEMBER ITEM (CDR L)))))          ; Recurse.
```

Evidently, OUR-MEMBER considers two situations to be basic: either the second argument, L, is an empty list, resulting in a value of NIL for OUR-MEMBER; or the first element of L is equal to the first argument, ITEM. If neither of the basic situations is in effect, OUR-MEMBER gives up and hands a slightly simplified problem to a copy of itself. The copy has a list to work with

---

[1] OUR-MEMBER does not behave exactly like MEMBER, because they use different equality tests, as explained in chapter 9.

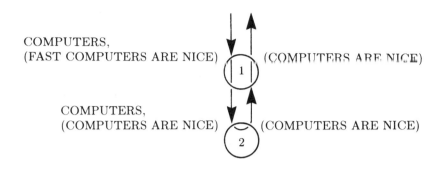

COMPUTERS,
(FAST COMPUTERS ARE NICE)   (COMPUTERS ARE NICE)

COMPUTERS,
(COMPUTERS ARE NICE)   (COMPUTERS ARE NICE)

Figure 4-3. A simulation of OUR-MEMBER at work on the symbol COMPUTERS and the list (FAST COMPUTERS ARE NICE).

that is one element shorter. Figure 4-3 shows OUR-MEMBER at work on the following problem:

```
(OUR-MEMBER 'COMPUTERS '(FAST COMPUTERS ARE NICE))
  (COMPUTERS ARE NICE)
```

Note that presenting the LISP definition of OUR-MEMBER is a way of describing what OUR-MEMBER does. Such a description is a useful alternative to a description in English. But because OUR-MEMBER acts much like MEMBER, the official LISP primitive, we see that it is possible to describe part of LISP using LISP itself. In chapter 23, this idea will be developed to a surprising extreme, with the whole of LISP evaluation incestuously defined in terms of a LISP program.

Tail Recursion Can Be Efficient

Note also that OUR-MEMBER either considers a situation basic, or hands a simplified problem to a copy of itself. OUR-MEMBER does not need to remember anything while the copy is at work. The value returned is just the value returned by the copy. Conceptually, the copy does not have to return to the original procedure. Instead, the copy could return directly to the caller of the original procedure.

- A procedure is said to be *tail recursive* if the value returned is either something computed directly or the value returned by a recursive call.

Because a tail-recursive procedure does nothing with the value returned by the recursive call, it need not remember anything.[2]

---

[2] To be precise, a tail-recursive procedure can be evaluated using a fixed amount of control memory, independent of the arguments given.

The recursive form need not be the last form in the procedure body. It just has to be the last form that gets evaluated, given that the recursive form is evaluated at all. In fact, recursive forms may appear in more than one place in the procedure body. Recursion may also be indirect, of course, via another procedure.

Consider the following procedure, which trims off the first N elements of a list and returns the rest:

```
(DEFUN TRIM-TAIL (L N)
  (COND ((ZEROP N) L)
        (T (TRIM-TAIL (CDR L) (- N 1)))))
```

This procedure is tail recursive, because it does nothing with the result returned by the call to TRIM-TAIL inside the COND. Now suppose that we instead wanted the other part of the list; that is, a list of the first N elements. The following does the trick:

```
(DEFUN TRIM-HEAD (L N)
  (COND ((ZEROP N) NIL)
        (T (CONS (CAR L) (TRIM-HEAD (CDR L) (- N 1))))))
```

This procedure is not tail recursive, because it uses the result returned by the call to TRIM-HEAD as an argument to CONS. It also has to remember the value of (CAR L) while the form containing TRIM-HEAD is being evaluated.

By defining an auxiliary function, we can introduce a variable that allows us to hang onto the partially assembled result:

```
(DEFUN TRIM-CLEVER (L N)  (TRIM-AUX L NIL N))
```

```
(DEFUN TRIM-AUX (L RESULT N)
  (COND ((ZEROP N) (REVERSE RESULT))
        (T (TRIM-AUX (CDR L) (CONS (CAR L) RESULT) (- N 1)))))
```

The auxiliary procedure is tail recursive, because the value returned by the call to TRIM-AUX inside the COND is used directly as the value of the procedure.

In subsequent chapters, there are many examples of tail recursive procedures that hand partial results down to lower-level copies without doing anything to the values returned by these lower-level copies. We exhibit them, because many LISP programmers are wild about programming in this tail-recursive style, arguing that tail-recursive procedures are elegant and that the values of tail-recursive procedures can be computed efficiently.[3]

---

[3] A tail-recursive procedure can be converted *automatically* into a procedure that computes the same thing without recursion. This means that the programmer writing a procedure may use the perspicuous recursive form, without a penalty in performance, if the LISP system converts to the equivalent nonrecursive form internally. Not all LISP systems take advantage of this possibility, however.

Recursion Can Be Used To Analyze Nested Expressions

Now consider COUNT-ATOMS, a procedure that counts the atoms in some given expression:

```
(DEFUN COUNT-ATOMS (L)
  (COND ((NULL L) 0)                      ; List empty?
        ((ATOM L) 1)                      ; Atom rather than a list?
        (T (+ (COUNT-ATOMS (CAR L))       ; T forces recursion.
              (COUNT-ATOMS (CDR L)))))))
```

The first two clauses of the COND form deal with the very simplest cases, returning 0 for empty lists and 1 for atoms. If COUNT-ATOMS gets NIL as its argument, then it returns 0, because NIL ≡ ( ), and the empty-list test is done before the atom test.

The third clause handles other situations by converting big problems into smaller ones. Lists are broken up using CAR and CDR, and COUNT-ATOMS is applied to each of the two resulting fragments. Because every atom in the list is either in the CAR or the CDR, every atom gets counted. The + combines the results. Eventually, after perhaps many applications of itself, COUNT-ATOMS reduces the hard cases to something that either the first or the second clause of the conditional can handle.

At this point it is helpful to see how COUNT-ATOMS can take an expression apart and reduce it successively to the simple cases. As shown in figure 4-4, the particular expression whose atoms are to be counted is (* X (SQRT 4)). Note that the data expression in this case is itself a form, something that one might think of evaluating. Here then is an example of a procedure, COUNT-ATOMS, examining a piece of another procedure and performing a computation on it.

At each stage, COUNT-ATOMS's argument gets broken into two smaller pieces. Once the answers for both pieces are at hand, + adds the results together and returns the value to a higher-level place further up the tree.

Now consider this variant of COUNT-ATOMS:

```
(DEFUN COUNT-ATOMS (L)
  (COND ((NULL L) 0)                      ; List empty?
        ((ATOM L) 1)                      ; Atom rather than a list?
        ((+ (COUNT-ATOMS (CAR L))         ; No T, first is also last.
            (COUNT-ATOMS (CDR L)))))))
```

This works because COND triggers on anything but NIL, not just on T. NIL can never be produced by +, and the clause therefore triggers just as if the T were there. Because the clause has only one form, that form is both first and last and so provides both the test and the value returned.

Using a clause whose first element is T is better programming practice, however, because it clearly signals the fact that the programmer expects the last clause to be used when all else fails. Using a T clearly indicates that there can be no falling right through the conditional, with the default value of NIL.

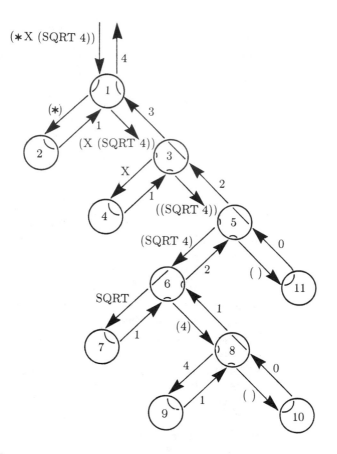

Figure 4-4. Again a simulation helps illuminate the strategy of a recursive procedure. Here the expression (* X (SQRT 4)) is broken up into its constituent pieces
by the procedure COUNT-ATOMS. The arrows show how control moves from one
numbered application of the procedure to another. Arguments are shown on the
downward pointing arrows; values returned, on the upward.

We have seen singly recursive procedures, like OUR-EXPT and OUR-MEMBER,
and doubly recursive procedures, like FIBONACCI and COUNT-ATOMS. Generally, singly recursive procedures are natural for working with various types
of sequences, such as the top-level element of a list. Doubly recursive procedures are natural when it comes to exploring trees, such as *all* parts of an
expression, even those deeply embedded. In these situations, the amount of
work a singly recursive procedure does is proportional to the length of the
list it works on, as measured by LENGTH, while the amount of work a doubly
recursive procedure does is proportional to the total number of elements
in the expression, as measured by COUNT-ATOMS.

Typically then, doubly recursive procedures tend to require more work than those that are singly recursive. Note, however, that it is a particular *procedure* that is said to be singly or doubly recursive; many different procedures often can compute the desired result, possibly even without using recursion at all.

Problems

Problem 4-1: Suppose for the moment that + and - can be used only to increment and decrement a number by one. Write a recursive procedure for adding two numbers. Assume that both numbers are positive.

Problem 4-2: Define a version of OUR-EXPT that is tail recursive. It may help to define an auxiliary procedure, OUR-EXPT-AUX, that has one more argument than OUR-EXPT itself and does the actual recursion. The extra argument can be used as a kind of accumulator for partial results, to be passed on to the next copy of the procedure. This approach represents a common way of turning a singly recursive procedure into a tail-recursive one. The tail-recursive one then easily can be turned into one that does not use recursion at all, as we will see later when we look at iterative versions of OUR-EXPT.

Problem 4-3: Define OUR-REVERSE, a tail-recursive version of REVERSE. Use the same approach as in the previous problem.

Problem 4-4: The algorithm we have been using for computing powers of numbers is not particularly efficient. Write a version of OUR-EXPT that considers its second argument to be a binary number and looks at one bit of it at a time. Use these identities:

$$m^n = \begin{cases} (m^2)^{n/2}, & \text{for } n \text{ even;} \\ m \times (m^2)^{(n-1)/2}, & \text{for } n \text{ odd.} \end{cases}$$

Problem 4-5: Define a version of COUNT-ATOMS that uses an auxiliary variable to hang onto the count accumulated so far in exploring one part of the tree.

Problem 4-6: Describe the evident purpose of the following procedure:

```
(DEFUN MYSTERY (S)
  (COND ((NULL S) 1)
        ((ATOM S) 0)
        (T (MAX (+ (MYSTERY (CAR S)) 1)
                (MYSTERY (CDR S))))))
```

Problem 4-7: Describe the evident purpose of the following procedure:

```
(DEFUN STRANGE (L)
  (COND ((NULL L) NIL)
        ((ATOM L) L)
        (T (CONS (STRANGE (CAR L))
                 (STRANGE (CDR L))))))
```

Problem 4-8:   Define `PRESENTP` a predicate that determines whether a given atom occurs *anywhere* in an expression. `PRESENTP` differs from `MEMBER`, in that `MEMBER` looks only for top-level instances. Symbolic-mathematics systems make use of a procedure like `PRESENTP` to determine if an expression contains a particular variable. Consider these examples:

```
(SETQ FORMULA '(SQRT (/ (+ (EXPT X 2) (EXPT Y 2)) 2.0)))

(PRESENTP 'X FORMULA)
  T

(PRESENTP 'Z FORMULA)
  NIL
```

Problem 4-9:   Define `SQUASH`, a procedure that takes an expression as its argument and returns a nonnested list of all atoms found in the expression. Here is an example:

```
(SQUASH '(A (A (A (A B))) (((A B) B) B) B))
  (A A A A B A B B B B)
```

Essentially, this procedure explores the *fringe* of the tree represented by the list given as its argument, and returns a list of all the leaves.

Problem 4-10:   The version of `FIBONACCI` given in the text is the obvious, but wasteful, implementation. Many computations are repeated. Write a version that does not have this flaw. It may help to have an auxiliary procedure with some extra parameters in order to be able to pass along more than one Fibonacci number.

Problem 4-11:   A particular definition of a mathematical *function*, like the Fibonacci function, may directly suggest a LISP *procedure* for computing it, as the version of `FIBONACCI` shown in this section. This is of course not the only, and quite often not the best, procedure, as the previous problem already shows. In this particular case, we can go even further and solve the linear recurrence relation for $f(n)$. We obtain Binet's formula in terms of the golden ratio, $(1 + \sqrt{5})/2$, and its inverse, $(\sqrt{5} - 1)/2$:

$$f(n) = \frac{1}{\sqrt{5}} \left[\left(\frac{1 + \sqrt{5}}{2} \right)^{n+1} - \left(\frac{1 - \sqrt{5}}{2} \right)^{n+1} \right]$$

Write yet another version of `FIBONACCI`, this time doing the computation directly, without recursion or iteration. There may, perhaps, be some hidden recursion or iteration in the LISP primitives you use.

Problem 4-12:   An association list is a list of correspondences of items from one set with items of another. We will see them a lot later on. Write OUR-PAIRLIS, a procedure that takes two lists as arguments, and returns a list of sublists each containing two elements.[4] In each sublist, the first element is to come from the first argument, while the second element is to be the corresponding element from the second argument:

```
(OUR-PAIRLIS '(X Y Z) '(1 2 3))
  ((X 1) (Y 2) (Z 3))
```

Problems about Sets

We now divert ourselves by looking at some problems involving sets. This section can be skipped without harm by the hasty reader.

A *set* is a collection of elements, each of which is said to be a member of the set. A set can be represented as a list, with each element of the set represented by an atom. Each atom occurs only once in the list, and no significance is attached to the order of the atoms in the list.[5]

Problem 4-13:   Define OUR-UNION.[6] The union of two sets is a set containing all the elements that are in either of the two sets.

Define OUR-INTERSECTION. The intersection of two sets is a set containing only the elements that are in both of the two sets.

Define OUR-SET-DIFFERENCE. The difference of two sets, the IN set and the OUT set, is what remains of the set IN after all elements that are also elements of set OUT are removed.

Problem 4-14:   Define INTERSECTP, a predicate that tests whether two sets have any elements in common. It is to return NIL if the two sets are disjoint.

Problem 4-15:   Define SAMESETP, a predicate that tests whether two sets contain the same elements. Note that the two lists representing the sets may be arranged in different orders, so you cannot just use EQUAL.

---

[4] The COMMON LISP primitive PAIRLIS uses CONS. Consequently, the result is a list of dotted pairs, entities that we discuss in chapter 9.

[5] A simple list representation for sets is *not* optimal in terms of access efficiency. If it is possible to impose some ordering on the elements, then one can do better using binary trees, to be discussed in the next section.

[6] COMMON LISP has primitives UNION, INTERSECTION, and SET-DIFFERENCE.

Problems about Binary Trees

We now look at some problems involving binary trees. This section can be skipped without harm by the hasty reader.

A *binary tree* can be defined recursively either as a leaf, or as a node with two attached binary trees. Such a binary tree can be represented using atoms for the leaves and three-element lists for the nodes. The first element of each list is an atom representing a node, and the other two elements are the subtrees attached to the node.

Thus the following is the representation of a particular binary tree with six nodes (N-1 TO N-6) and seven leaves (L-A TO L-G):

```
(N-1 (N-2 L-A L-B) (N-3 (N-4 L-C L-D) (N-5 L-E (N-6 L-F L-G))))
```

The following group of problems make use of this representation.

Problem 4-16: A mobile is a kind of abstract sculpture consisting of parts that may move relative to one another. Usually it contains objects suspended in mid-air by fine wires hanging from horizontal beams. We can define a particularly simple type of mobile recursively either as a suspended object or as a beam with a submobile hanging from each end. If we assume that each beam is suspended from its midpoint, we can represent such a mobile as a binary tree. Single suspended objects are represented by numbers equal to their weights, whereas more complicated mobiles are represented by a three-element list. The first element is a number equal to the weight of the beam, and the other two elements represent submobiles attached at the two ends of the beam.

A mobile should be balanced. This means that the two mobiles suspended from opposite ends of each beam must be equal in weight. Define MOBILEP, a procedure that determines whether a mobile is balanced. It returns NIL if it is not, and its total weight if it is:

```
(MOBILEP '(6 (4 (2 1 1) 4) (2 5 (1 2 2))))
   30
```

Problem 4-17: Binary trees can also be used to represent arithmetic expressions, as for example:

```
(* (+ A B) (- C (/ D E)))
```

Part of the work of a compiler is to translate such an arithmetic expression into the machine language of some computer. Suppose for example that the target machine has a set of sequentially numbered registers that can hold temporary results.

Further suppose that the target machine has a `MOVE` instruction for getting values into these registers, and `ADD`, `SUB`, `MUL`, and `DIV` instructions for arithmetically combining values in two registers. Our example expression could be translated into the following:

```
((MOVE 1 A)
 (MOVE 2 B)
 (ADD 1 2)
 (MOVE 2 C)
 (MOVE 3 D)
 (MOVE 4 E)
 (DIV 3 4)
 (SUB 2 3)
 (MUL 1 2))
```

The result is left in register number one. Define `COMPILE-ARITHMETIC`, a procedure that performs this translation.

Problem 4-18: In this problem, we define the *weight* of a binary tree to be equal to 1 when it is just a leaf. If the binary tree is not a leaf, its weight is the larger of the weights of the two subtrees if these are not equal. If the weights of the two subtrees are equal, the weight of the tree is the weight of either subtree plus 1. The tree representing the arithmetic expression shown in the previous problem, for example, has weight 3. Define `TREE-WEIGHT`, a procedure that computes the weight of a tree.

Problem 4-19: The number of registers used to compute an arithmetic procedure depends on whether the left or the right subtree is computed first. The procedure `TREE-WEIGHT`, defined in the previous problem, actually determines the minimum number of registers required to compute a particular arithmetic expression. It is clear that our compiler is not optimal, because it used four registers for a tree with weight 3. Assume that another instruction, `COPY`, is available for moving the contents of one register into another. Improve `COMPILE-ARITHMETIC`, using `TREE-WEIGHT`, to minimize the number of registers used.

Project 4-1: Develop procedures for adding members to sets, and for removing them, using a binary tree representation for sets. If possible, try to arrange for the trees to be nearly *balanced*, that is, at each node, about an equal number of leaves are found below to the left, as there are to the right.

**Problems about C
Curves and Dragon
Curves**

We now look at some problems involving curves. This section can be
skipped without harm by the hasty reader.

William Gosper first drew our attention to certain recursively defined
drawings. Consider the following recursive procedure:

```
(DEFUN C-CURVE (LENGTH ANGLE MIN-LENGTH)
  (COND ((< LENGTH MIN-LENGTH) (PLOT-LINE LENGTH ANGLE))
        (T (C-CURVE (/ LENGTH (SQRT 2.0))
                    (+ ANGLE (/ PI 4.0))
                    MIN-LENGTH)
           (C-CURVE (/ LENGTH (SQRT 2.0))
                    (- ANGLE (/ PI 4.0))
                    MIN-LENGTH))))
```

Assume that (PLOT-LINE LENGTH ANGLE) plots a straight line whose length
is the value of LENGTH at an angle ANGLE with respect to some standard
reference axis. The line is drawn from wherever the last line ended. Also,
assume again that the value of the global free variable PI is π. It may help
to simulate the result with paper and pencil for cases where the recursion
is only two or three layers deep. Compare the results with figure 4-5.

Problem 4-20: Write the procedure PLOT-LINE using LINE, a procedure
that takes four arguments, X-START, Y-START, X-END and Y-END, specifying
the coordinates of the end points of a line to be drawn. Use the global
free variables X-OLD and Y-OLD to remember where the previous line ended.
Assume that the procedures SIN and COS calculate the sine and cosine of
their single arguments given in radians.

Problem 4-21: Lines end up being drawn in only one of eight directions.
(Actually only four, for any particular set of values of LENGTH and MIN-
LENGTH.) Write PSEUDO-SIN, a procedure that takes an integer and produces
the result previously offered up by SIN. The corresponding angle is $\pi/4$
times the integer.

Problem 4-22: One can view the recursive step in C-CURVE as one in
which a straight line is replaced by a pair of shorter straight lines at right
angles to each other, connecting the end points of the original line. There
are two ways of doing this, depending on which side of the original line
one decides to place the elbow so formed. In C-CURVE, the shorter lines are
consistently placed on the same side of the longer line being replaced. If
the elbows are placed on *opposite* sides of their respective lines, one obtains
instead a figure called a dragon curve.[7]

This figure can also be constructed from a strip of paper that has
been folded in half repeatedly. The folded strip is opened up so that each
crease forms a 90° angle. A dragon curve is shown in figure 4-6. Write
DRAGON-CURVE, a procedure similar to C-CURVE.

---

[7] A ceramic tile design, based on the dragon curve of order 9, graces the entrance
to Donald and Jill Knuth's house.

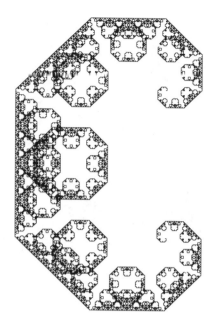

Figure 4-5. The C curve, a recursively defined drawing.

Problems about Rewriting Logical Expressions

We now look at some problems involving digital hardware. This section can be skipped without harm by the hasty reader.

When working with digital hardware, people often use more than the minimum number of logic functions. This is convenient, because it is tedious to work in terms of a minimal set. At the same time, only a minimal set of logic gate types may be available for actually building electronic circuits. There is, then, a need for automatic translation from the form preferred by the designer to that required when actually building something. In particular, designers may prefer to think in terms of logical functions like NOT, AND, OR, and XOR, whereas the basic hardware modules may be just NAND gates.

The procedure REWRITE will translate from one form to the other by rewriting the logical functions at the head of the expression handed to it. The arguments of this logical function are translated using recursive applications of REWRITE.

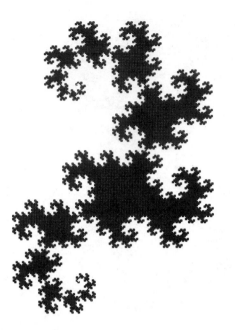

Figure 4-6. The Dragon curve, another recursively defined drawing.

The REWRITE procedure depends on well-known identities between log-ical expressions, such as de Morgan's laws:

```
(NOT (OR X Y))    ≡    (AND (NOT X) (NOT Y))

(NOT (AND X Y))   ≡    (OR (NOT X) (NOT Y))
```

Problem 4-23:   Do the equivalences that express de Morgan's laws apply to LISP expressions in general, or only to forms whose values are restricted to be either NIL or T?

Problem 4-24:   The following implementation of REWRITE shown is some-times wasteful. In certain cases, composite operands may be rewritten several times. Develop a new version of REWRITE that avoids this by ap-plying REWRITE recursively to lists constructed using NAND and *untranslated* arguments of the logical functions.

```
(DEFUN REWRITE (L)
  (COND ((ATOM L) L)
        ((EQUAL (CAR L) 'NOT)
         (LIST 'NAND
               (REWRITE (CADR L)) T))
        ((EQUAL (CAR L) 'AND)
         (LIST 'NAND
               (LIST 'NAND
                     (REWRITE (CADR L))
                     (REWRITE (CADDR L)))
               T))
        ((EQUAL (CAR L) 'OR)
         (LIST 'NAND
               (LIST 'NAND (REWRITE (CADR L)) T)
               (LIST 'NAND (REWRITE (CADDR L)) T)))
        ((EQUAL (CAR L) 'XOR)
         (LIST 'NAND
               (LIST 'NAND
                     (LIST 'NAND (REWRITE (CADR L)) T)
                     (LIST 'NAND (REWRITE (CADDR L)) T))
               (LIST 'NAND
                     (REWRITE (CADR L))
                     (REWRITE (CADDR L))))
         T))
        (T (LIST 'ERROR L))))
```

Dealing with Lists May Call for Iteration Using MAPCAR

A somewhat more elegant way to define procedures like COUNT-ATOMS is by means of the primitives MAPCAR and APPLY, two new procedures that are very useful and very special in the way they handle their arguments.

Iterate is a technical term meaning to repeat. MAPCAR can be used to iterate when the same procedure is to be performed over and over again on a whole list of things. Suppose, for example, that it is useful to record which numbers in a list are odd. From the list (1 2 3), we expect to get (T NIL T).

To accomplish such transformations with MAPCAR, you supply the name of the procedure together with a list of things to be handed to the procedure, one after the other. Consider the following, for example, where the primitive ODDP has the obvious definition:

```
(MAPCAR 'ODDP                    ;Procedure to work with.
        '(1 2 3))                ;Arguments to be fed to the procedure.
  (T NIL T)
```

MAPCAR is said to cause iteration of ODDP, because the MAPCAR causes ODDP to be used over and over again.

There is no restriction to procedures of one parameter, but if the procedure does have more than one parameter, there must be a corresponding number of lists of things from which to extract arguments that can be fed to the procedure.

As shown in the following example, MAPCAR works like an assembly machine, taking one element from each list of arguments and assembling them for the procedure:

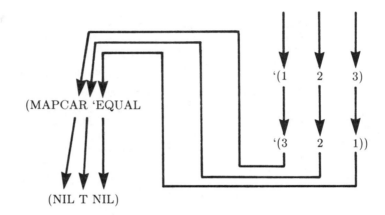

In a moment, we will use MAPCAR in a new definition of COUNT-ATOMS, but first, you must understand why the primitive APPLY is necessary. Suppose we want to add up a list of numbers, L.

```
(SETQ L '(4 7 2))
   (4 7 2)
```

It would be wrong to evaluate the form (+ L). The primitive + expects arguments that are numbers. But here + gets one argument that is a list of numbers, rather than an actual number. The primitive + does not know what to do with the unexpected argument. It is as if we tried to evaluate the incorrect form (+ '(4 7 2)) instead of (+ 4 7 2).

To make + work, we must use APPLY, which takes two arguments, a procedure name and a list, and arranges to have the procedure act on the elements in the list as if they appeared as proper arguments. Thus the particular form (APPLY '+ L) is a special case of the following general form:

```
(APPLY <procedure description>
       <list of arguments>)
```

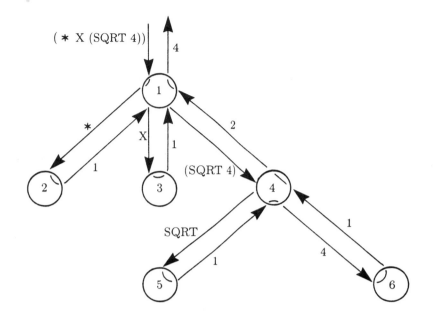

Figure 4-7. A version of COUNT-ATOMS using MAPCAR instead of CARs and CDRs exhibits less recursion.

Now, using APPLY and MAPCAR, we can work up a more elegant way of counting atoms:

```
(DEFUN COUNT-ATOMS (L)
  (COND ((NULL L) 0)
        ((ATOM L) 1)
        (T (APPLY '+ (MAPCAR 'COUNT-ATOMS L)))))
```

As suggested by the first two COND clauses, simple cases are handled as before. Once again, the objective is to reduce the more complex expressions to the simple ones. Only now MAPCAR is used to simplify expressions rather than CAR and CDR. This version of COUNT-ATOMS exploits MAPCAR's talent for going after every top-level element of a list with a specified procedure, in this case a recursive application of COUNT-ATOMS itself.

Now, assuming for a moment that the procedure works, we see that MAPCAR comes back with a list of numbers that must be added together. This is why APPLY appears. The primitive + wants numbers, not a list of numbers. APPLY does the appropriate interfacing and hands the list of numbers to + as if each element in the list were itself an argument to +.

Simulating this version of COUNT-ATOMS is easier than simulating the other one, because the recursion is less deep and complicated. See figure 4-7.

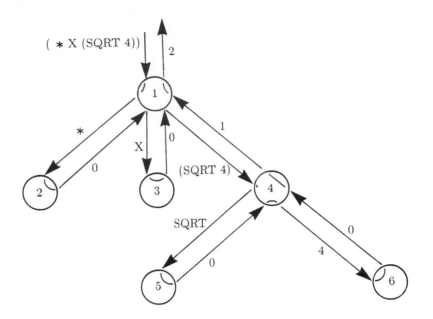

Figure 4-8. The recursion pattern for DEPTH is the same as the one for COUNT-ATOMS shown in figure 4-7.

Now it is easy to modify COUNT-ATOMS to do other things. For example, to determine the depth of nesting of an expression, the following simple modifications to COUNT-ATOMS are all that is necessary: change the name to DEPTH, change the empty list and atom results, change + to MAX, and increment the result:

```
(DEFUN DEPTH (L)
  (COND ((NULL L) 1)
        ((ATOM L) 0)
        (T (+ (APPLY 'MAX (MAPCAR 'DEPTH L)) 1))))
```

Figure 4-8 shows how DEPTH works on the expression previously used to illustrate COUNT-ATOMS. Again, at each branching, we see how MAPCAR splits up an expression into simpler elements to be worked on.

The iteration involved in the use of MAPCAR is a special case of iteration, because it is restricted to the repeated application of a procedure to the top-level elements of a list. In the section after the next, we look at DO, a special form that makes it possible to do iteration in general.

Problems

Problem 4-25: Define DYNAMIC-RANGE, a procedure that takes one argument, a list of numbers, and returns the ratio of the biggest to the smallest.

**MAPCAN Behaves
Like MAPCAR
Followed by APPEND**

MAPCAN acts much as if it were a combination of MAPCAR and APPEND.[8] Thus, for our present purpose, these are equivalent:

```
(MAPCAN <some procedure specification> <some list>))
≡
(APPLY 'APPEND (MAPCAR <some procedure specification> <some list>))
```

Suppose, for example, that we have a procedure, PARENTS, that returns the parents of any person, if known, or NIL otherwise.

Given PARENTS, the following is a procedure that is supposed to compute all known ancestors of a given person:

```
(DEFUN ANCESTORS-WITH-BUG (PERSON)        ;BUGGED!
  (LET ((P (PARENTS PERSON)))
    (COND ((NULL P) NIL)
          (T (APPEND P (MAPCAR 'ANCESTORS-WITH-BUG P)))))))
```

Unfortunately, however, there is a bug. If John and Sara are the parents of William, and if Isaac and Mary are the parents of Sara, and if nothing else is known, the result is as follows:

```
((JOHN SARA) NIL (ISAAC MARY))
```

The problem, of course, is that MAPCAR returns lists of lists of ancestors, instead of a simply lists of ancestors. The problem can be solved by appending together the results produced by MAPCAR:

```
(DEFUN ANCESTORS (PERSON)                 ;OK, but ugly.
  (LET ((P (PARENTS PERSON)))
    (COND ((NULL P) NIL)
          (T (APPEND P (APPLY 'APPEND (MAPCAR 'ANCESTORS P))))))))
```

Now the result is the desired one:

```
(JOHN SARA ISAAC MARY)
```

---

[8] Actually, MAPCAN acts as if it were a combination of MAPCAR and NCONC, a primitive that will be explained later, in chapter 9. This makes MAPCAN a dangerous primitive for novices, because the NCONC can cause unexpected things to happen.

The more elegant way to do the appending is to substitute MAPCAN for the combination of APPLY, APPEND, and MAPCAR:

```
(DEFUN ANCESTORS (PERSON)                    ; Nice version.
  (LET ((P (PARENTS PERSON)))
    (COND ((NULL P) NIL)
          (T (APPEND P (MAPCAN 'ANCESTORS P))))))
```

DO Binds Parameters and Supports Explicit Iteration

DO is a popular special form, particularly with those who do a lot of numerical computation, because it provides one way to write procedures that iterate explicitly.

The syntax for DO is easier to explain through an immediate example, rather than through a recitation of DO's syntax. For illustration, we use the procedure that computes powers of numbers again, this time specified in a way that suggests iteration rather than recursion:

$$m^n = m \times m \times \ldots m$$

Here, then, is another way to write OUR-EXPT:

```
(DEFUN OUR-EXPT (M N)
  (DO ((RESULT 1)                      ; Bind and assign parameters.
       (EXPONENT N))                   ; Bind and assign parameters.
      ((ZEROP EXPONENT) RESULT)        ; Test and return.
    (SETQ RESULT (* M RESULT))         ; Body.
    (SETQ EXPONENT (- EXPONENT 1))))   ; Body.
```

Several things must be explained. Keep in mind that the objective is to multiply n m's together. This will be accomplished by passing n times through the *body*, which in this example consists of the two SETQ forms following the DO's test-and-return section.

- The first part of a DO is always occupied by a list of parameters that are all bound and assigned to initial values on entering the DO.

Each parameter that has a value before evaluation of the DO is restored to its old value on exit. If there are no parameters, ( ) must be in the first position.

- The second part of a DO is the place that determines when the loop will be terminated and what will be returned. This part consists of a list whose initial form is a termination test. The forms that follow in this list are evaluated in turn. The value returned by DO is the value of the last form in this list.

The test is attempted before each pass through the body, including the first pass. The forms after the test form are evaluated only when the test succeeds. All forms between the first and the last are evaluated for side effects only. If there is only one form, it is the test, and DO returns NIL. Consequently, the iteration-terminating part of a DO is not exactly like a clause in a COND, although there are strong similarities.

- The third part of a DO, the body, consists of forms that are evaluated sequentially. All values are ignored, so the evaluations are done only for possible side effects.

- Whenever an expression starting with RETURN is encountered in the body of a DO, the DO is terminated immediately. The value of the terminated DO is the value of the argument in the RETURN expression that stopped the DO.

Thus the following is another way of defining OUR-EXPT, albeit an awkward way.

```
(DEFUN OUR-EXPT (M N)
  (DO ((RESULT 1)                        ;Bind and assign parameters.
       (EXPONENT N))                     ;Bind and assign parameters.
      (NIL)                              ;Test always fails.
      (COND ((ZEROP EXPONENT)            ;Test.
             (RETURN RESULT)))           ;Return.
      (SETQ RESULT (* M RESULT))         ;Body.
      (SETQ EXPONENT (- EXPONENT 1))))   ;Body.
```

- The parameter specifications can include update assignments in addition to variable names and initial values.

Using (RESULT 1 (* M RESULT)), instead of (RESULT 1), in DO's parameter list not only makes 1 the value of RESULT on the first pass, but also makes (* M RESULT) the value of RESULT on subsequent passes. This means that still another way to define OUR-EXPT is as follows:

```
(DEFUN OUR-EXPT (M N)
  (DO ((RESULT 1 (* M RESULT))           ;Bind, assign, and update parameters.
       (EXPONENT N (- EXPONENT 1)))      ;Bind, assign, and update parameters.
      ((ZEROP EXPONENT) RESULT)))        ;Test and return.
```

Note that this DO has no body. In this version of OUR-EXPT, all the necessary computation is specified in the parameter update descriptions.

The syntax of DO can be shown in its full-blown glory as follows:

```
(DO (((<parameter 1> <initial value 1> <update form 1>)
     (<parameter 2> <initial value 2> <update form 2>)
     ...
     (<parameter n> <initial value n> <update form n>))
    (<termination test> <zero or more intermediate forms> <result form>)
  <body>)
```

- All initialization forms are evaluated before binding and assignment. Similarly, all update forms are evaluated before reassignment.

Consequently, DO is said to handle its parameters in *parallel*. In this respect, DO is similar to LET and PSETQ. This becomes critical when an initialization or update form has side effects. Consider this somewhat silly and definitely defective definition for OUR-EXPT:

```
(DEFUN OUR-EXPT (M N)                  ;BUGGED!
  (DO ((RESULT M (* M RESULT))         ;Result starts as M not 1.
       (EXPONENT N (- EXPONENT 1))
       (COUNTER (- EXPONENT 1)         ;User expects COUNTER to be
                (- EXPONENT 1)))        ; one less than exponent.
      ((ZEROP COUNTER) RESULT)))       ;Loses on N = 0 as well.
```

As written, OUR-EXPT will report an error, because there is no value assigned to EXPONENT at the time of the first attempt to evaluate (- EXPONENT 1).

The following version runs, but it gives an incorrect answer:

```
(DEFUN OUR-EXPT (M N)                  ;BUGGED!
  (DO ((RESULT M (* M RESULT))         ;Result starts as M not 1.
       (EXPONENT N (- EXPONENT 1))
       (COUNTER (- N 1)                ;User expects COUNTER to be
                (- EXPONENT 1)))        ; one less than exponent.
      ((ZEROP COUNTER) RESULT)))       ;Loses on N = 0 as well.
```

Now the initial value is calculated correctly, but all subsequent values are computed using an old value of EXPONENT, rather than the value just established for the next iteration. Remember the parallel way DO does assignment: the value of EXPONENT is not actually changed until all the update forms are evaluated.

There are two ways to rescue the situation. The first simply decouples the computation of the EXPONENT and COUNTER update values:

```
(DEFUN OUR-EXPT (M N)
  (DO ((RESULT M (* M RESULT))         ;Result starts as M not 1.
       (EXPONENT N (- EXPONENT 1))     ;Not used!
       (COUNTER (- N 1)                ;COUNTER is one less than exponent.
                (- COUNTER 1)))
      ((ZEROP COUNTER) RESULT)))       ;Happens to lose on N = 0.
```

Still another way to fix the problem is to employ DO*, a special form similar to DO, which does a serial, rather than parallel, assignment of values. Because DO* is to DO as LET* is to LET, this works:

```
(DEFUN OUR-EXPT (M N)
   (DO* ((RESULT M (* M RESULT))        ;Result starts as M not 1.
         (EXPONENT N (- EXPONENT 1))
         (COUNTER (- EXPONENT 1)        ;COUNTER is actually
                  (- EXPONENT 1)))      ; one less than exponent.
        ((ZEROP COUNTER) RESULT)))      ;Happens to lose on N = 0.
```

Using PROG Is an Old-fashioned Way To Do Iteration

At one time, PROG was used a lot, because it was the only way to create explicit loops before DO was introduced. We include a brief discussion here for historical purposes. In the next edition, we will leave it out.

As with DO, the syntax for PROG is easier to explain through an immediate example rather than through discussion. We will use the procedure that computes powers of numbers once more:

```
(DEFUN OUR-EXPT (M N)
   (PROG (RESULT EXPONENT)             ;Bind parameters to NIL.
      (SETQ RESULT 1)                  ;Initialize.
      (SETQ EXPONENT N)                ;Initialize.
    LOOP                               ;Start loop.
      (COND ((ZEROP EXPONENT)          ;Test.
             (RETURN RESULT)))         ;Return.
      (SETQ RESULT (* M RESULT))       ;Reset.
      (SETQ EXPONENT (- EXPONENT 1))   ;Reset.
      (GO LOOP)))                      ;Repeat.
```

This use of PROG arranges to multiply n m's together by passing repeatedly through the part of the PROG just after LOOP.

- The first position in a PROG is always occupied by a list of parameters, which are all bound on entering the PROG. Each parameter that has a value before the PROG is evaluated is restored to its previous value upon exit. If there are no parameters, NIL or ( ) must be in first position. The parameters are each initialized to NIL automatically—other values cannot be supplied.

- The forms in the body of a PROG are evaluated one after the other. The values are ignored, so the evaluations are only useful for side effects. If control runs off the end of a PROG, then NIL is returned. just as with COND.

- Whenever a RETURN expression is reached when evaluating a PROG, the PROG is terminated immediately. The value of the terminated PROG is the value of the argument in the RETURN expression that stopped the PROG, just as with DO.

- Any top-level symbol in the body of a PROG is considered to be a position marker. These symbols, called *tags*, are not evaluated. They mark places to which control can be transferred by GO expressions. That is, (GO <TAG>) transfers control to the form following <TAG>.

- PROGs can be nested.[9]

It is clear that the procedure that computes powers of numbers works by looping back through the tag named LOOP until the parameter N is counted down to 0. Each time through the loop, RESULT is changed through multiplication by M. The conditional tests for the stop condition, N = 0, and evaluates a RETURN when the test succeeds. RESULT starts with a value of NIL, as all PROG parameters do, but is set to 1 before the loop is entered.

PROG-based Iteration Should Be Avoided

One reason PROG-based iteration can be hard to understand is that the description of a loop tends to be spread out. Parameter initialization, parameter incrementing SETQs, and termination tests with RETURNs can be scattered everywhere. Worse yet, multiple PROG tags and GOs ensure that the actual path a procedure takes may look like a badly tangled up length of string.

Consequently, using DO is better. All of the loop description is given at the beginning, before the body of the loop and not interdigitated with it. Whereas PROG begins with a parameter list, DO begins with a parameter list, initialization information, descriptions of how to increment the parameters each time around the loop, and a loop termination test. Importantly, it can be shown that anything using PROG can be rewritten using DO. Consequently, PROG, strictly speaking, is unnecessary.

Problems

Problem 4-26: Define FACTORIAL, using the iterative version of OUR-EXPT as a model. Factorial of n is to be 1, if n is 0, and n times the factorial of $(n-1)$ otherwise. That is:

$$n! = \begin{cases} n * (n-1)!, & \text{for } n > 0; \\ 1, & \text{for } n = 0. \end{cases}$$

---

[9] GO can tranfer control to a tag in a lexically enclosing PROG, but *not* one that is lexically enclosed.

Problem 4-27: Simple tail-recursive procedures can be rewritten easily in an iterative form using DO. Write an iterative version of this:

```
(DEFUN OUR-MEMBER (ITEM L)
  (COND ((NULL L) NIL)
        ((EQUAL ITEM (CAR L)) L)
        (T (OUR-MEMBER ITEM (CDR L)))))
```

Problem 4-28: Write an iterative version of REVERSE. You may want to base your solution on the tail-recursive OUR-REVERSE of a previous problem.

Problem 4-29: Some elements of a set may be equivalent. Such equivalences can be expressed using a list of pairs of equivalent elements. If A is equivalent to B, then B is equivalent to A. Further, if A is equivalent to B, and B is equivalent to C, then A is also equivalent to C. *Equivalence classes* are maximal subsets, all elements of which are equivalent. In the case just described, the set (A B C) forms an equivalence class. Define COALESCE, a procedure that takes a set of pairwise equivalences and returns a set of equivalence classes. A typical application of COALESCE is the following:

```
(COALESCE '((A E) (Z F) (M B) (P K)
            (E I) (F S) (B D) (T P)
            (I O) (S V) (D G) (K P)
            (O U) (V Z) (G M) (P T)))
((A E I O U) (F S V Z) (B D G M) (K P T))
```

It may be helpful to employ UNION and INTERSECTION. Also, the solution may make use of both recursion and iteration.

PROG1 and PROGN Handle Sequences Explicitly

The simplest way of getting things done may be to evaluate a series of forms sequentially, returning the value of one of them. This is arranged *implicitly* when we use DEFUN, because the body of a defined procedure can consist of any number of forms, with the last form determining the procedure's value. Similarly, the bodies of LET forms can consist of any number of forms, with the last again determining the LET expression's value.

Sometimes, however, it is desirable to combine forms *explicitly* into sequences. PROG1 and PROGN do this, as shown by the following examples:

```
(PROG1 (SETQ A 'X) (SETQ B 'Y) (SETQ C 'Z))
  X

(PROGN (SETQ A 'X) (SETQ B 'Y) (SETQ C 'Z))
  Z
```

As with DEFUN-defined procedures and LET forms, all but one of the forms is evaluated for side-effects only. Evidently, the one that establishes the value is the first for PROG1 and the last for PROGN.

Because the bodies of DEFUNs and LETs can contain any number of forms, PROG1 and PROGN are not much used. Nevertheless, they can be handy, particularly when it is desirable to combine side effects and a test in the test position of a COND or a DO.

Here, for example, is a way to define OUR-EXPT, using a DO with an embedded PROG1 in the exit-test position:

```
(DEFUN OUR-EXPT (M N)
  (DO ((RESULT 1)                          ;Bind and assign parameters.
       (EXPONENT N))                       ;Bind and assign parameters.
      ((PROG1 (ZEROP EXPONENT)             ;Compute value for test first.
              (SETQ EXPONENT (- EXPONENT 1)))  ;Then increment parameter.
       RESULT)
    (SETQ RESULT (* M RESULT)))))
```

Note that the PROG1 appears in the DO's test position. Because PROG1 returns the value of its first form, the first form determines whether the DO is terminated. Fortunately, this first form is evaluated before EXPONENT is decremented.

Problems and Their Representation Determine Proper Control Structure

We can now state some rough guidelines for determining how to select alternatives from the repertoire of control structures introduced so far.

- The definition of a mathematical function may suggest an appropriate control structure. If so, use it.

- If solving a problem involves diving into list structure, recursion probably makes sense.

- If solving a problem involves doing something to every element in a list, iteration using MAPCAR is often the right thing.

- When working with arrays, to be introduced later, try iteration using DOs.

These rules are only rough guidelines to be augmented as experience increases. Keep in mind that control selection is partly a matter of personal style. One person's recursion may be another person's DO.

Also keep in mind that implementation details may force a control selection. Recursion may be ruled out by limits on the depth of recursion permitted, forcing the use of DO. Similarly, recursion may be ruled out by speed considerations, again forcing the use of DO.

In this book, however, we have leaned toward recursion rather than iteration. We have done this, in part, to counterbalance the natural tendency of many people to write strictly iteratively.[10]

Summary

- Programming requires control structure selection.
- Recursion allows procedures to use themselves.
- Tail recursion can be efficient.
- Recursion can be used to analyze nested expressions.
- Dealing with lists may call for iteration using MAPCAR.
- MAPCAN behaves like MAPCAR followed by APPEND.
- DO binds parameters and supports explicit iteration.
- Using PROG is an old-fashioned way to do iteration.
- PROG-based iteration should be avoided.
- PROG1 and PROGN handle sequences explicitly.
- Problems and their representation determine proper control structure.

References

Knuth [1968] gives many examples of recursive procedures, including examples involving the Fibonacci function.

Special forms in LISP are discussed by Pitman [1980].

The conversion of recursive procedures into iterative ones is discussed by Auslander and Strong [1976] as well as Darlington and Burstall [1976], and Burstall and Darlington [1977]. Burge [1975] discusses recursive programming at length.

Waters [1983] discusses an alternate iteration construct for LISP.

Davis and Knuth [1970], as well as Knuth and Knuth [1973] discuss dragon curves.

Algorithms involving sets are analyzed by Aho, Hopcroft, and Ullman [1974]. The equivalence class problem can be solved using a transitive closure algorithm also found in Aho, Hopcroft, and Ullman [1974]. They also discuss binary trees. Hu [1982] goes into all sorts of combinatorial algorithms.

Knuth [1974] discusses structured programming with GO-TO statements. Ramshaw [1983] shows how to get rid of GO-TOs.

---

[10] Because we typically resort to tail recursion rather than iteration, our procedures may be evaluated somewhat less efficiently in implementations that do not exploit the equivalence of tail-recursive and iterative procedures.

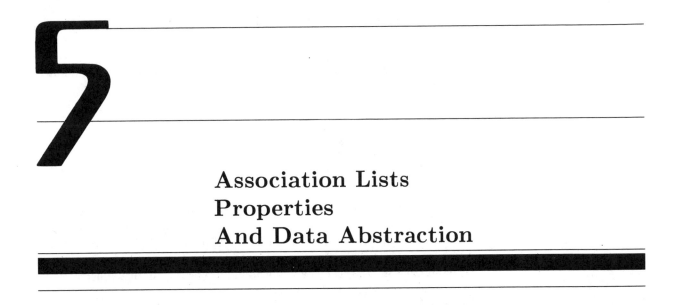

Association Lists
Properties
And Data Abstraction

So far, we know how to give a symbol a value and how to get the value back. The purpose of this chapter is to introduce other methods for remembering and recalling things. For illustration, we exhibit three new ways to remember and recall facts about simple blocks.

Our first objective is to work on certain lists called association lists. One of the features of association lists is that they enable groups of symbol values to be remembered, suppressed, or restored, all at once.

Then we generalize the notion of value, making it possible to give a symbol many different values, each of which is associated with an explicitly named property.

Finally, we discuss the key idea of data abstraction, showing how access procedures improve the quality of programs. This enables us to race past the use of structures, showing how it is possible to create and to manipulate new data types.

ASSOC Retrieves Elements from Association Lists

An *association list* is a list of embedded sublists, in which the first element of each sublist is a *key*.[1]

---

[1] Certain primitives assume that association lists, also called *a-lists*, are lists whose elements are dotted pairs, to be described in chapter 9.

The following creates an association list describing some facts about a particular block:

```
(SETQ BRICK-A '((COLOR RED)
                (SUPPORTED-BY BRICK-B)
                (IS-A BRICK)))
  ((COLOR RED) (SUPPORTED-BY BRICK-B) (IS-A BRICK))
```

ASSOC is a procedure of two arguments. ASSOC looks for the key, specified by its first argument, in the association list, specified by its second argument. ASSOC moves down the association list until it finds a sublist whose CAR is equal to the key. The value of the ASSOC is the *entire* element so discovered, key and all, or NIL if the key is not found.[2] These examples illustrate:

```
(ASSOC 'COLOR BRICK-A)
  (COLOR RED)

(ASSOC 'IS-A BRICK-A)
  (IS-A BRICK)

(ASSOC 'SIZE BRICK-A)
  NIL
```

Note that an association list can contain two elements with the same key. ASSOC returns the first one that it finds:

```
(SETQ BRICK-A '((SUPPORTED-BY BRICK-C)
                (COLOR RED)
                (SUPPORTED-BY BRICK-B)
                (IS-A BRICK)))
  ((SUPPORTED-BY BRICK-C) (COLOR RED) (SUPPORTED-BY BRICK-B) (IS-A BRICK))

(ASSOC 'SUPPORTED-BY BRICK-A)
  (SUPPORTED-BY BRICK-C)
```

The existence of the sublist (SUPPORTED-BY BRICK-B), further down the association list, does not affect the value returned by ASSOC.

---

[2] When successful, ASSOC returns the entire element, key and all, to avoid ambiguity. If only the CDR of the element were returned, there would be no way to determine whether there was no matching key or whether there was a matching key associated with NIL. This sort of ambiguity does occur using GET, a primitive introduced in the next section.

Problems

Problem 5-1: Write FETCH, a procedure that takes a key and an association list. If the key is found as the first element of an item on the association list, then the second item is to be returned. Otherwise FETCH is to return a question mark. The following examples illustrate:

```
(SETQ CHART '((TEMPERATURE 100) (PRESSURE (120 60)) (PULSE 72)))
   ((TEMPERATURE 100) (PRESSURE (120 60)) (PULSE 72))

(FETCH 'TEMPERATURE CHART)
   100

(FETCH 'COMPLAINTS CHART)
   ?
```

Problem 5-2: Write LIST-KEYS, a procedure that takes an association list and returns a list of all the keys in it. Recall that the keys are the things that ASSOC checks its first argument against.

Problem 5-3: Write TREND, a procedure that takes two association lists that record temperature, among other things. TREND is to return either IMPROVING or STABLE or SINKING depending on whether the patient's temperature is moving toward normal, at normal, or moving away. Assume the first association list records the older data. Further assume that there is always an entry for temperature on both association lists. Use FETCH as defined in a previous problem, if you like.

Problem 5-4: The procedure OUR-SUBLIS is to perform substitutions.[3] It is to take two arguments: the first is an association list and the second, an expression. OUR-SUBLIS replaces all occurrences of the first element of each of the sublists in the association list with the corresponding second element. In effect, OUR-SUBLIS can perform several SUBSTs simultaneously. Consider the following version:

```
(DEFUN OUR-SUBLIS (A-LIST L)         ;BUGGED!
   (COND ((NULL A-LIST) L)           ;Done all substitutions?
         (T (OUR-SUBLIS (CDR A-LIST) ;Apply remaining changes
                  (SUBST (CADAR A-LIST) ; after substitution of this,
                         (CAAR A-LIST)  ; for that,
                         L)))))         ; in the expression.
```

What is wrong with this? Think about conflicting variable names, and the difference between sequential and parallel assignment. Consider the dependence of the result on the order in which sublists appear in the association list. Write a version of OUR-SUBLIS, using ASSOC, that does not suffer from this problem.

---

[3] The built in primitive SUBLIS behaves slightly differently, in that it expects an association list to contain dotted pairs instead of two-element lists.

**Properties and
Property Values
Generalize the Notion
of Symbol and Value**

Symbols can have *properties*. Property names and property values are left to the imagination of the user. An example is the COLOR property. The value of the COLOR property of the symbol PYRAMID-D could be RED, for example, capturing the same sort of facts previously recorded on an association list. In general, the value of a property can be any expression.

Note, incidentally, that the word *value* is used in three senses: first, we talk of the value returned when a form is evaluated; second, we talk of the value of some particular property of a symbol; and third, we talk of the value of a symbol.

**GET Is the Custodian
of Property Lists**

To retrieve property values, GET is used. In contrast to ASSOC, the GET primitive returns only the value, not a combination of the property and the value:

```
(GET 'PYRAMID-D 'COLOR)
  RED
```

```
(GET 'PYRAMID-D 'SUPPORTED-BY)
  BRICK-B
```

```
(GET 'PYRAMID-D 'IS-A)
  PYRAMID
```

It is important to note that GET returns NIL if no property with the given name exists. This suggests, first of all, that NIL is a poor choice for the value of a property, because the result returned by GET cannot be distinguished from what GET returns when it does not find the property asked for.

Properties are removed using the primitive REMPROP, which takes the symbol name and property name as arguments.

```
(REMPROP <symbol name> <property name>)
```

SETF can be used to place or replace a property value.[4] The first argument to SETF, the *access form*, is always a form that, if evaluated, would produce the current property value, and the second argument supplies the replacement value. The value returned by SETF is the replacement value:

```
(SETF (GET 'PYRAMID-D 'COLOR) 'RED)
  RED
```

```
(SETF (GET 'PYRAMID-D 'SUPPORTED-BY) 'BRICK-C)
  BRICK-C
```

---

[4] Later we see that SETF can be used for purposes other than the modification of property lists.

Thus the first argument to SETF identifies the symbol and the property to work with. SETF must examine this argument, but need not and does not evaluate it.

Note that as far as GET is concerned, properties can be removed using SETF, although it is better programming practice to use REMPROP.

```
(SETF (GET <symbol name> <property name>) NIL)
```

Problems

Problem 5-5: Suppose each city in a network of cities and highways is represented by a symbol. Further suppose that each city is to have a property named NEIGHBORS. The value of the NEIGHBORS property is to be a list of the other cities for which there is a direct highway connection.

Define a procedure, CONNECT, that takes two cities as arguments and puts each on the property list of the other under the NEIGHBORS property. Write CONNECT such that nothing changes if a connection is already in place.

Problem 5-6: Suppose X and Y are properties used to specify the position of cities in some reference coordinate system. Assuming a flat earth, write a procedure that calculates the distance between two cities. Remember that SQRT calculates square roots.

Problem 5-7: Assume that if a person's father is known, the father's name is given as the value of the FATHER property. Define GRANDFATHER, a procedure that returns the name of a person's paternal grandfather, if known, or NIL otherwise.

Problem 5-8: Define ADAM, a procedure that returns the most distant male ancestor of a person through the paternal line, working through the FATHER property. If no male ancestor is known, the procedure is to return the name given as its argument.

Problem 5-9: Define ANCESTORS, a procedure that returns a list consisting of the person given as its argument together with all known ancestors of the person. It is to work through both the FATHER and MOTHER properties. You may assume that related people do not have children together; that is, there is never a way to get to any ancestor by two distinct paths.

Data Abstraction Simplifies Data Interactions

Depending on circumstances, a programmer may use straight values, property lists, association lists, or intricate combinations. Experienced programmers often think in different terms, however. They isolate themselves from low-level details, and they concentrate on high-level concepts.

Consider an analogy between building design and program design. Architects tend to think about abstract concepts like walls and rooms more than they think about concrete concepts like bricks and mortar. Similarly, experienced programmers think more about abstract data objects than they think about detailed descriptions of how those abstract data objects are built, changed, and accessed with lower-level data primitives.

Thinking on the higher level is possible because it is easy to write procedures called *data constructors*, *data selectors*, and *data mutators*. Constructors make abstract data objects, selectors get information from those abstract objects, and mutators make changes. Together, constructors, selectors, and mutators are called *access procedures*.

For illustration, let us return to our descriptions of bricks and pyramids. Recall that we happened to put all brick information on an association list and all pyramid information on a property list. Assume now, however, that the association list for each brick is kept under its A-LIST property:

```
(SETF (GET 'BRICK-A 'A-LIST) '((COLOR RED)
                              (SUPPORTED-BY BRICK-B)
                              (IS-A BRICK)))
  ((COLOR RED) (SUPPORTED-BY BRICK-B) (IS-A BRICK))
```

As it stands, to get at the color of a brick, we have to remember to use GET and ASSOC with CADR, and to get at the color of a pyramid, we have to remember to use GET alone:

```
(CADR (ASSOC 'COLOR (GET 'BRICK-A 'A-LIST)))
  RED
(GET 'PYRAMID-D 'COLOR)
  RED
```

Keeping track of such detail can cause brain damage. Consequently, we think of bricks and pyramids as data types. For each data type, we define a selector procedure that extracts color:

```
(DEFUN BRICK-COLOR (BRICK)
  (CADR (ASSOC 'COLOR (GET BRICK 'A-LIST))))

(DEFUN PYRAMID-COLOR (PYRAMID)
  (GET PYRAMID 'COLOR))
```

Now we can forget about the details of how color is recorded, and we need only remember the mnemonically-principled names of the selector procedures.

Naturally, a similar story is told for creating and modifying instances of bricks and pyramids. We eliminate the need to remember the details using two type-specific constructor procedures:

```
(DEFUN MAKE-BRICK (OBJECT COLOR SUPPORT)
  (SETF (GET OBJECT 'A-LIST)
        (LIST (LIST 'IS-A 'BRICK)
              (LIST 'COLOR COLOR)
              (LIST 'SUPPORTED-BY SUPPORT)))
  OBJECT)

(DEFUN MAKE-PYRAMID (OBJECT COLOR SUPPORT)
  (SETF (GET OBJECT 'IS-A) 'PYRAMID)
  (SETF (GET OBJECT 'COLOR) COLOR)
  (SETF (GET OBJECT 'SUPPORTED-BY) SUPPORT)
  OBJECT)
```

To change data, we repeat, creating two mutators:

```
(DEFUN SET-BRICK-COLOR (BRICK COLOR)
  (SETF (GET BRICK 'A-LIST)
        (CONS (LIST 'COLOR COLOR) (GET BRICK 'A-LIST)))
  COLOR)

(DEFUN SET-PYRAMID-COLOR (PYRAMID COLOR)
  (SETF (GET PYRAMID 'COLOR) COLOR))
```

When selector and mutator procedures are written that cover two or more abstract data types, we say that we have a *compound data type*. As it stands, we need selector procedures for both bricks and pyramids and we need to know which one to use. Let us therefore create another abstract data type, the block, which encompasses both bricks and pyramids. The block data type is therefore said to be a compound data type. The selector and mutator procedures associated with blocks do the right thing for both bricks and pyramids. Here is a selector example:

```
(DEFUN BLOCK-COLOR (BLOCK)
  (COND ((EQUAL (GET BLOCK 'IS-A) 'PYRAMID)
         (PYRAMID-COLOR BLOCK))
        (T (BRICK-COLOR BLOCK))))
```

In summary, *data abstraction* is the process of building abstract data types. Data abstraction isolates programmers from representational details by hiding existing lower-level data storage, modification, and retrieval primitives underneath a layer of higher-level constructor, selector, and mutator procedures collectively called *access procedures*.

Data abstraction makes programs easier to modify. Given some need to change the way data is arranged, it is easier to change the definitions of a few access procedures than to find and change each place that data is used. This is particularly important when many programmers are working on the same programs.

Each access procedure may involve complicated combinations of lower-level procedures.   Access procedures are easier to remember and think about than the equivalent combinations.

A set of access procedures can become quite elaborate. Consequently, LISP gives us considerable help by way of DEFSTRUCT, described in the next section.

DEFSTRUCT Is a Powerful Mechanism for Data Abstraction

Conceptually, a *structure* is a collection of *fields* and *field values*. We are allowed to define new structures by specifying their particular field names and default field values. We are further allowed to construct individual structures of any already defined type, to access those individual structures, and to revise them. However, in keeping with the spirit of data abstraction, we are not allowed to look at the way individual structures are represented internally, for we are supposed to be isolated from that internal representation.[5]

To understand all this, consider the problem of describing blocks. To provide for color, support, and type information, we reserve a field for each when the block-describing structure is defined. To be more specific, we use DEFSTRUCT to define a suitable structure:

```
(DEFSTRUCT (BLOCK)              ;Define the BLOCK data type.
   (COLOR NIL)                  ;It has a field for color—default value is NIL.
   (DIRECTLY-SUPPORTS NIL)      ;Another field, with default value NIL.
   (IS-A 'BRICK))               ;Another field, with default value BRICK.
```

Evaluating this structure-defining primitive, DEFSTRUCT, has dramatic effects. First, DEFSTRUCT creates three selector procedures: one is the selector BLOCK-COLOR, another is the selector BLOCK-DIRECTLY-SUPPORTS, and a third is the selector BLOCK-IS-A. These procedures are used to get information out of the various fields of block-describing structures.

Second, DEFSTRUCT creates MAKE-BLOCK, a constructor procedure. This procedure is used to make new structures. When used with no arguments, MAKE-BLOCK constructs a block-describing structure with three fields, each filled by evaluating the default-value forms given to DEFSTRUCT when the BLOCK structure type was defined. Consider this:

```
(SETQ EXAMPLE1 (MAKE-BLOCK))

(BLOCK-COLOR EXAMPLE1)
   NIL
```

---

[5]   As a matter of fact, the internal representation of a structure is implementation dependent, and a program that fools with it is not portable.

```
(BLOCK-DIRECTLY-SUPPORTS EXAMPLE1)
  NIL

(BLOCK-IS-A EXAMPLE1)
  BRICK
```

It is easy to override the defaults: simply supply arguments to the MAKE-BLOCK structure-constructing procedure together with field-identifying *keywords*. For example, the following describes a red pyramid:

```
(SETQ EXAMPLE2 (MAKE-BLOCK :COLOR 'RED :IS-A 'PYRAMID))

(BLOCK-COLOR EXAMPLE2)
  RED

(BLOCK-DIRECTLY-SUPPORTS EXAMPLE2)
  NIL

(BLOCK-IS-A EXAMPLE2)
  PYRAMID
```

Note that a keyword consists of a field name prefixed by a colon.

Of course we need a way of altering existing field values. The structure-defining DEFSTRUCT takes care of this too. However, it creates no new procedures. Instead, DEFSTRUCT generalizes SETF, making it do more than we have indicated so far by working with structure fields. In fact, SETF is a mnemonic for set field:

```
(SETF (BLOCK-IS-A EXAMPLE2) 'PYRAMID)

(BLOCK-IS-A EXAMPLE2)
  PYRAMID
```

Again, as with ordinary property retrieval, the first argument to SETF is always an access form that, were it to be evaluated, would produce the field value, and the second is the field replacement value.

The use of structures is often the most appropriate, most elegant way to do data abstraction.

Summary

- ASSOC retrieves elements from association lists.
- Properties and property values generalize the notion of symbol and value.
- GET is the custodian of property lists.
- Data abstraction simplifies data interactions.
- DEFSTRUCT is a powerful mechanism for data abstraction.

References   For an excellent treatment of data abstraction, see Abelson and Sussman [1984].

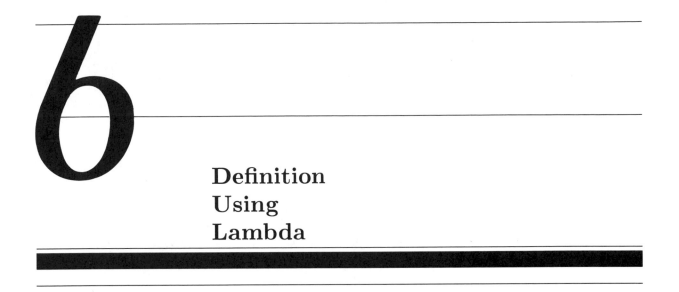

Definition
Using
Lambda

The descriptions of procedures are recorded using DEFUN so that they can be recalled later, using their name. In this chapter, we see that it is possible to use a procedure description in places where ordinarily there would be a procedure name. This is useful in a variety of ways.

LAMBDA Defines Anonymous Procedures

Suppose, for some bizarre reason, we have a list of groceries:

```
GROCERIES
  (BROCCOLI MILK APPLE BREAD BUTTER PEAR STEAK)
```

Consider FRUITP, a procedure that checks whether something is a fruit using its A-KIND-OF property:

```
(DEFUN FRUITP (X) (EQUAL (GET X 'A-KIND-OF) 'FRUIT))
```

With FRUITP, we can check which elements in a list are fruit:

```
(MAPCAR 'FRUITP GROCERIES)
  (NIL NIL T NIL NIL T NIL)
```

This is a little painful, if there is only one occasion to test for fruit. Passing over a list with a simple procedure should not require going off somewhere else to define a procedure. Why not make the programmer's intention more transparent by laying out the procedure at the spot where it is to be used:

```
(MAPCAR (DEFUN FRUITP (X) (EQUAL (GET X 'A-KIND-OF) 'FRUIT))
        GROCERIES)
  (NIL NIL T NIL NIL T NIL)
```

DEFUN works, because MAPCAR wants a procedure name, and the value of DEFUN is the name of the procedure defined. But to avoid the proliferation of useless names, the name can be dropped if it is used only here. In this event, the lack of a procedure name is signaled by using something different from DEFUN to define the procedure. For historical reasons, the new procedure definition is called a *lambda expression* and the symbol LAMBDA appears instead of DEFUN. One correct way to use a local definition, therefore, is as follows:

```
(MAPCAR '(LAMBDA (X) (EQUAL (GET X 'A-KIND-OF) 'FRUIT)) GROCERIES)
  (NIL T T T NIL NIL)
```

A longer but perhaps more informative name for introducing local definitions would be DEFINE-ANONYMOUS. We stick to LAMBDA because that is the accepted name, but if confusion ever sets in, a good heuristic for understanding LAMBDA is to translate it mentally to DEFINE-ANONYMOUS.

Note that the lambda expression that appears in the MAPCAR is quoted. Whereas the single quote is appropriate is some circumstances, it is more common to see a character sequence with a slightly different effect, namely, a hash mark followed by a single quote, #':

```
(MAPCAR #'(LAMBDA (X) (EQUAL (GET X 'A-KIND-OF) 'FRUIT)) GROCERIES)
  (NIL T T T NIL NIL)
```

The #' is a standard abbreviation for a primitive named FUNCTION. Thus #' provides a form of syntactic sugaring, just as ' does:

```
#'<expression>    ≡    (FUNCTION <expression>)
```

```
'<expression>    ≡    (QUOTE <expression>)
```

The form #'<LAMBDA EXPRESSION> differs from '<LAMBDA EXPRESSION> because something called a *lexical closure* is associated with #'<EXPRESSION>. When the lambda expression associated with a lexical closure is evaluated, the rules of lexical scoping are obeyed. If evaluation is to obey the rules of dynamic scoping instead, ' is used in place of #'. In this book, we use #', but we usually could use ' just as well, because we rarely use free variables in our lambda expressions, and where we do, the same result would be obtained using either scoping rule. Attention to scoping rules is necessary only when there is a question of where free-variable values are to be found.

Note that a lambda expression can go just about anywhere a procedure name can go. In particular, a lambda expression can be the first element in a form to be evaluated, even though it is much more common to see the name of a procedure there. The following are exactly equivalent, given the existing definition of FRUITP:

```
(FRUITP 'APPLE)
  T

((LAMBDA (X) (EQUAL (GET X 'A-KIND-OF) 'FRUIT)) 'APPLE)
  T

(FUNCALL 'FRUITP 'APPLE)
  T

(FUNCALL #'(LAMBDA (X) (EQUAL (GET X 'A-KIND-OF) 'FRUIT)) 'APPLE)
  T
```

For further illustration, suppose we want to actually count the number of fruit on the list GROCERIES. There are several methods involving MAPCAR. The first involves building a new procedure around FRUITP that returns 1 or 0 instead of T or NIL:

```
(DEFUN ONE-IF-FRUIT (X)
  (COND ((FRUITP X) 1) (T 0)))
```

Then it is easy to count the apples by using MAPCAR to run ONE-IF-FRUIT down the list, adding the results by applying +:

```
(MAPCAR 'ONE-IF-FRUIT GROCERIES)
  (0 1 1 1 0 0)

(APPLY '+ (MAPCAR 'ONE-IF-FRUIT GROCERIES))
  3
```

Alternatively, the action now embedded in ONE-IF-FRUIT can be specified locally, using a lambda expression in the MAPCAR:

```
(APPLY '+ (MAPCAR #'(LAMBDA (X) (COND ((FRUITP X) 1)
                                      (T 0)))
                  GROCERIES))
  3
```

Indeed, the guts of FRUITP can be brought in too:

```
(APPLY '+ (MAPCAR #'(LAMBDA (X) (COND ((EQUAL (GET X 'A-KIND-OF)
                                              'FRUIT)
                                       1)
                                      (T 0)))
                  GROCERIES))
  3
```

Of course it is easy to bottle all of this up and make a procedure out of it:

```
(DEFUN COUNT-FRUIT (GROCERIES)
   (APPLY '+ (MAPCAR #'(LAMBDA (X) (COND ((EQUAL X 'APPLE) 1)
                                         (T 0)))
                     GROCERIES)))

(COUNT-FRUIT GROCERIES)
   3
```

Incidentally, a lambda expression can have any number of parameters. Also, a lambda expression can have any number of forms in its body, just like an ordinary procedure definition. Only the last determines the value. The rest are evaluated for side effects.

LAMBDA Helps REMOVE-IF and REMOVE-IF-NOT Do Filtering

Having just seen lambda expressions at work with MAPCAR, now is a good time to explain REMOVE-IF and REMOVE-IF-NOT. Often REMOVE-IF and REMOVE-IF-NOT are used to do *filtered accumulations*. To see what this means, suppose we want to make a list out of the fruit in a list of groceries. Then it is natural to think of using FRUITP on every element in the grocery list. MAPCAR can arrange this for us, but the result is not quite what we want:

```
(MAPCAR 'FRUITP GROCERIES)
   (NIL NIL T NIL NIL T NIL)
```

The primitive REMOVE-IF-NOT does the job, however, keeping only those items on which FRUITP has a nonNIL result:

```
(REMOVE-IF-NOT 'FRUITP GROCERIES)
   (APPLE PEAR)
```

Just as MAPCAR is happy with lambda expressions, so is REMOVE-IF-NOT. Consequently, this will work too:

```
(REMOVE-IF-NOT #'(LAMBDA (X) (EQUAL (GET X 'A-KIND-OF) 'FRUIT))
               GROCERIES)
   (APPLE PEAR)
```

Using REMOVE-IF-NOT, we can define KEEP-FRUIT like this:

```
(DEFUN KEEP-FRUIT (GROCERIES)
   (REMOVE-IF-NOT #'(LAMBDA (X) (EQUAL (GET X 'A-KIND-OF) 'FRUIT))
                  GROCERIES))
```

**LAMBDA Helps
Interface Procedures
to Argument Lists**

The next example develops a procedure that determines how many times atoms with a specified property are found in some given expression. Unlike COUNT-FRUIT, this new procedure is expected to work on any expression, not just lists of atoms.

The plan is to make a recursive procedure that can work its way into the expression that is given. This alternate version of COUNT-FRUIT counts all instances of fruit:

```
(DEFUN COUNT-DEEP-FRUIT (L)
  (COND ((ATOM L)
         (COND ((EQUAL (GET L 'A-KIND-OF) 'FRUIT) 1)    ;It is a fruit?
               (T 0)))                                  ;No, it is not.
        (T (APPLY '+ (MAPCAR 'COUNT-DEEP-FRUIT L)))))    ;Recurse.
```

Now we attempt to generalize this by adding another parameter, making a procedure that counts any desired type, not just fruit. The new procedure counts the instances of the first argument appearing in the second argument. Our first attempt fails:

```
(DEFUN COUNT (TYPE L)                              ;BUGGED!
  (COND ((ATOM L)
         (COND ((EQUAL (GET L 'A-KIND-OF) TYPE) 1) ;Is it one?
               (T 0)))                             ;No, it is not.
        (T (APPLY '+ (MAPCAR 'COUNT L)))))          ;Blunder!
```

This is wrong, because COUNT is defined as a procedure of two arguments, TYPE and L. If it does not get two, it is unhappy. But the MAPCAR only has one list of things to channel into COUNT; hence, disaster. There is a fatal mismatch between the parameter list in COUNT and the arguments that COUNT is supplied by the MAPCAR.

The solution is to replace the COUNT that appears in the MAPCAR by a new procedure definition, one that uses COUNT appropriately. Again, this new, nameless procedure definition is announced by LAMBDA:

```
(DEFUN COUNT (TYPE L)
  (COND ((ATOM L)
         (COND ((EQUAL (GET L 'A-KIND-OF) TYPE) 1) (T 0)))
        (T (APPLY '+ (MAPCAR #'(LAMBDA (E) (COUNT TYPE E)) ;Lambda definition.
                      L)))))
```

Here the lambda expression matches COUNT, a procedure with two parameters, to a single list of MAPCAR arguments. Note that TYPE is a free variable with respect to the lambda expression.[1]

---

[1] It is tempting to deal with COUNT's interfacing problem by defining an auxiliary procedure, COUNT1, with a free variable, TYPE, but that would be wrong. The problem is that the auxiliary procedure would be looking for the value of TYPE in the wrong environment, because our LISP uses lexical scoping, as explained in chapter 3.

Problems

Problem 6-1: Using MAPCAR, define a version of PRESENTP, a procedure defined in an earlier problem, which determines if a particular atom exists *anywhere* in an expression.

Problem 6-2: We can study the application of procedures to given arguments, now that we know about lambda expressions. Remember that parameters are part of a procedure's definition, whereas arguments occur where the procedure definition is used. Write SUBSTITUTE-FOR-PARAMETERS, a procedure that replaces occurrences of parameters in the body of a lambda expression with corresponding arguments. SUBSTITUTE-FOR-PARAMETERS is to take two arguments, the first is a list of arguments and the second the lambda expression:

```
(SUBSTITUTE-FOR-PARAMETERS '(1 2 3)
                           #'(LAMBDA (X Y Z) (+ (* X Y) (* Y Z) (* Z X))))
   (+ (* 1 2) (* 2 3) (* 3 1))
```

Presumably, if we feed the result produced by SUBSTITUTE-FOR-PARAMETERS to EVAL, we get the same answer as if we feed the original lambda expression and its arguments to APPLY. This is a nice illustration of a LISP procedure treating another LISP procedure as data. Note that PAIRLIS and SUBLIS, introduced in the problems of chapters 4 and 5, may come in handy here.

Project 6-1: Suppose that DEFUN works by attaching lambda expressions to procedure names. Suppose further that the primitive SYMBOL-FUNCTION retrieves lambda expressions from procedure names. Using the procedure SUBSTITUTE-FOR-PARAMETERS from the previous problem, expand the lambda expression of a procedure whose name is given as an argument. Your procedure, EXPAND-OUT, should attempt to retrieve the lambda expression of procedures appearing in forms in the body of the lambda expression. One can test whether a symbol is associated with a procedure definition by using FBOUNDP. Also, the result produced by SYMBOL-FUNCTION can be tested using LISTP to make sure that it is a lambda expression. If a procedure is a primitive, or a special form, no lambda expression will be found, and so no expansion should take place.

Suppose that the following is typed at LISP:

```
(DEFUN NOUGHT (U V W) (+ (SQ-DIF U V) (SQ-DIF V W) (SQ-DIF W U)))

(DEFUN SQ-DIF (K L) (* (+ K L) (- K L)))
```

Then EXPAND-OUT applied to NOUGHT produces a procedure that happens to always return 0:

```
(LAMBDA (U V W)
  (+ (* (+ U V) (- U V))
     (* (+ V W) (- V W))
     (* (+ W U) (- W U))))
```

Improve EXPAND-OUT to deal separately with the special form COND.
Now suppose that the following procedures are defined:

```
(DEFUN MEDIAN-OF-THREE (A B C)
  (COND ((> A B) (MEDIAN-THREE 1 D A C))          ;Arrange for A < B.
        (T (MEDIAN-THREE-1 A B C))))

(DEFUN MEDIAN-THREE-1 (A B C)
  (COND ((> B C) (MEDIAN-THREE-2 A C B))          ;Arrange for B < C.
        (T (MEDIAN-THREE-2 A B C))))

(DEFUN MEDIAN-THREE-2 (A B C)
  (COND ((> A B) A) (T B)))                        ;Arrange for A < B.
```

What happens if you apply EXPAND-OUT to MEDIAN-OF-THREE?

Summary

- LAMBDA defines anonymous procedures.
- LAMBDA helps REMOVE-IF and REMOVE-IF-NOT do filtering.
- LAMBDA helps interface procedures to argument lists.

References

The calculus of lambda conversion was introduced by Church [1941]. See also Landin [1964, 1965].

7

Printing
And Reading

The purpose of this chapter is to introduce PRINT and READ, primitives that help procedures communicate with the user. Without PRINT, the only way a user can learn about what a LISP procedure is doing is to wait for a value to appear. Without READ, the only way a procedure can get information is through its arguments and through free variables. PRINT and READ therefore open the door to much more communication. Happily, both are very simple.

PRINT and READ Facilitate Communication

PRINT evaluates its single argument and prints it on a new line. Thus the following procedure prints out the squares of the integers until something drops dead:[1]

```
(DEFUN BORE-ME ()
  (DO ((N 0 (+ N 1)))
      (NIL)
    (PRINT (* N N))))
```

---

[1] LISP systems usually have some kind of interrupt method that allows the user to terminate evaluations that appear to be stuck in a loop. It is important to find out early on what that method is.

```
(BORE-ME)
  0
  1
  4
  9
```

The value returned by PRINT is the unaltered value of its argument.[2] In BORE-ME, PRINT's value is not used.

When (READ) is encountered, LISP stops and waits for the user to type an expression. That expression, without evaluation, becomes the value of (READ). Consequently, using READ by itself causes total inactivity until the user types some expression. In this example, the user types EXAMPLE, followed by a space:

```
(READ)EXAMPLE
    EXAMPLE
```

Because READ prints nothing to indicate that it is waiting, not even a carriage return, it is usually a good idea to use PRINT first to prompt the user and to indicate what kind of response is expected.

Problems about Stacking Disks on Pins

We now tackle the celebrated Tower-of-Hanoi problem. An ancient myth has it that in some temple in the Far East, time is marked off by monks engaged in the transfer of 64 disks from one of three pins to another. The universe as we know it will end when they are done. The reason we do not have to concern ourselves about the cosmological implications of this is that their progress is kept in check by some clever rules:

- Only one disk can be moved at a time.

- The disks all have different diameters, and no disk can ever be placed on top of a smaller one.

Initially all disks are on one pin and each disk rests on a larger one.

The insight leading to the correct sequence of moves comes from the realization that a set of n disks can be transferred from pin A to pin B in these stages: first move the top $(n-1)$ disks from A to the spare pin C; then move the large bottom disk from A to B; and finally, move the $(n-1)$ disks from the spare pin, C, onto pin B. Naturally, moving the $(n-1)$ disks can be done by the same trick, using the third pin (not involved in the transfer) as workspace. By means of recursion, we postpone the actual work until n equals 1.

---

[2] In some older dialects of LISP, PRINT returns T, a useless value.

```
(DEFUN TOWER-OF-HANOI (N) (TRANSFER 'A 'B 'C N))           ;N disks on A first.

(DEFUN MOVE-DISK (FROM TO)
  (LIST (LIST 'MOVE 'DISK 'FROM FROM 'TO TO)))             ;Build instruction.

(DEFUN TRANSFER (FROM TO SPARE NUMBER)
  (COND ((= N 1) (MOVE-DISK FROM TO))                      ;Easy case - one disk.
        (T (APPEND (TRANSFER FROM                          ;Move from FROM
                             SPARE                         ; to SPARE
                             TO                            ; using TO as spare,
                             (- N 1))                      ; (n-1) disks.
                   (MOVE-DISK FROM TO)                     ;Move lowest disk.
                   (TRANSFER SPARE                         ;Move from SPARE
                             TO                            ; to TO using
                             FROM                          ; FROM as spare,
                             (- N 1))))))                  ; (n-1) disks.
```

This is what the resulting list of instructions looks like for a typical case:

```
(TOWER-OF-HANOI 3)
  ((MOVE DISK FROM A TO B)
   (MOVE DISK FROM A TO C)
   (MOVE DISK FROM B TO C)
   (MOVE DISK FROM A TO B)
   (MOVE DISK FROM C TO A)
   (MOVE DISK FROM C TO B)
   (MOVE DISK FROM A TO B))
```

Problem 7-1: The above solution may not be very convincing, because everything seems to be done blindly, without checking whether disks are ever placed on smaller disks, or for that matter, whether any disks are left on the pin from which they are supposed to be removed. What is needed is a *simulation* of the pin transfer steps. There is a need also to print detailed information about the steps as they are taken.

It would be more informative if the final instructions included some identification of which disk is being moved. Let us assume that the disks are numbered in order of increasing size. Further, let A, B, and C be global free variables bound to lists of numbers representing the stacks of disks currently on each of the three pins. Rewrite MOVE-DISK to include checking on the legality of proposed moves, appropriate modification of the lists that are the values of A, B, and C, as well as generation of more informative output.

Consider the following example:

```
(SETQ A '(1 2 3)  B NIL  C NIL)

(TOWER-OF-HANOI)
  (MOVE 1 FROM A TO B)
  (MOVE 2 FROM A TO C)
  (MOVE 1 FROM B TO C)
  (MOVE 3 FROM A TO B)
  (MOVE 1 FROM C TO A)
  (MOVE 2 FROM C TO B)
  (MOVE 1 FROM A TO B)
```

Special Conventions Make Weird Symbol Names Possible

Sometimes it is useful to have symbols that consist wholly or partly of characters that ordinarily are not allowed in symbols. Spaces and parentheses are examples of such characters. Placing vertical bars around such special symbols is the best way to do this:

```
(SETQ SYMBOL1 '|(|)
  |(|

(SETQ SYMBOL2 '|WEIRD SYMBOL|)
  |WEIRD SYMBOL|

(PRINT SYMBOL1)
  |(|
  |(|

(PRINT SYMBOL2)
  |WEIRD SYMBOL|
  |WEIRD SYMBOL|
```

The vertical bar, |, is called a multiple escape character. Another method uses a backslash, \, called a single escape character. It indicates that just the following character is to lose any special syntactic properties it might otherwise have had.[3] We could have used '\(instead of SYMBOL1 and 'WEIRD\ SYMBOL instead of SYMBOL2 in the above examples. For output, LISP uses the vertical bar convention, not slashes.

Symbols Can Be Created

If there is a program that wants a fresh symbol without bothering the user to get it, GENSYM can be used. In some sense, GENSYM is an input primitive that creates new symbols rather than reading them in:

---

[3] This means that when we really want a single \ we have to use two, \\.

```
(GENSYM)
  G1

(GENSYM)
  G2
```

In chapter 15, these GENSYMed symbols are used to build tree structures that record how the procedures in a blocks-world manipulation system call one another to solve problems. The trees make it possible to answer questions about how things were done, as well as why and when.

Exotic Input/Output Primitives Lie Beyond PRINT and READ

It is possible to go through a career of LISP programming without using any printing and reading primitives other than PRINT and READ. Eventually, however, most people like to use other primitives that enable better-looking, more presentable input and output. It does not make much sense to dwell on those other printing and reading primitives, however, because they tend to vary from system to system. The following are given mainly to show what is available.

TERPRI is a primitive that starts a new line. PRIN1 is another primitive, like PRINT, except that PRIN1 does not start with a new line nor does it finish with a space. Thus:

```
(PROGN (TERPRI) (PRIN1 X) (PRIN1 '| |))    ≡    (PRINT X)
```

PRINC is like PRIN1 except that vertical bars, if any, are suppressed. The idea is that PRIN1 produces output that is suitable to be fed back into LISP, whereas PRINC is better suited to present formatted output to be read by people:[4]

```
(PRINT SYMBOL2)
  |WEIRD SYMBOL|
  |WEIRD SYMBOL|

(PRIN1 SYMBOL2)|WEIRD SYMBOL|
  |WEIRD SYMBOL|

(PRINC SYMBOL2)WEIRD SYMBOL
  |WEIRD SYMBOL|
```

Note that because PRIN1 and PRINC do not start a new line, the things they print are on the same line the user typed on.

---

[4] It is possible to read input from a source other than the user terminal keyboard, and it is possible to send the output of a program to a sink other than the user terminal screen. In COMMON LISP sinks and sources, called streams, are specified by an optional argument to PRINT, PRINC, PRIN1, TERPRI, and READ.

**Formatted Printing
Can Be Arranged**

As an example of what can be done with vertical bars and exotic printing primitives, let us consider a procedure that takes two arguments—a list of items to be printed and a list of columns where printing is to start:[5]

```
(DEFUN TABLE-PRINT (ITEMS COLUMNS)
   (TERPRI)                               ;Go to beginning of line.
   (TABLE-PRINT1 ITEMS COLUMNS 0))

(DEFUN TABLE-PRINT1 (ITEMS COLUMNS N)
   (COND ((NULL ITEMS) T)                 ;Stop when all items printed.
         ((< N (CAR COLUMNS))             ;Check current position.
          (PRINC '| |)                    ;Print blank space if needed.
          (TABLE-PRINT1 ITEMS             ;Repeat.
                        COLUMNS
                        (+ N 1)))
         (T (PRINC (CAR ITEMS))           ;Print next atom.
            (TABLE-PRINT1 (CDR ITEMS)     ;Repeat.
                          (CDR COLUMNS)
                          (+ N (LENGTH (SYMBOL-NAME (CAR ITEMS)))))))))
```

LENGTH, working with the primitive SYMBOL-NAME, returns the number of characters in a symbol's name. You may think of this as a miracle for now: actually, SYMBOL-NAME returns something called a *string*, and LENGTH is willing to work with strings as well as lists. We will not discuss strings in detail.[6]

The following is an example in which several TABLE-PRINTs are used to print a timetable in columns determined by the value of TABS.

```
(DEFUN TIME-TABLE ()
  (LET ((TABS '(0 12 24 36 48)))
    (TABLE-PRINT '(CONCORD LINCOLN WALTHAM CAMBRIDGE BOSTON) TABS)
    (TABLE-PRINT '(6-11 6-17 6-29 6-41 6-55) TABS)
    (TABLE-PRINT '(6-46 6-52 7-05 7-17 7-31) TABS)))
TIME-TABLE

(TIME-TABLE)
CONCORD     LINCOLN     WALTHAM     CAMBRIDGE   BOSTON
6-11        6-17        6-29        6-41        6-55
6-46        6-52        7-05        7-17        7-31
   T
```

----

[5] Normally, printed output is in *free format*, using up as much or as little space as is needed to print out a number or name of a symbol. COMMON LISP, however, also has FORMAT, a complicated primitive that allows one to specify in agonizing detail just how to assemble output to be printed.

[6] Strings are vectors of characters. Vectors are one dimensional arrays, briefly mentioned later. A *sequence* is a list or a vector. Several primitives, like LENGTH, will work on any sequence, not just a list.

Problems

Problem 7-2: Define ECHO1, a procedure that reads expressions and returns them without evaluation, and define ECHO2, a procedure that returns with evaluation.

Problem 7-3: It is often handy to have a way of printing information without too many parentheses to confuse things. Define a procedure P that takes one argument and prints the atoms in it as a single list without nesting. This illustrates:

```
(SETQ L '(A (B (C D) E) (F (G (H I) J) K) L))
  (A (B (C D) E) (F (G (H I) J) K) L)

(P (LIST '(THE SYMBOLS IN L ARE) L))
  (THE SYMBOLS IN L ARE A B C D E F G H I J K L)
```

Then define PC, a procedure that takes two arguments and prints only if the first evaluates to nonNIL. When PC does print, it is to print the second argument as a nonnested list. And finally define RQ, a procedure that prints its argument as a nonnested list, reads a form given by the user, and returns its value. These examples illustrate:

```
(SETQ N 'ROBBIE)
  ROBBIE

(PC (NOT (NUMBERP N)) (LIST 'WARNING N '(IS NOT A NUMBER)))
  (WARNING ROBBIE IS NOT A NUMBER)

(RQ '(PLEASE SUPPLY A VALUE FOR E))
  (PLEASE SUPPLY A VALUE FOR E) 2.718281828
  2.718281828
```

Problem 7-4: Define PSENTENCE, a procedure that behaves like P except that it prints no parentheses at all, with a period at the end.

```
(SETQ L '(A B C D E F G H I J K L))
  (A B C D E F G H I J K L)

(PSENTENCE (LIST '(THE SYMBOLS IN L ARE) L))
  THE SYMBOLS IN L ARE A B C D E F G H I J K L.
```

Problem 7-5: The examples throughout this book indicate that PRINT indents two spaces before starting. This is done for clarity only, and in actual LISP systems, PRINT does not indent. Define BOOK-PRINT, a procedure that does indent two spaces.

Problem 7-6: A program's requests for information and the user's replies can be arranged neatly on the screen of a display terminal. The desired format for the requests can be described by a list in which each sublist specifies where some words are to be printed:

```
(<list of words> <row> <column>)
```

Similarly the location where information typed by the user is to appear can be described by a list consisting of sublists like the following:

```
(<word> <row> <column>)
```

The symbol <WORD> is to be set, using SET, to the number or word typed by the user. SET is somewhat like SETQ except that SET *does* evaluate its first argument. Note, however, that SET only works with dynamic variables, not lexical variables. Since all variables are lexical by default, you must make a proclamation specifically declaring which variables are not to be lexical:

```
(PROCLAIM '(SPECIAL LAST-NAME FIRST-NAME ...))
```

Also, SET takes only two arguments, the first of which must be the name of a free variable.

Define DATA-ENTRY, a procedure that prints and reads according to such formatting instructions. Assume that items are ordered, so that a cursor can always be positioned by spacing forward and going to the next line. A cursor is a mark that indicates where the next character is to appear on the screen. Further assume that TOP-OF-SCREEN clears the display screen and positions the cursor in the top left-hand corner.[7] The following is a test case for your procedure:

```
(DATA-ENTRY '(((LAST NAME) 1 0) (LAST-NAME 1 11)
              ((FIRST NAME) 1 30) (FIRST-NAME 1 43)
              ((AGE) 3 0) (AGE 3 6)
              ((SEX) 3 14) (SEX 3 20)
              ((OCCUPATION) 3 30) (OCCUPATION 3 43)
              ((YOUR ADDRESS NEXT) 6 0)
              ((STREET) 9 0) (STREET 9 9)
              ((NUMBER) 9 30) (NUMBER 9 39)
              ((CITY:) 10 0) (CITY 10 9)
              ((STATE) 10 30) (STATE 10 38)
              ((ZIP CODE) 10 52) (ZIP 10 63)
              ((THANK YOU VERY MUCH) 13 0)))
```

Problem 7-7: It is essential, when using LISP, to have some tools to help get the layout of expressions right. Otherwise the parentheses become snares. LISP-oriented editors are a big help in this regard. Such editors have various procedures including one that does what is called pretty-printing. Write a simple OUR-PPRINT. If OUR-PPRINT's argument is a list, it is to print the first element, then the second, and then the third, neatly lining up the third and the rest under the second. Any elements that are themselves lists are to be printed in the same way, recursively; recursion is to stop when

---

[7] In some dialects of LISP, programmers can control the position of the cursor on the screen of the display terminal explicitly and read its position when desired. Such facilities simplify the writing of fancy printing procedures.

atoms are encountered. Assume that you will not encounter numbers or symbols with weird names.

```
(<element-1> <element-2>
            <element-3>
            .
            .
            .
            <element-n>)
```

Each element itself should be pretty-printed so that the overall printed result makes the structure of the expression clearly apparent.

Project 7-1:   Write a simple screen editor in LISP. Special single character commands should move the cursor around.

Summary

- PRINT and READ facilitate communication.
- Special conventions make weird symbol names possible.
- Symbols can be created.
- Exotic input/output primitives lie beyond print and read.
- Formatted printing can be arranged.

References

Pretty-printing is discussed by Goldstein [1973], Oppen [1979], Hearn and Norman [1979], Mikelson [1981], as well as Waters [1981]. A powerful real time editor written in LISP is described by Greenberg [1979, 1980].

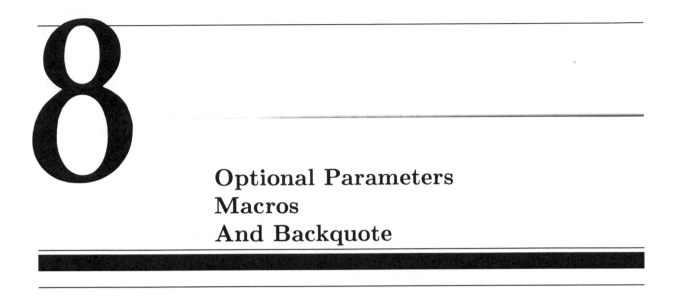

Optional Parameters
Macros
And Backquote

So far we know how to define ordinary procedures with a fixed number of arguments that are always evaluated. Their purpose has been either to produce values as output or to produce useful side effects.

The first purpose of this chapter is to show how to define procedures that take additional, *optional arguments*, if supplied. The second purpose is to show how to define *macro procedures*, which do their work in two steps: first, one or more argument expressions are used to build an intermediate form; and second, the intermediate form is evaluated to produce an output value.

Using macros, we can define idiomatic procedures that are easy to work with even though the evaluation of those procedures involves complicated LISP forms.[1]

Finally, the third purpose of this chapter is to introduce the backquote mechanism, which often simplifies many sorts of programming tasks drastically, particularly macro writing.

---

[1] Using a macro does not involve any extra inefficiencies in a compiled program. During compilation, each macro is translated into an intermediate form, which is then spliced into the place where the macro appears. The macro evaluation occurs only once. Also, some interpreters avoid repeated macro evaluation by splicing intermediate macro forms into appropriate places.

Optional Parameters
Allow Optional
Arguments

Suppose, for the sake of illustration, that we have a procedure that attaches the symbol PERIOD to the end of a list:

```
(DEFUN PUNCTUATE (L)
  (APPEND L '(PERIOD)))
```

Here is an example of its use:

```
(PUNCTUATE '(THIS IS AN EXAMPLE))
  (THIS IS AN EXAMPLE PERIOD)
```

Naturally, it is easy to add other procedures that add QUESTION-MARK or EXCLAMATION-MARK instead. Alternatively, we can rewrite PUNCTUATE so that it takes a second argument:

```
(DEFUN PUNCTUATE (L MARK)
  (APPEND L (LIST MARK)))
```

Most sentences end with a period, however, so supplying the second argument every time is annoying. Happily, the optional arguments feature enables us to supply the second argument only when needed. Here is our definition of PUNCTUATE with an optional argument:

```
(DEFUN PUNCTUATE (L &OPTIONAL MARK)
  (COND ((NOT MARK) (APPEND L '(PERIOD)))
        (T (APPEND L (LIST MARK)))))
```

The & of &OPTIONAL signals that &OPTIONAL is a parameter separator rather than a parameter. Parameters following &OPTIONAL are bound on procedure entry just like any other parameters. If there is no matching argument, the optional parameter is set to NIL. Thus the value of MARK in the following example is QUESTION-MARK, because there is a matching argument:

```
(PUNCTUATE '(IS THIS AN EXAMPLE) 'QUESTION-MARK)
  (IS THIS AN EXAMPLE QUESTION-MARK)
```

But the value of MARK in the next example is NIL, the default, because there is no matching argument. Consequently, PERIOD is added:

```
(PUNCTUATE '(THIS IS AN EXAMPLE))
  (THIS IS AN EXAMPLE PERIOD)
```

The following is another, simpler version of PUNCTUATE, this time with a default value for the optional parameter.

```
(DEFUN PUNCTUATE (L &OPTIONAL (MARK 'PERIOD))
  (APPEND L (LIST MARK)))
```

If no matching argument is supplied, then PERIOD, by default, becomes the value for MARK, rather than NIL.

There can be any number of optional parameters. There also can be a single optional parameter, signaled by &REST, whose value becomes a list of all arguments given beyond those that match required and optional parameters. Consider the appearance of the &REST-signaled parameter in this version of PUNCTUATE, for example:

```
(DEFUN PUNCTUATE (L &REST MARKS)
  (COND ((NULL MARKS) (APPEND L '(PERIOD)))
        (T (APPEND L MARKS))))
```

In the following example, PUNCTUATE operates as before:

```
(PUNCTUATE '(THIS IS AN EXAMPLE))
  (THIS IS AN EXAMPLE PERIOD)
```

But here, MARKS's value is a list of the extra arguments, SO, TO, SPEAK, and EXCLAMATION-MARK, producing a longer result:

```
(PUNCTUATE '(THIS IS AN EXAMPLE) 'SO 'TO 'SPEAK 'EXCLAMATION-MARK)
  (THIS IS AN EXAMPLE SO TO SPEAK EXCLAMATION-MARK)
```

Ordinary Procedures Always Evaluate Their Arguments

Now suppose that you find yourself constantly writing simple conditionals of the following simple form:

```
(COND (<test> <result if test succeeds>)
      (T <result if test fails>))
```

You then conjecture that the following is a nicer, more streamlined way to express the same idea:[2]

```
(OUR-IF <test> <result if test succeeds> <result if test fails>)
```

Consequently, you are tempted to write a procedure, OUR-IF, like this:

```
(DEFUN OUR-IF (TEST SUCCESS-RESULT FAILURE-RESULT)        ;BUGGED!
  (COND (TEST SUCCESS-RESULT)
        (T FAILURE-RESULT)))
```

Unfortunately, this OUR-IF procedure evaluates all three arguments before doing anything else, whereas the intent is for it to be a substitute for a conditional that evaluates either one expression or another, but *not* both.

The difference is not just a matter of efficiency. If either result form has side effects, then the use of OUR-IF, as defined, produces a different computation from the conditional that OUR-IF is intended to replace.

---

[2] COMMON LISP has the primitive IF, which is similar to OUR-IF.

For another example, consider this use of OUR-IF, which is intended to return the value of X if the value is an atom, and the first element in the value of X if the value is a list:

```
(OUR-IF (ATOM X) X (CAR X))          ;BUGGED!
```

The current version of OUR-IF does the wrong thing because there will be an attempt to evaluate (CAR X) even when X is an atom.

Happily, macros provide just the flexibility we need. Soon you will see OUR-IF defined as a macro that first *translates* OUR-IF forms into a conditional:

```
(OUR-IF <test> <result if test succeeds> <result if test fails>)


↓


(COND (<test> <result if test succeeds>)
      (T <result if test fails>))
```

Once the translation is done, the resulting conditional is evaluated as if the COND had been there in the first place.

Macros Do Not Evaluate Their Arguments

Macros never evaluate any of their arguments. An example makes this clear. Suppose DEMONSTRATION-MACRO is defined as a macro using the macro-defining procedure DEFMACRO:

```
(DEFMACRO DEMONSTRATION-MACRO (PAR)
  (PRINT PAR))
```

Evidently, macros are defined using the same syntax as ordinary procedures:

```
(DEFMACRO <macro name> <parameter list> <macro body>)
```

Now suppose DEMONSTRATION-MACRO is used as follows:

```
(SETQ THIS 'VALUE-OF-THIS)
```

```
(DEMONSTRATION-MACRO THIS)
```

No attempt is made to evaluate THIS. Instead THIS becomes the value of PAR. The PRINT therefore causes THIS to be printed, after which PRINT returns THIS as its value, which becomes the value of the macro's intermediate form. When THIS, the intermediate form, is evaluated, it produces VALUE-OF-THIS:

```
(DEMONSTRATION-MACRO THIS)
  THIS
  VALUE-OF-THIS
```

Note that this is quite different from the behavior of the similar-looking procedure DEMONSTRATION-PROCEDURE:

```
(DEFUN DEMONSTRATION-PROCEDURE (PAR)
  (PRINT PAR))
```

DEMONSTRATION-PROCEDURE produces this:

```
(DEMONSTRATION-PROCEDURE THIS)
  VALUE-OF-THIS
  VALUE-OF-THIS
```

Macros Translate and Then Execute

Now let us consider a more ambitious example by doing OUR-IF as a macro. Thinking in terms of macros, the overall idea is to translate OUR-IF forms into equivalent conditional forms. Remember, for a three-argument use of OUR-IF, we want to translate OUR-IF forms into a conditional as follows:

```
(OUR-IF <test> <result if test succeeds> <result if test fails>)
```

↓

```
(COND (<test> <result if test succeeds>)
      (T <result if test fails>))
```

When evaluated, the equivalent conditional yields the desired result. Evaluating the body of the following macro, OUR-IF, builds the required conditional using SUBST, together with the raw material supplied in OUR-IF's parameters:

```
(DEFMACRO OUR-IF (TEST SUCCESS-RESULT FAILURE-RESULT)
  (SUBST TEST 'TEST
         (SUBST SUCCESS-RESULT 'SUCCESS-RESULT
                (SUBST FAILURE-RESULT 'FAILURE-RESULT
                       '(COND (TEST SUCCESS-RESULT) (T FAILURE-RESULT)))))))
```

The resulting conditional is then evaluated, because OUR-IF is a macro and therefore, by special privilege, the result of evaluating the body is itself evaluated.

- Given a piece of procedure, a macro computes a new piece of procedure from it, which is then evaluated. Thus macros exploit the fact that LISP procedures and data have the same form.

Now it is easy to generalize OUR-IF so that it is happy with either two or three arguments: We simply retain TEST and SUCCESS-RESULT as required parameters, but make FAILURE-RESULT optional using &OPTIONAL:

```
(DEFMACRO OUR-IF (TEST SUCCESS-RESULT &OPTIONAL FAILURE-RESULT)
  (SUBST TEST 'TEST
         (SUBST SUCCESS-RESULT 'SUCCESS-RESULT
                (SUBST FAILURE-RESULT 'FAILURE-RESULT
                       '(COND (TEST SUCCESS-RESULT) (T FAILURE-RESULT)))))))
```

The value of FAILURE-RESULT is NIL if no third argument is supplied. Consequently, the COND construction gets the right value inserted for the false result whether or not the OUR-IF has a third argument.

Note, incidentally, that there is a subtle danger due to *variable name conflict* in using SUBST. Suppose, for example, that the third argument to OUR-IF coincidentally contains either of the symbols TEST or SUCCESS-RESULT. Such symbols will be replaced, happily but foolishly, because the second and third evaluations of SUBST cannot tell the difference between instances appearing by virtue of the first evaluation of SUBST and the instances appearing explicitly in the macro body. Similarly, if the second argument to OUR-IF coincidentally contains TEST, it too will be replaced.

Backquote Simplifies Template Filling

In general, the backquote mechanism provides an easy way to create expressions in which most of the expression is fixed, and in which only a few, variable, details need to be filled in. The backquote, `, acts just like the normal quote, ', except that any commas that appear within the scope of the backquote have the effect of *unquoting* the following expression.

```
(SETQ VARIABLE 'EXAMPLE)
  EXAMPLE

`(THIS IS AN ,VARIABLE)
  (THIS IS AN EXAMPLE)
```

Backquote also allows a comma conjoined to an at sign; that is, ,@. This combination unquotes the following expression, just as comma does, but in contrast to comma, the resulting value must be a list. The elements in this list are *spliced* into the list in which the ,@ appears, rather than strung together:

```
(SETQ VARIABLE '(MORE DIFFICULT EXAMPLE))
  (MORE DIFFICULT EXAMPLE)

(THIS IS A ,VARIABLE)
  (THIS IS A (MORE DIFFICULT EXAMPLE))
```

```
`(THIS IS A ,@VARIABLE)
  (THIS IS A MORE DIFFICULT EXAMPLE)
```

Using the backquote mechanism simplifies macro writing, because the intermediate form of many macros can often be thought of as a filled-in template. For OUR-IF, the intermediate template looks like this:

```
(COND (<test> <result if test succeeds>)
      (T <result if test fails>))
```

Expressed as a backquote expression, the template becomes:

```
`(COND (,TEST ,SUCCESS-RESULT) (T ,FAILURE-RESULT))
```

Consequently it is natural to define OUR-IF as follows:

```
(DEFMACRO OUR-IF (TEST SUCCESS-RESULT &OPTIONAL FAILURE-RESULT)
  `(COND (,TEST ,SUCCESS-RESULT) (T ,FAILURE-RESULT)))
```

Suppose the arguments of OUR-IF are (MALEP X), 'MALE, and 'FEMALE, as in (OUR-IF (MALEP X) 'MALE 'FEMALE), then the filled-in intermediate template becomes:

```
(COND ((MALEP X) 'MALE) (T 'FEMALE))
```

Evaluating this filled-in template produces the desired value, MALE or FEMALE.

Backquote Simplifies Printing

Backquote appears widely, not just in macros, because the backquote mechanism is useful whenever it is natural to think of template filling. For example, backquote helps make transparent arguments for PRINT forms from a hodgepodge of atoms, lists, and informative glue. In chapter 13, for example, a procedure contains this PRINT form:

```
(PRINT `(,SUPPORT SUPPORTS ,KRUFT))
```

Without backquote, the same effect would require something more awkward, full of CONSs, LISTs, or APPENDs, like these alternatives:

```
(PRINT (CONS SUPPORT (CONS 'SUPPORTS (LIST KRUFT))))

(PRINT (APPEND (LIST SUPPORT) '(SUPPORTS) (LIST KRUFT)))
```

Problems

Problem 8-1:   In addition to IF, COMMON LISP has WHEN and UNLESS, defined as follows:

```
(WHEN <test> <forms>)    ≡    (COND (<test> <forms>))

(UNLESS <test> <forms>)  ≡    (COND ((NOT <test>) <forms>))
```

Define macros OUR-WHEN and OUR-UNLESS.

Problem 8-2:   Not all LISP systems have the backquote mechanism. Define BACKQUOTE such that it has the effect of backquote and allows for the appropriate handling of expressions with COMMA and COMMA-AT, as in the following:

```
(BACKQUOTE (A B (LIST 'C 'D) (COMMA (LIST 'E 'F)) (COMMA-AT (LIST 'G 'H))))
  (A B (LIST 'C 'D) (E F) G H)
```

Problem 8-3:   The syntax of DEFUN is somewhat unfortunate. It would be prettier to combine the procedure name with the parameters so that the first argument would be a list that closely resembles what an application of the procedure looks like. Define DEFINE, a macro that uses DEFUN, but has the following syntax:

```
(DEFINE (<procedure name> <parameter 1> . . . <parameter n>)
  <body>)
```

Problem 8-4:   Some people are annoyed by the nonmnemonic character of the critical primitives CAR, CDR, and CONS. Define new procedures, OUR-FIRST, OUR-REST, and CONSTRUCT, as macros that do the same things. Note that OUR-SECOND, OUR-THIRD, and similar procedures are equally easy to create.

Problem 8-5:   In COMMON LISP a number of simple iteration constructs are available for the case when the full generality of DO is unnecessary. DOLIST, for example, permits one to step easily through all the elements of a list:

```
(DOLIST (<var> <list> <result>) <body>)
```

First <LIST> is evaluated, which should produce a list. Then each of the elements of the list is assigned to <VAR> in turn, while <BODY> is evaluated. Finally, the value of <RESULT> is returned. An explicit RETURN may be used to terminate the iteration and to return a specified value.

Devise a form involving DO that is equivalent. Then write the macro OUR-DOLIST.

Problem 8-6: Another simple iteration construct is DOTIMES. It allows you to do something for every integer from 0 up to, but not including, some specified value:

```
(DOTIMES (<var> <count> <result>) <body>)
```

First <COUNT> is evaluated, which should produce an integer, then <VAR> is successively bound to the integers from 0 to the value of <COUNT> minus 1. The <BODY> is evaluated each time, and the value of <RESULT> is returned at the end. An explicit RETURN may be used to terminate the iteration and to return a specified value.

Devise a form involving DO that is equivalent. Then write the macro OUR-DOTIMES.

Problem 8-7: A *stack* is a linearly ordered set of things that can be accessed using push and pop operations. OUR-PUSH adds a new item to the top of the stack, while OUR-POP removes the item on top of the stack. A list can be used to represent a stack, with the first element corresponding to the item on top. Define OUR-PUSH and OUR-POP as macros. OUR-PUSH takes two arguments, the item to be pushed and the name of a variable whose value is the list representing the stack. The value returned is the enlarged list. OUR-POP takes a single argument, the name of the variable whose value is the list. The value returned is the item popped. In both cases the value of the variable is changed to reflect the new state of the stack.

Problem 8-8: Suppose LET did not exist. Define your own OUR-LET as a macro using LAMBDA.

Project 8-1: The following two procedures are equivalent; that is, they compute the same result, given valid arguments:

```
(DEFUN <name> (<arg>)
  (COND (<test> <result>)
        (T <body> (<name> <new>))))
≡
(DEFUN <name> (INITIAL)
  (DO ((<arg> INITIAL <new>))
      ((<test> <result>)
    <body>))
```

The first procedure is tail recursive, the second iterative. Define a macro, DEFITER, that takes a definition in the first form, meant for DEFUN, and translates it into the second.

Summary

- Optional parameters allow optional arguments.
- Ordinary procedures always evaluate their arguments.
- Macros do not evaluate their arguments.
- Macros translate and then execute.
- Backquote simplifies template filling.
- Backquote simplifies printing.

9

List Storage
Surgery
And Reclamation

This chapter describes how atoms and lists can be represented in a computer. There are two reasons for needing to know about this. First, understanding list representation clears away some of the fog. Second, an understanding of list representation enables one to understand certain primitives that can surgically alter existing expressions, such as NCONC, RPLACA, RPLACD, and DELETE.

Networks of Memory Cells Represent Lists

Conceptually, the memory of an ordinary computer consists of numbered memory cells. The number of a particular memory cell is called its address. In the following diagram, for example, the address of the first cell is 2000 and its contents is 9037:

Address	Contents
2000	9037
2001	9100
2002	9025
2003	9001
2004	9050

Note that the memory-cell contents are numbers, just as addresses are. Consequently the contents of one memory cell may be said to contain the address of another. If the contents are interpreted this way, then the first memory cell is said to contain a *pointer* to the other. Memory cell 2001, by this terminology, contains a pointer to memory cell 9100.

Atoms and lists can be represented as collections of memory cells whose contents are mainly pointers to other memory cells. Each LISP system has some set of conventions for interpreting such collections. For example, memory cells may be large enough to hold two pointers, a left-half pointer and a right-half pointer. Straightforward LISP implementations treat such memory cells as two-pointer places:

Address	Contents
2000	[9037 | 2001]
2001	[9100 | 2002]
2002	[9025 | 2004]
2003	[9001 | 0000]
2004	[9050 | 2003]

Using such two-pointer cells, a list can be represented as a set of memory cells that are threaded together by their right-half pointers. Left-half pointers would specify the elements of the list. Some special reserved number, typically 0, would be in the right-half of the last memory cell in each list to signal its end. Thus NIL is represented by 0.

Usually it is convenient to represent the contents of memory in an abstract way that stands above any particular set of implementation choices. In *box-and-arrow notation*, each pointer is represented by an arrow. Lists are represented by groups of boxes connected together by their right pointers and terminated by a slash. It is not necessary to keep the cells in any particular pattern. They can be arranged in a diagram so as to make the connections clear:

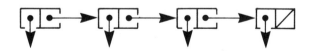

In box-and-arrow notation, an atom is represented by simply writing down its name. When a list element is an atom, a left-half arrow is drawn to the atom's name. An arrow drawn from an atom that is a symbol, rather than a number, gives that symbol's value. Thus the following is a way of representing the list (THIS IS A LIST), which happens to be the value of the symbol EXAMPLE1:

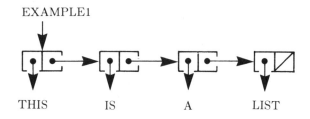

EXAMPLE1

THIS   IS   A   LIST

Of course, the elements of a list may be lists, rather than atoms. This means that left-half arrows may represent pointers to other lists, as in this example for the list, ((THIS IS) (TWO LISTS)), the value of EXAMPLE2:

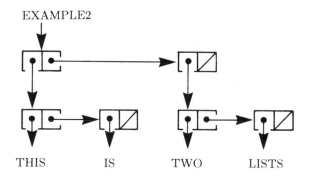

EXAMPLE2

THIS   IS   TWO   LISTS

The key thing is that there are atoms and there are two-pointer entities, sometimes called CONS boxes, that tie things together. In computer memory, the pointers may be packed two to a memory cell, or one each, in two consecutive memory cells. Said another way, an abstract CONS box may be implemented as one real memory cell or two. Box-and-arrow notation stands above such detail.

In some LISP implementations, including a demonstration LISPlike language developed in chapter 23, each symbol is paired with a value on an association list. In other LISPs, a special little chunk of memory is set aside for each symbol, with the current value found offset by a standard distance from the beginning of the chunk.[1]

---

[1] Values saved when a variable is lambda-bound may be kept on a stack.

**CONS Builds New
List Structure by
Depositing Pointers
in Free Cells**

LISP maintains a list of spare memory cells for use in constructing list structures. This list of spare memory cells is called the free storage list. If CONS boxes are implemented by single memory cells, the CONS primitive operates by removing the first cell on the free storage list and by depositing new pointers into this first cell. The following shows what happens when evaluating (SETQ EXAMPLE3 (CONS 'A EXAMPLE3)), given that the value of EXAMPLE3 is (B C):

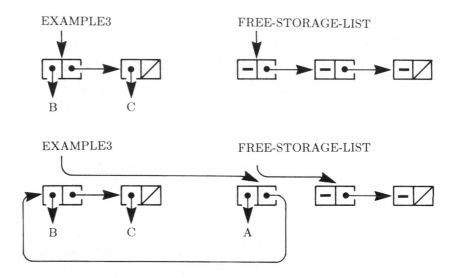

Curiously, CONS need not really have a list as its second argument. Noting that CONS simply connects its two arguments together, there is no reason to panic if the second is an atom. Here is the result of doing (CONS 'A 'B):

There is, of course, the issue of how to represent such structures in printed form. The fact is, they are neither atoms nor lists. Historically, they have been called *dotted pairs* and they are written, indeed, with a dot.[2] Note

---

[2] An ordinary list is terminated by NIL. A list terminated by some nonNIL atom is called a *dotted list*.

that there must be a space on either side of the dot, by the way, to avoid confusion:

```
(CONS 'A 'B)
  (A . B)
```

Sometimes dotted pairs make sense.[3] For the most part, however, dotted pairs are mainly a source of insidious bugs. Most programmers avoid them completely and still lead worthwhile lives.

APPEND Builds New List Structure by Copying

In a moment we consider how APPEND works. First let us set up some values that will help. For mnemonic value, let the variables ABC and XYZ have the lists (A B C) and (X Y Z) as their values:

```
(SETQ ABC '(A B C))
  (A B C)

(SETQ XYZ '(X Y Z))
  (X Y Z)
```

The box-and-arrow diagrams for ABC and XYZ are as follows:

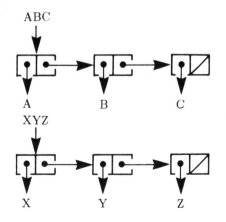

---

[3] In some implementations of LISP, a dotted pair takes less storage than a list of two elements does.

It might seem that responding to (SETQ ABCXYZ (APPEND ABC XYZ)) should involve alteration of the last memory cell in the representation of the list (A B C):

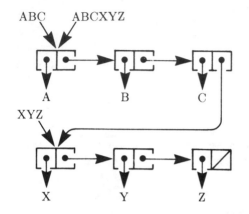

As far as the variable ABCXYZ is concerned, the result is just fine: the newly revised list structure would represent the list (A B C X Y Z), as desired. Also, the value of XYZ is unchanged. The trouble is, the value of ABC has been changed. It is now, unexpectedly, (A B C X Y Z), no longer (A B C)! Given that APPEND should leave the values of its arguments intact, it must work in some other way.

The following diagram illustrates what APPEND really does. The first list is copied, using spare memory cells from the free storage list, and then the second list is attached to the copy:

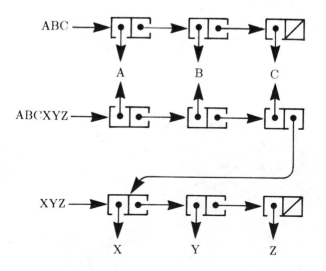

NCONC, RPLACA, RPLACD, and DELETE Dangerously Alter Memory-cell Contents

NCONC does exactly what was just described as what APPEND should not do. It smashes two lists together by a surgical change to the last cell in the first list, altering the value of any variable whose value is represented by a pointer into that first list. Note the following contrast:

```
(SETQ ABC '(A B C))
  (A B C)

(SETQ XYZ '(X Y Z))
  (X Y Z)

(SETQ BC (CDR ABC))
  (B C)

(SETQ YZ (CDR XYZ))
  (Y Z)

(SETQ ABCXYZ (APPEND ABC XYZ))
  (A B C X Y Z)

ABC
  (A B C)

XYZ
  (X Y Z)

BC
  (B C)

YZ
  (Y Z)

(SETQ ABCXYZ (NCONC ABC XYZ))
  (A B C X Y Z)

ABC
  (A B C X Y Z)

XYZ
  (X Y Z)

BC
  (B C X Y Z)

YZ
  (Y Z)
```

NCONC, like APPEND, can take more than two lists. The last cells of each of the lists, except the last one, are altered by NCONC.

MAPCAN does an NCONClike operation after making up a list of results:

```
(MAPCAN <some procedure specification> <some list>)
≡
(APPLY 'NCONC (MAPCAR <some procedure specification> <some list>))
```

Hence MAPCAN also requires careful use.

RPLACA, like NCONC, does surgery. It takes two arguments, the first of which must be a list. It alters this list by replacing the left half of its first cell by a pointer to the second argument. The value returned is the altered list. Consider, for example, what happens when we do the following:

```
(SETQ FACT1 '(BIG COMPUTERS ARE NICE))
   (BIG COMPUTERS ARE NICE)

(RPLACA FACT1 'FAST)
   (FAST COMPUTERS ARE NICE)
```

The first cell representing (BIG COMPUTERS ARE NICE) has the pointer to BIG replaced by one to FAST:

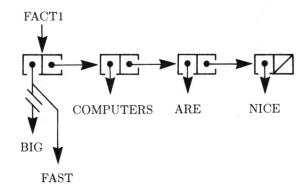

From the box-and-arrow diagram, we see that the value of FACT1 is changed even though there is no SETQ.

```
FACT1
   (FAST COMPUTERS ARE NICE)
```

Note that the following yields the same value, even though it is produced in a very different way, without a structure-altering side effect, leaving the value of FACT1 unchanged.

```
(SETQ FACT1 '(BIG COMPUTERS ARE NICE))
   (BIG COMPUTERS ARE NICE)
```

```
(CONS 'FAST (CDR FACT1))
  (FAST COMPUTERS ARE NICE)

FACT1
  (BIG COMPUTERS ARE NICE)
```

RPLACA, incidentally, is a mnemonic for replace CAR. Its complement, RPLACD, is a mnemonic for replace CDR. The primitive RPLACD, like RPLACA, surgically alters its first argument, which must be a list, and then returns the altered list. The alteration is to the other half, however. Consider these:

```
(SETQ FACT2 '(APPLES ARE GOOD FOR YOU))
  (APPLES ARE GOOD FOR YOU)

(RPLACD FACT2 '(WERE BAD FOR ADAM))
  (APPLES WERE BAD FOR ADAM)
```

Now only APPLES is retained from FACT2, as the following diagram shows:

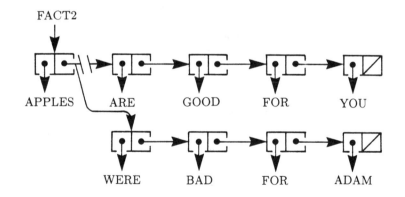

Note that the following yields the same value, even though the value is produced, once more, in a very different way:

```
(CONS (CAR FACT2) '(WERE BAD FOR ADAM))
  (APPLES WERE BAD FOR ADAM)
```

You can create re-entrant list structures using RPLACA and RPLACD. That is, a list structure can be altered so that it has pointers back into itself. If you attempt to print out such a *circular* list, you should be prepared to interrupt LISP, for it will get stuck in a loop and never stop.

DELETE gets rid of instances of its first argument that appear at the top level in its second:[4]

```
(DELETE 'HEADS '(HEADS TAILS TAILS HEADS TAILS))
  (TAILS TAILS TAILS)
```

If the first element in the list is a matching element, DELETE simply skips over it when handing back a value. Otherwise, DELETE does its job by splicing the matching elements out of the list structure. Consequently, DELETE can alter symbol values peculiarly as a side effect:

```
(SETQ TOSSES '(HEADS TAILS TAILS HEADS TAILS))
  (HEADS TAILS TAILS HEADS TAILS)

(DELETE 'HEADS TOSSES)
  (TAILS TAILS TAILS)

TOSSES
  (HEADS TAILS TAILS TAILS)
```

It is best to combine the DELETE with a SETQ, to insure that the value of TOSSES is properly changed, independent of which elements happened to get deleted.

Note that the idiosyncrasies of DELETE can be avoided. The thing to do is to use REMOVE, a primitive that copies list structure, rather than altering it. REMOVE is similar to, but simpler than REMOVE-IF and REMOVE-IF-NOT, primitives that were introduced earlier.

Now let us look at why NCONC, RPLACA, RPLACD, and DELETE can, on occasion, be useful and warranted. Suppose a procedure is desired that substitutes the symbol PERSON for every instance of MAN in any expression given as an argument. Call this procedure LIBERATE1. It can be defined as follows using CAR, CDR, and CONS:

```
(DEFUN LIBERATE1 (S)                    ;First version.
  (COND ((EQUAL S 'MAN) 'PERSON)        ;Replace MAN.
        ((ATOM S) S)                    ;Keep other atoms.
        (T (CONS (LIBERATE1 (CAR S))    ;Recurse on CAR
                 (LIBERATE1 (CDR S)))))) ; and CDR.
```

The CAR and CDR rip the given argument apart again and again until the atoms are reached, and then reassemble a near copy using CONS to build it. If the list structure is deeply nested, this can take a lot of time even if there are few instances of MAN to replace. The CONS operation itself takes time, and in addition, CONS depletes free storage. The more free storage is used, the more reclamation is needed later.

---

[4] The first argument for DELETE need not be an atom; it can be any expression. As for SUBST and MEMBER, however, this is typically useful only if a nonstandard test is specified using a keyword.

In the next version, RPLACA is used instead of CONS. The original list structure is not copied. Instead, local surgery is performed whenever an instance of MAN is encountered. If a lot of liberation is to be done, time can be saved.

```
(DEFUN LIBERATE2 (S)                    ;First version.
  (COND ((EQUAL S 'MAN) 'PERSON)        ;Replace MAN.
        ((ATOM S) S)                    ;Keep other atoms.
        ((EQUAL (CAR S) 'MAN)           ;If MAN spotted,
         (RPLACA S 'PERSON)             ; replace with PERSON
         (LIBERATE2 S))                 ; and do the rest.
        (T (LIBERATE2 (CAR S))          ;Recurse on CAR
           (LIBERATE2 (CDR S))          ; and CDR.
           S)))                         ;Return result.
```

However, using this version of LIBERATE can be dangerous, because it alters the list structure that is supplied by an argument. Examples using LIBERATE1 and LIBERATE2 show how:

```
(SETQ TEST '(CHAIR MAN))
  (CHAIR MAN)

(LIBERATE1 TEST)
  (CHAIR PERSON)

TEST
  (CHAIR MAN)
```

Evidently, doing (LIBERATE1 TEST) does not change the value of TEST. Now consider this:

```
(LIBERATE2 TEST)
  (CHAIR PERSON)

TEST
  (CHAIR PERSON)
```

Now the value of TEST has changed because LIBERATE2 alters list structure.

- LISP does not completely prevent the abuse of arguments. Efficiency considerations may argue in favor of using the dangerous primitives. Flexibility sometimes provides hanging rope.

In general, the use of NCONC, RPLACA, RPLACD, and DELETE is to be discouraged, because of possibly unexpected side effects.

- It is a good idea to leave the use of NCONC, RPLACA, RPLACD, and DELETE to risk-loving programmers. Unless desperate for time or space saving, using them can lead to unnecessary bugs.

**EQUAL Is Not the
Same as EQL**

EQL takes two arguments. If both are atoms, EQL returns T if they are the same. In this respect EQL is similar to EQUAL. If the two arguments are lists, however, things are a bit more complicated. Consider the following:

```
(SETQ L1 (LIST 'A 'B 'C))
  (A B C)

(SETQ L2 (LIST 'A 'B 'C))
  (A B C)

(SETQ L3 L2)
  (A B C)
```

Each time LIST is used, it assembles a list using new memory cells drawn from the free storage list repository. Consequently, while the values of L1 and L2 are both (A B C), the two values are represented by distinct memory cells.[5] SETQ, on the other hand, simply attaches a pointer from its first argument to the structure that is pointed to by its second. Hence the values of L2 and L3 are not only both (A B C), but also the two values are represented by the same memory cells. All of this is illustrated in this diagram:

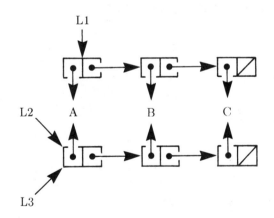

Now certainly, both (EQUAL L1 L2) and (EQUAL L2 L3) return T, because on the one hand, the values of L1 and L2 are exact copies of one another, and on the other hand, the values of L2 and L3 are even represented by exactly the same memory-cell structure. They are equal in a slightly different sense, but EQUAL could not care less.

---

[5] To be more precise, two expressions that print out the same way need not be the same object in terms of memory storage. Thus EQL may not consider them to be equal. EQUAL, however, generally will.

The primitive EQL does care. For EQL, two lists are equal only if they are represented by the same memory cells. Copies are not considered equal in the EQL sense. Thus (EQL L1 L2) returns NIL whereas (EQL L2 L3) returns T.

- Two lists that are EQUAL may not be EQL.
- Any two lists that are EQL are also always EQUAL.

Why use EQL? The answer again is that it is a matter of efficiency. It takes longer to see if a structure is a copy than to see if it is exactly the same. In the examples in this book, EQUAL is always used, whether strictly necessary or not, just to avoid raising the question of what sense of *equal* is appropriate. After all, if two lists are EQL, they will certainly be EQUAL as well.

We make an exception when comparing numeric arguments, where we use =, the special equality test for numbers. Generally, it is better to use =, because it makes it clear what kinds of things are being compared. Also, = automatically converts all its arguments to the same number type before comparing them. EQUAL is happy with two equal numbers only if they are of the same type. The following examples illustrate:

```
(EQUAL 1 1.0)
  NIL
```

```
(= 1 1.0)
  T
```

Using = with arguments other than numbers results in an error.

A Keyword Alters MEMBER To Use EQUAL instead of EQL

The first argument given to the primitive MEMBER need not be an atom. However, by convention, MEMBER normally uses EQL as its equality test. Consequently, the unwary may be a little surprised by this apparent anomaly:

```
(MEMBER '(A B) '((A B) (B C)))
  NIL
```

MEMBER returns NIL, even though (A B) is an element of ((A B) (B C)), because MEMBER tests for equality using EQL. This is reasonable, surprisingly. EQL is normally good enough, and EQL is typically much faster than EQUAL is.

Fortunately, when we do want MEMBER to use EQUAL, we can override the EQL default. This is done by signaling MEMBER with a keyword, :TEST, followed by 'EQUAL, as follows:

```
(MEMBER '(A B) '((A B) (B C)) :TEST 'EQUAL)
  T
```

The test predicate to be used need not be built in—we are free to define our own standard of comparison, if we like.

- Advanced programmers often use various keywords to pull primitives away from default assumptions, particularly in the case of primitives like ASSOC, SUBST, DELETE, and others, that, like MEMBER, involve some sort of specifiable equality test.

Single Quote Marks Are a Shorthand Form for QUOTE Expressions

At first, it might seem that the single quote mark lies outside of what box-and-arrow notation can handle. But actually, when a LISP system absorbs text from a terminal or from a file, single quote marks are translated into applications of the primitive QUOTE. This is necessary, because LISP internally requires all data to be expressed strictly and uniformly in the form of an expression. The single-quote device does not fit into the expression definition, although it makes programs clearer and learning easier. LISP is therefore buffered from text prepared by programmers by a reading program that, among other things, effects the following translation:

```
'<expression>   →   (QUOTE <expression>)
```

This same reading program also handles any semicolons that appear to mark comments. The reading program discards the semicolons and ignores the text on the rest of the line.

Of course, the principal task of the reading program is to translate LISP character sequences, full of parentheses, into the corresponding internal representation. Symmetrically, the printing program translates the other way. READ and PRINT give users direct access to these printing and reading programs.

In some cases it may be desirable to recreate proper list structure from the character sequences that PRINT has placed in a file. This means that PRINT has to produce material in a format that READ can accept. That is why some output primitives, like PRINT and PRIN1 use escape characters when faced with symbol names that contain unusual characters. Others, like PRINC are oriented more toward producing output that is to be interpreted by the user. They do not insert the escape characters.

Garbage Collection Reclaims Memory Cells for the Free Storage List

Consider this sequence:

```
(SETQ EXAMPLE4 (LIST 'A 'B 'C))
  (A B C)

(SETQ EXAMPLE4 (LIST 'X 'Y 'Z))
  (X Y Z)
```

Like CONS, the primitive LIST builds a new list by taking material from the free storage list. The structure is accessible via the value of EXAMPLE4. But we changed the value of EXAMPLE4 immediately. The previous structure is no longer accessible. To be sure, the value of EXAMPLE4 can be made to be (A B C) again, but only by taking new cells from the free storage list and rebuilding.

There is no point in wasting the cells in the now inaccessible list. Somehow they should be returned to the free storage list so that they can be used again. Note, however, that we cannot just return the cells when they are snipped off by SETQ: other structures may be pointing to them. Instead, we just continue using up new cells, allowing the no-longer used ones to languish. When we finally do run out of space, we perform a complete sweep to determine which cells can be reused. *Garbage collection* is the technical term for what needs to be done.

Typical garbage collectors have two phases. In the first phase, the garbage collector runs through memory, starting from the values, properties, and procedure definitions of all symbols, together with all the forms used in the current computation, somehow marking all of the memory cells representing the expressions encountered.

The marking may be done by altering one of the bits in the memory cells, if any are unused, or by maintaining a table containing one bit per cell of list storage. The choice is influenced strongly by the architecture of the computer. Figure 9-1 illustrates what the garbage collector's marker does in an area that contains the cells representing the current value of EXAMPLE4 and nothing else.

Once the marking phase is finished, a sweep phase passes through memory sequentially, taking note of unmarked cells and returning them to the free storage list. Figure 9-2 illustrates how the sweep phase handles a previously marked area.

To clarify exactly what happens in garbage collection, it may be helpful to see a simple garbage collector specified as a LISP procedure. Keep in mind, however, that our simple garbage collector should not be taken seriously, because a lot depends on the details of a particular LISP implementation.

Assume that there is a predicate named MARKEDP that tells us whether a cell is marked. Further, let MARKIT set the mark on a cell, while UNMARK resets the mark. Finally, we need a way to access cells sequentially, rather

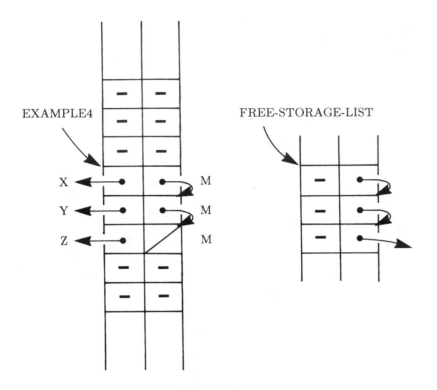

Figure 9-1. Results of a garbage collector's marking phase.

than by following list structures. Suppose (CELL I) produces a pointer to the cell in memory whose address is the value of I. The global free variable FREE points to the head of the free storage list, from which CONS grabs cells when it combines pointers to existing list structures.

The first step is to trace along all active list structures and mark all cells encountered. Naturally, cells already marked need not be considered further.

```
(DEFUN MARK (L)
  (COND ((MARKEDP L))              ;Already marked.
        ((ATOM L) (MARKIT L))      ;Just mark atom.
        (T (MARKIT L)              ;Mark cell,
          (MARK (CAR L))           ; and trace CAR
          (MARK (CDR L)))))        ; and trace CDR.
```

When everything of importance has been protected by marking, a linear sweep through memory can pick up cells that were not reached by the marking phase.

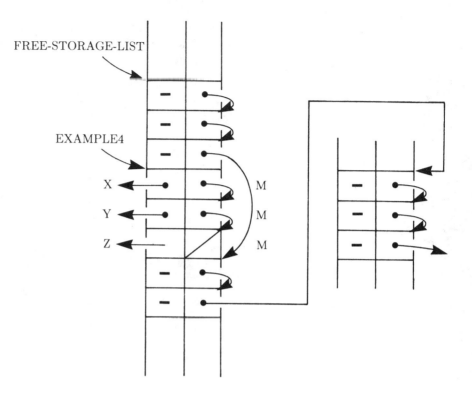

Figure 9-2. Results of a garbage collector's sweeping phase.

```
(DEFUN SWEEP ()
  (DO ((I 0 (+ I 1))) ((= I TOP))          ;Scan through all cells.
    (COND ((MARKEDP (CELL I))              ;If marked,
           (UNMARK (CELL I)))              ; then unmark them,
          (T (RPLACD (CELL I) FREE)        ; otherwise, add to
             (SETQ FREE (CELL I)))))))      ; list of free cells.
```

Here TOP is a global free variable whose value is the total number of cells in memory. Suppose, for simplicity, that the global free variable KEEP-LIST contains pointers to all structures currently relevant, as determined by looking at the values, properties, and procedure definitions of all symbols. Then the following will work:

```
(DEFUN GC () (MARK KEEP-LIST) (SWEEP))
```

Typically, a garbage collector is invoked automatically when the free storage list is near exhaustion. Users never know, unless they become suspicious because the computer seems to drop dead suddenly but temporarily.

Some newer garbage collectors do not use the global mark-and-sweep idea. Instead they do a little garbage collection with each CONS. They never stop for a complete purge.

To further illustrate some of the ideas in this chapter, we present a marking procedure used in garbage collection. The nonrecursive garbage collector presented here is based on Floyd's modification of an algorithm independently discovered by Deutsch and by Schorr and Waite. A procedure based on this algorithm avoids recursive calls by modifying the list structure being marked. LISP pointers are reversed on the way downward, only to be restored on the way upward. This is a clever way of building a doubly recursive procedure that does *not* require saving a lot of information on a stack.

```
(DEFUN MARK (P)
  (PROG (N Q)
    (COND ((ATOM P) (RETURN P)))        ; Easy case.
  LOOPCAR
    (SETQ Q (CAR P))                    ; Track down CAR.
    (COND ((ATOM Q))
          ((MARKEDP Q))
          (T (RPLACA P N)               ; Reverse pointer.
             (SETQ N P P Q)
             (GO LOOPCAR)))             ; Continue down CAR.
  LOOPCDR
    (MARKIT P)                          ; Indicate CAR is done.
    (SETQ Q (CDR P))                    ; Track down CDR.
    (COND ((ATOM Q))
          ((MARKEDP Q))
          (T (RPLACD P N)               ; Reverse pointer.
             (SETQ N P P Q)
             (GO LOOPCAR)))             ; Go down CAR first.
  LOOPCONS
    (COND ((NULL N) (RETURN P)))        ; Finished marking?
    (SETQ Q N)
    (COND ((MARKEDP Q                   ; Was CAR of this done?
             (SETQ N (CDR Q))
             (RPLACD Q P)               ; Undo pointer reversal.
             (SETQ P Q)
             (GO LOOPCONS))             ; Continue upward.
          (T (MARKIT Q)
             (SETQ N (CAR Q))
             (RPLACA Q P)               ; Undo pointer reversal.
             (SETQ P Q)
             (GO LOOPCDR)))))           ; Still have to do CDR.
```

Understanding and debugging a procedure like this nonrecursive version of MARK is difficult, because such procedures alter existing list structures extensively.

Problems

Problem 9-1: The primitive REVERSE copies the top-level of the list given as its argument. Write OUR-NREVERSE, a procedure that reverses a list without copying.

Problem 9-2: We have already seen two uses of the primitive SETF and will see more still. Basically SETF just wants a form it can use to determine what to change or create. It even makes sense to do (SETF (CAR L) A), albeit dangerous sense. What are the equivalents, in terms of SETF, of (RPLACA X Y) and (RPLACD X Y)?

Problem 9-3: A *queue* is a linearly ordered set of things that can be accessed using enqueuing and dequeuing operations. ENQUEUE adds a new item to the tail of the queue, while DEQUEUE removes an item from the head of the queue. A list can be used to represent a queue, with the first element corresponding to the item at the head of the queue. Define ENQUEUE and DEQUEUE as macros. ENQUEUE takes two arguments, the item to be enqueued and the name of a variable whose value is the list representing the queue. The value returned is the enlarged list. DEQUEUE takes a single argument, the name of the variable whose value is the list. The value returned is the item dequeued. In both cases the value of the variable is changed to reflect the new contents of the queue. Do not copy the list when enqueuing a new item.

Problem 9-4: In order to try out a procedure like MARK, it is convenient to *simulate* list structure and the flags that are used to mark memory cells. Suppose a cell and its mark are represented by a list of four elements: the atom PAIR, a flag that indicates whether the cell has been marked or not, then the CAR, and finally the CDR. The flag can be either T or NIL. Atoms in turn are represented by lists containing three elements: the atom ATOM and a flag followed by the atom itself.

Write N-ATOM, a predicate that checks whether an expression is an atom or not. Also write MARKEDP, MARKIT and UNMARK. Then proceed to write N-CAR, N-CDR, N-RPLACA, and N-RPLACD. They are to manipulate the simulated list structure in ways analogous to normal LISP primitives with corresponding names. To build a list structure you will also need to define MAKE-ATOM and N-CONS. The following recursive version of MARK then can be applied to it:

```
(DEFUN MARK (L)
  (COND ((MARKEDP L))                ; Already marked.
        ((N-ATOM L) (MARKIT L))      ; Just mark atom.
        (T (MARKIT L)                ; Mark cell,
           (MARK (N-CAR L))          ;  and trace CAR,
           (MARK (N-CDR L)))))       ;  and trace CDR.
```

Problem 9-5: Unlike nearly all the other procedures in this book, the marking procedure introduced in the last section uses PROG. It could instead be written in a recursive form. The problem with that approach is that recursive calls require memory space to save information needed on return from the recursive calls, but memory space is the very commodity that is in short supply when a garbage collection cycle is initiated. Tail recursion, however, can be implemented in an efficient way, because nothing needs to be saved. Write a tail-recursive version of MARK that does not use PROG. Use the procedures, introduced in the last problem, that simulate list structure to check the solution.

Project 9-1: None of our versions of COUNT-ATOMS was tail recursive. Use the pointer-reversing approach to define a tail-recursive version. You may have to destroy the list structure in the process of counting the atoms in it.

Summary

- Networks of memory cells represent lists.

- CONS builds new list structure by depositing pointers in free cells.

- APPEND builds new list structure by copying.

- NCONC, RPLACA, RPLACD, and DELETE dangerously alter memory-cell contents.

- EQUAL is not the same as EQL.

- A keyword alters member to use EQUAL instead of EQL.

- Single quote marks are a shorthand form for QUOTE expressions.

- Garbage collection reclaims memory cells for the free storage list.

References

Knuth [1969] discusses representations for lists.

Queues are discussed in Aho, Hopcroft, and Ullman [1974]. See also Hood and Melville [1980].

Garbage collection is covered by Pratt [1975, chapter 7] and Knuth [1969]. See also, Baker [1977, 1979], Barth [1977], Conrad [1974], Deutsch and Bobrow [1976], Dijkstra [1978], Fenichel [1969], Hansen [1969], Kung [1977], Lieberman and Hewitt [1980], Minsky [1963], Morris [1978], Schorr and Waite [1967], Steele [1975], and Wadler [1976].

10

Examples Involving Arrays
And Binary Images

In this chapter, we explore algorithms used in binary image processing. We deal with binary image processing for three reasons: first, the programs involved illustrate some of the features of arrays; second, the programs demonstrate that it is possible to use LISP in a style that is like that of other programming languages if you so choose; and third, simple programs allow us to get quickly to interesting things. Specifically, the programs find the position and orientation of an object, as well as doing classification. Even binary images with multiple objects can be analyzed.

AREF and SETF Are Used with Arrays

Conceptually, an *array* is a data structure in which information is located in slots, each of which is associated with a particular set of numbers called indices. Sometimes it is useful to think of the indices as the coordinates of a point in a space. The coordinates are measured along axes corresponding to the indices. The number of axes is called the dimension of the array.

Suppose, for illustration, that we sample the brightness in an image on a regular grid of points. Each point will be referred to as a *picture cell* and the quantized measurement of the brightness there as a *gray level*. Picture cells are arranged in rows and columns, so each has two coordinates. It is natural to store the gray levels in a two-dimensional array, using the row and column numbers to specify exactly where the values should go.

If an image is stored in an array that is the value of the symbol `IMAGE`, evaluating (`AREF IMAGE 314 271`) will retrieve the gray level of the picture cell at the intersection of the 314th row and the 271th column. Which index corresponds to which coordinate is, of course, quite arbitrary. In the case of matrices, it is customary to let the first index be the row number and the second, the column number.[1]

Arrays are created using `MAKE-ARRAY`. You have to specify the dimension, that is the number of indices to be used, as well as the range of each of the indices.[2] For example, the following creates a two-dimensional array:

```
(SETQ IMAGE (MAKE-ARRAY '(1024 1024)))
```

Each of the two indices can range over the values from `0` to `1023`.[3] We hang onto the array by making it the value of the symbol `IMAGE`, as shown above. The variable `IMAGE` can now be used to refer to the array when we want to access or alter entries.

Once an array has been created, information can be stored in it. For example, we can store `88` in the array location at the intersection of the 314th row and 271th column as follows:

```
(SETF (AREF IMAGE 314 271) 88)
    88
```

In this context, the form involving `AREF` only identifies a place in the array, whose contents are then altered by `SETF`. Note the generalization of `SETF` to yet another situation.

The array in this example happens to hold only numbers, but LISP array slots may hold arbitrary expressions.[4]

It is often useful to be able to discover the range of the indices of an array. The primitive `ARRAY-DIMENSION`, helps us here. The first argument identifies the array and the second specifies an axis of the array. For the array we have been working with so far, we have the following:

```
(ARRAY-DIMENSION IMAGE 0)
    1024
```

---

[1] The ordering of array indices leads to some confusion, as it seems equally natural to specify the x coordinate before the y coordinate. Yet the convention is that x corresponds to column number, whereas y corresponds to row number.

[2] One-dimensional arrays are particularly simple and are called vectors. Some specialized primitives, which we do not discuss at length, apply only to vectors.

[3] In COMMON LISP, indices start at `0`; this is different from some other programming languages in which they start at `1`.

[4] In COMMON LISP, the user can specify that an array will be used to hold only particular data types by means of keywords. Such information may be used to make array storage more efficient.

```
(ARRAY-DIMENSION IMAGE 1)
  1024
```

Note that the numbering of the axes starts at 0.

Problems

Problem 10-1: Define PRINT-IMAGE, a procedure that prints out the elements of a two-dimensional array, passed as the single argument. Each row is to appear on a separate line. Use ARRAY-DIMENSION to ascertain the ranges of the two indices.

Problem 10-2: One way to represent a matrix is as a list of lists, each sublist corresponding to a row. Define STUFF-IMAGE, a procedure that makes an array of appropriate size, and then fills it in from a matrix represented as a list of lists. The array created is returned as the value of the procedure. Assume that all sublists have the same length. Here is a test case for STUFF-IMAGE:

```
(STUFF-IMAGE  '((0 0 0 0 0 0 0 0 0 0 0 0 0 0 0 0 0 0)
                (0 0 1 1 1 1 1 1 1 1 1 1 1 0 0 0 0 0)
                (0 0 1 1 1 1 1 1 1 1 1 1 1 1 0 0 0 0)
                (0 0 0 1 1 0 0 0 0 0 0 0 1 1 0 0 0 0)
                (0 0 0 1 1 0 0 0 0 0 0 0 1 1 0 0 0 0)
                (0 0 0 1 1 1 1 1 1 1 1 1 1 0 0 0 0 0)
                (0 0 0 1 1 1 1 1 1 1 1 1 1 1 1 0 0 0)
                (0 0 0 1 1 0 0 0 0 0 0 0 1 1 0 0 0 0)
                (0 0 0 1 1 0 0 0 0 0 0 0 1 1 0 0 0 0)
                (0 0 0 1 1 0 0 0 0 0 0 0 1 1 0 0 0 0)
                (0 0 1 1 1 1 1 1 1 1 1 1 1 1 1 0 0 0)
                (0 0 1 1 1 1 1 1 1 1 1 1 1 1 0 0 0 0)
                (0 0 0 0 0 0 0 0 0 0 0 0 0 0 0 0 0 0))))
```

Binary Images Are Easy to Process

Sometimes lighting can be arranged so that there is a clear separation in image brightness between an object of interest and the background. In this case, a simple thresholding operation can turn measured brightness values into 0s and 1s depending on whether a particular picture cell is judged to be part of the image of the object or not. If the image is sampled on a rectangular raster of points, we obtain a two-dimensional array of numbers, each of which is 0 or 1, constituting a *binary image*, as shown in figure 10-1. This binary image is quantized both spatially and in brightness level. If significant information about the object is contained in this compressed, two-dimensional representation, then binary image-processing techniques are appropriate.

Figure 10-1. Binary image of an object. The black squares correspond to 1s, and the white squares correspond to 0s.

Suppose, for example, that we want to find out where a single object lies and how it is oriented. This is useful if the object is passing by an image sensor on a conveyor belt, because information about the position and orientation of the object then can be used to direct a mechanical manipulator to pick it up.[5] We assume initially that there is only one object in the field of view. Methods for labeling multiple objects will be explored later.

An Object Can Be Found Using Binary Image Analysis

We will refer to the set of picture cells in the binary image that have the value 1 as the *region of interest*. The center of area of this region provides a reasonable definition of the position of the region in the image, and hence indirectly the position of the object.

How can we find the center of area of the region of interest from the binary image? Let $p_{i,j}$ be the value of the picture cell at the intersection

---

[5] Somehow positions in images must be translated into coordinates that are appropriate for robot arms. This can pose additional subtle problems.

of the ith row and the jth column. First of all, the total number of picture cells in the region of interest, its area, is simply

$$A = \sum_{i=0}^{n-1} \sum_{j=0}^{m-1} p_{i,j},$$

where n is the number of rows, and m is the number of columns in the binary image array. Then, by matching first moments, we find that the center of area is at

$$i_o = \frac{1}{A} \sum_{i=0}^{n-1} \sum_{j=0}^{m-1} i\, p_{i,j} \quad \text{and} \quad j_o = \frac{1}{A} \sum_{i=0}^{n-1} \sum_{j=0}^{m-1} j\, p_{i,j}.$$

The center of area can be computed as follows:

```
(DEFUN CENTER (IMAGE)
  (LET ((N (ARRAY-DIMENSION IMAGE 0))         ;N rows and
        (M (ARRAY-DIMENSION IMAGE 1))         ; M columns.
        (SUM 0) (SUM-I 0) (SUM-J 0))          ;Accumulators.
    (DO ((I 0 (+ I 1)))                       ;Step through rows.
        ((= I N)                              ;Done all rows?
         (COND ((ZEROP SUM) 'NO-OBJECT)       ;All zero, else
               (T (LIST (/ (FLOAT SUM-I) (FLOAT SUM))      ; compute i-0,
                        (/ (FLOAT SUM-J) (FLOAT SUM))))))  ; compute j-0.
      (DO ((J 0 (+ J 1)))                     ;Step through columns.
          ((= J M))                           ;Done all columns?
        (COND ((ZEROP (AREF IMAGE I J)))      ;Ignore zeros.
              (T (SETQ SUM (+ SUM 1)          ;Total up p(i, j), &
                       SUM-I (+ SUM-I I)      ; total i * p(i, j),
                       SUM-J (+ SUM-J J))))))))    ; total j * p(i, j).
```

In the above, SUM, SUM-I, and SUM-J are integer quantities. The center of area, however, need not fall exactly on a picture cell (that is SUM-I and SUM-J need not be integer multiples of SUM). Consequently, we used FLOAT when computing the center of area.[6]

Note that we determine the number of rows and columns, N and M, only once. We hang onto their values using LET, so that they need not be recomputed every time we apply the termination test in the DOs.

Orientation is not quite so easy to determine, or even define, as position. If the object is elongated, it will have a natural axis lying in the direction of elongation. In fact, there will be an axis about which the region of interest has least inertia. Mechanical engineers refer to the axes of least and greatest inertia as the principal axes of an object. We can use the direction of the axis of least inertia to define the orientation of the object.

---

[6] A ratio is returned if / is given two integers that do not divide evenly.

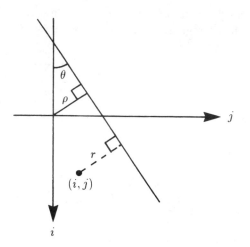

Figure 10-2. The distance of a point (i, j) from a line is $i \sin \theta - j \cos \theta + \rho$ where θ is the inclination of the line with respect to the i-axis, and ρ is the perpendicular distance of the line from the origin $(0, 0)$.

This will fail only if the object has no unique axis of least inertia, as will be the case with a centrally symmetric object like a circular disk.

Finding this axis requires mathematical manipulations that we will only hint at here. The axis of least inertia passes through the center of area. It is convenient, therefore, to change to a new coordinate system, parallel to the old one, but with the origin at the center of area:

$$i' = i - i_o \qquad \text{and} \qquad j' = j - j_o.$$

The inertia of the region about a line is just the sum of squares of the distances of the picture cells in that region from the line. This distance can be found as shown in figure 10-2. The inertia about a line, inclined θ relative to the i'-axis, through the center of area, is as follows:

$$I = \sum_{i=0}^{n-1} \sum_{j=0}^{m-1} p_{i,j} (i' \sin \theta - j' \cos \theta)^2,$$
$$= a \sin^2 \theta - 2b \sin \theta \cos \theta + c \cos^2 \theta,$$

where,

$$a = \sum_{i=0}^{n-1} \sum_{j=0}^{m-1} (i')^2 \, p_{i,j}, \quad b = \sum_{i=0}^{n-1} \sum_{j=0}^{m-1} (i'j') \, p_{i,j}, \quad c = \sum_{i=0}^{n-1} \sum_{j=0}^{m-1} (j')^2 \, p_{i,j}.$$

We can find the orientation, θ_o, of the axes of least and greatest moment of inertia by differentiating with respect to θ and setting the result equal to 0. This way we obtain the following:

$$\tan 2\theta_o = \frac{2b}{a - c}.$$

The procedure ORIENTATION returns a list containing the center of area and the angle of the axis of least inertia.

```
(DEFUN ORIENTATION (IMAGE)
  (LET ((N (ARRAY-DIMENSION IMAGE 0))            ;N rows and
        (M (ARRAY-DIMENSION IMAGE 1))            ; M columns.
        (C-O-A (CENTER IMAGE)))                  ;Center of area.
    (COND ((ATOM C-O-A) C-O-A)                   ;No object found.
          (T (LET ((IO (CAR C-O-A)) (JO (CADR C-O-A))
                   (A 0.0) (B 0.0) (C 0.0))      ;Accumulators.
               (DO ((I 0 (+ I 1)))
                   ((= I N)                       ;Step, rows.
                    (COND ((AND (ZEROP B) (= A C)) ;Symmetrical.
                           (APPEND C-O-A '(SYMMETRICAL)))
                          (T (APPEND C-O-A         ;Direction of axis.
                                (LIST (/ (ATAN (* 2.0 B) (- A C))
                                         2.0))))))
                 (DO ((J 0 (+ J 1))) ((= J M))     ;Step, columns.
                   (COND ((ZEROP (AREF IMAGE I J))) ;Ignore zeros.
                         (T (SETQ A (+ A (* (- I IO) (- I IO)))
                                  B (+ B (* (- I IO) (- J JO)))
                                  C (+ C (* (- J JO) (- J JO)))))))))))))
```

Here, the value of (ATAN Y X) is an angle, θ, in radians, between $-\pi$ and $+\pi$, such that

$$y = r \sin\theta \qquad \text{and} \qquad x = r \cos\theta,$$

for some r, where x and y are the values of X and Y, respectively. Thus ATAN finds the arc tangent of y/x in the quadrant determined by the signs of x and y. This primitive has no trouble when the angle approaches $+\pi/2$ or $-\pi/2$. The result is undefined *only* when both x and y are 0. This happens here if the object lacks an axis of least inertia.[7]

Note that in the above, IO and JO, obtained from the procedure CENTER, are floating-point numbers. Thus the differences and products computed using them also are floating-point numbers, because of floating-point contagion.

---

[7] Given a single argument, ATAN uses a default second argument of 1.

Problems

Problem 10-3:   Simplify ORIENTATION by using the following identities:

$$a = \sum_{i=0}^{n-1} \sum_{j=0}^{m-1} i^2\, p_{i,j} - A\, i_o^2,$$

$$b = \sum_{i=0}^{n-1} \sum_{j=0}^{m-1} ij\, p_{i,j} - A\, i_o j_o,$$

$$c = \sum_{i=0}^{n-1} \sum_{j=0}^{m-1} j^2\, p_{i,j} - A\, j_o^2.$$

These formulas allow a, b, and c to be calculated directly, without resorting to the transformed coordinates i' and j'.

Problem 10-4:   In order to get adequate accuracy, an image should be sampled finely, producing a huge array of bits. We therefore should be a little sensitive to issues of computational efficiency. Although the equations given correctly define the center of area, they suggest procedures that are unnecessarily slow.

It turns out that the position of the center of area along the i-direction is not altered by projecting the image onto a line parallel to this direction. That is, i_o can be found from the one-dimensional array of row sums. A similar projection can be made onto a line parallel to the j-direction, and j_o can be found from the one dimensional array of column sums. If we let the row and column sums be

$$r_i = \sum_{j=0}^{m-1} p_{i,j} \quad\text{and}\quad c_j = \sum_{i=0}^{n-1} p_{i,j},$$

then the center of area can be computed using

$$i_o = \frac{1}{A} \sum_{i=0}^{n-1} i\, r_i \quad\text{and}\quad j_o = \frac{1}{A} \sum_{j=0}^{m-1} j\, c_j.$$

Note that the row and column sums can be found using nothing more sophisticated than counting. A tremendous data reduction occurs once the row and column sums are known, and we need pay less attention to issues of speed. By the way, A is equal to the total of the row sums r_i, and is also equal to the total of the column sums c_j.

Rewrite CENTER to use PROJECT, a procedure that returns a list of two arrays containing the row and column sums.

Problem 10-5: It would be useful to speed up the calculation of *orientation* as well, using row and column sums. Here we need to calculate the sums a, b, and c. Two of these, a and c, can be obtained easily from the row and column sums using the following identities:

$$\sum_{i=0}^{n-1}\sum_{j=0}^{m-1} i^2\, p_{i,j} = \sum_{i=0}^{n-1} i^2 \sum_{j=0}^{m-1} p_{i,j} = \sum_{i=0}^{n-1} i^2\, r_i,$$

$$\sum_{i=0}^{n-1}\sum_{j=0}^{m-1} j^2\, p_{i,j} = \sum_{j=0}^{m-1} j^2 \sum_{i=0}^{n-1} p_{i,j} = \sum_{j=0}^{m-1} j^2\, c_i.$$

But what about the sum of the product of i and j, needed to calculate b? Another projection of the binary image is needed. Note this:

$$(i+j)^2 = i^2 + 2ij + j^2.$$

This suggests the use of a diagonal projection:

$$d_k = \sum_{i=i_o}^{i_m} p_{i,k-i} = \sum_{j=j_o}^{j_m} p_{k-j,j},$$

where k ranges from 0 to $(n+m-2)$. The indices i and j are restricted in the sums, so that only points that actually lie in the binary image are accessed. Clearly,

$$\sum_{i=0}^{n-1}\sum_{j=0}^{m-1} (i+j)^2 p_{i,j} = \sum_{k=0}^{n+m-2} k^2\, d_k,$$

and so

$$2\sum_{i=0}^{n-1}\sum_{j=0}^{m-1} ij\, p_{i,j} = \sum_{k=0}^{n+m-2} k^2\, d_k - \left[\sum_{i=0}^{n-1} i^2\, r_i + \sum_{j=0}^{m-1} j^2\, c_j\right].$$

The last two terms have been calculated already while finding a and c.

Rewrite ORIENTATION to make use of row, column, and diagonal sums. A new version of PROJECT will be needed.

Features Found in Binary Images Can Be Used for Classification

In many cases more than one type of object may appear in the field of view of a machine vision system. How can we distinguish these? We have already calculated some information that might be useful. Different objects may differ in both their areas and in their least and greatest moments of inertia.

Substituting the direction θ_o of the axis of least inertia and a direction at right angles in the formula for the inertia, we get the extreme values:

$$I = \frac{a + c}{2} \pm \frac{\sqrt{b^2 + (a - c)^2}}{2}.$$

The sum and difference of the least and the greatest inertia are thus

$$(I_{\max} + I_{\min}) = (a + c), \quad \text{and} \quad (I_{\max} - I_{\min}) = \sqrt{b^2 + (a - c)^2},$$

respectively. Dividing the sum of the least and greatest inertia by the area squared provides a measure of how spread out the region of interest is. A circular disk has the least possible value for this quantity, namely, $1/(2\pi)$. Dividing the difference of the least and the greatest moment of inertia by the sum provides a measure of how elongated the region appears to be. In many cases, measurements of area and moments of inertia allow distinguishing among different objects.

If these features do not provide enough discrimination, it is necessary to measure a few more. Some useful measurements can be obtained by counting the outcomes of simple local logical operations. Measurements that can be determined this way are area, perimeter, and something called the Euler number. The Euler number is the difference between the number of objects and the number of holes. Thus a single blob has an Euler number of 1; the object shown in figure 10-1 has Euler number 0. A binary image of the uppercase letter "B," as in the test data for STUFF-IMAGE in an earlier example, has Euler number -1. We already know how to calculate the area:

```
(DEFUN AREA (IMAGE)
  (LET ((N (ARRAY-DIMENSION IMAGE 0))      ;N rows and
        (M (ARRAY-DIMENSION IMAGE 1))      ; M columns.
        (SUM 0))                           ;Accumulated total.
    (DO ((I 0 (+ I 1))) ((= I N) SUM)      ;Step through rows.
      (DO ((J 0 (+ J 1))) ((= J M))        ;Step through columns.
        (SETQ SUM (+ SUM (AREF IMAGE I J))))))))  ;Count nonzero ones.
```

This calculation, by the way, can be accomplished entirely within the parameter specifications of the DOs, leaving the bodies of the DOs empty:

```
(DEFUN AREA (IMAGE)
  (LET ((N (ARRAY-DIMENSION IMAGE 0))          ;N rows and
        (M (ARRAY-DIMENSION IMAGE 1)))         ; M columns.
    (DO ((I 0 (+ I 1))
         (ISUM 0 (+ ISUM
                    (DO ((J 0 (+ J 1))
                         (JSUM 0 (+ JSUM (AREF IMAGE I J))))
                        ((= J M) JSUM)))))
        ((= I N) ISUM))))
```

Which of these forms is considered more readable seems to be a matter of personal taste.

The perimeter can be estimated by counting the number of places where 0s are adjacent to 1s.

```
(DEFUN PERIMETER (IMAGE)
  (LET ((N (ARRAY-DIMENSION IMAGE 0))          ;N rows and
        (M (ARRAY-DIMENSION IMAGE 1))          ; M columns.
        (SUM 0))                               ;Accumulated total.
    (DO ((I 1 (+ I 1))) ((= I N) SUM)          ;Step through rows.
      (DO ((J 1 (+ J 1))) ((= J M))            ;Step through columns.
        (COND ((NOT (= (AREF IMAGE I J)
                       (AREF IMAGE I (- J 1))))
               (SETQ SUM (+ SUM 1))))          ;0-1 & 1-0 vertical.
        (COND ((NOT (= (AREF IMAGE I J)
                       (AREF IMAGE (- I 1) J)))
               (SETQ SUM (+ SUM 1)))))))))     ;0-1 & 1-0 horizontal.
```

The number calculated here will tend to overestimate the true perimeter of the binary image, because of the jaggedness of the outline in a quantized image. The number computed is still useful, however, for distinguishing among objects differing greatly in perimeter.

The Euler number is found by looking for the distinctive patterns:

$$
\begin{array}{cc} 0 & 0 \\ 0 & 1 \end{array} \qquad \begin{array}{cc} 0 & 1 \\ 1 & 1 \end{array}
$$

The Euler number is the difference of the number of occurrences of the first pattern and the number of occurrences of the second pattern. For example, in figure 10-1, each pattern occurs 15 times. For that object the Euler number is 0, as already noted.

The Euler number is sensitive to isolated noise points, but provides useful information in a clean, smoothed binary image.

The Euler number can be computed as follows:

```
(DEFUN EULER (IMAGE)
  (LET ((N (ARRAY-DIMENSION IMAGE 0))            ;N rows and
        (M (ARRAY-DIMENSION IMAGE 1))            ; M columns.
        (SUM 0))                                 ;Accumulated total.
    (DO ((I 1 (+ I 1))) ((= I N) SUM)            ;Step through rows.
      (DO ((J 1 (+ J 1))) ((= J M))              ;Step through columns.
        (COND ((ZEROP (AREF IMAGE I J)))         ;Ignore  p(i, j)=0,
              ((NOT (ZEROP (AREF IMAGE (- I 1) (- J 1))))) ; p(i-1, j-1)=1.
              ((AND (ZEROP (AREF IMAGE I (- J 1)))   ;Increment if p(i, j-1)
                    (ZEROP (AREF IMAGE (- I 1) J)))  ; and p(i-1, j)=0.
               (SETQ SUM (+ SUM 1)))
              ((OR (ZEROP (AREF IMAGE I (- J 1)))
                   (ZEROP (AREF IMAGE (- I 1) J))))  ;Decrement if p(i, j-1)
              (T (SETQ SUM (- SUM 1)))))))))          ; and p(i-1, j)=1.
```

At this point, we assume that a list of such measurements can be derived from a binary image. The recognition system can be trained by presenting it with examples of each of the classes and asking it to remember the feature measurements. A list of classes and feature vectors might look like this:

```
((BOLT (25.0 2.3 0.2 9.0 1.0))
 (NUT (12.0 1.1 1.0 3.9 0.0))
 (WRENCH (65.0 3.1 0.75 25.0 1.0))
 (PRETZEL (40.0 1.1 0.5 12.0 -1.0)))
```

Each feature list can be thought of as a point in an n-dimensional space. In figure 10-3 only two dimensions are used, corresponding to the third and fifth elements in the lists above. An unknown object can be classified by comparing its feature vector with the known ones. Although sophisticated methods have been developed to carry out this classification, in some cases it is enough to measure the distance between two feature vectors. The unknown is assigned to the class whose representative has the closest feature vector. In figure 10-3, for example, the unknown, indicated by the question mark, would be assigned to class N. The following procedure does the trick:

```
(DEFUN CLASSIFY (CLASSES UNKNOWN)
  (CLASS-AUX (CDR CLASSES)                        ;Rest of classes.
             UNKNOWN                              ;Unknown.
             (CAR CLASSES)                        ;Head of list.
             (DISTANCE (CAR CLASSES) UNKNOWN)))   ;Distance to that one.

(DEFUN CLASS-AUX (CLASSES UNKNOWN BEST BEST-DIST)
  (COND ((NULL CLASSES) BEST)                     ;No more to test?
        (T (LET ((NEW (CAR CLASSES))              ;Head of list.
                 (NEW-DIST (DISTANCE (CAR CLASSES) UNKNOWN)))
             (COND ((< NEW-DIST BEST-DIST)        ;Better than old?
                    (CLASS-AUX (CDR CLASSES) UNKNOWN NEW NEW-DIST))
                   (T (CLASS-AUX (CDR CLASSES) UNKNOWN BEST BEST-DIST)))))))
```

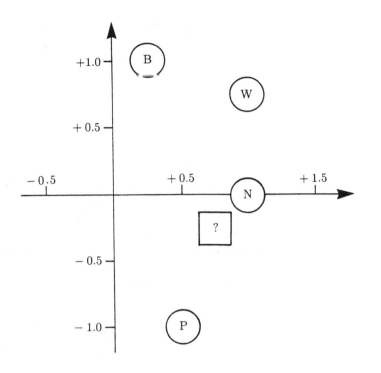

Figure 10-3. Four classes of objects represented by positions of points in feature space. A simple classification procedure assigns the unknown indicated by the question mark to class N. This illustrates how measurements on binary images can be used to identify an object.

Problems

Problem 10-6: Write DISTANCE, a procedure for calculating the distance between two feature vectors. Because the result is only used in comparisons, it is reasonable to have DISTANCE actually calculate the square of the distance instead.

Problem 10-7: Classification can be improved considerably if information is available on the variability of each of the components of the feature vector. Modify the representation of classes to include variance in addition to mean and modify the procedure DISTANCE to weight the square of the difference of two components inversely with the stored variance value.

**Components of a
Binary Image Can Be
Labeled in Two Passes**

So far we have assumed that there is only one object in the field of view. If there are several, we may want to assign a label to each one and perform the sort of calculation discussed so far separately for each component of the image. The idea is to assign a different number to every connected component of the image. The labeling operation can be performed by scanning a 2×2 window over the binary image and observing the pattern found therein.

$$C \quad B$$
$$D \quad A$$

We scan along each row from left to right, starting at the top. When we inspect cell A, cells B, C, and D have already been labeled with a number. This number will be 0 if the binary image was 0 at the corresponding point. Otherwise it identifies the image component.

Let us carefully analyze all possible cases. First of all, if the three neighbors of A are all 0, a new label is assigned to A. Next, if C has been labeled, we label A similarly. It does not matter in this case whether B or D have been labeled because these two cells touch C and therefore must have the same label. If C is 0 and either B or D has been labeled, we label A similarly.

The most difficult case arises when B and D have different labels. This occurs at a place where two components of an object, thought of as parts of separate objects, are seen to be connected. In figure 10-4, for example, the top right-hand arm of the object has been labeled 1, whereas the left-hand arm appeared to be part of another object and has been labeled 2. When the procedure attempts to label the point marked with a question mark, it becomes apparent that the two pieces are connected and belong to one object. Not only must one of the two labels be used to label A, but a note must be made to remember that the two labels seen are equivalent. Later, a second pass over the labeled image will map each label into the smallest one that is equivalent.

These rules can be summarized as follows:

- If A is 0, it remains 0; otherwise,

- if C is labeled n, so is A; otherwise,

- if B, C, and D are 0, A is assigned a new label; otherwise,

- if D is 0 and B is labeled n, so is A; otherwise,

- if B is 0 and D is labeled m, so is A; otherwise,

- if B and D are labeled n, so is A; otherwise,

- if B is labeled n and D is labeled m, then A is labeled n, and a note is made that m is equivalent to n.

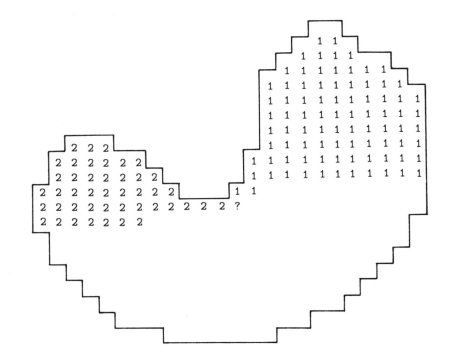

Figure 10-4. When objects in a binary image are labeled, it may be found that pieces with different labels actually are connected. In this case an entry must be made in a list that records the equivalence of the two labels. Here the program notes when attempting to label the point marked with a question mark that the two arms are connected.

To simplify matters we assume that the edges of the array are 0s. Then the following program works:

```
(DEFUN LABEL-COMPONENTS (IMAGE)
  (LET ((N (ARRAY-DIMENSION IMAGE 0))              ;N rows and
        (M (ARRAY-DIMENSION IMAGE 1))              ; M columns.
        (NEXT 1)                                   ;Next label.
        (EQ-LIST NIL))                             ;Equivalence list.
    (DO ((I 1 (+ I 1)))
        ((= I N) (LIST (- NEXT 1) EQ-LIST))
      (DO ((J 1 (+ J 1))) ((= J M))
        (LABEL-COMPONENTS-AUX IMAGE I J            ;Pick up window.
                              (AREF IMAGE I J)
                              (AREF IMAGE (- I 1) J)
                              (AREF IMAGE (- I 1) (- J 1))
                              (AREF IMAGE I (- J 1)))))))
```

```
(DEFUN LABEL-COMPONENTS-AUX (IMAGE I J A B C D)
  (COND ((ZEROP A))                              ;Ignore zeros.
        ((NOT (ZEROP C))                         ;If C ≠ 0,
         (SETF (AREF IMAGE I J) C))              ; use C.
        ((AND (ZEROP B) (ZEROP D))               ;If B & D = 0,
         (SETF (AREF IMAGE I J) NEXT)            ; pick new label.
         (SETQ NEXT (+ NEXT 1)))
        ((ZEROP D) (SETF (AREF IMAGE I J) B))    ;If D = 0, use B.
        ((ZEROP B) (SETF (AREF IMAGE I J) D))    ;If B = 0, use D.
        ((= B D) (SETF (AREF IMAGE I J) B))      ;If B = D, use 'em,
        (T (SETF (AREF IMAGE I J) B)             ; note equivalence.
           (SETQ EQ-LIST (CONS (LIST D B)
                               EQ-LIST)))))
```

At this point some objects may be labeled with more than one label. Another pass corrects this. First a lookup table for labels is constructed. The lookup table is then used to reassign each picture cell to the smallest equivalent label:

```
(DEFUN REASSIGN (IMAGE MAPPING)
  (LET ((N (ARRAY-DIMENSION IMAGE 0))            ;N rows and
        (M (ARRAY-DIMENSION IMAGE 1)))           ; M columns.
    (DO ((I 0 (+ I 1))) ((= I N))
      (DO ((J 0 (+ J 1))) ((= J M))
        (SETF (AREF IMAGE I J) (AREF MAPPING (AREF IMAGE I J)))))))
```

Problems

Problem 10-8:   Define MAKE-TABLE, a procedure that uses the equivalence list returned by LABEL-COMPONENTS to construct a lookup table needed by REASSIGN.

Project 10-1:   If the edge of an object is nearly horizontal and very jagged, it may give rise to several false starts. A large number of labels will be used. In fact it is possible that the largest number used cannot be stored in the image array. Combine the procedures above so that label equivalence is resolved after each row has been labeled.

Project 10-2:   Often multiple labels for a single component of a binary image are created when the left hand edge of the region is tilted slightly to the right. Modify the labeling procedure to take into account the label of the picture cell E in the following pattern:

C B E
D A

Summary
- AREF and SETF are used with arrays.

- Binary images are easy to process.

- An object can be found using binary image analysis.

- Features found in binary images can be used for classification.

- Components of a binary image can be labeled in two passes.

References

For a general introduction to vision, see *Robot Vision*, by Berthold K. P. Horn [1985]. Also see Ballard and Brown [1982].

For an introduction to the methods of pattern recognition, see Duda and Hart [1973].

Gray [1971] gives an excellent discussion of what can and cannot be done using binary image processing methods. Minsky and Papert [1969] also discuss the limitations of so-called local methods on binary images. Work on hexagonal image arrays is described in Golay [1969] and Preston [1971]. Also of interest are Nagy [1969], Stefanelli and Rosenfeld [1971], Deutsch [1972], and Levialdi [1972].

Industrial applications of these methods can be found in Baird [1978], Ejiri *et al.* [1973], Gleason and Agin [1979], Holland, Rossol, and Ward [1979], and Horn [1975]. Also see the chapters by Brady, Villers, and Russo in *The AI Business: The Commercial Uses of Artificial Intelligence* edited by Patrick H. Winston and Karen A. Prendergast [1984].

Other approaches to machine vision are discussed by Horn [1970, 1974, 1977, 1979, 1980].

Examples
Involving
Search

In this chapter, we turn our attention to the well-known problem of search, because search is ubiquitous in one form or another.

The search problem is illustrated in figure 11-1. In each of the versions shown, there is a starting place, many intermediate places, and some number of finish places, from 0 to many. The problem is to find a path from the starting place, through some of the intermediate places, to a finish place. We will see that various strategies for search look much alike when reduced to program form.

Breadth-First and Depth-First Searches Are Basic Strategies

Places are called *nodes*. The connections between nodes are called *arcs*. Arrowheads on arcs indicate that only one-way travel is permitted. If it is possible to go directly from a node P to node C, then P is called a parent of C, and C is called a child of P.

- Collections of arcs and nodes are called *nets*. Figure 11-1a shows a net with loops that make it possible to leave a node and return to it again. Figure 11-1b shows a net without any loops.

- If every node in a net has a unique parent, with only one exception, then the net is called a *tree*. The exception node, which has no parent, is called the root node. Figure 11-1c shows a tree.

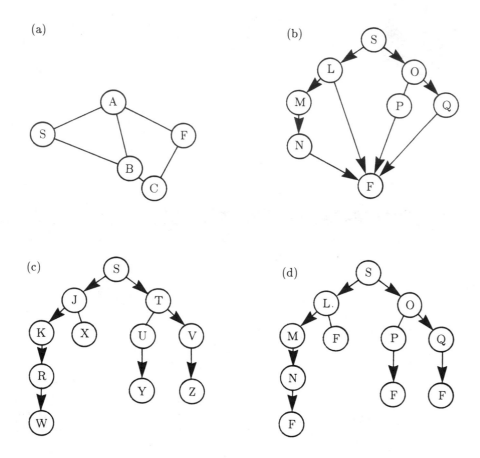

Figure 11-1. The search problem. In *a* and *b* the problem is to move through a net. In *c*, the problem is to move through a tree. The tree in *d* was made from the net of *b* by drawing multiple copies of nodes that are reached from different paths.

We will have occasion to transform nets into related trees using two rules:

- A new copy is made of a node whenever it is about to be reached in more than one way.

- A path is terminated when it is about to close on itself.

Figure 11-1d illustrates.

First, let us consider *breadth-first* search on the tree in figure 11-1d, which happens to be equivalent to the net in figure 11-1b. In breadth-first search, movement is level-by-level, with each node at one level examined before looking at those on the next level, as shown in figure 11-2.

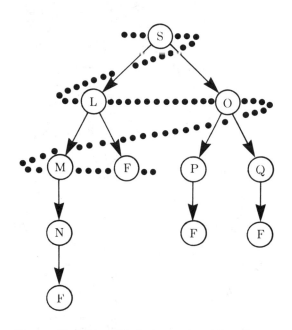

Figure 11-2. Breadth-first search. All nodes on one level are examined before any on the next lower level are considered.

Figure 11-3 illustrates *depth-first* search on the same tree. At first only one of the children of the starting node is examined. If it is not the finish node, one of its children is examined, again ignoring the rest. At each level, the idea is to pick an exit from each node arbitrarily when there is a choice, always moving down. If there are no exits left to explore at some node, attention moves back to the last place where there was a choice. Then downward motion begins again.

A Node Queue Facilitates Depth-First Search and Breadth-First Search

It is particularly easy to write a program for depth-first search. In fact, there have been many examples already of doubly recursive procedures that rip into list structure, moving in depth-first fashion.

Unfortunately, it is not easy to modify those procedures to implement breadth-first and other varieties of search. We will therefore develop a queue-oriented depth-first search program. Our queue is to consist of partial paths. Using a queue of partial paths makes things harder at first, but once we have done depth-first search, modification to do other searches will be easy.

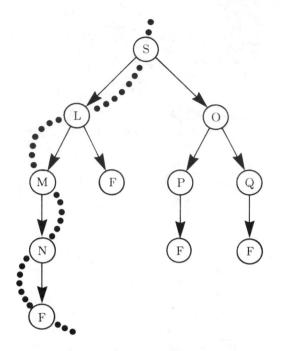

Figure 11-3. Depth-first search. Only one node at each level is examined unless failure requires the search to back up to explore alternatives previously ignored.

SEARCH simply converts its first argument into a one-element queue for the benefit of SEARCH1. Then SEARCH1 examines the queue, testing the first path in the queue for success. If the last node in the first path is not the finish node, then SEARCH1 extends that first path, modifies the queue, and hands the modified queue to another copy of SEARCH1. Thus one copy of SEARCH1 tests one node:

```
(DEFUN SEARCH (START FINISH)
   (SEARCH1 (LIST START) FINISH))              ; Initialize.

(DEFUN SEARCH1 (QUEUE FINISH)
   (COND ((NULL QUEUE) NIL)                    ; Return NIL if queue is empty.
         ((EQUAL FINISH (CAR QUEUE)) T)        ; Return T if goal is found.
         (T (SEARCH1                           ; Try again with new queue.
            <appropriate merge of (EXPAND (CAR QUEUE)) and QUEUE>
            FINISH))))
```

Note that EXPAND is presumed to return the children of a node, given that node as its argument. Before EXPAND can be written, we must deal with the problem of representing the data. Nested lists would do nicely if we were only interested in trees. For nets, it is better to use symbols and properties. The symbols can represent nodes and their CHILDREN properties can represent arcs.

Thus the following SETFs capture the structure of the tree shown in figure 11-1d.

```
(SETF (GET 'S 'CHILDREN) '(L O))

(SETF (GET 'L 'CHILDREN) '(M F))

(SETF (GET 'M 'CHILDREN) '(N))

(SETF (GET 'N 'CHILDREN) '(F))

(SETF (GET 'O 'CHILDREN) '(P Q))

(SETF (GET 'P 'CHILDREN) '(F))

(SETF (GET 'Q 'CHILDREN) '(F))
```

Having recorded the node connections as entries on property lists, EXPAND is easy to write:

```
(DEFUN EXPAND (NODE) (GET NODE 'CHILDREN))
```

The method of merging the new children into the old queue depends, of course, on the search strategy involved. For simple depth-first search, the appropriate form is just this:

```
(APPEND (EXPAND (CAR QUEUE)) (CDR QUEUE))
```

Thus depth-first search is done by the following program:

```
(DEFUN DEPTH (START FINISH)
  (DEPTH1 (LIST START) FINISH))

(DEFUN DEPTH1 (QUEUE FINISH)
  (COND ((NULL QUEUE) NIL)              ;Return NIL if queue is empty.
        ((EQUAL FINISH (CAR QUEUE)) T)  ;Return T if goal is found.
        (T (DEPTH1                      ;Try again with new queue.
           (APPEND (EXPAND (CAR QUEUE)) ;New nodes at head.
                   (CDR QUEUE))         ;Rest of queue.
           FINISH))))
```

Although there is nothing wrong with this search program, it does not do much. For one thing, it only returns T or NIL, whereas it would usually be desirable to have some clue about the path if the search is successful. Moreover, although it works fine on trees, it cannot handle nets, because there is no check to prevent it from getting stuck in endless loop traversal.

Let us first arrange for a successful path to be returned, if there is one, rather than just T or NIL. One approach is to pack more information into the elements of QUEUE. Heretofore the elements have been the nodes remaining to be tested. Given the nodes in figure 11-1d, the `QUEUE` has developed like this:

```
(S)
(L O)
(M F O)
(N F O)
(F F O)
```

Now the elements will consist of paths rather than just nodes. Each path will extend from the starting node to a node whose children are not yet explored. The `QUEUE` develops like this:

```
((S))
((L S) (O S))
((M L S) (F L S) (O S))
((N M L S) (F L S) (O S))
((F N M L S) (F L S) (O S))
```

Thus each element in `QUEUE` is now a list. The elements, in reverse order, give the path from the starting node to some other node. The search proceeds as the first path on the `QUEUE` is extended, through the children of the path's last node.

The changes required in `DEPTH` to use and exploit the new format for the `QUEUE` are simple. First, `FINISH` is compared with (`CAAR QUEUE`) rather than (`CAR QUEUE`). Second, if the finish node is reached, the path on which it was found is returned instead of `T`:

```
(DEFUN DEPTH (START FINISH)
  (DEPTH1 (LIST (LIST START)) FINISH))        ;Note slight change.

(DEFUN DEPTH1 (QUEUE FINISH)
  (COND ((NULL QUEUE) NIL)
        ((EQUAL FINISH (CAAR QUEUE))          ;Note other
         (REVERSE (CAR QUEUE)))               ; slight changes.
        (T (DEPTH1 (APPEND (EXPAND (CAR QUEUE))
                           (CDR QUEUE))
                   FINISH))))
```

Of course `EXPAND` also must be changed. Rather than take a node and return a list of its children, it must take a path, find the children of the node at the end of the path, and return a list of new paths. Each new path will consist of the original path with one of the children tacked on. The number of new paths will equal the number of children.

```
(DEFUN EXPAND (PATH)                          ;Initial version.
  (MAPCAR #'(LAMBDA (CHILD) (CONS CHILD PATH))
          (GET (CAR PATH) 'CHILDREN)))
```

The MAPCAR arranges for a new path to be constructed for each child found just beyond the end of the old path.

Lamentably, our program still risks disaster if given a net with closed loops, because there is nothing to prevent it from going around them again and again. If nets are to be handled, any path offered up by the EXPAND operation must be checked to see if it has a new node that is already present elsewhere in the path. If so, that path must be purged. To arrange for this to happen, we improve EXPAND using REMOVE-IF:

```
(DEFUN EXPAND (PATH)                                          ;Improved version.
  (REMOVE-IF
    #'(LAMBDA (PATH) (MEMBER (CAR PATH) (CDR PATH)))   ;Flush circular paths.
    (MAPCAR #'(LAMBDA (CHILD) (CONS CHILD PATH))
            (GET (CAR PATH) 'CHILDREN))))
```

Rather than keeping a list of nodes visited for each path, we could have marked each node that had been visited. The problem with that approach is that a given search strategy may require us to explore several possible paths simultaneously, and so we would need several different markers. It is easier to keep track of each trail using a list, much like the thread left by Theseus when exploring the labyrinth of the Minotaur.

With the new version of EXPAND, DEPTH will work on nets such as the one shown in figure 11-1a and captured by the SETFs here:

```
(SETF (GET 'S 'CHILDREN) '(A B))

(SETF (GET 'A 'CHILDREN) '(S B F))

(SETF (GET 'B 'CHILDREN) '(S A C))

(SETF (GET 'C 'CHILDREN) '(B F))

(SETF (GET 'F 'CHILDREN) '(A C))
```

For this, the queue develops as follows:

```
((S))
((A S) (B S))
((B A S) (F A S) (B S))
((C B A S) (F A S) (B S))
((F C B A S) (F A S) (B S))
```

Note that the expansion is much like that for the tree in figure 11-1d. Indeed, the tree in figure 11-1d can be made from the net in figure 11-1a by doing the following: first, trace out all paths leading from the starting node; and second, give separate names to each instance of nodes A, B, and C encountered. The result is that node A became L and P, B became M and O, and C became Q.

This has been a lot of work, but now it is simple to make modifications that capture other search ideas. For example, by adding the new paths to the end of the QUEUE instead of the front, we have breadth-first search, as defined earlier:

```
(DEFUN BREADTH (START FINISH)
  (BREADTH1 (LIST (LIST START)) FINISH))

(DEFUN BREADTH1 (QUEUE FINISH)
  (COND ((NULL QUEUE) NIL)
        ((EQUAL FINISH (CAAR QUEUE))
         (REVERSE (CAR QUEUE)))
        (T (BREADTH1 (APPEND (CDR QUEUE)           ;New nodes to the rear.
                             (EXPAND (CAR QUEUE)))
                     FINISH))))
```

Best-First Search and Hill-Climbing Require Sorting

Sometimes it is possible to make a good guess about how far a given node is from the finish. If so, it may make sense to extend the path that leads to a place closest to the finish. This strategy is called best-first search.

Identifying the path that leads to the best place so far can be done, albeit somewhat wastefully, by ordering the paths completely. This is done here using SORT, a primitive that orders a list on the basis of any two-argument predicate that can accept any two of the elements on the list.[1]

```
(DEFUN BEST (START FINISH)
  (BEST1 (LIST (LIST START)) FINISH))

(DEFUN BEST1 (QUEUE FINISH)
  (COND ((NULL QUEUE) NIL)
        ((EQUAL FINISH (CAAR QUEUE))
         (REVERSE (CAR QUEUE)))
        (T (BEST1 (SORT (APPEND (EXPAND (CAR QUEUE))     ;Sort whole queue.
                                (CDR QUEUE))
                        #'(LAMBDA (X Y) (CLOSERP X Y FINISH)))
                  FINISH))))
```

Now let us work on CLOSERP. First we will need a way of estimating the distance remaining. For a map traversal problem, the straight-line distance is good enough for illustration:

```
(DEFUN DISTANCE (N1 N2)
  (SQRT (+ (SQUARE (- (GET N1 'X) (GET N2 'X)))
           (SQUARE (- (GET N1 'Y) (GET N2 'Y))))))
```

---

[1] Actually, SORT will sort any *sequence*, where a sequence is either a list or a vector.

```
(DEFUN SQUARE (X) (* X X))
```

Given DISTANCE, it is easy to decide if one partial path terminates closer to the finish than another:

```
(DEFUN CLOSERP (A B WITH-RESPECT-TO)
  (< (DISTANCE (CAR A) WITH-RESPECT-TO)
     (DISTANCE (CAR B) WITH-RESPECT-TO)))
```

For hill-climbing in a tree, the necessary program differs from the one for best-first search in that the new queue is made by sorting the new children and placing them at the head of the queue, rather than by sorting the whole queue.

Note that all of the above search procedures are tail recursive. All the information they need to remember is kept in the queue, which is simply handed from copy to copy.

Problems

Problem 11-1: A tree can be represented by a list in several ways. One way is to have the list consist of the name of the root followed by lists representing each of the subtrees sprouting from the root. The subtrees themselves are represented similarly. Using this notation, the tree in figure 11-1d corresponds to the following:

```
(S (L (M (N (F))) F) (O (P (F)) (Q (F))))
```

Depth-first search in such a tree can be implemented easily using a doubly recursive procedure. Write SIMPLE-SEARCH, a procedure that determines whether the goal, its second argument, can be reached by traversing the tree, given as its first argument. Your procedure should return a list giving the first path found from the root of the tree to the goal or NIL if none is found. You may wish to model your solution on PRESENTP, first defined in a problem in chapter 4, or on one of the many versions of COUNT-ATOMS.

Problem 11-2: Define HILL, a search program that does hill climbing in a tree, such that the new elements of the queue are sorted and then added to the head of the queue.

Problem 11-3: Define PATH-LENGTH such that it returns the length of a path through a list of cities, assuming that the distance between adjacent cities on the list is the straight line distance.

Then define SHORTERP, a predicate on two paths that holds if the first path is shorter than the second.

Finally, define BRANCH-AND-BOUND, a search program that extends the shortest path on the queue. It is guaranteed to produce the shortest path from start to finish, even though all paths may not be fully extended to the finish.

Problem 11-4:   Define BEAM, a search program that extends a specified number of the best paths on the queue and makes the results into a new queue after sorting. *Best* means ends closest to the goal. The name BEAM is used because BEAM looks at a small number of ways to continue, just as a person with a flashlight looks at a small part of the world.

Problems about Sorting

In the previous section we needed a procedure for sorting a list. There are many different methods for sorting things. Naturally, we will be tempted to think here in terms of a recursive, divide-and-conquer strategy.

One such algorithm is called the radix exchange sorting method. It sorts numbers by looking at them one digit at a time, starting at the high order digit. Having sorted on one digit, the process is repeated on the next lower one, after dividing the list of numbers according to the digit just sorted. Each sublist so formed contains numbers with the same high order digits. This makes it possible to sort each sublist separately according to its low order digits, without disturbing the order already created.

The following list of numbers has been sorted on the left-most digit and is ready to be broken up into four lists to be sorted on the next digit to the right:

```
521
543
542
451
467
371
332
318
337
121
172
```

If we choose to use binary representation for numbers (radix equals two), the list of numbers will be divided into two sublists at each step. One sublist contains numbers that have a 1 in the bit position just sorted on, the other containing numbers with a 0 in that position.

Let us assume that the numbers are stored in an array. The procedure RADIX-SORT will sort the part of the array, from index BOTTOM to one less than index TOP on the bit that is a 1 in the number NUM.[2] After sorting on this bit, the procedure calls itself to sort the array on the next bit to the right. The recursive calls include the correct boundary positions, so that

---

[2] In COMMON LISP lower limits are usually inclusive, whereas upper limits are exclusive.

the part of the array where the bit specified by NUM is 0 is sorted separately from that part of the array where this bit is 1.

```
(DEFUN RADIX-SORT (TABLE BOTTOM TOP NUM)
  (COND ((ZEROP NUM))                            ;Terminate after rightmost bit.
        ((= BOTTOM TOP))                         ;Nothing left to sort here.
        ((= BOTTOM (- TOP 1)))                   ;Sorting one item is easy!
        (T (DO ((BO BOTTOM) (TO TOP))            ;Up and down scan pointers.
               ((= BO TO)                        ;Done at this level?
                (RADIX-SORT TABLE BOTTOM TO (TRUNCATE NUM 2))    ;Divide and
                (RADIX-SORT TABLE BO TOP (TRUNCATE NUM 2)))      ; conquer.
             (SETQ BO (DO ((BB BO (+ BB 1)))     ;Up till 1
                          ((OR (= BB TOP)        ; or top.
                               (ODDP (TRUNCATE (AREF TABLE BB) NUM)))
                           BB))
                   TO (DO ((TT TO (- TT 1)))     ;Down till 0
                          ((OR (= TT BOTTOM)     ; or bottom.
                               (EVENP
                                 (TRUNCATE (AREF TABLE (- TT 1)) NUM)))
                           TT)))
             (COND ((< BO TO)
                    (LET ((X (AREF TABLE BO))     ;Indices unequal?
                          (Y (AREF TABLE (- TO 1))))
                      (SETF (AREF TABLE (- TO 1)) X)     ;Exchange
                      (SETF (AREF TABLE BO) Y)))))))))   ; the two.
```

In this procedure, we need to know if a particular bit in a number is a 1. One way to do this is to divide the number by the appropriate power of two and then check whether the result is even or odd. An alternative is to use primitives that perform bit-wise logical operations on binary numbers, also commonly available in LISP.

In the initial call, BOTTOM and TOP should point to the beginning and one past the end of the array, while NUM should be some power of two larger than any number in the array.

Problem 11-5: Rewrite RADIX-SORT using LOGTEST, a predicate that determines whether the logical *and* of its two arguments is nonzero. Use ASH to shift the single bit in the binary number NUM to the right. ASH is a primitive that shifts its first argument left by a number of bit positions specified by its second argument. If the second argument is negative, the shift is to the right.

Problem 11-6: Two sorted lists can be combined into a single ordered list by a simple process called merging. Write the procedure OUR-MERGE that does this.[3] A sorting procedure can operate by merging short lists into larger and larger ones. The overall task is accomplished by breaking

---

[3] COMMON LISP has a primitive MERGE that is more general than our version, and that takes four arguments, not two.

a list into two parts, sorting each, and merging the results. Define SORT-MERGE appropriately. Assume that the list given to SORT-MERGE contains sublists that are to be sorted on their first element. Here is a test case for SORT-MERGE:

```
(SORT-MERGE '((1.0 AVOCADO)
              (5.0 MANGO)
              (2.0 PAWPAW)
              (4.0 PINEAPPLE)
              (3.0 COCONUT)
              (6.0 BANANA)
              (0.0 ORANGE)))
```

Problem 11-7: Define your own version, OUR-SORT, of the primitive SORT, introduced in the previous section. The first argument is a list to be sorted using the predicate given as the second argument. Base your solution on a simple insertion sorting method as follows: start by defining SPLICE-IN, a recursive procedure that takes three arguments, an element to be spliced in, an ordered list to splice it into, and a predicate that takes two arguments. The new element is to be spliced in just before the first element on the list for which the following evaluates to T:

```
(FUNCALL <predicate> <new element> <list element>)
```

Project 11-1: Change the radix exchange sorting routine to operate with a base of 4. That is, sort on two bits of the number at each level.

Problems about Measuring Out a Volume of Water

Imagine being given two crocks of different volumes, A and B. The crocks may be filled from a source or emptied into a sink. In addition, water can be poured from one into the other until it is filled or until the crock from which water is being poured is emptied. The problem is to measure out a given volume, C.

First of all, we will insist that this volume fit into one or the other of the two crocks. Thinking about it carefully, it is clear that only certain volumes can be measured out this way. For example, if B is twice A, it is not possible to measure out amounts other than A and twice A. In fact, if both A and B are multiples of X, only multiples of X can be measured out. We can now deduce the general rule that only multiples of the greatest common divisor of A and B can be achieved.

```
(DEFUN WATER-CROCK (A B C)
  (COND ((AND (> C A) (> C B)) 'C-TOO-LARGE)
        ((NOT (ZEROP (REM C (OUR-GCD A B)))) 'C-NOT-POSSIBLE)
        (T (WATER-MAKE 0 0 A B C))))
```

We will discuss in a moment what WATER-MAKE has to do. First, however let us define OUR-GCD, a procedure that finds the greatest common divisor of two numbers using Euclid's algorithm.[4] The basic idea is that the greatest common divisor of two numbers is not changed by subtracting the smaller one from the larger:

$$\gcd(u, v) = \gcd(u, v - u) \qquad \text{if} \qquad v > u.$$

We can use this reduction again and again, until $v < u$. In the process, we have computed the remainder of the division of v by u. In LISP, the remainder can be obtained in one step using the primitive REM.

At this point, we repeat the process, with the roles of the two numbers interchanged. This continues until one of them becomes 0, at which point the answer is at hand: it is the other number. To summarize:

- If one of the numbers is 0, the greatest common divisor equals the other.

- Otherwise, the greatest common divisor equals the greatest common divisor of the smaller number and the remainder obtained by dividing the larger number by the smaller.

Sound mysterious? Here is the LISP procedure:

```
(DEFUN OUR-GCD (U V)
   (COND ((ZEROP U) V)               ; Termination test.
         (T (OUR-GCD (REM V U) U)))) ; Recursive call.
```

Note that (REM V U) is just V, if U happens to be larger than V. That means that no special check is needed to determine which of the two given numbers is larger. It took Euclid many sentences to describe the method, in part, because proof by induction, the mathematical analog of the concept of recursion, was not then recognized as an acceptable mathematical argument.

Now let us return to the water-crock problem. Assuming that C is achievable, let us proceed to consider sequences of possible moves. A little thought makes it clear that it never makes sense to back up, undoing what has been achieved so far. As a result, water always moves in one direction: from the source it goes into one crock; from there, into the other; and from there, it is finally poured out. We do not have to search a huge tree of possible moves, because most moves do not make sense. It is sufficient to repeat a series of transfers in one direction, checking at each step whether one of the two crocks happens to contain the correct amount of water.

---

[4] COMMON LISP has a built-in GCD primitive.

Recalling that A and B are the capacities of the two crocks, we may construct the following procedure:

```
(DEFUN WATER-MAKE (X Y A B C)                    ;Current contents are X & Y.
  (COND ((= X C) '((CORRECT AMOUNT IN A)))       ;Right amount in crock A.
        ((= Y C) '((CORRECT AMOUNT IN B)))       ;Right amount in crock B.
        ((= X A) (CONS '(EMPTY A)                 ;Crock A is full, empty it.
                       (WATER-MAKE O Y A B C)))
        ((= Y O) (CONS '(FILL B)                  ;Crock B is empty, fill it.
                       (WATER-MAKE X B A B C)))
        ((> (- A X) Y)                            ;Will what is in B fit into A?
         (CONS '(EMPTY B INTO A)                  ;Yes, empty B into A.
               (WATER-MAKE (+ X Y) O A B C)))
        (T (CONS '(FILL A FROM B)                 ;No, fill A from B.
                 (WATER-MAKE A (- Y (- A X)) A B C)))))
```

Note the use of recursion when WATER-MAKE is called with arguments reflecting the current contents of the two crocks. The procedure shown will return a list of instructions that lead to the desired result. Consider this:

```
(WATER-CROCK 3 5 2)
  ((FILL B) (FILL A FROM B) (CORRECT AMOUNT IN B))
```

Problem 11-8:   The list of instructions produced by WATER-CROCK may not be the shortest possible one. Note, for example, that interchanging A and B in the above example leads to this:

```
(WATER-CROCK 5 3 2)
  ((FILL B) (EMPTY B INTO A) (FILL B) (FILL A FROM B)
   (EMPTY A) (EMPTY B INTO A) (FILL B) (EMPTY B INTO A)
   (FILL B) (FILL A FROM B) (CORRECT AMOUNT IN B))
```

This happens because we arbitrarily chose to transfer water in the direction:

$$\text{SOURCE} \quad \rightarrow \quad \text{CROCK B} \quad \rightarrow \quad \text{CROCK A} \quad \rightarrow \quad \text{SINK}$$

About half of the time it is better to go the other way:

$$\text{SINK} \quad \leftarrow \quad \text{CROCK B} \quad \leftarrow \quad \text{CROCK A} \quad \leftarrow \quad \text{SOURCE}$$

Write WATER-CROCK-OPTIMUM, a procedure that returns the shorter of the two possible sequences of instructions. Avoid using two different versions of WATER-CROCK.

Project 11-2:   Write a program that finds the greatest common divisor of two polynomials. Assume that the polynomials are represented by lists of their coefficients. Naturally, procedures for adding, subtracting, multiplying, and dividing polynomials will be needed.

**Problems about
Placing Queens on a
Chess Board**

How is it possible to place eight queens on a chess board so that they do not threaten each other? This well-known problem can be solved conveniently by a tree-search method.

First, we have to write a predicate that will determine whether two queens threaten each other. A queen in chess can move along the column, the row, and the two diagonals through her present position. We can encode the positions on the board by numbering the rows and columns. Then the following predicate will do:

```
(DEFUN THREAT (I J A B)
  (OR (= I A)                     ;Same row.
      (= J B)                     ;Same column.
      (= (- I J) (- A B))         ;SW-NE diagonal.
      (= (+ I J) (+ A B))))       ;NW-SE diagonal.
```

Next, we can represent the configuration of several queens on the board using a list of two-element sublists, each sublist containing the row and column number of one queen on the board. Suppose now that we plan to add a queen to a board. The following predicate will tell us whether the position (N, M) for the new queen is safe:

```
(DEFUN CONFLICT (N M BOARD)
  (COND ((NULL BOARD) NIL)
        ((OR (THREAT N M (CAAR BOARD) (CADAR BOARD))
             (CONFLICT N M (CDR BOARD)))))))
```

With these preliminaries out of the way we can tackle the search problem.

Problem 11-9:   Write QUEEN such that starting at row 0, an attempt is made to place a queen in column 0. After placing the first queen, it does not make sense to place another queen in the same row, so attention shifts to the next row. A safe square is then found there. This process is to continue until all queens are placed on the board. If, at some stage, all squares on a particular row are threatened, the program has to back up. It is to do this by removing the last queen placed on the board.

Let the single argument, SIZE, specify the size of the board. This will be eight for a full chess board, but it is interesting to watch the program at work on smaller boards too. There are no solutions for 2×2 and 3×3 boards, for example, but there are two for a 4×4 board:

```
(QUEEN 4)
  ((0 1) (1 3) (2 0) (3 2))
  ((0 2) (1 0) (2 3) (3 1))
  FINISH
```

There are 92 solutions, by the way, for the full 8×8 board.

Problem 11-10:   Write BOARD-PRINT, a procedure to print out a board configuration given as a list of sublists of row and column numbers. Assume that the sublists are ordered appropriately in the list, and that there is exactly one sublist for every row.

```
(BOARD-PRINT '((0 0) (1 4) (2 7) (3 5) (4 2) (5 6) (6 1) (7 3)))
  Q . . . . . . .
  . . . . Q . . .
  . . . . . . . Q
  . . . . . Q . .
  . . Q . . . . .
  . . . . . . Q .
  . Q . . . . . .
  . . . Q . . . .
```

Problem 11-11:   Simplify QUEEN so that it turns into PERMUTATIONS, a procedure that prints out all of the permutations of the set of integers from 0 up to one less than the value of its single argument.

Summary

- Breadth-first and depth-first searches are basic strategies.
- A node queue facilitates depth-first search and breadth-first search.
- Best-first search and hill-climbing require sorting.

References

For a general introduction to search, see *Artificial Intelligence (Second Edition)* by Patrick H. Winston.

Knuth [1973] and Aho, Hopcroft, and Ullman [1974] cover methods for searching more deeply. Both books also provide extensive discussion of sorting methods, as does Ullman [1982]. The radix exchange sorting method is discussed by Knuth [1973].

Some LISP systems employ an algorithm called quicksort, due to Hoare [1962] and mentioned by Knuth [1973], as well as Aho, Hopcroft, and Ullman [1974], when sorting arrays. For lists, they usually use a merge sort, due to Cohen and Levitt [1965], and discussed by Knuth [1973].

Euclid's algorithm for finding the greatest common divisor is discussed in Brown [1971]. Hu [1982] and Segdewick [1983] go into combinatorial algorithms, like sorting and searching, as well as many other useful ones.

12

Examples
From
Mathematics

The purpose of this chapter is to explore procedures for numerical computations. For many, the first exposure to programming is through examples of this kind. We therefore believe it may be helpful to see LISP in action on certain of these problems. Those who find the mathematical details of the examples here distracting, however, should omit this chapter on first reading.

It Is Easy To Translate Infix Notation to Prefix

Many find it inconvenient and error-prone to translate mathematical formulas into prefix notation. Therefore let us develop a simple LISP procedure that performs this translation automatically.

An arithmetic expression will be represented as a list of operands and operators, as in this example:

(A + B * C)

The usual precedence among arithmetic operators will be enforced. In the above expression, for example, * has higher precedence than +, so that the expression indicates a computation where B and C are multiplied first and then the result is added to A. Ordering can be enforced by enclosing a subexpression in parentheses, making it a sublist.

Consequently, we have the following equivalence:

```
(A + (B * C))   ≡   (A + B * C)
```

In this case, the extra parentheses are not really needed. The parentheses become important, however, in the following example:

```
((A + B) * (C + D))
```

We start by exhibiting WEIGHT, a procedure that returns the precedence weighting of an operator:

```
(DEFUN WEIGHT (OPERATOR)                    ;Determine weight of operator.
  (COND ((EQUAL OPERATOR '=) 0)
        ((EQUAL OPERATOR '+) 1)
        ((EQUAL OPERATOR '-) 1)
        ((EQUAL OPERATOR '*) 2)
        ((EQUAL OPERATOR '/) 2)
        ((EQUAL OPERATOR '\\) 2)
        ((EQUAL OPERATOR '^) 3)
        (T (PRINT `(,OPERATOR NOT AN OPERATOR)) 4)))
```

Note that the actual values of the weights are of no significance, only the ordering of the weights matters. In the given procedure, operators that are not recognized are arbitrarily given the greatest weight.

Above we provided for an operator, \, that computes the remainder. Recall that the back-slash, \, is used to signal an unusual treatment for the next character—it is a way to prevent a space from being interpreted as a separator, for example. As a result, it is necessary to use \\ to get the equivalent of a single \ in the above.

Next, we must look up the appropriate LISP primitive to implement each of the operators:

```
(DEFUN OPCODE (OPERATOR)                    ;Get appropriate LISP primitive.
  (COND ((EQUAL OPERATOR '=) 'SETQ)
        ((EQUAL OPERATOR '+) '+)
        ((EQUAL OPERATOR '-) '-)
        ((EQUAL OPERATOR '*) '*)
        ((EQUAL OPERATOR '/) '/)
        ((EQUAL OPERATOR '\\) 'REM)
        ((EQUAL OPERATOR '^) 'EXPT)
        (T (PRINT `(,OPERATOR NOT AN OPERATOR)) OPERATOR)))
```

The symbols denoting the primitives that perform simple arithmetic operations happen to be the symbols normally used to represent those operations in ordinary mathematical formulas. This correspondence is convenient, but perhaps slightly confusing here. In OPCODE, + is used in two ways: in the first instance we are checking to see whether the given formula contains this symbol; in the second instance we are referring to the primitive that performs addition.[1]

Also note that a message is printed when an error occurs. It would be better to provide the user with more information about the computation going on at the time the error happened. In fact, the user should be allowed to inspect the variable bindings in effect at that point as well.

Techniques for debugging that make this possible are introduced in chapter 14. Here we are content with simple messages indicating the general nature of the error.

Now then, the *prefix* form of an arithmetic expression can be represented as a tree. Figure 12-1, for example, shows a tree corresponding to the following expression:

```
(SETQ TOTAL (* PRINCIPAL (EXPT (+ 1.0 INTEREST) YEARS)))
```

The *infix* form is essentially a linear string obtained by a depth-first exploration of the tree representing the arithmetic expression.

By tracing along the outer boundary of the tree in figure 12-1, for example, we obtain this:

```
(TOTAL = PRINCIPAL * (1.0 + INTEREST) ^ YEARS)
```

There are many methods for translating from one form to the other. We will employ a linear left-to-right scan, where operands and operators not yet used in producing the output are kept on a list. For clarity, we actually use two separate lists, OPERANDS and OPERATORS, to stack up operands and operators.

Things are added to the fronts of the lists when the operator at the head of what remains of the arithmetic expression, AE, has a larger weight than the operator at the head of the list OPERATORS. Otherwise, the operator at the head of OPERATORS is combined with the two top operands at the head of OPERANDS. Whenever a piece of procedure has been assembled in this fashion, that piece is added to the front of the operand list as a new, composite operand.

---

[1] In some older versions of LISP, the generic primitive for addition is called PLUS, rather than +.

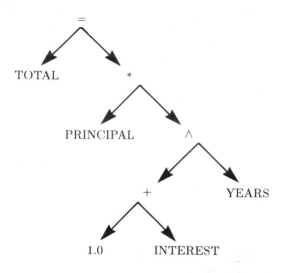

Figure 12-1. An arithmetic expression in prefix form can be represented as a tree. The operators lie at the nodes, and the leaves are the operands. The equivalent infix form can be found by a simple depth-first exploration of this tree.

The following simple example illustrates by showing successive stages in the translation of the arithmetic expression (A + B * C):

OPERATORS	OPERANDS	AE
()	()	(A + B * C)
()	(A)	(+ B * C)
(+)	(A)	(B * C)
(+)	(B A)	(* C)
(* +)	(B A)	(C)
(* +)	(C B A)	()
(+)	((* B C) A)	()
()	((+ A (* B C)))	()

When precedence is forced using sublists, the procedure simply calls itself recursively on the sublist. The value returned is the translated result. Here is the procedure INF-TO-PRE that does the translation:

```
(DEFUN INF-TO-PRE (AE)
  (COND ((ATOM AE) AE)                        ;Easy case first,
        (T (INF-AUX AE NIL NIL))))            ; else stacks start empty.

(DEFUN INF-AUX (AE OPERATORS OPERANDS)
  (INF-ITER (CDR AE)                          ;Work on CDR after
            OPERATORS
            (CONS (INF-TO-PRE (CAR AE)) OPERANDS)))  ; recursion on CAR.
```

```
(DEFUN INF-ITER (AE OPERATORS OPERANDS)
  (COND ((AND (NULL AE) (NULL OPERATORS))          ; Finished?
         (CAR OPERANDS))
        ((AND (NOT (NULL AE))
              (OR (NULL OPERATORS)
                  (> (WEIGHT (CAR AE))             ; Compare weights of
                     (WEIGHT (CAR OPERATORS)))))   ;  operator & list head.
         (INF-AUX (CDR AE)
                  (CONS (CAR AE) OPERATORS)        ; Push operator
                  OPERANDS))                       ;  and continue.
        (T (INF-ITER AE
                     (CDR OPERATORS)               ; Pop operator,
                     (CONS (LIST (OPCODE (CAR OPERATORS))
                                 (CADR OPERANDS)   ;  construct sublist
                                 (CAR OPERANDS))
                           (CDDR OPERANDS))))))     ;  and pop operands.
```

Here is an example of INF-TO-PRE in action:

```
(INF-TO-PRE '(TOTAL = PRINCIPAL * (1.0 + INTEREST) ^ YEARS))
  (SETQ TOTAL (* PRINCIPAL (EXPT (+ 1.0 INTEREST) YEARS))))
```

Problems

Problem 12-1: It is simple to translate from prefix to infix. Write PRE-TO-INF without worrying about removing unnecessary parentheses.

Problem 12-2: Improve PRE-TO-INF so that it will not put in redundant levels of parentheses. It should do the following, for example:

```
(PRE-TO-INF '(SETQ TOTAL (* PRINCIPAL (EXPT (+ 1.0 INTEREST) YEARS)))
  (TOTAL = PRINCIPAL * (1.0 + INTEREST) ^ YEARS)
```

Problem 12-3: Add a tracing mechanism to INF-TO-PRE that prints the values of AE, OPERANDS, and OPERATORS whenever they change. Let the tracing operation be under the control of TRACE-FLAG, a global free variable.

Problem 12-4: Operators of the same weight now lead to code that nests left to right. While this is the usual convention for most programming languages able to accept arithmetic expressions, it may at times be desirable to have operations nested right to left. Change one line to modify INF-TO-PRE appropriately.

Problem 12-5: Sometimes it is convenient to indicate multiplication by simply juxtaposing two operands without an intervening *. Modify INF-TO-PRE to permit implicit multiplication by checking for the presence of an operand where an operator is expected. Note that the operand may be an atom or a list.

Problem 12-6:   To make it possible to add new operators easily, it is better to store information on their property lists instead of encasing them in procedures like WEIGHT and OPCODE. Make INF-TO-PRE extensible by looking up the precedence weight and the appropriate primitive on the property lists of the operators.

Problem 12-7:   Add comparison operators, like < and >, and logical operators, like & (for AND) and | (for OR), noting the convention that logical operators have less weight than comparison operators, which in turn have less weight than the usual arithmetic operators. Also, & has more weight than |. Here is an example of the modified program at work:

```
(INF-TO-PRE '(A + B < C + D  &  A + C > B + D))
  (AND (< (+ A B) (+ C D)) (> (+ A C) (+ B D)))
```

Project 12-1:   We have not allowed unary operators like -, SQRT, and SIN. Add a check for the presence of an operator where INF-TO-PRE is looking for an operand, to implement this extension. Unary operators have highest precedence weight.

It Is Useful To Represent Sparse Matrices as Lists of Lists

Matrices are conveniently represented using arrays. When they get large this can become unwieldy. In the case of sparse matrices, storage is wasted on the large number of 0 entries, which also lead to useless arithmetic operations. Adding 0 and multiplying by 0 can be avoided if just the nonzero elements are stored. Lists are well suited to this task.

A sparse vector can be represented conveniently as a list of two-element sublists. Each sublist contains an index and the corresponding component. So the vector expressed as $[1.2, 0.0, 3.4, 0.0, 0.0, -6.7, 0.0]$ can be represented by the list ((1 1.2) (3 3.4) (6 -6.7)).

Locating a particular component requires additional work, but storage and computation is conserved when large sparse vectors are manipulated.

First, let us develop a procedure that multiplies a sparse vector by a scalar. This can be done easily by multiplying one component and recursively applying the same procedure to the rest of the vector.

```
(DEFUN SPARSE-SCALE-V (SCALE V)
  (COND ((ZEROP SCALE) NIL)                    ;Special case.
        ((NULL V) NIL)                         ;Termination?
        (T (CONS (LIST (CAAR V)                ;Copy index.
                       (* SCALE (CADAR V)))     ;Scale component.
                 (SPARSE-SCALE-V SCALE (CDR V)))))) ;Recurse.
```

Note the special treatment of the case when the scale factor equals 0. Next we apply a similar program structure to the problem of calculating the dot product of two sparse vectors. At each step we check whether the components at the head of the lists have matching indices. If they do, the product of the corresponding components is calculated. Otherwise the component with the lower index is discarded, and the procedure is applied recursively to what remains.

```
(DEFUN SPARSE-DOT-PRODUCT (A B)
  (COND ((NULL A) 0)                          ;Termination?
        ((NULL B) 0)                          ;Termination?
        ((< (CAAR A) (CAAR B))
         (SPARSE-DOT-PRODUCT (CDR A) B))      ;Discard A component.
        ((< (CAAR B) (CAAR A))
         (SPARSE-DOT-PRODUCT (CDR B) A))      ;Discard B component.
        (T (+ (* (CADAR A) (CADAR B))         ;Multiply components.
              (SPARSE-DOT-PRODUCT (CDR A) (CDR B))))))
```

We do not need much more than this to add two sparse vectors, as long as we are careful to construct the representation of the result correctly:

```
(DEFUN SPARSE-V-PLUS (A B)
  (COND ((NULL A) B)                          ;Termination?
        ((NULL B) A)                          ;Termination?
        ((< (CAAR A) (CAAR B))
         (CONS (CAR A)                        ;Copy A component.
               (SPARSE-V-PLUS (CDR A) B)))
        ((< (CAAR B) (CAAR A))
         (CONS (CAR B)                        ;Copy B component.
               (SPARSE-V-PLUS (CDR B) A)))
        (T (CONS (LIST (CAAR A)
                       (+ (CADAR A) (CADAR B)))  ;Add components and
                 (SPARSE-V-PLUS (CDR A) (CDR B)))))) ; recurse.
```

Sparse matrices can be represented as lists of sublists too. Now each sublist contains a row index and a sparse vector representing the corresponding row. So for example,

```
((1 ((1 1.0)))
 (2 ((2 1.0)))
 (3 ((3 1.0))))
```

is a representation of the 3×3 identity matrix.

By definition, the product of a vector by a matrix is a vector obtained by listing the dot products of the vector with each of the columns of the matrix. Our representation is organized around rows, so to make use of the definition, we would have to transpose the matrix. This may be inefficient or inconvenient, so we look for an alternative. If we scale each row of the matrix by the corresponding component of the vector, and then add up the rows, treating each as a vector, we also obtain the product of the vector and the matrix.

This next procedure clarifies:

```
(DEFUN SPARSE-V-TIMES-M (V M)
  (COND ((NULL V) NIL)                                ;Termination?
        ((NULL M) NIL)                                ;Termination?
        ((< (CAAR V) (CAAR M))
         (SPARSE-V-TIMES-M (CDR V) M))                ;Discard piece of V.
        ((< (CAAR M) (CAAR V))
         (SPARSE-V-TIMES-M V (CDR M)))                ;Discard piece of M.
        (T (SPARSE-V-PLUS (SPARSE-SCALE-V (CADAR V) (CADAR M))
                          (SPARSE-V-TIMES-M (CDR V) (CDR M)))))))
```

Now we are ready for matrix multiplication. There are a number of ways of looking at the product, C, of two matrices A and B. The $(i, j)^{th}$ element of C is the dot product of the ith row of A and the jth column of B, for example. Thus the ith row of C is the product of the ith row of A and the matrix B.

```
(DEFUN SPARSE-M-TIMES (A B)
  (COND ((NULL A) NIL)
        (T (CONS (LIST (CAAR A)
                       (SPARSE-V-TIMES-M (CADAR A) B))
                 (SPARSE-M-TIMES (CDR A) B)))))
```

We see that multiplication of sparse matrices is simple, given all the auxiliary procedures.

Problems

Problem 12-8:   Write a procedure to extract the nth component of a sparse vector.

Problem 12-9:   There is no special provision in SPARSE-V-PLUS for the situation when the sum of two components happens to be 0. Change the procedure SPARSE-V-PLUS so that this component is not inserted in the result.

Problem 12-10:   Does it matter whether we let the indices of the components of a sparse vector run from 0 to $(n-1)$ or from 1 to n?

Problem 12-11:   Write SPARSE-M-PRINT, a procedure that prints each row of a sparse matrix on a separate line.

Problem 12-12:   Using SPARSE-V-PLUS as a model, write SPARSE-M-PLUS for adding two sparse matrices.

Problem 12-13:   The product of a matrix by a vector is a vector obtained by listing the dot products of each row of the matrix with the vector. Write SPARSE-M-TIMES-V.

Problem 12-14: Write SPARSE-M-TRANSPOSE, a procedure for transposing a sparse matrix.

Problem 12-15: The jth column of C, the product of two matrices A and D, is the product of A and the jth column of B. Write another version of SPARSE-M-TIMES based on this observation. Use SPARSE-M-TRANSPOSE and SPARSE-M-TIMES-V defined in earlier problems.

Project 12-2: Extend the above set of procedures to deal with objects of higher dimensionality.

Roots of Numbers Can Be Found Using Tail Recursion

LISP typically comes equipped with SQRT, a primitive that takes the square root of a number. COMMON LISP also has a special integer version, ISQRT, that computes the greatest integer less than or equal to the exact positive square root of the integer argument.

Suppose we want to write our own version of ISQRT. We can restate its purpose: it is to compute the largest integer whose square is no larger than the given integer argument. One approach would be to implement the digit by digit method, similar to long division, that was once taught in school. Other alternatives are faster, however. One such alternative is based on Heron's rule, a special case of the Newton-Raphson iterative method for finding zeros of a function:

$$x_{n+1} = \frac{1}{2}\left[x_n + \frac{y}{x_n}\right].$$

The new estimate of the square root, x_{n+1}, is computed using the current estimate, x_n, and the argument y.

This method usually is used in an iterative fashion on floating-point numbers to obtain increasingly better approximations. In the case of integer arithmetic, a *finite* number of steps leads to a result, x, that satisfies the constraint, $x^2 \leq y < (x+1)^2$.

Generally, x_{n+1} eventually will equal x_n, terminating the iteration after a few steps. However, if y happens to be one less than a perfect square, successive values of x will cycle between the correct answer and a number one larger. This condition can be detected by checking whether $x_{n+1} = y/x_n$.

One remaining problem is that we must use integer division. Remember that TRUNCATE does just the right thing, whereas / produces an integer only when the ratio of its arguments happens to be a whole number. TRUNCATE takes the true ratio and *truncates* it toward 0, that is, finds the integer of the same sign that has the greatest integral magnitude not greater than that of the argument.

We can now write the procedure OUR-ISQRT for integer arguments:

```
(DEFUN OUR-ISQRT (Y)
  (COND ((MINUSP Y) 'NEGATIVE-SQUARE-ROOT)      ;Error.
        (T (OUR-ISQRT-AUX Y                      ;Argument.
              1                                  ;First estimate.
              (TRUNCATE (+ Y 1) 2)))))           ;Second estimate.

(DEFUN OUR-ISQRT-AUX (Y XN XN1)                  ;y, x(n), x(n+1)
  (COND ((= XN1 XN) XN1)                         ;x(n+1) = x(n) ?
        ((= XN1 (TRUNCATE Y XN)) XN1)            ;x(n+1) = y/x(n) ?
        (T (OUR-ISQRT-AUX
            Y                                    ;Argument.
            XN1                                  ;Old estimate.
            (TRUNCATE (+ XN1 (TRUNCATE Y XN1))
                      2)))))                     ;New estimate.
```

Successive values of x_n are 1, 7, 4, 3, and 3 when given an argument of 15. Note the use of tail recursion in the above implementation.

Problems

Problem 12-16:   Write ICURT, a procedure to compute the integer cube root of an integer. Be careful about negative arguments. Use the Newton-Raphson iteration:

$$x_{n+1} = \frac{1}{3}\left[2x_n + \frac{y}{x_n^2}\right].$$

Representing Complex Numbers Is Straightforward

In the following sections we often deal with complex numbers. COMMON LISP implementations may have built-in primitives for dealing with complex numbers, just as they are supposed to have primitives for dealing with rational numbers, but some implementations are not complete. Consequently, we develop our own complex-number procedures, rather than depend on the COMMON LISP primitives. This development also provides some exercise in working with access procedures. Of course, if your LISP *does* support these extended features, you can easily omit the OUR- prefixes, as appropriate.

A natural representation for a complex number is a list of two numbers, the first representing the real part, and the second the imaginary part. Then we can make a complex number this way:

```
(DEFUN FORCE-COMPLEX (REAL IMAGINARY)            ;Make complex number.
  (LIST REAL IMAGINARY))
```

Why the procedure has a slightly peculiar name will become apparent later. We can extract the real and imaginary parts this way:

```
(DEFUN OUR-REALPART (COMPLEX) (CAR COMPLEX))      ;Extract real part.

(DEFUN OUR-IMAGPART (COMPLEX) (CADR COMPLEX))     ;Extract imaginary part.
```

If the imaginary part of a computed result is 0, we can represent the result just as an ordinary number. This is called complex canonicalization.[2] Thus we will have to be able to distinguish between real and complex numbers. For our representation, the following does the trick:

```
(DEFUN OUR-COMPLEXP (X) (NOT (NUMBERP X)))        ;Within this context.
```

To take advantage of the idea of complex canonicalization, we need a slightly different version of the procedure that builds complex numbers:

```
(DEFUN OUR-COMPLEX (REAL IMAGINARY)               ;More imaginative version.
  (COND ((ZEROP IMAGINARY) REAL)                  ;Real simple.
        (T (LIST REAL IMAGINARY))))               ;Make complex number.
```

When an arithmetic procedure is given one number that is complex and one that is not, it should first convert the noncomplex number into an equivalent complex number with a 0 imaginary part. This is called complex contagion.[3] Note that we must use FORCE-COMPLEX to do this, because the form (OUR-COMPLEX X 0) just returns the number X.

We could directly embed the primitive, LIST, found in the constructor FORCE-COMPLEX, and the primitives CAR and CADR, found in the the access procedures OUR-REALPART and OUR-IMAGPART, into any procedures that manipulate complex numbers. Direct embedding would cause some loss of readability, but more importantly, if we were ever to change our mind about how to represent complex numbers, many error-prone changes would have to be made. On the other hand, if we use the access procedures, changing from list representation to dotted pairs, for example, is easy. All we have to do is to change LIST to CONS in FORCE-COMPLEX, and CADR to CDR in OUR-IMAGPART.[4]

---

[2] In COMMON LISP complex canonicalization actually applies only to complex numbers whose real and imaginary parts are ratios. For illustrative purposes, we perform complex canonicalization when the components are floating point numbers.

[3] Complex contagion is similar to floating contagion, where an integer is converted to the equivalent floating-point number before entering into a relationship with a floating-point number.

[4] We could use DEFSTRUCT to implement our representation for complex numbers. We did not, but we cannot think why.

Problems

Problem 12-17: Write `OUR-+`, `OUR--`, `OUR-*`, `OUR-/`. These arithmetic operators are to compute the sum, difference, product, and quotient of two complex numbers. When given two numbers that are not complex, these procedures should just apply `+`, `-`, `*`, and `/`. It may help to remember this:

$$\frac{a + \iota b}{c + \iota d} = \frac{(ac + bd) + \iota(bc - ad)}{c^2 + d^2}.$$

Problem 12-18: We can obtain the negative of a complex number by subtracting it from 0, but that would be a little inefficient. Write `NEGATE` which does the right thing. Also write `OUR-CONJUGATE`, a procedure that negates just the imaginary part. The inverse of a complex number can be found easily by dividing 1 by it. Write `RECIPROCAL`, a procedure that takes the inverse more efficiently.

Problem 12-19: Write `OUR-ABS` and `OUR-PHASE`, which compute radius and angle of the polar form of a complex number.

Problem 12-20: Write `OUR-SQRT`, a procedure that can take the square root of a complex number represented as a list of two numbers. The two numbers are the real and imaginary parts.[5] Use the fact that if

$$(a + \iota b)^2 = c + \iota d,$$

then, because $c = (a^2 - b^2)$ and $d = 2ab$:

$$a = \pm\sqrt{\frac{\sqrt{c^2 + d^2} + c}{2}} \qquad \text{and} \qquad b = \pm\sqrt{\frac{\sqrt{c^2 + d^2} - c}{2}}.$$

The signs of a and b must be chosen so that $2ab = d$. Also, arrange for `OUR-SQRT` to call upon `SQRT` only when given a number that is not complex.

Project 12-3: Do what we did above for rational numbers. To allow for rationals as well as complex numbers, invent new representations for both. It would be nice if the components of complex numbers could be any other type of number: integers, ratios or floating-point numbers.

Problems about Calculating Impedances of Electrical Nets

Two-terminal nets of resistors, inductors, and capacitors can be represented conveniently as list structures. Components are denoted by two-element lists, a component type, `R`, `L`, or `C`, and the component value, in ohms, henries, and farads. Series connections of two components can be indicated by lists containing the symbol `SERIES` and the two things connected in series.

---

[5] Note that `SQRT` in COMMON LISP produces the principal square root of a complex number, if complex numbers have been implemented.

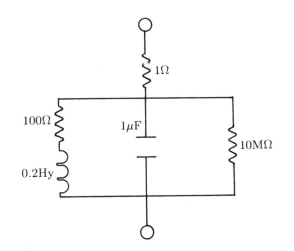

Figure 12-2. A two-terminal net of resistors, capacitors, and inductors can be represented as a list structure. The impedance of the circuit can then be calculated easily.

Similarly, the symbol PARALLEL indicates parallel connection. The following describes the simple circuit shown in figure 12-2:

```
(SETQ CIRCUIT-A '(SERIES (R 1.0)
                        (PARALLEL (SERIES (R 100.0)
                                          (L 0.2))
                                  (PARALLEL (C 0.000001)
                                            (R 10000000.0)))))
```

Suppose now that we wish to compute the impedance of a circuit. This is simple if the circuit consists of just one component:

```
(DEFUN R (X) X)                                        ;Resistor is easy.

(DEFUN L (X) (OUR-COMPLEX 0.0 (* X OMEGA)))            ;Inductor.

(DEFUN C (X) (OUR-COMPLEX 0.0 (/ -1.0 (* X OMEGA))))   ;Capacitor.
```

Here OMEGA, a global free variable, is the angular frequency in radians per second. Lists containing real and imaginary parts are used, because impedance is a complex quantity.

The series and parallel connections are treated next:

```
(DEFUN SERIES (A B) (OUR-+ A B))

(DEFUN PARALLEL (A B)
  (RECIPROCAL (OUR-+ (RECIPROCAL A) (RECIPROCAL B))))
```

Here OUR-+ and RECIPROCAL are the addition and multiplicative-inverse operations on complex numbers, introduced in the problems in the last section.

The following procedure will compute the impedance of a given circuit at an arbitrary frequency:

```
(DEFUN IMPEDANCE (CIRCUIT FREQUENCY)
  (SETQ OMEGA (* 2 PI FREQUENCY))
  (EVAL CIRCUIT))
```

So for example, near the resonance of CIRCUIT-A, we find these results:

```
(IMPEDANCE CIRCUIT-A 346.87)
  (2000.6 0.0)

(IMPEDANCE CIRCUIT-A 351.4)
  (2025.911 -223.177)
```

The first example above is taken at a frequency where the imaginary part is 0, while the second is taken where the real part is largest.

Problem 12-21:   Write ADMITTANCE, a procedure that will calculate the admittance of a circuit described as above. The admittance is the inverse of the impedance.

Project 12-4:   Develop a representation for nets with one input and one output port. Write a procedure that will calculate the transfer function of such a net.

Roots of Algebraic Equations Can Be Found Easily

Now let us construct a collection of procedures for finding the roots of algebraic equations with real coefficients. These roots may be complex, so the procedures should return a list, each element of which may be either a floating point number or a complex number.

Finding the roots of an equation from its coefficients by means of a finite number of rational operations and extraction of roots is called solution by radicals. The solutions by radicals of algebraic equations of the third and fourth degree were discovered in the sixteenth century. Early in the nineteenth century, P. Ruffini and N. H. Abel showed that the general algebraic equation whose degree is greater than four cannot be solved by radicals. We will confine our attention to equations of degree four or less so that we will be able to find the roots without resorting to approximation or iteration. It may help to remember at this point that complex roots, if any, will occur in conjugate pairs if we allow only algebraic equations with *real* coefficients.

We will have to be careful about special cases that arise when some of the coefficients are 0. Naturally, conditionals will be useful in sorting out these exceptions. We start with the innocent-looking linear equation in one unknown, $ax + b = 0$. For this, we could just write the following:

```
(DEFUN LINEAR (A B) (LIST (/ (- B) A)))      ;Inadequate version.
```

But this solution does not deal properly with the special cases. If both a and b are 0, we do not have much of an equation. It is said to be homogeneous, and any value of x is a solution. The user should be warned and an empty list returned. If a is 0 but b is not, the equation is inconsistent. There are no solutions, and again a warning is called for. Finally, if neither a nor b is 0, we have the obvious result,

$$x = -\frac{b}{a}.$$

Remembering that the value returned should be a list of roots, we arrive at the following procedure:

```
(DEFUN LINEAR (A B)
  (COND ((ZEROP A)
         (COND ((ZEROP B) (PRINT 'HOMOGENEOUS) NIL)      ;a = 0 & b = 0.
               (T (PRINT 'INCONSISTENT) NIL)))           ;a = 0 & b ≠ 0.
        ((ZEROP B) '(0.0))                               ;a ≠ 0 & b = 0.
        (T (LIST (/ (- B) A)))))                         ;a ≠ 0 & b ≠ 0.
```

Note that the penultimate line could be omitted at the cost of two unnecessary arithmetic operations in the case that b is 0. Also, simple messages are printed when the equation does not have roots or has an infinite number of roots. Instead of returning an empty list in these cases, the user could be permitted more elaborate interaction using the debugging techniques introduced in chapter 14.

We are now ready to tackle quadratic equations like $ax^2 + bx + c = 0$. If a is 0, this is not really a quadratic equation and the solutions are those of the remaining linear equation $bx + c = 0$. If c is 0, one of the roots is 0 and the other can be found by solving the linear equation $ax + b = 0$. In these two cases we can call on the procedure already defined. If neither a nor c is 0, we can remove the linear term using the transformation $y = 2ax + b$, obtaining this equation:

$$y^2 + (4ac - b^2) = 0.$$

Using the fact that $x = (y - b)/(2a)$, we could just write the following procedure:

```
(DEFUN QUADRATIC (A B C)                      ;Inadequate version.
  (LET ((DISROOT (OUR-SQRT (- (* B B) (* 4.0 A C)))))
    (LIST (OUR-/ (OUR-+ (- B) DISROOT) (* 2.0 A))
          (OUR-/ (OUR-- (- B) DISROOT) (* 2.0 A)))))
```

We use the complex versions of the arithmetic operators here, because DISROOT may be complex. This version of QUADRATIC, although easy to understand, once again does not deal separately with the special cases that may arise. It is also wasteful in computation and does not produce the most accurate result possible. We proceed more carefully now. The part of the program that deals with the special cases and computes the discriminant is as follows:

```
(DEFUN QUADRATIC (A B C)
  (COND ((MINUSP A) (QUADRATIC (- A) (- B) (- C)))
        ((ZEROP A) (LINEAR B C))                        ;a = 0.
        ((ZEROP C) (CONS 0.0 (LINEAR A B)))             ;c = 0.
        (T (QUADRATIC-AUX A
                          B
                          C
                          (- (* B B) (* 4.0 A C))))))   ;Discriminant.
```

The first clause in the conditional above is to ensure that a is not negative. This makes it easier afterwards to pick the best method for numerical accuracy and also to order real roots, if any, so that the most positive appears first in the list.

Now $x = (y - b)/(2a)$, so if the discriminant is negative, the original equation has the complex conjugate pair of solutions:

$$-\frac{b}{2a} \pm \iota \frac{\sqrt{4ac - b^2}}{2a}.$$

If the discriminant happens to be 0, the two roots coincide at $-b/(2a)$. Finally, when it is positive, there are two real roots, usually given in this form:

$$\frac{-b \pm \sqrt{b^2 - 4ac}}{2a}.$$

Curiously, by viewing the original equation as an equation in the variable $1/x$, we find an alternate form:

$$\frac{2c}{-b \mp \sqrt{b^2 - 4ac}}.$$

This is quickly verified by noting that the sum of the roots must equal $-(b/a)$, and their product must equal (c/a). Why bother with the second form if both are correct? It is a question of numerical accuracy: if b^2 is much larger than the magnitude of $4ac$, the square root of the discriminant will be only a little different from the magnitude of b.

The floating-point methods used to represent real numbers in a computer have only limited accuracy, and that accuracy is degraded when two quantities that are nearly equal are subtracted. Thus one of the two roots will be known with considerably less accuracy than the other if we recklessly apply either of the two formulas alone. Consequently, we pick between the two formulas for the solution judiciously.

We now test the discriminant to see what is to be done next:

```
(DEFUN QUADRATIC-AUX (A B C DISCRIMINANT)
  (COND ((MINUSP DISCRIMINANT)                              ;Conjugate pair.
         (QUADRATIC-CONJUGATE (/ (- B) (* 2.0 A))
                              (/ (SQRT (- DISCRIMINANT)) (* 2.0 A))))
        ((ZEROP DISCRIMINANT)                               ;Double root.
         (QUADRATIC-EQUAL (/ (- B) (* 2.0 A))))
        ((MINUSP B)                                         ;Real roots b < 0.
         (QUADRATIC-REAL-P A
                           (- (SQRT DISCRIMINANT) B)
                           C))
        (T (QUADRATIC-REAL-M A                              ;Real roots b ≥ 0.
                             (- (+ (SQRT DISCRIMINANT) B))
                             C)))))
```

Note that the special treatment of the case when the discriminant is 0 can be omitted if the cost of taking the square root of 0 is of no concern and exact equality of the two roots is not imperative. Similarly, special treatment of the case when c is 0 can be removed with only minor loss in accuracy of the result.

We are now ready to write the rest. To make it easier to see what is going on, the work has been divided among four procedures.

```
(DEFUN QUADRATIC-EQUAL (X) (LIST X X))

(DEFUN QUADRATIC-CONJUGATE (REAL IMAGINARY)
  (LIST (OUR-COMPLEX REAL IMAGINARY)
        (OUR-COMPLEX REAL (- IMAGINARY))))
```

```
(DEFUN QUADRATIC-REAL-P (A RAT C)        ;Two real roots & b < 0.
  (LIST (/ RAT (* 2.0 A))                ;If a > 0, most positive first.
        (/ (* 2.0 C) RAT)))
```

```
(DEFUN QUADRATIC-REAL-M (A RAT C)        ;Two real roots & b > 0.
  (LIST (/ (* 2.0 C) RAT)                ;If a > 0, most positive first.
        (/ RAT (* 2.0 A))))
```

The program required for this simple exercise may seem surprisingly large. This results from the careful attention to the special cases, use of the best methods for numerical accuracy, a desire to avoid repeating calculations, and the use of mnemonic, but long, procedure and parameter names.

Someone familiar with certain other languages would no doubt have written this procedure quite differently, perhaps as a single procedure using a large PROG. Several local variables would have been declared and set using SETQ. The other way, illustrated here, is by means of many procedure definitions. It is quite common to find LISP programs predominantly employing this multiple-definition, procedural-abstracting method. This leads to a division of programs into a large number of procedures, each short enough to be easy to understand.

Next we tackle cubic equations like $ax^3 + bx^2 + cx + d = 0$. These either have one real root and a complex conjugate pair of roots or three real roots. It is helpful to remove the quadratic term using the substitution, $y = 3ax + b$, producing the equation:

$$y^3 + 3(3ac - b^2)y + (2b^3 - 9abc + 27a^2d) = 0.$$

In order to find the roots of this simplified cubic, we first find the roots of the quadratic resolvent:

$$t^2 + (2b^3 - 9abc + 27a^2d)t - (3ac - b^2)^3 = 0.$$

The roots are found using CUBIC:

```
(DEFUN CUBIC (A B C D)
  (COND ((MINUSP A) (CUBIC (- A) (- B) (- C) (- D)))
        ((ZEROP A) (QUADRATIC B C D))                 ;a = 0.
        ((ZEROP D) (CONS 0.0 (QUADRATIC A B C)))      ;d = 0.
        (T (CUBIC-AUX A
                      B
                      (QUADRATIC 1.0                   ;Resolvent.
                                 (+ (* 2.0 B B B)
                                    (* 9.0 A (- (* 3.0 A D) (* B C))))
                                 (EXPT (- (* B B) (* 3.0 A C))
                                       3)))))))
```

If the roots of the resolvent are complex, the cubic has three real roots. If the roots of the resolvent are real, the cubic has one real root and a complex conjugate pair of roots.

```
(DEFUN CUBIC-AUX (A B ROOTS)
  (COND ((NOT (OUR-COMPLEXP (CAR ROOTS)))      ;Check resolvent roots.
         (CUBIC-CONJUGATE A                    ;Resolvent roots real.
                          B
                          (CURT (CAR ROOTS))   ;Pick out
                          (CURT (CADR ROOTS))))  ; the two roots.
        (T (CUBIC-REAL A                       ;Roots complex.
                       B
                       (OUR-ABS (CAR ROOTS))   ;Modulus, and
                       (OUR-PHASE (CAR ROOTS)))))) ; argument.
```

Here we have used CURT, a procedure that calculates the cube root of a number. Because this is not a primitive of LISP, it must be defined.

As we go along, we must be careful to avoid disasters like dividing by 0 or taking the square root of a negative number.[6] Now, hidden inside

---

[6] We have, however, not worried about floating point over- and under-flow, issues that would be a concern to someone attempting to write a robust package to be used by others.

the procedure OUR-PHASE, defined in an exercise earlier, is a call to ATAN. As mentioned before, the primitive ATAN fails only if both arguments are 0. This cannot happen in OUR-PHASE, because the arguments to ATAN are the real and imaginary parts of the root, and if the root *was* 0, it would have been represented as a floating point number and so triggered the first clause of the conditional in the procedure above.

Now we can use Cardano's formula. If the roots of the quadratic resolvent are α and β, then the roots of the simplified cubic are as follows, where ω is one of the three cube roots of unity:

$$y = \omega \alpha^{1/3} + \omega^2 \beta^{1/3}.$$

The complex number ω is given by this:

$$\omega = \cos \frac{2\pi k}{3} + \iota \sin \frac{2\pi k}{3} \quad \text{for} \quad k = 0, 1, \text{ and } 2.$$

Expanding this result and using the substitution $x = (y - b)/(3a)$, we can write the following:

```
(DEFUN CUBIC-CONJUGATE (A B R S)                        ;r & s are cube roots.
  (CUBIC-CONJUGATE-AUX (/ (- (+ R S) B) (* A 3.0))
                       (/ (- (- (/ (+ R S) 2.0)) B) (* A 3.0))
                       (/ (* (- R S) (/ (SQRT 3.0) 2.0)) (* A 3.0)))))

(DEFUN CUBIC-CONJUGATE-AUX (REAL-ROOT REAL IMAGINARY)
  (LIST REAL-ROOT                                       ;Real root first,
        (OUR-COMPLEX REAL IMAGINARY)                    ; then comes the
        (OUR-COMPLEX REAL (- IMAGINARY)))))             ; conjugate pair.
```

We could, but did not, treat specially the case when the two roots of the quadratic resolvent are equal. In this case two of the roots of the cubic are equal too.

If the roots of the quadratic resolvent are complex, the cubic has three real roots. This is the celebrated *casus irreducibilis* which can *not* be solved using only rational operations and real roots. We proceed trigonometrically and find the roots given by the following, where ρ is the modulus of one of the complex roots of the resolvent and θ is the argument of this complex root:

$$y = 2\rho^{1/3} \cos \left(\frac{\theta + 2\pi k}{3} \right) \quad \text{for} \quad k = 0, 1, \text{ and } 2.$$

Expanding this result and using the substitution $x = (y - b)/(3a)$, we can write this:

```
(DEFUN CUBIC-REAL (A B RHO THETA)         ;Rho & theta of complex root.
  (CUBIC-REAL-AUX A
                  B
                  (* 2.0 (CURT RHO))
                  (/ (COS (/ THETA 3.0)) -2.0)
                  (/ (* (SIN (/ THETA 3.0)) (SQRT 3.0)) 2.0)))
```

The primitives SIN and COS calculate the sine and cosine of their single argument, given in radians.

```
(DEFUN CUBIC-REAL-AUX (A B RD CD SD)              ;If a > 0, most positive first.
  (LIST (/ (- (* -2.0 RD CD) B) (* 3.0 A))
        (/ (- (* RD (+ CD SD)) B) (* 3.0 A))
        (/ (- (* RD (- CD SD)) B) (* 3.0 A))))
```

We now, with our last breath of air, proceed to quartic equations like $ax^4 + bx^3 + cx^2 + dx + e = 0$. Textbooks advertise several solutions to this type of equation. Unfortunately most, like Ferrari's formula, suffer from poor numerical stability. That is, although formally correct, procedures based on them generate results that are of low accuracy. This, once again, has to do with the inexact nature of the computer's representation for real numbers. One method that does not suffer from this problem is to reduce the quartic to a product of two quadratics with real coefficients. In order to find these quadratics, it is first necessary to solve the cubic resolvent:

$$t^3 - ct^2 + (bd - 4ae)t - (ad^2 + b^2e - 4ace) = 0.$$

If s is the most positive real root of this resolvent, then the quadratics are as follows:

$$2ax^2 + (b \pm \sqrt{b^2 - 4a(c - s)})x + (s \pm \sqrt{s^2 - 4ae}) = 0.$$

The signs of the two square roots must be picked carefully so that their product equals $(bs - 2ad)$. Note that the product of the two quadratics is actually a nonzero constant times the original quartic, but that does not change the roots.

Fortunately, we arranged for CUBIC to return the real root first in the list, if there is only one, and to return the most positive root first, if there are three real roots. Finally, we can write this:

```
(DEFUN QUARTIC (A B C D E)
  (COND ((MINUSP A) (QUARTIC (- A) (- B) (- C) (- D) (- E)))
        ((ZEROP A) (CUBIC B C D E))                  ;a = 0.
        ((ZEROP E) (CONS 0.0 (CUBIC A B C D)))       ;e = 0.
        (T (QUARTIC-AUX A
                        B
                        C
                        D
                        E
                        (CAR (CUBIC 1.0                  ;Resolvent cubic.
                                    (- C)
                                    (- (* B D) (* 4.0 A E))
                                    (- (* 4.0 A C E)
                                       (+ (* A D D) (* B B E)))))))))
```

```
(DEFUN QUARTIC-AUX (A B C D E S)                              ; s is root of resolvent.
  (QUARTIC-SPLIT A
                 B
                 (SQRT (- (* B B) (* 4.0 A (- C S))))
                 S
                 (SQRT (- (* S S) (* 4.0 A E)))
                 (- (* B S) (* 2.0 A D))))

(DEFUN QUARTIC-SPLIT (A B R1 S R2 BS-2AD)
  (COND ((MINUSP (* R1 R2 BS-2AD))                            ; r1 r2 same  as bs-2ad?
         (APPEND (QUADRATIC (* 2.0 A) (- B R1) (+ S R2))         ; No.
                 (QUADRATIC (* 2.0 A) (+ B R1) (- S R2))))
        (T (APPEND (QUADRATIC (* 2.0 A) (- B R1) (- S R2))      ; Yes.
                   (QUADRATIC (* 2.0 A) (+ B R1) (+ S R2))))))
```

Problems

Problem 12-22:   Write CURT using the primitives LOG and EXP, which produce the natural logarithm and natural anti-logarithm, respectively. The result will not be as accurate as we might hope for. Add one step of the Newton-Raphson iteration, given earlier in the problem on the integer cube root, ICURT.

Problem 12-23:   To check the roots of algebraic equations, it is helpful to have a procedure that finds the coefficients of a polynomial given its roots. Write MAKE-POLY, a procedure that produces a list of possibly complex coefficients of a polynomial given a list of its possibly complex roots. Arrange for the higher order coefficients to appear first in the list. You must allow for complex coefficients, because they may occur in intermediate terms, even if the final polynomial is reputed to have only real coefficients.

Problem 12-24:   Another way to check a root is to plug it into the original polynomial to see if the polynomial evaluates to 0. Write POLY-VALUE, a procedure that will evaluate a polynomial at a possibly complex value given as a second argument. Assume the polynomial is given as a list of possibly complex coefficients, with the high order coefficients appearing first.

Problem 12-25:   You may have wondered about the initial clauses in the conditionals of QUADRATIC, CUBIC, and QUARTIC. These assure that the first coefficient, a, is positive. That makes it much easier to keep track of what sign intermediate terms and roots of resolvents will have. It is part of an attempt to return the most positive root first in the list of roots. This is important, because the solution of the quartic depends on having the most positive root of the cubic resolvent, for example.

There is a bug, however. The problem is that when the last coefficient of a polynomial is found to be 0, the root 0.0 is CONSed onto the list of roots computed by a call to a lower-order solver. Thus the most positive root may be hidden behind a `0.0`. Write `INSERT-ROOT`, a procedure that inserts a new root in a list of roots so that the ordering is maintained. That is, the most positive real root comes first in the list. Now all you have to do is replace the appropriate `CONS`es in `QUADRATIC`, `CUBIC`, and `QUARTIC` with `INSERT-ROOT`. Although when used this way, the procedure will not be asked to insert a complex value, make it general enough to deal with this case too so that it can be used in the next problem.

Problem 12-26:   If we use `INSERT-ROOT` as above, then all procedures except `QUARTIC` return their roots in order. Using `INSERT-ROOT`, replace the two `APPEND`s in `QUARTIC-SPLIT`, so that it returns its list of roots ordered as well.

Project 12-5:   In the solutions above we sometimes needed only one root of a resolvent equation in order to proceed, yet all roots were calculated and the unused ones discarded. Write `CUBIC-S`, which only returns the most positive real root.

Summary

- It is easy to translate infix notation to prefix.
- It is useful to represent sparse matrices as lists of lists.
- Roots of numbers can be found using tail recursion.
- Representing complex numbers is straightforward.
- Roots of algebraic equations can be found easily.

References

Methods for numerical computations in general are discussed by Conte and de Boor [1972], Forsythe, Malcomb and Moler [1977], Hamming [1962], and Hildebrand [1974]. Matrix operations are analyzed in Aho, Hopcroft, and Ullman [1974].

Methods for solving algebraic equations can be found in Burington [1973], Abramowitz and Stegan [1964], and Iyanga and Kawada [1977]. Polynomial arithmetic is discussed by Aho, Hopcroft, and Ullman [1974].

Cody and Waite [1980] provide a cookbook for implementors of mathematical function subroutines. Seminumerical algorithms are treated in detail in Knuth [1969]. Hu [1982] and Segdewick [1983] discuss many algorithms, including ones for dealing with some of the problems presented here.

Part II

LISP Applications

13

The
Blocks
World

Here we describe a program that creates simple plans. The plans are for an imaginary, one-handed robot operating in a world that consists of a table and a few bricks, boxes, pyramids, and balls. Our purpose is to exhibit a program that is larger than those in earlier chapters and to prepare for a discussion of good programming practice.

The Blocks-World Program Creates a Plan

In the course of moving things, it is often necessary to move obstructions out of the way and to make sure every object is properly supported at all times. Let us assume the blocks world's one-handed robot can grasp only objects that have nothing on them. Furthermore, let us assume that all objects rest on only one support. The key planning procedure, PUT-ON, initiates the activity that adds to the plan:

```
(PUT-ON <object name> <support name>)
```

The plan has the form of a list of instructions for a physical arm or a simulated one. It is a series of MOVE-OBJECT, GRASP, and UNGRASP instructions.

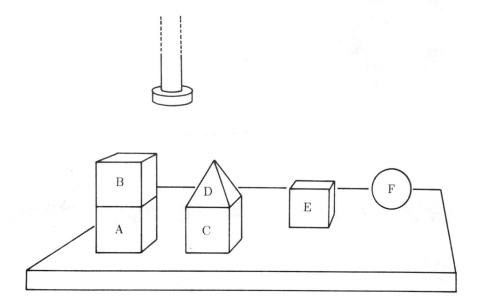

Figure 13-1. A particular situation in the blocks world.

The following plan contains the series of instructions created in response to the command (PUT-ON 'A 'C) for the situation illustrated in figure 13-1:

```
((GRASP D) (MOVE-OBJECT D <space above TABLE for D>) (UNGRASP D)
 (GRASP B) (MOVE-OBJECT B <space above TABLE for B>) (UNGRASP B)
 (GRASP A) (MOVE-OBJECT A <space above C for A>) (UNGRASP A))
```

Each particular object is represented by a symbol that carries information in the form of property-value pairs. This is a typical property list for a brick:

Symbol	Property	Value
A	IS-A	BRICK
	POSITION	(1 1 0)
	SIZE	(2 2 2)
	SUPPORTED-BY	TABLE
	DIRECTLY-SUPPORTS	(B)
	COLOR	RED

For the robot's hand, we have something like this:

Symbol	Property	Value
HAND	GRASPING	NIL
	POSITION	(2.5 3.8 4.1)

The Blocks-World Program Requires Number-crunching Procedures

Shortly we will look at the procedures required by the plan-creating program. First we list some auxiliary procedures for which program definitions will not be given:

- FIND-SPACE is a procedure that tries to find a place for a given object on top of a given support. FIND-SPACE returns NIL if it fails to find space.

- GET-OBJECT-UNDER is a procedure that looks at the size and position properties of all objects to determine if there is one lying directly under a given ~~object~~. PLACE

- TOP-CENTER is a procedure that determines the position of the top of a given block.

- NEW-TOP-CENTER is a procedure that determines the position of the top of a given block after it is moved to a given place.

The Blocks-World Program's Procedures Are Relatively Transparent

The plan itself is manufactured using the procedures shown in figure 13-2 along with those listed above. The solid arrows represent procedure calls that always happen. Dotted-line arrows represent procedure calls that may or may not happen depending on the state of the blocks world. Let us examine these procedures.

The goal of PUT-ON is to place one object on another. The work is done by finding a place using GET-SPACE and then putting the object at that place. If FIND-SPACE, called by GET-SPACE, cannot locate a suitable place, then MAKE-SPACE gets a chance. MAKE-SPACE is more powerful than FIND-SPACE because it can clear away obstructions to make room:

```
(DEFUN PUT-ON (OBJECT SUPPORT)
  (PUT-AT OBJECT (GET-SPACE OBJECT SUPPORT))      ;Put object at place.
  (REVERSE PLAN))                                 ;Return up-to-date plan.

(DEFUN GET-SPACE (OBJECT SUPPORT)
  (COND ((FIND-SPACE OBJECT SUPPORT))             ;Space exists.
        ((MAKE-SPACE OBJECT SUPPORT))))           ;Make some space.
```

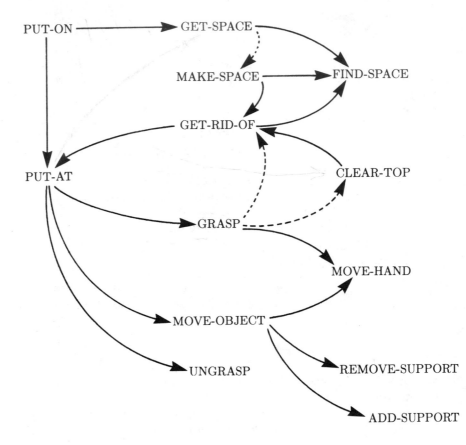

Figure 13-2. The robot's planning program uses many short goal-oriented procedures. **PUT-ON** means put one block on another. **PUT-AT** means put a block at a specified location. **PUT-AT** is used both to accomplish the main goal and to help clear away obstacles on the block to be moved. **MAKE-SPACE** is more powerful than **FIND-SPACE** because it will move things if no room is available. **REMOVE-SUPPORT** and **ADD-SUPPORT** are auxiliary procedures that do bookkeeping. **ADD-SUPPORT** refuses to act if the supporting object is a ball or pyramid.

PLAN is a global free variable, initially set to NIL, that the blocks-world program extends as it works out ways to obey commands.

PUT-AT differs from PUT-ON in that its second argument is a specific point in space rather than the name of an object. The work is accomplished straightforwardly by the commands GRASP, MOVE-OBJECT, and UNGRASP:

```
(DEFUN PUT-AT (OBJECT PLACE)
   (GRASP OBJECT)                                    ; Grasp object.
   (MOVE-OBJECT OBJECT PLACE)                        ; Move it to a place.
   (UNGRASP OBJECT))                                 ; Let go.
```

Note that PUT-AT must certainly accomplish its purpose by way of side effects. As with most of the procedures in the program, the value returned is ignored by the higher-level calling procedure.

Moving on, one might be surprised at GRASP's complexity, but GRASP has things to check:

```
(DEFUN GRASP (OBJECT)
   (LET ((KRUFT (GET 'HAND 'GRASPING))
         (CLUTTER (GET OBJECT 'DIRECTLY-SUPPORTS)))
      (COND (KRUFT (GET-RID-OF KRUFT)))              ; Holding something?
      (COND (CLUTTER (CLEAR-TOP CLUTTER OBJECT)))    ; Top not clear?
      (MOVE-HAND (TOP-CENTER OBJECT))                ; Position hand.
      (SETF (GET 'HAND 'GRASPING) OBJECT)            ; Grab.
      (SETQ PLAN (CONS (LIST 'GRASP OBJECT) PLAN)))) ; Extend plan.
```

First, it may be that the hand is currently grasping something else that must be dispensed with. GET-RID-OF does the job. Next, the property list of the object is examined to see if the property DIRECTLY-SUPPORTS indicates that the object is free to be grasped by the hand. If it is not, a call is made to CLEAR-TOP.

After all of these tests are done and responses are made, GRASP passes off responsibility to MOVE-HAND, which moves the hand into position over the object to be grasped. Finally, GRASP makes a note that the hand is grasping the object by appropriately modifying the GRASPING property of HAND.

Once an object has been grasped, PUT-AT uses MOVE-OBJECT to get it into position. REMOVE-SUPPORT and ADD-SUPPORT take care of keeping the SUPPORTED-BY properties up-to-date:

```
(DEFUN MOVE-OBJECT (OBJECT NEWPLACE)
   (REMOVE-SUPPORT OBJECT)                           ; Bookkeeping.
   (MOVE-HAND (NEW-TOP-CENTER OBJECT NEWPLACE))
   (SETF (GET OBJECT 'POSITION) NEWPLACE)
   (ADD-SUPPORT OBJECT NEWPLACE)                     ; Bookkeeping.
   (SETQ PLAN (CONS (LIST 'MOVE-OBJECT OBJECT NEWPLACE) PLAN)))
```

MOVE-HAND simply changes the POSITION property of the hand:

```
(DEFUN MOVE-HAND (POSITION)
  (SETF (GET 'HAND 'POSITION) POSITION))
```

UNGRASP lets go by modifying the GRASPING property. Note, however, that these changes happen only if UNGRASP is sure there is a support. If the SUPPORTED-BY property has a NIL value, then UNGRASP does nothing but return NIL:

```
(DEFUN UNGRASP (OBJECT)
  (COND ((NOT (GET OBJECT 'SUPPORTED-BY)) NIL)         ;Do nothing!
        (T (SETF (GET 'HAND 'GRASPING) NIL)            ;Drop it.
           (SETQ PLAN (CONS (LIST 'UNGRASP OBJECT) PLAN)))))
```

GET-RID-OF is simple. It puts an object on the table by finding a place for it and moving it to that place. Note the use of PUT-AT, which completes a loop in the network of procedures, giving the program thoroughly recursive behavior:

```
(DEFUN GET-RID-OF (OBJECT)
  (PUT-AT OBJECT (FIND-SPACE OBJECT 'TABLE)))
```

Now we turn to CLEAR-TOP. Its purpose is to remove all the objects directly supported by something the hand is supposed to grasp. This is done by looping until each object found under the DIRECTLY-SUPPORTS property is placed on the table by GET-RID-OF:

```
(DEFUN CLEAR-TOP (CLUTTER OBJECT)
  (DO ((CLUTTER CLUTTER (CDR CLUTTER)))          ;Select next item.
      ((NULL CLUTTER))                           ;No more items.
    (GET-RID-OF (CAR CLUTTER))))                 ;Move it.
```

REMOVE-SUPPORT changes the support relationships that existed at the old place:

```
(DEFUN REMOVE-SUPPORT (OBJECT)
  (LET ((SUPPORT (GET OBJECT 'SUPPORTED-BY)))
    (SETF (GET SUPPORT 'DIRECTLY-SUPPORTS)         ;Put back right stuff.
          (REMOVE OBJECT                           ;Purge wrong stuff.
                  (GET SUPPORT 'DIRECTLY-SUPPORTS)))  ;Get existing stuff.
    (SETF (GET OBJECT 'SUPPORTED-BY) NIL)))         ;Fix other stuff.
```

ADD-SUPPORT is more complicated. Its purpose is to put in new support relationships corresponding to the new position of the object just moved.

It refuses to do this, however, if there is no object in a position to do some supporting or if the object proposed as a support is neither the table, nor a box, nor a brick. Pyramids and balls will not do:

```
(DEFUN ADD-SUPPORT (OBJECT PLACE)
  (LET ((SUPPORT (GET-OBJECT-UNDER PLACE)))
    (COND ((OR (EQUAL SUPPORT 'TABLE)                    ;Support ok?
               (EQUAL (GET SUPPORT 'IS-A) 'BOX)
               (EQUAL (GET SUPPORT 'IS-A) 'BRICK))
           (SETF (GET SUPPORT 'DIRECTLY-SUPPORTS)        ;Put back right stuff.
                 (CONS OBJECT                            ;Add right stuff.
                       (GET SUPPORT                      ;Get old stuff.
                            'DIRECTLY-SUPPORTS)))
           (SETF (GET OBJECT 'SUPPORTED-BY) SUPPORT))))) ;Fix other stuff.
```

MAKE-SPACE is nothing more than a repeated appeal to GET-RID-OF to clear away space for a new object. The loop containing GET-RID-OF returns as soon as enough clutter has been cleared away to make enough room for FIND-SPACE to succeed:

```
(DEFUN MAKE-SPACE (OBJECT SUPPORT)
  (DO ((CLUTTER (GET SUPPORT 'DIRECTLY-SUPPORTS)      ;Get items.
                (CDR CLUTTER))                        ;Select next item.
       (PLACE NIL))
      (PLACE PLACE)                                   ;Return place if any.
    (GET-RID-OF (CAR CLUTTER))                        ;Remove something.
    (SETQ PLACE (FIND-SPACE OBJECT SUPPORT))))
```

The Number-Crunching Procedures Can Be Faked

Actually writing FIND-SPACE and the other procedures that deal with geometry is a big job. If only the planning is of interest, as it is here, the big job can be avoided by deflecting certain procedures away from geometry toward a simulation of the geometry. The faked data-base procedures enable the others to be run, debugged, and experimented with.

By one approach, FIND-SPACE would ask some human partner to supply the coordinates that it itself is supposed to find. In the following version, even this is avoided. Instead of working with numbers, the program is led to work with descriptions. Instead of returning a list of three numbers, FIND-SPACE returns a description of what the numbers would be:

```
(FIND-SPACE 'A 'C)
  (SPACE ABOVE C FOR A)
```

Of course if the support has anything on it, FIND-SPACE may not be expected
to succeed. The human partner decides:[1]

```
(DEFUN FIND-SPACE (OBJECT SUPPORT)
  (LET ((KRUFT (GET SUPPORT 'DIRECTLY-SUPPORTS)))
    (COND ((OR (EQUAL SUPPORT 'TABLE)                    ;Always space on table.
               (NULL KRUFT))                             ;Always space if clear.
           `(SPACE ABOVE ,SUPPORT FOR ,OBJECT))
          (T (PRINT `(,SUPPORT SUPPORTS ,@KRUFT))
             (PRINT '(TYPE T IF FIND-SPACE SHOULD SUCCEED))    ;Ask.
             (COND ((NOT (EQUAL T (READ))) NIL)          ;Deny?
                   (T `(SPACE ABOVE ,SUPPORT FOR ,OBJECT)))))))
```

Given this version of FIND-SPACE, the GET-OBJECT-UNDER procedure will get
places that are represented by lists in which the third element is the object
GET-OBJECT-UNDER is after:

```
(DEFUN GET-OBJECT-UNDER (PLACE)
  (CADDR PLACE))
```

TOP-CENTER and NEW-TOP-CENTER also can be arranged to return descriptions
of places rather than coordinates:

```
(DEFUN TOP-CENTER (OBJECT)
  (LIST 'TOP-CENTER OBJECT))

(DEFUN NEW-TOP-CENTER (OBJECT PLACE)
  (LIST 'NEW-TOP-CENTER OBJECT PLACE))
```

As we noted in chapter 5, it is good for a program to interact with its
data-base through just a few access procedures like FIND-SPACE, GET-OBJECT-
UNDER, TOP-CENTER, and NEW-TOP-CENTER. There are two reasons:

- The actual activity in the data base can be simulated, thus allowing
  independent debugging of the action programs and the data-base programs.

- The data base and the data-base procedures can be changed easily,
  thus enabling action programs to work with more than one data base.

**Simulation Is
Straightforward**

At this point it is helpful to walk through the actions that follow from an
effort to place brick A on brick C given the situation in figure 13-1. Both
the procedures themselves and the connections shown in figure 13-2 are
helpful. The diagram in figure 13-3 gives the result.

---

[1] We do not use the COMMON LISP primitive Y-OR-N-P in FIND-SPACE because
we have not introduced the format strings involved.

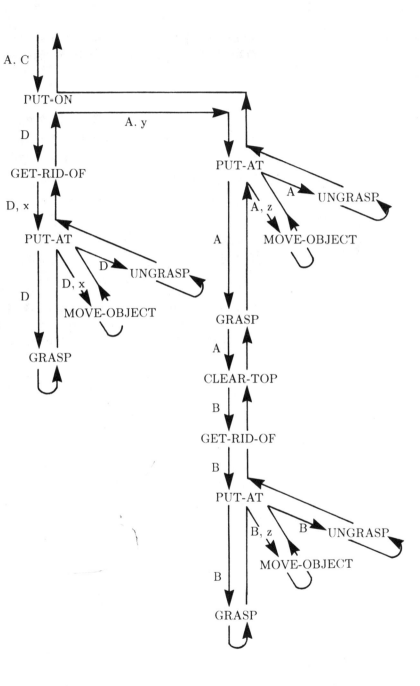

Figure 13-3. The procedures and arguments involved in doing (PUT-ON A C). The x is to be read as (SPACE ABOVE TABLE FOR D); the y, as (SPACE ABOVE C FOR A); and the z, as (SPACE ABOVE TABLE FOR B).

Problems   **Project 13-1:**   Implement FIND-SPACE, GET-OBJECT-UNDER, TOP-CENTER,
                      and NEW-TOP-CENTER, the procedures that actually do geometric calculations.

Summary   • The blocks-world program creates a plan.
                      • The blocks-world program requires number-crunching procedures.
                      • The blocks-world program's procedures are relatively transparent.
                      • The number-crunching procedures can be faked.
                      • Simulation is straightforward.

References   The blocks world appeared as the domain of discourse in Winograd's thesis
                      [1972] on natural language. Winograd worked with a simulated world, not
                      a real one with real blocks, a vision system, and a manipulator. Work on an
                      early system that manipulated real blocks is described in Winston [1972].

                      For a general introduction to problem solving paradigms, see *Artificial
                      Intelligence (Second Edition)* by Patrick H. Winston [1984].

14

Rules For Good Programming And Tools For Debugging

Good programming and good debugging go hand in hand because attention to some basic rules of good programming practice both eliminates some debugging and simplifies the rest. We begin by enumerating some of our favorite rules of good programming practice and finish by discussing three debugging primitives, BREAK, TRACE, and STEP.

The Blocks-World Program Illustrates Some Rules of Good Programming Practice

Some languages make such a big fuss out of procedure interaction that having one procedure call on another is a major event. The connections among procedures written in such languages tend to resemble the example of figure 14-1, where there is one major procedure with a few subprocedures shallowly arrayed under it.

In other languages, particularly LISP, the notion of subprocedure is so intimately involved with the language's fundamental structure that essentially everything is best thought of as a subprocedure call. A deep hierarchy of subprocedure arrangements is natural. Superior procedures accept tasks and hand them to subordinate procedures. Along the way the original task is perhaps simplified a bit or at least is divided up. When all of the subordinates are through, the superior passes the results upward, perhaps adding a bit of embellishment. Consequently, LISP is a language that is said to promote procedure abstraction. In fact, LISP's talent for

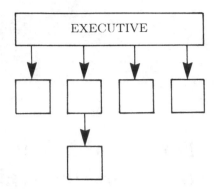

Figure 14-1. Most programming languages encourage shallow program organization with little subprocedure depth.

procedure abstraction helps facilitate data abstraction, described in chapter 5. Because it is particularly important to use abstraction, let us start a list of rules for good programming practice this way:

- Procedures should be layered, with procedure abstraction used liberally.

- Procedures should be insulated from the details of data representation, with data abstraction used liberally.

- Procedures should be commented liberally. Put descriptive paragraphs before definitions and staccato notes inside them.

- Procedures should be short. In the blocks-world program, the modules interact like a community of experts.

- Procedures should be built around goals. In the blocks-world program, goals are satisfied by invoking a small number of subgoals for other procedures to handle or by calling a few primitives directly.

- Procedures should presume as little as possible about the situation in effect when they are called. In the blocks-world program, the procedures themselves contain some of the necessary machinery to set up conditions that are required before they do their jobs.

- Procedures should stop and report on what is going on when bad but predictable situations occur.

The next section discusses stopping.

It Is Often Useful To Stop Procedures using BREAK

Recall that the procedure `ADD-SUPPORT` in the blocks-world program keeps `DIRECTLY-SUPPORTS` and `SUPPORTED-BY` properties up to date:

```
(DEFUN ADD-SUPPORT (OBJECT PLACE)
  (LET ((SUPPORT (GET-OBJECT-UNDER PLACE)))
    (COND ((OR (EQUAL SUPPORT 'TABLE)                      ;Support ok?
               (EQUAL (GET SUPPORT 'IS-A) 'BOX)
               (EQUAL (GET SUPPORT 'IS-A) 'BRICK))
           (SETF (GET SUPPORT 'DIRECTLY-SUPPORTS)          ;Put back right stuff.
                 (CONS OBJECT                              ;Add right stuff.
                       (GET SUPPORT                        ;Get old stuff.
                            'DIRECTLY-SUPPORTS)))
           (SETF (GET OBJECT 'SUPPORTED-BY) SUPPORT)))))   ;Fix other stuff.
```

As it stands, `ADD-SUPPORT` does nothing if the value of `SUPPORT` is an object that is neither the table nor a brick. The following version, responding to the same situation, calls the procedure `OUR-BREAK` with an error message:[1]

```
(DEFUN ADD-SUPPORT (OBJECT PLACE)
  (LET ((SUPPORT (GET-OBJECT-UNDER PLACE)))
    (COND ((OR (EQUAL SUPPORT 'TABLE)                      ;Support ok?
               (EQUAL (GET SUPPORT 'IS-A) 'BOX)
               (EQUAL (GET SUPPORT 'IS-A) 'BRICK))
           (SETF (GET SUPPORT 'DIRECTLY-SUPPORTS)          ;Put back right stuff.
                 (CONS OBJECT                              ;Add right stuff.
                       (GET SUPPORT                        ;Get old stuff.
                            'DIRECTLY-SUPPORTS)))
           (SETF (GET OBJECT 'SUPPORTED-BY) SUPPORT))      ;Fix other stuff.
          (T (OUR-BREAK '(ADD-SUPPORT CANNOT ARRANGE FOR SUPPORT)))))))
```

`OUR-BREAK`, if encountered, prints its argument and enters a loop. Within the loop, the user supplies expressions that the user is curious about. `OUR-BREAK` prints their value. The user types `CONTINUE` to get out of the loop. `OUR-BREAK` then terminates, returning `NIL`.

To see how `OUR-BREAK` is used, suppose we try to put a brick on top of a pyramid, as in this example:

```
(PUT-ON 'A 'D)
  (BREAK: ADD-SUPPORT CANNOT ARRANGE FOR SUPPORT)
  >
```

---

[1] `OUR-BREAK` is similar in spirit to `BREAK`, a built-in, but implementation-dependent, COMMON LISP primitive.

At this point, the blocks-world program is inside a call to OUR-BREAK waiting for the user to type something. Here is how the user might discover what is wrong:

```
(PUT-ON 'A 'D)
  (BREAK: ADD-SUPPORT CANNOT ARRANGE FOR SUPPORT)
  > OBJECT
  A
  > SUPPORT
  D
  > (GET SUPPORT 'IS-A)
  PYRAMID
  > CONTINUE
```

Evidently the user wanted to know the values for the variables OBJECT and SUPPORT. Finding that SUPPORT has the value D, the user elects to find out what D is. Discovering that its IS-A property has the value PYRAMID, the user understands why ADD-SUPPORT stumbled and decides to go on. The user arranges for OUR-BREAK to terminate by typing CONTINUE, causing OUR-BREAK to return NIL.

Problems

Problem 14-1: Implement OUR-BREAK as a macro. Why is it that OUR-BREAK must be implemented as a macro rather than as an ordinary procedure?

Problem 14-2: PUT-ON was defined to have two arguments, OBJECT and SUPPORT. If the values of OBJECT and SUPPORT are the same, then PUT-ON would attempt to put one block on top of itself. This clearly would be a cause for alarm. Define PUT-ON such that OUR-BREAK is called if OBJECT and SUPPORT have the same value.

TRACE Causes Procedures To Print their Arguments and their Values

Suppose for some reason that things are just not working out. Things drop dead, perhaps with an error message that is too opaque to help. For the sake of illustration, suppose the user is suspicious about REMOVE-SUPPORT. The user thinks it may not be getting called or that it is called with a strange argument. A primitive approach to testing such a theory would be to modify REMOVE-SUPPORT so that it prints useful information, both on its entry and exit:

```
(DEFUN REMOVE-SUPPORT (OBJECT)
  (PRINT `(ENTERING REMOVE-SUPPORT ,OBJECT))
  (LET ((RESULT
         (LET ((SUPPORT (GET OBJECT 'SUPPORTED-BY)))
           (SETF (GET SUPPORT 'DIRECTLY-SUPPORTS)
                 (REMOVE OBJECT
                         (GET SUPPORT 'DIRECTLY-SUPPORTS)))
           (SETF (GET OBJECT 'SUPPORTED-BY) NIL))))
    (PRINT `(EXITING REMOVE-SUPPORT ,RESULT))
    RESULT))
```

In a set of problems in the next chapter, we will define a procedure named
OUR-TRACE. It will arrange for entry and exit information to be printed for
a list of procedures supplied as arguments.[2] This OUR-TRACE procedure will
have the additional feature of indenting lines in proportion to depth of
procedure call. The following illustrates its use on FACTORIAL:

```
(DEFUN FACTORIAL (N) (COND ((ZEROP N) 1) (T (* N (FACTORIAL (- N 1))))))

(OUR-TRACE FACTORIAL)


(FACTORIAL 10.)
  (ENTERING FACTORIAL (10.))
   (ENTERING FACTORIAL (9.))
    (ENTERING FACTORIAL (8.))
     (ENTERING FACTORIAL (7.))
      (ENTERING FACTORIAL (6.))
       (ENTERING FACTORIAL (5.))
        (ENTERING FACTORIAL (4.))
         (ENTERING FACTORIAL (3.))
          (ENTERING FACTORIAL (2.))
           (ENTERING FACTORIAL (1.))
            (ENTERING FACTORIAL (0.))
            (EXITING FACTORIAL 1.)
           (EXITING FACTORIAL 1.)
          (EXITING FACTORIAL 2.)
         (EXITING FACTORIAL 6.)
        (EXITING FACTORIAL 24.)
       (EXITING FACTORIAL 120.)
      (EXITING FACTORIAL 720.)
     (EXITING FACTORIAL 5040.)
    (EXITING FACTORIAL 40320.)
   (EXITING FACTORIAL 362880.)
  (EXITING FACTORIAL 3628800.)
3628800.
```

---

[2] OUR-TRACE is similar to TRACE, a built-in COMMON LISP primitive. Note that
different COMMON LISP implementations may have a slightly different TRACE.

The blocks world supplies another illustration. Consider again the use of PUT-ON in the situation shown back in figure 13-1, this time with some tracing. Returned values are suppressed as they are both verbose and dull.

```
(OUR-TRACE PUT-ON PUT-AT GRASP MOVE-OBJECT UNGRASP CLEAR-TOP GET-RID-OF)
(PUT-ON 'A 'C)
  (ENTERING PUT-ON A C)
  (C SUPPORTS D)
  (TYPE T IF FIND-SPACE SHOULD SUCCEED)
NIL
    (ENTERING GET-RID-OF D)
     (ENTERING PUT-AT D (SPACE ABOVE TABLE FOR D))
      (ENTERING GRASP D)
      (EXITING GRASP)
      (ENTERING MOVE-OBJECT D (SPACE ABOVE TABLE FOR D))
      (EXITING MOVE-OBJECT)
      (ENTERING UNGRASP D)
      (EXITING UNGRASP)
     (EXITING PUT-AT)
    (EXITING GET-RID-OF)
    (ENTERING PUT-AT A (SPACE ABOVE C FOR A))
     (ENTERING GRASP A)
      (ENTERING CLEAR-TOP A)
       (ENTERING GET-RID-OF B)
        (ENTERING PUT-AT B (SPACE ABOVE TABLE FOR B))
         (ENTERING GRASP B)
         (EXITING GRASP)
         (ENTERING MOVE-OBJECT B (SPACE ABOVE TABLE FOR B))
         (EXITING MOVE-OBJECT)
         (ENTERING UNGRASP B)
         (EXITING UNGRASP)
        (EXITING PUT-AT)
       (EXITING GET-RID-OF)
      (EXITING CLEAR-TOP)
     (EXITING GRASP)
     (ENTERING MOVE-OBJECT A (SPACE ABOVE C FOR A))
     (EXITING MOVE-OBJECT)
     (ENTERING UNGRASP A)
     (EXITING UNGRASP)
    (EXITING PUT-AT)
  (EXITING PUT-ON)
  ((GRASP D) (MOVE-OBJECT D (SPACE ABOVE TABLE FOR D)) (UNGRASP D)
   (GRASP B) (MOVE-OBJECT B (SPACE ABOVE TABLE FOR B)) (UNGRASP B)
   (GRASP A) (MOVE-OBJECT A (SPACE ABOVE C FOR A)) (UNGRASP A))
```

OUR-UNTRACE will stop the tracing of the procedures supplied as arguments, turning off the effect of OUR-TRACE.

**STEP Causes
Procedures To Proceed
One Step at a Time**

Once you have a good idea which procedure is causing trouble, perhaps by tracing, it is time to start watching the performance of that suspect procedure in detail, following its action one step at a time. This can be done using OUR-STEP [3]

In stepping mode, each expression is printed out before evaluation, whereupon LISP pauses. After you type N, for next, LISP proceeds into the expression to work on the expression's arguments. Consider using OUR-STEP on FACTORIAL, for example:

```
(OUR-STEP '(FACTORIAL 2))
(FACTORIAL 2)                        ;Expression printed, LISP waits for N.
  2                                  ;Argument is a number—number is printed.
  (COND ((ZEROP N) 1) (T (* N (FACTORIAL (- N 1)))))
    (ZEROP N)                        ;Next expression—user types N.
      N = 2                          ;Value of argument symbol is 2.
    NIL                              ;Value of expression is NIL.
    (* N (FACTORIAL (- N 1)))        ;Next expression—user types N.
      N = 2                          ;Value of argument symbol is 2.
      (FACTORIAL (- N 1))            ;Next expression—user types N.
        (- N 1)                      ;Next expression—user types N.
          N = 2                      ;Value of argument symbol is 2.
          1                          ;Argument is a number—number is printed.
        1                            ;Value of expression is 1.
        (COND ((ZEROP N) 1) (T (* N (FACTORIAL (- N 1)))))
          (ZEROP N)                  ;Next expression—user types N.
            N = 1
          NIL
          (* N (FACTORIAL (- N 1)))  ;Next expression—uscr types N.
            N = 1
            (FACTORIAL (- N 1))      ;Next expression—user types N.
              (- N 1)                ;Next expression—user types N.
                N = 1
                1
              0
              (COND ((ZEROP N) 1) (T (* N (FACTORIAL (- N 1)))))
                (ZEROP N)            ;Next expression—user types N.
                  N = 0
                T                    ;T stops recursion.
                1                    ;Recursion starts unwinding.
              1
            1
          1
        1
      2
    2
  2
```

---

[3] OUR-STEP is similar to STEP, a built-in COMMON LISP primitive. Note that different COMMON LISP implementations may have a slightly different STEP.

While wonderful for the patient, this example involves too much detail for the impatient. Consequently, OUR-STEP allows you to step along at the same level, rather than recursing into arguments, by typing a space instead of an N:

```
(OUR-STEP '(FACTORIAL 2))
(FACTORIAL 2)                        ;Expression printed, LISP waits for N.
  2                                  ;Argument is a number—number is printed.
  (COND ((ZEROP N) 1) (T (* N (FACTORIAL (- N 1)))))
    (ZEROP N)                        ;Next expression—user types N.
      N = 2                          ;Value of argument symbol is 2.
    NIL                              ;Value of expression is NIL.
    (* N (FACTORIAL (- N 1)))        ;Next expression—user types space, so
    2                                ;  the stepper no longer moves into
  2                                  ;  deeper evaluations.
2
```

Most versions of STEP allow users to start stepping when a procedure is encountered. Some allow the specification of conditional step options when working with trace.

LISP Systems Offer Many Debugging Features

OUR-BREAK, OUR-TRACE, and OUR-STEP only scratch the surface of what can be done with interactive debugging in LISP systems. Unfortunately debugging procedures tend to be implementation-specific and therefore inappropriate for detailed discussion here. We must be content with the following overview of procedures and features that are typically available:

- More general BREAK, TRACE, and STEP procedures.
- A way of terminating all ongoing computation. This is useful when a program appears to be running for an excessive amount of time.
- A way of entering a debugging mode, fixing something, and continuing in response to errors signaled by built-in LISP procedures.
- A way of interrupting an ongoing evaluation, entering a debugging mode, fixing something, and continuing.

Summary

- The blocks-world program illustrates some rules of good programming practice.
- It is often useful to stop procedures using BREAK.
- TRACE causes procedures to print their arguments and their values.
- STEP causes procedures to proceed one step at a time.
- LISP systems offer many debugging features.

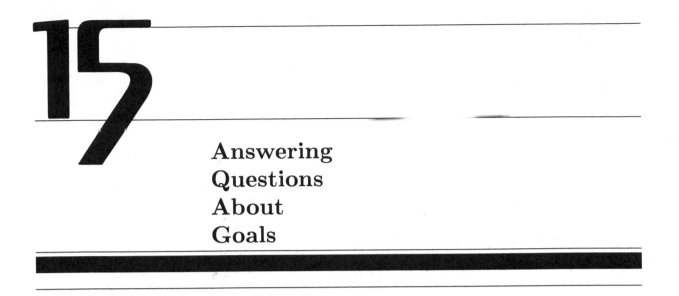

15

Answering
Questions
About
Goals

The plan produced by the blocks-world program is only a list of sequential instructions for a real or simulated hand. It does not offer any insight into how and why those instructions were given. If how and why questions are likely to come up, then it is useful for the program itself to have access to a tree structure showing how the program has moved from one procedure to another. Because the program is organized around procedures that each work toward an identifiable goal, it is easy for the program to answer many questions about its own behavior by looking into the tree structure and performing a sort of introspection.

The Blocks-World Program Can Introspect to a Degree

Figure 15-1 shows why some introspection is possible. It is another representation of the goal tree, similar to the one given back in figure 13-3. Each node represents an instance in which the named procedure was invoked. Most nodes branch out into other nodes that represent procedures called to help out.

Why questions are the first to think about. "Why did you put B on the table?" is correctly answered by finding a suitable instance of PUT-ON in the goal tree, looking up to the next higher node, and answering that the action was performed in order to get rid of B. The question, "Why did you do that?" then requires one more step up the tree, producing a remark

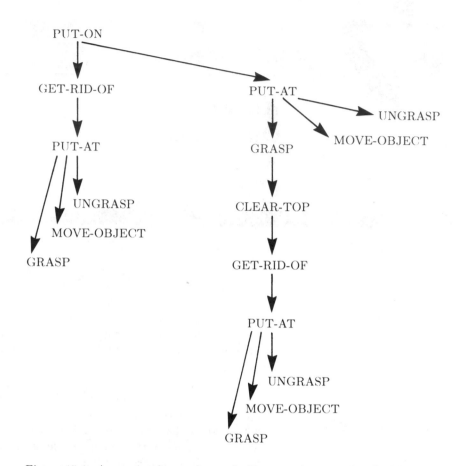

Figure 15-1. Answering how, why, and when questions requires building a goal tree. The goal tree shown here is one built by the blocks-world program. In general, moving one level down handles questions about how; one level up, why; and all the way to the top, when.

about clearing off **A**. Repeating the question eventually gets to an answer involving the need to put **A** on **C**, and repeating again leads to the universal, top-level response, "Because you told me to."

Questions about *how* go the other way. "How did you put **A** on **C**?" causes a response of, "I put it at space above **C** for **A**." Repeating causes recitation of the goals listed directly under the node that causes **A** to be put at space above **C** for **A**, namely, "First I grasped **A**; then I moved **A**; finally I let go of **A**."

Questions about *when* can be handled also. The trick is to trace up from the node asked about, all the way to the top of the tree to the node that represents the originating command. Thus "When did you grasp **B**?"

can be answered, "While I was putting A on C." If the question refers to a top-level node, then of course no upward tracing is possible, and it is necessary to nail down the time by reference to the next top-level command or the one done just before. "When did you put A on C?" might well be answered, "After I put B on A and before I picked up D." The following summarizes:

- *Why* questions are answered either by moving one step up the goal tree and describing the goal found there or by saying, "Because you told me to."

- *How* questions are answered by either enumerating the goals found one step down in the goal tree or by saying, "I just did it!"

- *When* questions are answered by either reference to a top-level goal or by reference to adjacent top-level goals in the recorded history.

Thus it is clear that a tree of procedure calls is a key element in answering how, why, and when questions related to accomplished actions. How can the blocks-world program construct such a tree? One way is to build some extra machinery into the procedures in the existing blocks-world program. So far all of the action is focused on creating the plan.

Remembering Procedure Calls Creates a Useful History

Each time a procedure is used, we want to record several associated things such as who called it, whom it calls, and the values of the arguments. One natural place to put such information is on the property list of some symbol. Consequently, we will arrange to create a new symbol each time a procedure is called. As illustrated in part in figure 15-2, created symbols and their property lists represent the history desired.

A call to PUT-AT, for example, does three things via calls to GRASP, MOVE-OBJECT, and UNGRASP. The node for a call to PUT-AT therefore has nodes representing calls to GRASP, MOVE-OBJECT, and UNGRASP on its property list under the property CHILDREN. In addition, the node for a call to PUT-AT will have a node representing PUT-ON on its property list under PARENT.

In complicated cases, the overall result is a deep structure in which each level corresponds to a layer of goals. The structure terminates at procedures that make no interesting calls to other procedures. The nodes representing calls to UNGRASP, for example, have no nodes listed under their CHILDREN property.

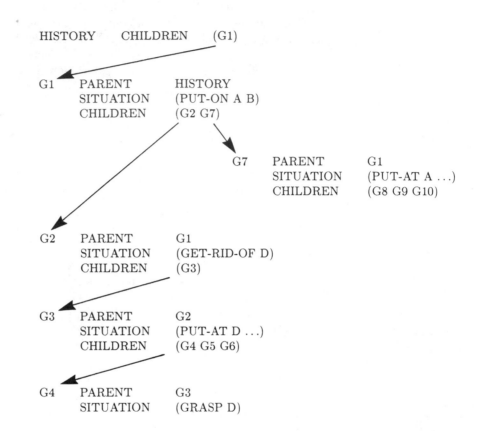

Figure 15-2. A goal tree can be stored by hanging appropriate properties and property values on symbols generated by GENSYM. This is a fragment of the same goal tree given before in a different form.

Now we must understand how the blocks-world program can be modified to generate such goal trees as it does its work. For illustration, we work with PUT-AT:

```
(DEFUN PUT-AT (OBJECT PLACE)
  (GRASP OBJECT)
  (MOVE-OBJECT OBJECT PLACE)
  (UNGRASP OBJECT))
```

Modifications will add two variables, PARENT and CHILD. By giving these variables appropriate values, it is easy to put the right things on the right property lists. ATTACH, helps take care of details:

```
(DEFUN ATTACH (C P)
  (SETF (GET C 'PARENT) P)              ;Attach parent to child.
  (SETF (GET P 'CHILDREN)               ;Attach child to parent.
      (APPEND (GET P 'CHILDREN) (LIST C))))
```

Using `ATTACH`, the necessary modification to `PUT-AT` involves only two new procedure calls:

```
(ATTACH CHILD PARENT)
```

```
(SETF (GET CHILD 'SITUATION)
    (LIST 'PUT-AT OBJECT PLACE))
```

There is no problem creating new symbols for each procedure call as desired. The procedure `GENSYM` can do that. The problem is to embed the `GENSYM` in a context where the appropriate things happen as one procedure calls another. For the situation in which `PUT-ON` calls `PUT-AT`, for example, we want the following:

- The symbol that was the value of `CHILD` inside `PUT-ON` becomes the value of `PARENT` inside `PUT-AT`.

- Inside `PUT-AT`, the value of `CHILD` becomes a new symbol generated by `GENSYM`.

These things are done conveniently by surrounding the body of `PUT-AT` by a `LET` expression that binds `PARENT` and `CHILD` to the correct values:

```
(DEFUN PUT-AT (OBJECT PLACE)
  (LET ((PARENT CHILD)
        (CHILD (GENSYM)))
    <manipulation of PARENT and CHILD>
    <previous body of PUT-AT>))
```

Importantly, the entry value of `CHILD` must be determined dynamically, rather than lexically. This is because the value desired is the value determined by the calling procedure, `PUT-ON`, not by the environment in force when `PUT-AT` is defined.

One way to arrange for `CHILD` to be a dynamic variable is to supply the following declaration, declaring `CHILD` to be a dynamic variable everywhere it is used:

```
(PROCLAIM '(SPECIAL CHILD))
```

Now remember how `LET` forms are evaluated. First the `LET`s parameter-assignment forms are evaluated, offering up the current value for `CHILD` and a new symbol via the call to `GENSYM`. Then the new value for the `LET` parameter `PARENT` becomes the value of `CHILD`, and the new value for the `LET` parameter `CHILD` becomes the value supplied by `GENSYM`. The value returned by `PUT-AT` is not changed by this maneuver because the value returned by the `LET` expression is the value returned by the last expression in the body of the LET, which is certainly the same as the last expression in the previous body of PUT-AT.

Putting all of this together, we have the following new, tree-building version of PUT-AT:

```
(DEFUN PUT-AT (OBJECT PLACE)
  (LET ((PARENT CHILD)
        (CHILD (GENSYM)))
    (ATTACH CHILD PARENT)
    (SETF (GET CHILD 'SITUATION)
          (LIST 'PUT-AT OBJECT PLACE))
    (GRASP OBJECT)                       ;Old body.
    (MOVE-OBJECT OBJECT PLACE)           ;Old body.
    (UNGRASP OBJECT)))                   ;Old body.
```

All other procedures that add nodes must have this modification done except PUT-ON. The modification to PUT-ON is slightly different because PUT-ON is the first procedure called, and hence it is the first to produce a value for CHILD. Consequently, there is no value for CHILD at the time PUT-ON is called. PARENT is bound to the symbol HISTORY instead:

```
(DEFUN PUT-ON (OBJECT SUPPORT)
  (LET ((PARENT 'HISTORY)
        (CHILD (GENSYM)))
    (ATTACH CHILD PARENT)
    (SETF (GET CHILD 'SITUATION)
          (LIST 'PUT-ON OBJECT SUPPORT))
    (PUT-AT OBJECT (GET-SPACE OBJECT SUPPORT))   ;Old body.
    (REVERSE PLAN)))                             ;Old body.
```

Problems

Problem 15-1:   Define TELL-HOW. It is to have one argument, a description of a procedure call. It is to look for the given description on the property lists of the nodes in the tree hanging from the node HISTORY. If the given description is found, it is to print descriptions of the nodes immediately below and return T. If the given description is not found, it returns NIL. Thus the following example describes TELL-HOW:

```
(TELL-HOW '(PUT-AT A (SPACE ABOVE C FOR A)))
  (GRASP A)
  (MOVE-OBJECT A (SPACE ABOVE C FOR A))
  (UNGRASP A)
  T
```

Assume that the properties PARENT, CHILDREN, and SITUATION are maintained as described before. It may help to adapt a search procedure described in chapter 11.

Problem 15-2: Define TELL-WHY. It also is to have one argument, again a description of a procedure call. If it finds the given description, it is to print the description of the node immediately above and return T. Otherwise it is to return NIL. Thus the following example describes TELL-WHY:

```
(TELL-WHY '(PUT-AT A (SPACE ABOVE C FOR A)))
  (PUT-ON A C)
  T
```

Problem 15-3: Define TELL-WHEN. It also is to have one argument, again a description of a procedure call. If it finds the given description, it is to print the description of the node above corresponding to the user command that led to the successful completion of the search and return T. Otherwise it is to return NIL.

Thus the following examples describe TELL-WHEN:

```
(TELL-WHEN '(PUT-AT A (SPACE ABOVE C FOR A)))
  (PUT-ON A C)
  T

(TELL-WHEN '(GRASP A))
  (PUT-ON A C)
  T
```

It Can Be Convenient To Define Procedure-Defining Procedures

It would be tiresome to modify all blocks-world procedures by hand because all of them need the same basic modification. The modification should be done by a new defining procedure instead. To accomplish this, we create DEFUN-WITH-HISTORY. When DEFUN-WITH-HISTORY is used instead of DEFUN, the definition supplied will be surrounded by the node-building machinery just developed. We assume that this creates a desired definition:

```
(DEFUN <procedure name> (<parameter 1> ...  <parameter n>)
  <procedure body>)
```

Now suppose DEFUN-WITH-HISTORY is substituted for DEFUN:

```
(DEFUN-WITH-HISTORY <procedure name> (<parameter 1> ...  <parameter n>)
  <procedure body>)
```

We then want DEFUN-WITH-HISTORY to behave as if we had this:

```
(DEFUN <procedure name> (<parameter 1> ...  <parameter n>)
  (LET ((PARENT CHILD)
        (CHILD (GENSYM)))
    (ATTACH CHILD PARENT)
    (SETF (GET CHILD 'SITUATION)
          (LIST '<procedure name> <parameter 1> ...  <parameter n>))
    <procedure body>))
```

Obviously, the way to build this desired structure is via a template-filling macro and backquote combination. Translating the desired structure into backquote form, we define the DEFUN-WITH-HISTORY macro this way:

```
(DEFMACRO DEFUN-WITH-HISTORY (NAME PARAMETERS &REST BODY)
  `(DEFUN ,NAME ,PARAMETERS
     (LET ((PARENT CHILD)
           (CHILD (GENSYM)))
       (ATTACH CHILD PARENT)
       (SETF (GET CHILD 'SITUATION)
             (LIST ',NAME ,@PARAMETERS))
       ,@BODY)))
```

Set up this way, consider the values for NAME, PARAMETERS, and BODY inside DEFUN-WITH-HISTORY given the following use:

```
(DEFUN-WITH-HISTORY PUT-AT (OBJECT PLACE)
  (GRASP OBJECT)
  (MOVE-OBJECT OBJECT PLACE)
  (UNGRASP OBJECT))
```

Clearly, the values are:

```
NAME
  PUT-AT
PARAMETERS
  (OBJECT PLACE)
BODY
  ((GRASP OBJECT)
   (MOVE-OBJECT OBJECT PLACE)
   (UNGRASP OBJECT))
```

Consequently, using DEFUN-WITH-HISTORY produces the following intermediate form, as desired:

```
(DEFUN PUT-AT (OBJECT PLACE)
  (LET ((PARENT CHILD)
        (CHILD (GENSYM)))
    (ATTACH CHILD PARENT)
    (SETF (GET CHILD 'SITUATION)
          (LIST 'PUT-AT (OBJECT PLACE)))
    (GRASP OBJECT)
    (MOVE-OBJECT OBJECT PLACE)
    (UNGRASP OBJECT)))
```

When evaluated, this gives us the desired definition for PUT-AT.

Problems

Problem 15-4:   It is usually better to use structures, rather than instances of GENSYM, to hold information. Create a suitable structure for nodes, together with structure-using versions of ATTACH and DEFUN-WITH-HISTORY.

Problem 15-5:   Create another version of DEFUN-WITH-HISTORY that does not use backquote. You will need to flail about a lot with CONS, LIST, and APPEND.

Problem 15-6:   Modify DEFUN-WITH-HISTORY such that it defines procedures that work equally well when entered with no value bound to CHILD. Assume that if CHILD has no value, the symbol HISTORY is to be used. You will need the procedure BOUNDP. When used, BOUNDP tests its argument to see whether it has a value. If it does, it returns T. Otherwise it returns NIL.

Problem 15-7:   Now we look at a different approach to seeing how procedures interact by defining a tracing procedure, TRACE1. It is to take one parameter, a procedure to be traced. A traced procedure will behave as described in the previous chapter. On entry it will print this:

```
(ENTERING <procedure name> <evaluated arguments>)
```

And on exit it will print this:

```
(EXITING <procedure name> <value returned>)
```

Each line is to be indented in proportion to the depth of the procedure calls that are traced.

This is a hard problem. The following suggestions therefore should be of great help:

• You may use INDENT-PRINT, a procedure to be defined in another problem, to print. Assume that INDENT-PRINT takes two arguments, the number of spaces to indent and the thing to be printed.

- You may use SYMBOL-FUNCTION, a built-in primitive, to recover definitions, in LAMBDA form, established using DEFUN.

Thus, in using SYMBOL-FUNCTION, we have the following:

```
(DEFUN FACTORIAL (N)
  (COND ((ZEROP N) 1)
        (T (* N (FACTORIAL (- N 1))))))
  FACTORIAL

(SYMBOL-FUNCTION 'FACTORIAL)
  (LAMBDA (N)
    (COND ((ZEROP N) 1)
          (T (* N (FACTORIAL (- N 1))))))
```

- Assume that TRACE1 is to copy the definition to the TRACED-PROCEDURE property. Further assume that it replaces the definition with the necessary procedure for printing the tracing information and for using the definition to be found under the TRACED-PROCEDURE property.

For FACTORIAL, the new value of the definition is to be as if the following had been executed:

```
(DEFUN FACTORIAL (N)
  (LET ((TRACE-RESULT)
        (TRACE-DEPTH (COND ((BOUNDP 'TRACE-DEPTH)
                            (+ TRACE-DEPTH 1))
                           (T 0))))
    (INDENT-PRINT TRACE-DEPTH (LIST 'ENTERING FACTORIAL N))
    (SETQ TRACE-RESULT (FUNCALL (GET FACTORIAL 'TRACED-PROCEDURE) N))
    (INDENT-PRINT TRACE-DEPTH (LIST 'EXITING FACTORIAL TRACE-RESULT))
    TRACE-RESULT))
```

Problem 15-8: Next, define UNTRACE1, a procedure that undoes the action of TRACE1.

Problem 15-9: Define INDENT-PRINT. It is to take two arguments, a number and something to be printed. The number determines how far to indent before printing.

Problem 15-10: Once TRACE1 is defined, it is relatively easy to write OUR-TRACE and OUR-UNTRACE. Do so. OUR-TRACE and OUR-UNTRACE are to get as arguments the procedures to be traced and untraced. If OUR-TRACE has no arguments, it prints the names of all traced procedures. If OUR-UNTRACE has no arguments, it untraces all traced procedures. OUR-TRACE is to return a list of those procedures supplied as its arguments that are not already traced. OUR-UNTRACE is to return a list of those procedures supplied as its arguments that are traced. Assume that the symbol TRACED-PROCEDURES is a global free variable whose value is a list of procedures currently traced.

Summary

- The blocks-world program can introspect to a degree.
- Remembering procedure calls creates a useful history.
- It can be convenient to define procedure-defining procedures.

References

For a general introduction to goal trees and their role in problem solving, see *Artificial Intelligence (Second Edition)* by Patrick H. Winston [1984].

16

Object-Centered Programming
Message Passing And Flavors

For many procedures, what happens depends on the classes of the particular things involved. Addition and multiplication, for example, are defined differently for numbers, complex numbers, matrices, and many other mathematical entities. Similarly, and perhaps more familiarly, the things a person does to greet someone or to buy someone a present depend on whether the other person involved is a relative, an ordinary friend, a romantic friend, or a robot.

Procedures and Object Classes Form a Table

Still another example, easy to develop in the blocks-world context, concerns putting blocks away. Assume that there are three different ways to put a block away depending on whether the block is a brick, a pyramid, or a ball. Keeping track of three special-purpose procedures is a chore, however. It is more convenient to have a general put-away procedure that defers to three specific procedures.

Assume that PUT-AWAY is the general-purpose procedure, and further assume that PUT-AWAY-BRICK is useful for putting away bricks, PUT-AWAY-PYRAMID is useful for pyramids, and PUT-AWAY-BALL is useful for balls.

Thus PUT-AWAY is to take some block and a box-specifying argument. If BLOCK-4 is a brick, evaluating (PUT-AWAY 'BLOCK-4 'RED-BOX) should arrange for (PUT-AWAY-BRICK 'BLOCK-4 'RED-BOX) to be evaluated.

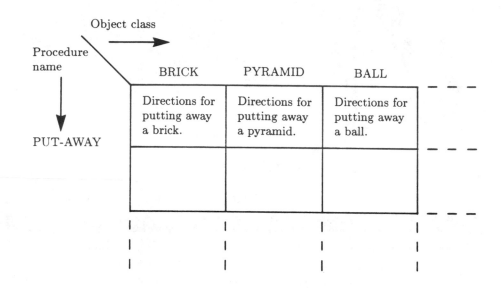

Figure 16-1. A table of procedures and object classes. In some circumstances it is better to record the table vertically, associating procedure information with the object classes, rather than horizontally, putting object class information into procedures.

Conceptually PUT-AWAY and its possible argument classes form part of a table as shown in figure 16-1. The embodiment of the table can be done in many ways. The simplest, and perhaps the worst, is to ask the programmer to keep track of things, using PUT-AWAY-BRICK, PUT-AWAY-PYRAMID, and PUT-AWAY-BALL as appropriate. This approach is bad because the programmer must know the class of the argument in order to select the right specialized procedure. This is usually inconvenient and may be impossible.

Consequently, it is better to ask a general PUT-AWAY procedure to figure out which procedure to use:

```
(DEFUN PUT-AWAY (OBJECT BOX)
  (COND ((EQUAL 'BRICK (GET OBJECT 'IS-A))      ;Class determines action.
         (PUT-AWAY-BRICK OBJECT BOX))
        ((EQUAL 'PYRAMID (GET OBJECT 'IS-A))
         (PUT-AWAY-PYRAMID OBJECT BOX))
        ((EQUAL 'BALL (GET OBJECT 'IS-A))
         (PUT-AWAY-BALL OBJECT BOX))))
```

Evidently, the particular special-purpose procedure selected depends on the result of examining the object's IS-A property.

**Objects May Supply
Their Own Procedures**

Another approach considerably changes the way the general procedure is connected to the special-purpose ones. The special-purpose procedure names are not reached by checking object classes in a COND clause. Instead, the special-purpose procedure names are accessed through the property lists of the class names. We give the symbol BRICK a PUT-AWAY property whose value is PUT-AWAY-BRICK. The general PUT-AWAY procedure therefore can decide that some object, say BLOCK-4, should be put away using PUT-AWAY-BRICK through the following steps:

- Object BLOCK-4 has an IS-A property.

- The value of the IS-A property is BRICK.

- BRICK has a PUT-AWAY property.

- The value of BRICK's PUT-AWAY property is PUT-AWAY-BRICK.

**FUNCALL and
APPLY Enable
Procedure Names or
Descriptions To Be
Computed**

Recall that FUNCALL uses its first argument to compute a procedure name or lambda expression and then applies the result to the other arguments. Similarly APPLY uses its first argument to compute a procedure name or lambda expression and then applies the result to a single argument, which contains a list of arguments for the procedure. Thus the following are equivalent:

```
(PUT-AWAY-BRICK 'BLOCK-4 'RED-BOX)

(FUNCALL 'PUT-AWAY-BRICK 'BLOCK-4 'RED-BOX)

(APPLY 'PUT-AWAY-BRICK (LIST 'BLOCK-4 'RED-BOX))
```

Conveniently, the FUNCALL and APPLY forms also allow alternatives like the following:

```
(FUNCALL (GET 'BRICK 'PUT-AWAY) 'BLOCK-4 'RED-BOX)

(FUNCALL (GET (GET 'BLOCK-4 'IS-A) 'PUT-AWAY) 'BLOCK-4 'RED-BOX)
```

Thus PUT-AWAY can be defined as follows:

```
(DEFUN PUT-AWAY (OBJECT BOX)
  (FUNCALL (GET (GET OBJECT 'IS-A)    ;Get class from object.
                'PUT-AWAY)            ;Get procedure from class.
           OBJECT
           BOX))
```

Importantly, the general idea works as well if lambda expressions are placed in the PUT-AWAY property slots instead of procedure names. There is no need to have procedure names for the special-purpose procedures unless they are referenced more than once and storage efficiency is important. Thus we need not necessarily do things this way:

```
(DEFUN PUT-AWAY-BRICK (OBJECT BOX) ...)

(DEFUN PUT-AWAY-PYRAMID (OBJECT BOX) ...)

(DEFUN PUT-AWAY-BALL (OBJECT BOX) ...)

(SETF (GET 'BRICK 'PUT-AWAY) 'PUT-AWAY-BRICK)

(SETF (GET 'PYRAMID 'PUT-AWAY) 'PUT-AWAY-PYRAMID)

(SETF (GET 'BALL 'PUT-AWAY) 'PUT-AWAY-BALL)
```

Instead, we can do things this way:

```
(SETF (GET 'BRICK 'PUT-AWAY)
      #'(LAMBDA (OBJECT BOX) ...))

(SETF (GET 'PYRAMID 'PUT-AWAY)
      #'(LAMBDA (OBJECT BOX) ...))

(SETF (GET 'BALL 'PUT-AWAY)
      #'(LAMBDA (OBJECT BOX) ...))
```

Using one approach, the procedure body is right there under the PUT-AWAY property. In the other, it is found one step removed through an intervening procedure name.[1]

One speaks of the general procedure *dispatching* to a special-purpose procedure name or lambda description on the basis of the object class observed. Conceptually this happens as if there were a table with general things to do on one axis, argument classes on the other, and special-purpose procedures in the cells. This abstract table is called a *dispatch table* when it is used to access object-dependent procedures through IS-A properties.

---

[1]   Although it is legal to store lambda expressions rather than procedure names on objects, there may be no convenient way to get those lambda expressions compiled, forcing interpretive use.

**Object-Centered
Programming Is
Becoming Popular**

Note that there are two major alternatives: we can record the procedure-object table horizontally, by stuffing class information into general-purpose procedures, or we can record it vertically, by stuffing procedural information into the class' property lists. Some people like to refer to traditional horizontal recording as *action centered* and to vertical recording as *object centered*.

Keeping the information in the body of general-purpose procedures requires procedure surgery whenever additions are to be made. Keeping it on property lists requires additions to the data base instead. Which is better depends on details of circumstance. Both techniques are in the tool bags of expert programmers.

The object-centered style of programming has been promoted through a number of successful procedures using it. Usually, however, object-centered programming is taken a bit further, to become message-centered programming, or two steps further, to become flavor-centered programming. We deal with these in the following sections.

Problems

Problem 16-1: Suppose that particular geometric objects such as circles and squares are represented as LISP symbols with appropriate property lists. For example:

Symbol	Property	Value
C	IS-A	CIRCLE
	RADIUS	3
S	IS-A	SQUARE
	LENGTH	1

Define two object-centered procedures, AREA and PERIMETER, that compute the area and perimeter of an object. They are to do their job by finding and using an appropriate lambda description on the property list of the class of the object involved. Place lambda descriptions on the property lists of CIRCLE and SQUARE under the properties AREA and PERIMETER so that AREA and PERIMETER will work on the examples given.

Problem 16-2:   In calculus, differentiation is defined in the following way for constants, sums, differences, products, quotients, and powers:

$$\frac{d}{dx}c = 0$$

$$\frac{d}{dx}x = 1$$

$$\frac{d}{dx}(u + v) = \frac{d}{dx}u + \frac{d}{dx}v$$

$$\frac{d}{dx}(u - v) = \frac{d}{dx}u - \frac{d}{dx}v$$

$$\frac{d}{dx}uv = u\frac{d}{dx}v + v\frac{d}{dx}u$$

$$\frac{d}{dx}\frac{u}{v} = \frac{d}{dx}uv^{-1}$$

$$\frac{d}{dx}u^n = nu^{n-1}\frac{d}{dx}u.$$

DIFFERENTIATE, below, is a LISP procedure that captures these formulas and makes it possible to differentiate expressions that are given in LISP prefix notation. The arguments of DIFFERENTIATE are E, an expression to be differentiated, and X, a variable to differentiate with respect to.

Note that OPERATOR, ARG1, and ARG2 are equivalent to CAR, CADR, and CADDR. They are used only to make the procedure somewhat clearer. Note also that DIFFERENTIATE expects all the arithmetic procedures it sees to have exactly two arguments:

```
(DEFUN DIFFERENTIATE (E X)
  (COND ((ATOM E) (COND ((EQUAL E X) 1)          ;Expression is x.
                        (T 0)))                  ;Expression is constant.
        ((OR (EQUAL (OPERATOR E) '+)
             (EQUAL (OPERATOR E) '-))
         `(,(OPERATOR E) ,(DIFFERENTIATE (ARG1 E) X)
                         ,(DIFFERENTIATE (ARG2 E) X)))
        ((EQUAL (OPERATOR E) '*)
         `(+ (* ,(ARG1 E) ,(DIFFERENTIATE (ARG2 E) X))
             (* ,(ARG2 E) ,(DIFFERENTIATE (ARG1 E) X))))
        ((EQUAL (OPERATOR E) '/)
         (DIFFERENTIATE `(* ,(ARG1 E) (EXPT ,(ARG2 E) -1)) X))
        ((EQUAL (OPERATOR E) 'EXPT)
         `(* ,(ARG2 E) (* (EXPT ,(ARG1 E) ,(- (ARG2 E) 1))
                          ,(DIFFERENTIATE (ARG1 E) X))))))
```

Write an object-centered version of DIFFERENTIATE that does its job by finding the appropriate lambda expression on the property lists of the operators +, -, *, /, and EXPT. Assume that the expressions are under the property DIFFERENTIATE. Write the required lambda-defined procedures for + and *.

Project 16-1: Write a program that simplifies expressions. Try your program on the incredibly bloated expressions produced by DIFFERENTIATE.

Messages Facilitate Object-Centered Programming

So far, we have a way of storing object-specific procedures such that those procedures can be retrieved when something general is to be done to something specific. In the example, the general PUT-AWAY procedure retrieves an object's specific procedure from the property list of the object's class:

```
(DEFUN PUT-AWAY (OBJECT BOX)
  (APPLY (GET (GET OBJECT 'IS-A) 'PUT-AWAY)
         (LIST OBJECT BOX)))
```

In this section, a series of changes and elaborations brings us from here to the notion of *message passing* as a programming paradigm.[2] So far, we can only write expressions like the following, whether or not the programming is action centered or object centered:

```
(PUT-AWAY 'BLOCK-4 'RED-BOX)
```

Soon, we will write something like the following instead, meaning "Send a message to the object named BLOCK-4, telling it to find a way to put itself into the box named RED-BOX:"

```
(SEND-MESSAGE 'BLOCK-4 'PUT-AWAY 'RED-BOX)
```

In this example, think of BLOCK-4 as the target of the message (PUT-AWAY RED-BOX).

SEND-MESSAGE uses the target to find the proper version of the procedure specified by the first element in the message:

```
(DEFUN SEND-MESSAGE (TARGET METHOD &REST ARGUMENTS)
  (APPLY (GET (GET TARGET 'IS-A) METHOD)
         (CONS TARGET ARGUMENTS)))
```

Assuming that BLOCK-4 is a brick and PUT-AWAY-BRICK is the value of BRICK's PUT-AWAY property, then the following are equivalent:

```
(PUT-AWAY-BRICK 'BLOCK-4 'RED-BOX)
```

```
(SEND-MESSAGE 'BLOCK-4 'PUT-AWAY 'RED-BOX)
```

Here is why: SEND-MESSAGE uses GET to discover that BLOCK-4 is a brick; another GET fetches PUT-AWAY-BRICK, which is the value of the PUT-AWAY property of BRICK. Then APPLY uses PUT-AWAY-BRICK on a list of arguments consisting of BLOCK-4 and RED-BOX.

---

[2] COMMON LISP does not yet offer a standard message-passing package.

Figure 16-2 summarizes what happens. Now note the following:

- A *method* is a procedure that is attached to an object and that is executed in response to an appropriate message.

Thus PUT-AWAY-BRICK is a method, attached to BRICK, relevant to dealing with PUT-AWAY messages sent to bricks.

Of course, making IS-A connections explicitly for all the blocks would be a pain. It is nicer to do it with a macro:

```
(DEFMACRO MAKE (OBJECT CLASS)
  `(SETF (GET ',OBJECT 'IS-A) ',CLASS))
```

Now we can make new instances of various classes at will:

```
(MAKE CUBE-5 BRICK)
```

```
(MAKE PYRAMID-8 PYRAMID)
```

```
(MAKE BALL-2 BALL)
```

Each of these blocks now has an IS-A property such that SEND-MESSAGE will find the right method in the right place.

Flavors Enable Procedures To Be Constructed from Inherited Parts

Now it is time to generalize our message-passing mechanism, turning it into a simple *flavor* system.[3] Here are the key ideas:

- Some procedures are so general, they work for a broad class of objects, rather than just a specific class.

Consequently, the method-fetching process should work by looking at the methods attached not only to a specific class, such as BRICK, but also to the more general classes reachable from the specific class via one or more METHOD-SOURCE properties, such as BLOCK. For example, the following method for keeping track of each box's contents will work for all blocks:

```
(DEFUN PUT-AWAY-AUX (OBJECT BOX)
  (SETF (GET BOX 'CONTENTS)
        (CONS OBJECT (GET BOX 'CONTENTS))))
```

Rather than somehow attaching PUT-AWAY-AUX to BRICK, PYRAMID, and BALL individually, it makes sense to attach PUT-AWAY-AUX to BLOCK instead.

---

[3] COMMON LISP does not yet offer a standard flavors package.

1. Superprocedure uses SEND-MESSAGE with an argument of BLOCK-4.

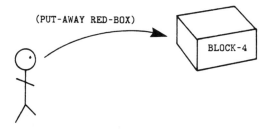

(PUT-AWAY RED-BOX)

BLOCK-4

2. SEND-MESSAGE finds BRICK on BLOCK-4's property list.

Symbol	Property	Value
BLOCK-4	A-KIND-OF	BRICK

3. SEND-MESSAGE finds PUT-AWAY-BRICK on BRICK's property list.

Symbol	Property	Value
BRICK	PUT-AWAY	PUT-AWAY-BRICK

4. PUT-AWAY-BRICK puts BLOCK-4 away in RED-BOX.

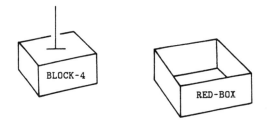

BLOCK-4

RED-BOX

Figure 16-2. The sequence of events involved in responding to a particular message.

- Some procedures can be broken into pieces: the preamble or *before* part, the *primary* part, and the epilogue or *after* part. Sometimes the primary part is object specific and the other parts, if any, are general. Sometimes it is the other way around.

Thus the method-fetching process should assemble procedures from before, primary, and after parts, all of which may be found anywhere in the set of symbols that is reachable by following METHOD-SOURCE properties.

For example, PUT-AWAY-AUX is a good object-general method to use after a block of any sort has been put away by an object-specific put-away method.

- Each method-bearing thing in an hierarchy of METHOD-SOURCE properties is called a *flavor*. Flavor systems mix together and execute various method parts found in various flavors in the hierarchy.

Suppose that CUBE-5 is a kind of cube and that a cube is a kind of brick. Consider the following message:

```
(SEND-MESSAGE 'CUBE-5 'PUT-AWAY 'BLUE-BOX)
```

Here is the appropriate response:

- The SEND-MESSAGE procedure looks for BEFORE methods attached to cube, brick, and block. There are none, so nothing is done. If there were some, all would be executed, starting with the one attached to the most specific object class.

- The SEND-MESSAGE procedure looks for PRIMARY methods. By convention, it uses only the first one it finds. There is no primary PUT-AWAY method attached to CUBE. Consequently SEND-MESSAGE uses PUT-AWAY-BRICK, the primary method attached to BRICK.

- The SEND-MESSAGE procedure looks for AFTER methods. There is only one, PUT-AWAY-AUX, attached to BLOCK as an AFTER method for PUT-AWAY. Consequently, SEND-MESSAGE just uses PUT-AWAY-AUX. If there were more, all would be executed, starting with the one attached to the most general object class.

- Finally, the SEND-MESSAGE procedure returns the value established by the single primary method used. This becomes the response to the message sent by SEND-MESSAGE.

All this is easy to arrange, given FETCH-METHODS, a procedure that crawls through METHOD-SOURCE properties, looking for the before, primary, and after parts of prescribed methods:

```
(FETCH-METHODS <object name>
               <method-name>
               <before, primary, or after indicator>)
```

Thus a new generalized version of SEND-MESSAGE looks like this:

```
(DEFUN SEND-MESSAGE (TARGET METHOD-NAME &REST ARGUMENTS)
  (PROG2 (DO ((BEFORES (FETCH-METHODS TARGET METHOD-NAME 'BEFORE)
                       (CDR BEFORES)))
             ((NULL BEFORES))
           (APPLY (CAR BEFORES) (CONS TARGET ARGUMENTS)))
         (APPLY (CAR (FETCH-METHODS TARGET METHOD-NAME 'PRIMARY))
                (CONS TARGET ARGUMENTS))
         (DO ((AFTERS (REVERSE (FETCH-METHODS TARGET
                                              METHOD-NAME
                                              'AFTER))
                      (CDR AFTERS)))
             ((NULL AFTERS))
           (APPLY (CAR AFTERS) (CONS TARGET ARGUMENTS)))))
```

The first DO handles all the BEFORE methods, fetched by using FETCH-METHODS. The second DO handles the AFTER methods. The intervening naked APPLY executes a single primary method, and the value returned by that APPLY is the value SEND-MESSAGE returns by virtue of the PROG2, which is like PROG1 and PROGN, except that PROG2 returns the value of its second form.

FETCH-METHODS gets the list of methods by crawling through the METHOD-SOURCE hierarchy, fetching methods. For the sake of illustration, let us assume that the methods are stored on association lists like these:

```
( ...  (PRIMARY PUT-AWAY-BRICK) ...  )

( ...  (AFTER PUT-AWAY-AUX) ...  )
```

Let us further assume that these association lists are attached to objects by method-indicating property names:

```
(SETF (GET BRICK 'PUT-AWAY)
      ( ...  (PRIMARY PUT-AWAY-BRICK) ...  ))

(SETF (GET BLOCK 'PUT-AWAY)
      ( ...  (AFTER PUT-AWAY-AUX) ...  ))
```

Plainly, we can use a combination of GET, ASSOC, and CADR to dig up the appropriate method name. FETCH-METHODS does this, working with the value returned from FETCH-FLAVORS:

```
(DEFUN FETCH-METHODS (OBJECT METHOD-NAME METHOD-TYPE)
  (DO ((FLAVORS (FETCH-FLAVORS OBJECT) (CDR FLAVORS))
       (METHODS NIL))
      ((NULL FLAVORS) (REVERSE METHODS))
    (SETQ METHODS
          (APPEND (CDR (ASSOC METHOD-TYPE              ;Dig out methods.
                              (GET (CAR FLAVORS)
                                   METHOD-NAME)))
                  METHODS))))

(DEFUN FETCH-FLAVORS (OBJECT)
  (LET ((FLAVORS (GET OBJECT 'METHOD-SOURCE)))
    (COND ((NULL FLAVORS) (LIST OBJECT))              ;No more.
          ((ATOM FLAVORS) (CONS OBJECT                ;A single link.
                                (FETCH-FLAVORS FLAVORS)))
          (T (CONS OBJECT (APPLY 'APPEND              ;Multiple links.
                                 (MAPCAR 'FETCH-FLAVORS
                                         FLAVORS)))))))
```

Note that FETCH-FLAVORS is happy to work with METHOD-SOURCE properties that are lists as well as those that are symbols. Thus methods can be inherited from a tree of classes, not just a chain.

Problem 16-3: Create DEFMETHOD, a procedure that attaches methods to an object under a given method name and a given before, primary, or after indicator. The method itself is to have no name; it is to be installed as a LAMBDA expression:

```
(DEFMETHOD <object name>
           <BEFORE, PRIMARY, or AFTER>
           <method name>
           <parameters> <body>)
```

Summary

- Procedures and object classes form a table.

- Objects may supply their own procedures.

- FUNCALL and APPLY enable procedure names or descriptions to be computed.

- Object-centered programming is becoming popular.

- Messages facilitate object-centered programming.

- Flavors enable procedures to be constructed from inherited parts.

References   Cannon [1982], in a landmark, but unpublished paper, discusses flavors
and object-oriented programming, as later implemented on various LISP
Machines.

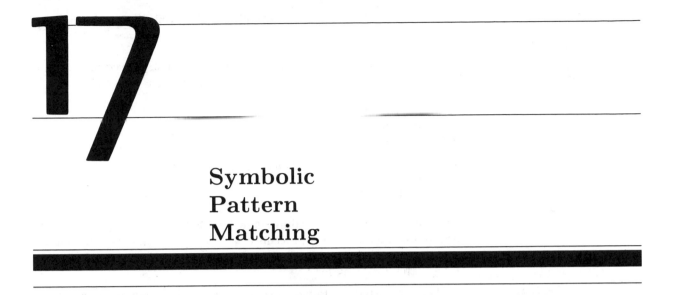

Symbolic Pattern Matching

Pattern matching is the process of comparing symbolic expressions to see if one is similar to another. The purpose of this chapter is to develop a pattern-matching procedure and to look at some examples. The pattern-matching procedure is a key element of a rule-based expert-system program to be developed in chapter 18. In action, that program does identification in the animal world.

Basic Pattern Matching Is Easy To Implement in LISP

Although LISP itself has no pattern matching built in, it is easy to write pattern-matching procedures in LISP. Hence, we say that LISP is a good implementation language for pattern matchers. Many of the matching sublanguages that have been embedded in LISP exhibit the sort of features developed here.

Matching Involves Comparison of Similar Expressions

Let us begin by thinking in terms of matching a pattern and a datum, both of which are lists. Often a datum will be used to represent an assertion about some real or supposed world. For the moment, each pattern and each datum will be restricted to be a list of atoms.

A pattern can contain certain special symbols not allowed in a datum. For example, the single character symbols `?` and `+`, are allowed:

```
(THIS IS A DATA LIST)        ;Data examples.
(COLOR APPLE RED)
(BOZO IS A CHEETAH)

(THIS + LIST)                ;Pattern examples.
(COLOR ? RED)
(BOZO IS A CHEETAH)
```

Soon we will develop a procedure named `MATCH` that will compare one pattern and one datum. This procedure will be used to illustrate matching-procedure implementation and use. First, however, let us see what basic things `MATCH` is to look for.

When a pattern containing no special symbols is compared to a datum, the two match only if they are exactly the same, with each corresponding position occupied by the same atom. If we match the pattern, (COLOR APPLE RED), against the identical datum, (COLOR APPLE RED), the match will of course succeed:

```
(MATCH '(COLOR APPLE RED) '(COLOR APPLE RED))
  T
```

But matching (COLOR APPLE RED) against (COLOR APPLE GREEN) fails:

```
(MATCH '(COLOR APPLE RED) '(COLOR APPLE GREEN))
  NIL
```

The special symbol `?` has the privilege of matching any atom. This greatly expands the usefulness of `MATCH`:

```
(MATCH '(COLOR APPLE ?) '(COLOR APPLE GREEN))
  T

(MATCH '(COLOR ? RED) '(COLOR APPLE RED))
  T
```

The `+` similarly expands the flexibility of `MATCH` by matching one or more atoms. A pattern with a `+` can match against a datum that has more atoms in it than the pattern:

```
(MATCH '(THIS + LIST) '(THIS IS A DATA LIST))
  T
```

Note that the matcher pays no attention to whether a datum is a fact in some real or imagined world. It tests only for form, ignoring meaning.

Now let us see how to implement MATCH. We adopt a strategy of moving down both the pattern and the datum, atom by atom, making sure that the pattern atom and the datum atom match in every position. Translated into LISP terms, we create a procedure that checks the first elements of two lists, and if satisfied, moves on by calling itself recursively on the CDR of the lists:

```
(DEFUN MATCH (P D)                         ;Initial preliminary version.
  (COND ((AND (NULL P) (NULL D)) T)        ;P and D both empty?
        ((OR (NULL P) (NULL D)) NIL)       ;One list shorter?
        ((EQUAL (CAR P) (CAR D))           ;First elements same?
          (MATCH (CDR P) (CDR D)))))        ;Recurse if so.
```

The first clause in the COND checks for whether the end of the lists is reached, thus terminating the recursion. The second clause checks for whether one of the two lists is shorter than the other.

Now because we want to proceed not only if the pattern atom and datum atom are the same, but also if the pattern atom is a ?, we generalize slightly:

```
(DEFUN MATCH (P D)                         ;Preliminary version.
  (COND ((AND (NULL P) (NULL D)) T)
        ((OR (NULL P) (NULL D)) NIL)
        ((OR (EQUAL (CAR P) '?)            ;First element is ?
             (EQUAL (CAR P) (CAR D)))
          (MATCH (CDR P) (CDR D)))))
```

Suppose we try some examples:

```
(MATCH '(COLOR ? RED) '(COLOR APPLE RED))
  T
```

We get a T as the ultimate result as indicated in figure 17-1. But consider this:

```
(MATCH '(COLOR ORANGE RED) '(COLOR APPLE RED))
  NIL
```

The result is NIL as shown in figure 17-2.

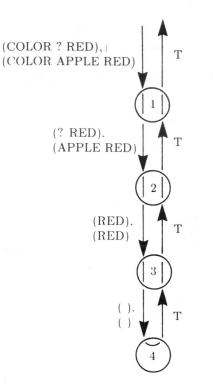

Figure 17-1. MATCH recurses as long as the first atom in the pattern is a ? or is the same as the first atom in the datum. On reaching the end of the pattern and the datum simultaneously, T is returned by the lowest level and passes up to the top.

Now to expand the power of the matching procedure, we incorporate a feature by which a + will match against one or more atoms:

```
(DEFUN MATCH (P D)                        ;Preliminary version.
  (COND ((AND (NULL P) (NULL D)) T)
        ((OR (NULL P) (NULL D)) NIL)
        ((OR (EQUAL (CAR P) '?)
             (EQUAL (CAR P) (CAR D)))
         (MATCH (CDR P) (CDR D)))
        ((EQUAL (CAR P) '+)               ;First element +?
         (OR (MATCH (CDR P) (CDR D))      ;Drop +.
             (MATCH P (CDR D)))))))       ;Keep +.
```

The COND clause testing for + initiates recursive calls to MATCH to see if one of two possibilities works out: the + matches one atom, in which case we chip off both the + and the atom it matches; or the + matches two or more atoms, in which case we work forward in the recursive spirit by retaining

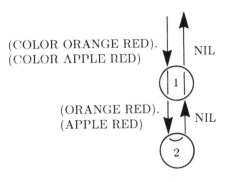

Figure 17-2. As soon as MATCH recurses to a pattern and datum that do not agree in the first position, NIL is returned by the lowest level and passes up to the top.

the + in the pattern while discarding the first of the atoms it matches before recursing.

A simulation helps to clarify how the recursion works under these circumstances. See figure 17-3.

Pattern Variables Add Expressive Power to Matching

The next dimension of improvement lies in generalizing MATCH so that certain pattern symbols are associated with values if match is successful. Pattern elements that are lists beginning with > and +, such as (> A) and (+ R), act as ? and + for matching purposes. The symbols seen in pattern elements with > and + are called *pattern variables*.

When MATCH succeeds, the pattern variables, if any, become associated with those parts of the datum that the pattern-variable elements match. The association is embodied in an association list of variable-value pairs returned by MATCH.

For example, if (EXPT (> A) (> B)) is matched to (EXPT 2 3), then the result is this list:

((A 2) (B 3))

Similarly, if ((+ L) MOTHER (+ R)) is matched to (SINCE MY MOTHER SPOKE), then the result will be this:

((L (SINCE MY)) (R (SPOKE)))

Thus the > variables come out associated with atoms while the + variables come out associated with lists. As before, MATCH is to return NIL if the match fails. MATCH is to return T if the match succeeds and the pattern contains no pattern variables.

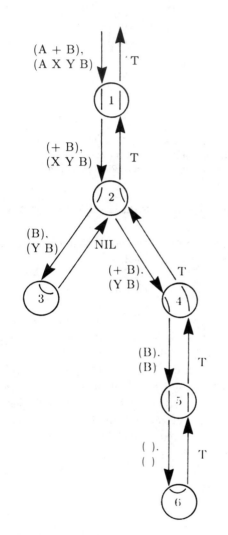

Figure 17-3. When a + appears in a pattern, it substitutes for one or more datum items.

Our generalized version of MATCH has a third argument, an association list of variable-value pairs. This association list is built by MATCH as it recursively chews its way down the pattern and the datum. The highest-level use of MATCH has the empty list as its third argument so there are no variable-value pairs yet:

```
(MATCH '(EXPT (> A) (> B)) '(EXPT 2 3) NIL)
  ((A 2) (B 3))

(MATCH '((+ L) MOTHER (+ R)) '(SINCE MY MOTHER SPOKE) NIL)
  ((L (SINCE MY)) (R (SPOKE)))
```

To generalize MATCH, we will use two access procedures, PATTERN-INDICATOR and PATTERN-VARIABLE. This enables us to add a clause to MATCH's COND in which PATTERN-INDICATOR digs the > or the + out of the pattern element for inspection.[1]

Given that the first element of a pattern is a list beginning with >, we add a variable-value pair to the association list argument in another, recursive use of MATCH using another new procedure, SHOVE-GR:

```
(DEFUN MATCH (P D ASSIGNMENTS)
  (COND
   ((AND (NULL P) (NULL D))
    (COND ((NULL ASSIGNMENTS) T)          ;If successful, return assignments,
          (T ASSIGNMENTS)))               ; if any.  Otherwise return T.
    .
    .
    .
   ((EQUAL (PATTERN-INDICATOR (CAR P)) '>)  ;Pattern item is a > variable?
    (MATCH (CDR P) (CDR D)                  ;Recurse with augmented a-list.
           (SHOVE-GR (PATTERN-VARIABLE (CAR P))
                     (CAR D)
                     ASSIGNMENTS)))
    .
    .
    .
   .))
```

---

[1] It would be syntactically nicer to use the symbol >A instead of the list, (> A). Instead of writing (MATCH '(EXPT (> A) (> B)) '(EXPT 2 3)), one would write (MATCH '(EXPT >A >B) '(EXPT 2 3)). However, the straightforward way to do this requires breaking up atoms into their characters constantly, a costly thing to do. The best alternative is offered by advanced LISP systems that permit characters to be declared to have certain special properties when moving from a file or a keyboard into active memory. Then it can be arranged that symbols beginning with the character > are converted into two-element lists beginning with >. The user sees only nice syntax, but internally, LISP exploits the ugly, efficient syntax.

Note the small change needed to ensure that the variable-value association list is returned when MATCH has successfully matched a pattern to a datum.

The auxiliary, data-abstracting SHOVE-GR program is easy to define:

```
(DEFUN SHOVE-GR (VARIABLE ITEM A-LIST)
  (APPEND A-LIST (LIST (LIST VARIABLE ITEM))))
```

Of course, PATTERN-INDICATOR and PATTERN-VARIABLE are also easy to define:

```
(DEFUN PATTERN-INDICATOR (L)
  (CAR L))

(DEFUN PATTERN-VARIABLE (L)
  (CADR L))
```

Just as it is useful to associate variables with values, it is often useful to get at those associations. In the following example, a symbol beginning with < demands that the datum element must correspond to the value of the pattern item, not the pattern item itself.

```
(MATCH '((> THIS) + (< THIS)) '(ABC IS THE SAME AS ABC) NIL)
  ((THIS ABC))

(MATCH '((> THIS) + (< THIS)) '(ABC IS THE SAME AS XYZ) NIL)
  NIL
```

With this addition, the > and < characters form a nicely mnemonic and complementary pair. One means *shove* a value into the variable after match; the other means *pull* a value out before match. Things are not always so mnemonic, however. Designers of matching languages are often quite baroque in their selection of syntax.

To implement < variables, we replace each < variable encountered by that variable's value, using MATCH on the result:

```
(DEFUN MATCH (P D ASSIGNMENTS)
  (COND .


        ((EQUAL (PATTERN-INDICATOR (CAR P)) '<)
         (MATCH (CONS (PULL-VALUE (PATTERN-VARIABLE (CAR P)) ASSIGNMENTS)
                      (CDR P))
                D
                ASSIGNMENTS))


    .))
```

The replacement employs PULL-VALUE to fetch the required value from the variable-value association list:

```
(DEFUN PULL-VALUE (VARIABLE A-LIST)
  (CADR (ASSOC VARIABLE A-LIST)))
```

All + variables are handled in the same spirit as the > variables, this time updating the association list using SHOVE-PL:

```
(DEFUN MATCH (P D ASSIGNMENTS)
  (COND .
        .
        .
        ((EQUAL (PATTERN-INDICATOR (CAR P)) '+)
         (LET ((NEW-ASSIGNMENTS (SHOVE-PL (PATTERN-VARIABLE (CAR P))
                                          (CAR D)
                                          ASSIGNMENTS)))
           (OR (MATCH (CDR P) (CDR D) NEW-ASSIGNMENTS)
               (MATCH P (CDR D) NEW-ASSIGNMENTS))))
        .
        .
        .))
```

Now consider this example:

```
(MATCH '(A (+ L) B) '(A X Y B) NIL)
  ((L (X Y)))
```

Figure 17-4 shows that (+ L) should match with X and Y, associating L with (X Y) in the process.

Note that SHOVE-PL is more complicated than SHOVE-GR. There must be a test in SHOVE-PL to see if the list of matching datum items already has been started by MATCH at a higher level:

```
(DEFUN SHOVE-PL (VARIABLE ITEM A-LIST)
  (COND ((NULL A-LIST) (LIST (LIST VARIABLE (LIST ITEM))))
        ((EQUAL VARIABLE (CAAR A-LIST))
         (CONS (LIST VARIABLE (APPEND (CADAR A-LIST) (LIST ITEM)))
               (CDR A-LIST)))
        (T (CONS (CAR A-LIST)
                 (SHOVE-PL VARIABLE ITEM (CDR A-LIST))))))
```

Restrictions Limit What a Pattern Variable Can Match

Another improvement may be made if we wish to specify that a position is to be filled by a member of some class of atoms. The class might be the numbers, or the atoms of a particular length, or the symbols with a particular property on their property list. We therefore introduce the restriction feature.

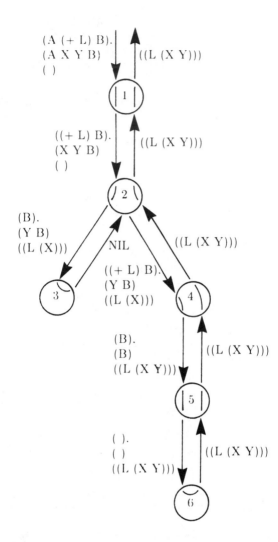

Figure 17-4. Variables prefaced by + substitute for one or more datum items. Successful matching leads to matching the + variables to the datum items they account for.

To use the restriction feature, a descriptive list is substituted into the pattern where previously only atoms were expected. The descriptive list has this form:

`(RESTRICT <either a ?  or a > variable> <predicate 1> ...  <predicate n>)`

The idea is that the corresponding position in the datum must be occupied by an atom that satisfies all of the predicates listed in the restriction. Thus we might define a predicate like COLORP or BAD-WORD-P.

```
(DEFUN COLORP (WORD) (MEMBER WORD '(RED WHITE BLUE)))

(DEFUN BAD-WORD-P (WORD) (MEMBER WORD '(SHUCKS DARN)))
```

Such predicates can be used in pattern restrictions to limit the class of acceptable symbols in the corresponding datum positions. In the following example, the restricted ? matches BLUE:

```
(MATCH '((+ L) (RESTRICT ? COLORP) (+ R))
       '(THE HOUSE IS BLUE AND WHITE)
     NIL)
  ((L (THE HOUSE IS)) (R (AND WHITE)))
```

Restrictions can be implemented for the ? as follows:

```
(DEFUN MATCH (P D ASSIGNMENTS)
  (COND .
        .
        .
        ((AND (EQUAL (PATTERN-INDICATOR (CAR P))
                     'RESTRICT)
              (EQUAL (RESTRICTION-INDICATOR (CAR P)) '?)
              (TEST (RESTRICTION-PREDICATES (CAR P)) (CAR D)))
         (MATCH (CDR P) (CDR D) ASSIGNMENTS))
        .
        .
        .))

(DEFUN RESTRICTION-INDICATOR (PATTERN-ITEM) (CADR PATTERN-ITEM))

(DEFUN RESTRICTION-PREDICATES (PATTERN-ITEM) (CDDR PATTERN-ITEM))
```

TEST is defined this way:

```
(DEFUN TEST (PREDICATES ARGUMENT)
  (COND ((NULL PREDICATES) T)                    ; All tests T?
        ((FUNCALL (CAR PREDICATES) ARGUMENT)     ; This test T?
         (TEST (CDR PREDICATES) ARGUMENT))
        (T NIL)))                                ; This test NIL?
```

Matchers Must Handle Many Cases

To summarize, a cumulative definition for MATCH follows. Note that although it is involved, it has nothing analogous to < to be used with + pattern variables, and it only handles one of four possible restrictions:

```
(DEFUN MATCH (P D ASSIGNMENTS)
  (COND ((AND (NULL P) (NULL D))                        ;Succeed.
         (COND ((NULL ASSIGNMENTS) T)
               (T ASSIGNMENTS)))
        ((OR (NULL P) (NULL D)) NIL)                    ;Fail.
        ((OR (EQUAL (CAR P) '?)                         ;Match ? pattern.
             (EQUAL (CAR P) (CAR D)))                   ;Identical elements.
         (MATCH (CDR P) (CDR D) ASSIGNMENTS))
        ((EQUAL (CAR P) '+)                             ;Match + pattern.
         (OR (MATCH (CDR P) (CDR D) ASSIGNMENTS)
             (MATCH P (CDR D) ASSIGNMENTS)))
        ((ATOM (CAR P)) NIL)                            ;Losing atom.
        ((EQUAL (PATTERN-INDICATOR (CAR P)) '>)         ;Match > variable.
         (MATCH (CDR P) (CDR D)
                (SHOVE-GR (PATTERN-VARIABLE (CAR P))
                          (CAR D)
                          ASSIGNMENTS)))
        ((EQUAL (PATTERN-INDICATOR (CAR P)) '<)         ;Substitute variable.
         (MATCH (CONS (PULL-VALUE (PATTERN-VARIABLE (CAR P)) ASSIGNMENTS)
                      (CDR P))
                D
                ASSIGNMENTS))
        ((EQUAL (PATTERN-INDICATOR (CAR P)) '+)         ;Match + variable.
         (LET ((NEW-ASSIGNMENTS (SHOVE-PL (PATTERN-VARIABLE (CAR P))
                                          (CAR D)
                                          ASSIGNMENTS)))
           (OR (MATCH (CDR P) (CDR D) NEW-ASSIGNMENTS)
               (MATCH P (CDR D) NEW-ASSIGNMENTS))))
        ((AND (EQUAL (PATTERN-INDICATOR (CAR P))        ;Match restriction.
                     'RESTRICT)
              (EQUAL (RESTRICTION-INDICATOR (CAR P)) '?)
              (TEST (RESTRICTION-PREDICATES (CAR P)) (CAR D)))
         (MATCH (CDR P) (CDR D) ASSIGNMENTS))))
```

Problems

Problem 17-1: Create a new kind of pattern variable, marked by <+, to work with + variables as the < variables work with > variables.

Problem 17-2: In many matching situations, it is desirable to use match values when matching is successful. In the following procedure fragment, for example, we want to use the match values of L and R following successful match.

```
(DEFUN TRANSLATE (E)
  (LET (A-LIST NIL)
    (COND ((SETQ A-LIST (MATCH '((+ L) IS (+ R)) E NIL))
                       .
                       '
                      .)
                       .
                       .
                      .)))
```

Evidently, TRANSLATE, arranges for matching, using MATCH, keeping the result as the value of A-LIST. To use the values, MATCH-VALUE is handy:

```
(DEFUN MATCH-VALUE (KEY A-LIST)
  (CADR (ASSOC KEY A-LIST)))
```

Write a procedure that converts Englishlike algebraic expressions into LISP-like prefix form. Use the following conversion example as a guide:

```
(THE NUMBER OF CUSTOMERS TOM GETS IS TWICE THE
     SQUARE OF THE NUMBER OF ADS HE RUNS)
```

↓

```
(= (THE NUMBER OF CUSTOMERS TOM GETS)
   (* 2
      (EXPT (THE NUMBER OF ADS HE RUNS)
            2)))
```

Your procedure will be similar to one in STUDENT, an early program that solved high-school algebra problems.

Problem 17-3: Many people do not like prefix notation for arithmetic expressions. They prefer infix notation, like this:

```
(A ^ B / (C * D) - E + F)
```

They dislike this:

```
(+ (- (/ (EXPT A B)
         (* C D))
      E)
   F)
```

Write INF-TO-PRE, a translation procedure that converts infix notation into prefix notation. Assume the precedence of operations is exponentiation, division, multiplication, subtraction, and then addition unless parentheses force something else. You will probably find that you need a restriction using the following procedure:

```
(DEFUN ONEPLUS (X)
  (EQUAL X '+))
```

Explain why.

Problem 17-4:   It is easy to write a simple version of a procedure that seems to interact with people at a terminal much like the way one type of psychiatrist interacts with people on the couch:

```
(DOCTOR)
  (SPEAK UP!)

(I AM WORRIED ABOUT THE WEATHER)
  (HOW LONG HAVE YOU BEEN WORRIED ABOUT THE WEATHER)

(SINCE MY MOTHER SPOKE)
  (TELL ME MORE ABOUT YOUR FAMILY)

(THEY ARE ALL INTO COMPUTERS THESE DAYS)
  (DO MACHINES FRIGHTEN YOU)

(NO)
  (PLEASE DO NOT BE SO SHORT WITH ME)

(GO TO HELL DARN IT)
  (PLEASE DO NOT USE WORDS LIKE THAT)

(YOU ARE FRUSTRATING ME)
  (EARLIER YOU SPOKE OF YOUR MOTHER)

(NOT NOW -- TELL ME ABOUT MY PROBLEM)
  (I AM SORRY OUR TIME IS UP)
  GOODBYE
```

Write DOCTOR as a loop through a COND that contains tests for key words and phrases, together with appropriate responses, as suggested in the sample dialogue.

Various versions of DOCTOR have been elaborated greatly. They typically have procedures that replace instances of MY with YOUR in the matched patterns, so that something like the following statement-response pair is possible:

```
(I AM WORRIED ABOUT MY HEALTH)
  (YOU SAY YOU ARE WORRIED ABOUT YOUR HEALTH)
```

It is important to note that the DOCTOR procedure has no real understanding of the user. It builds no model of the problems it seems to discuss, but depends instead on superficial key-word observations.

Many Matching Problems Remain

The matching described in this chapter is simple because no such thing as close match has been involved. Match either succeeds or fails. Dealing with matching in general can be much harder because the following possibilities arise:

- The matcher must deal with more general data structures. There is flexibility in how parts may correspond.
- The matcher is to report how the match scores on a scale ranging from not at all through poor and good all the way to perfect, perhaps giving a summary description of the match.

Summary

- Basic pattern matching is easy to implement in LISP.
- Matching involves comparison of similar expressions.
- Pattern variables add expressive power to matching.
- Restrictions limit what a pattern variable can match.
- Matchers must handle many cases.
- Many matching problems remain.

References

The STUDENT program was done by Bobrow [1962, 1964]. The DOCTOR program was done by Weizenbaum [1965].

18

Expert Problem Solving Using Rules And Streams

There are many problem-solving systems that are based on matching simple rules to given problems. They are often called rule-based expert systems, and sometimes they are called if-then systems or situation-action systems or production-rule systems. The purpose of this chapter is to summarize what rule-base expert systems are and to show how they can be implemented in LISP. Simultaneously, we introduce the concept of streams, a powerful programming idea that attracts much attention.

Our main example involves identification in the animal world. The key rule says that *if* an animal belongs to a certain species and *if* the animal has an offspring, then the offspring is of the same species.

Identification World Illustrates how Rule-based Systems Work

The following rules are typical of the things we learn as we become expert problem solvers:

- If an animal has pointed teeth, claws, and forward-pointing eyes, then it is a carnivore.

- If a tree is green in the winter, then it is a conifer.

- If an infection is a primary bacteremia, and it entered by way of the gastrointestinal tract, then there is evidence that the infecting organism is bacteroides.

- If an automobile engine will not start and fuel reaches the cylinders, then the ignition system is not working properly.
- If a silicon NPN transistor is on and the voltage at the base is V, then the voltage at the emitter is $(V - 0.6)$.

Evidently much expert knowledge can be represented as collections of rules, all of which have the following form:

```
IF      <antecedent assertion 1 is true>
        <antecedent assertion 2 is true>
          .
          .
          .

THEN    <consequent assertion 1 is true>
        <consequent assertion 2 is true>
          .
          .
          .
```

These rules are called *if-then* rules, *situation-action* rules, or *production* rules. Systems based on such rules do convincing medical diagnosis, understand electronic circuits, and even interpret the squiggles that come from instruments that people drop in oil wells.

Assertions and Rules Can Be Represented Easily

Let us agree that assertions are represented as lists of atoms. All of them are collected together in a list that is the value of ASSERTIONS. Here is how the value of ASSERTIONS could be initialized:

```
(SETQ ASSERTIONS
      '((BOZO IS A CHEETAH)
        (BOZO IS A PARENT OF SUGAR)
        (BOZO IS A PARENT OF BILLY)
        (SWEEKUMS IS A PENGUIN)
        (KING IS A PARENT OF REX)))
```

We need a procedure to get new assertions onto the assertions list. Let us call the procedure REMEMBER. Because REMEMBER works on a simple list, it is built around CONS and MEMBER. It returns the assertion if it manages to add it on and NIL if it is already there:

```
(DEFUN REMEMBER (NEW)
  (COND ((MEMBER NEW ASSERTIONS :TEST 'EQUAL) NIL)     ;If present, do nothing.
        (T (SETQ ASSERTIONS (CONS NEW ASSERTIONS))      ;If not, add.
           NEW)))                                        ;Return new assertion.
```

There are many ways to represent rules. The one illustrated below enables easy access to the rule parts. The symbols RULE, IF, and THEN are included only to make the representation more perspicuous.

```
(RULE <name>
    (IF <antecedent assertion 1>
        <antecedent assertion 2>
        ...
        <antecedent assertion n>)
    (THEN <consequent assertion 1>
          <consequent assertion 2>
          ...
          <consequent assertion n>)))
```

Problems

Problem 18-1:   Define RECALL, a procedure that finds all the assertions that match a given pattern. You must use MATCH from chapter 17.

Forward Chaining Means Working from Antecedents to Consequents

A problem solver is doing *forward chaining* if it starts with a collection of assertions and tries all available rules over and over, adding new assertions as it goes, until no rule applies.

The forward-chaining problem solver looks for rules that depend only on already known assertions. Here is a rule that says animals transmit their species to their offspring:

```
(RULE IDENTIFY16
    (IF ((> ANIMAL) IS A (> TYPE))
        ((< ANIMAL) IS A PARENT OF (> CHILD)))
    (THEN ((< CHILD) IS A (< TYPE))))
```

If it is known that an animal is a cheetah, a forward-chaining problem solver can conclude the animal's offspring are cheetahs too. Henceforward, the conclusion also is available for use and can help trigger other rules.

Our Forward-chaining Programs Use Streams

Pattern variables make it possible for a rule to match data in many ways. Keeping track of every possibility is a bit difficult. We need a powerful idea to help control the difficulty:

● A *stream* is a sequence of data objects.

The use of the stream idea is particularly common when talking about input/output operations: programs read information from streams connected to input files and write information to streams connected to output files.[1]

---

[1] COMMON LISP has special primitives to deal with input/output streams.

We will use the stream idea in a more general way, however. Sometimes programs are arranged like signal-processing systems: sequences of data objects flow through a series of procedures, just as electronic signals flow through a series of filters. In such situations, it is convenient to refer to the flowing data-object sequences as streams.

Here is a preview of how we use streams to build a rule-based expert system. We consider the use of a single rule with multiple antecedents:

- Match the first antecedent in the rule against each assertion in the data base. For each match, MATCH's initial association list is empty because there are no initial variable-value associations. Most matches will fail, but some may succeed. Each success produces an association list of variable-value associations. These association lists form an initial association list stream.

Let us have an example. Suppose the data base consists of these assertions:

```
(BOZO IS A CHEETAH)
(BOZO IS A PARENT OF SUGAR)
(BOZO IS A PARENT OF BILLY)
(SWEEKUMS IS A PENGUIN)
(KING IS A PARENT OF REX)
```

Suppose also that we are working with the parent-to-offspring rule:

```
(RULE IDENTIFY16
     (IF ((> ANIMAL) IS A (> TYPE))
         ((< ANIMAL) IS A PARENT OF (> CHILD)))
     (THEN ((< CHILD) IS A (< TYPE))))
```

Two assertions in the data base match ((> ANIMAL) IS A (> TYPE)), the first antecedent. One matching assertion is (BOZO IS A CHEETAH); the other matching assertion is (SWEEKUMS IS A PENGUIN). Together they determine the following stream of two association lists:

```
(((ANIMAL SWEEKUMS) (TYPE PENGUIN))
 ((ANIMAL BOZO) (TYPE CHEETAH)))
```

- Match the second antecedent in the rule against each assertion in the data base, but this time with an association list from the initial association list stream. Again, most matches will fail, but some may succeed. Consequently, some association lists from the initial stream may lead to one or more association lists in the second association-list stream. Other association lists from the initial association-list stream condemn the matcher to fail on all assertions and lead to nothing in the second association-list stream.

In our example, $((< \text{ANIMAL}) \text{ IS A PARENT OF } (> \text{CHILD}))$ is the second antecedent. Using the first association list in the input association-list stream, the pattern becomes (SWEEKUMS IS A PARENT OF (> CHILD)), which does not match anything in our data base, producing an empty output association-list stream. Using the second association list in the input stream, however, the pattern becomes (BOZO IS A PARENT OF (> CHILD)), which matches two items in the data base, producing an output stream with two elements. Combining the empty output stream with the two-element one, we have this:

```
(((ANIMAL BOZO) (TYPE CHEETAH) (CHILD BILLY))
 ((ANIMAL BOZO) (TYPE CHEETAH) (CHILD SUGAR)))
```

- Repeat for each antecedent.

For our example, there are only two antecedents, so we are already finished. Figure 18-1 illustrates what we have done.

Conceptually, it is best to think of filtering an association-list stream through a cascaded set of filters. The characteristics of each filter are jointly determined by one antecedent and by the existing data.

The sequence of association lists stretches and shrinks like a rubber band as it moves from filter to filter. For each way of matching the rule to the data, an association list emerges from the last filter. Each consequent must be processed for every such association list. Here is how:

- Replace all < variables in each consequent using an association list from the surviving association-list stream. Use these consequents to form an action stream.

In our example, there is only one consequent, $((< \text{CHILD}) \text{ IS A } (< \text{TYPE}))$. Using the first association list in the association-list stream, this becomes (BILLY IS A CHEETAH), which is placed in the data and into a single-element action stream.

- Repeat for each association list in the surviving association-list stream. Combine all of the resulting action streams.

The result, for our example, is two new assertions and a two-element action stream:

```
((BILLY IS A CHEETAH)
 (SUGAR IS A CHEETAH))
```

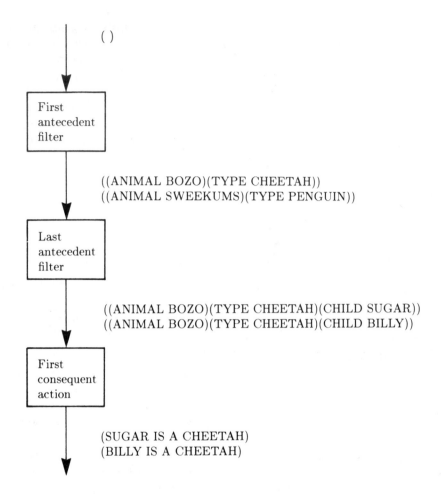

Figure 18-1. A diagram illustrating a particular example of rule use. The antecedents of a rule act as a set of cascaded filters. The input stream consists of one empty association list, which enters the first filter. The consequents of a rule act as a set of action boxes, in this case only one. The stream leaving the single action box consists of new assertions.

• If the action stream is not empty, report success.

Conceptually, it is best to think of splitting the association-list stream into multiple copies, passing a copy through each action box in parallel. The action sequences leaving the action boxes are combined to make a complete stream of all additions to the data. Figure 18-2 illustrates.

Input stream: a single empty-association list

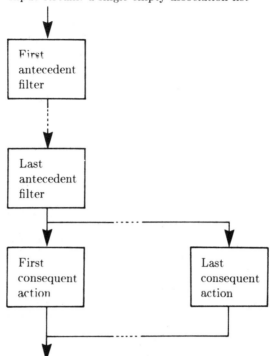

Output stream: a sequence of new assertions

Figure 18-2. A diagram illustrating rule use in general. The antecedents of a rule act as a set of cascaded filters. The input stream consists of one empty association list, which enters the first filter. The stream of association lists leaving the final filter embodies all possible ways the rule matches the data. The consequents of a rule act as a set of action boxes. The stream leaving the single action box consists of new assertions.

Constructors, Selectors, and Mutators Clarify Stream Use

For our purpose, it is adequate to represent streams as lists. Consequently, we could manipulate our streams using CAR, CDR, CONS, and APPEND. However, to make our programs clearer and easier to change, it is better to insulate ourselves from the details of stream representation by using some access procedures, making a new data type:

```
(DEFUN COMBINE-STREAMS (S1 S2) (APPEND S1 S2))

(DEFUN ADD-TO-STREAM (E S) (CONS E S))

(DEFUN FIRST-OF-STREAM (S) (CAR S))

(DEFUN REST-OF-STREAM (S) (CDR S))
```

```
(DEFUN EMPTY-STREAM-P (S) (NULL S))

(DEFUN MAKE-EMPTY-STREAM () NIL)
```

Some of these appear in `FILTER-ASSERTIONS`, one of the key procedures in our forward-chaining system. The first argument to `FILTER-ASSERTIONS` is a pattern taken from some rule's antecedents. The second is an initial association list taken from an association-list stream.[2]

```
(DEFUN FILTER-ASSERTIONS (PATTERN INITIAL-A-LIST)
  (DO ((ASSERTIONS ASSERTIONS (CDR ASSERTIONS))
       (A-LIST-STREAM (MAKE-EMPTY-STREAM)))
      ((NULL ASSERTIONS) A-LIST-STREAM)
    (LET ((NEW-A-LIST (MATCH PATTERN (CAR ASSERTIONS) INITIAL-A-LIST)))
      (COND (NEW-A-LIST (SETQ A-LIST-STREAM
                              (ADD-TO-STREAM NEW-A-LIST A-LIST-STREAM)))))))
```

Each call to `FILTER-ASSERTIONS` creates a new stream using `MAKE-EMPTY-STREAM`, to which it adds an association list for each way the pattern matches an assertion, given the initial association list supplied as an input. Recall that the association-list stream for the first filter consists of just one empty association list. Note the result when `FILTER-ASSERTIONS` has arguments of `((> ANIMAL) IS A (> TYPE))` and `NIL`:

```
(FILTER-ASSERTIONS '((> ANIMAL) IS A (> TYPE)) NIL)
  (((ANIMAL SWEEKUMS) (TYPE PENGUIN))
   ((ANIMAL BOZO) (TYPE CHEETAH)))
```

For subsequent filters, there may be many entering association lists or there may be few or none, depending on whether previously processed patterns match the data in many ways or in few or none. Obviously, for the second filter pattern in our example, `((< ANIMAL) IS A PARENT OF (> CHILD))`, there will be two association lists in the input stream. Here are the results for each:

```
(FILTER-ASSERTIONS '((< ANIMAL) IS A PARENT OF (> CHILD))
                   '((ANIMAL SWEEKUMS) (TYPE PENGUIN)))
  NIL

(FILTER-ASSERTIONS '((< ANIMAL) IS A PARENT OF (> CHILD))
                   '((ANIMAL BOZO) (TYPE CHEETAH)))
  (((ANIMAL BOZO) (TYPE CHEETAH) (CHILD BILLY))
   ((ANIMAL BOZO) (TYPE CHEETAH) (CHILD SUGAR)))
```

---

[2] We often use DO in this chapter because we are working with lists that may be too long to move through with recursion. Some implementations of LISP permit only a few hundred recursive procedure calls; with such an implementation, a recursive procedure would drop dead when trying to move through a list of a thousand assertions or a thousand rules.

Because each association list fed into `FILTER-ASSERTIONS` produces a stream of association lists, possibly empty, the results of the many applications must be combined. This is done by `FILTER-A-LIST-STREAM`:

```
(DEFUN FILTER-A-LIST-STREAM (PATTERN A-LIST-STREAM)
  (COND ((EMPTY-STREAM-P A-LIST-STREAM) (MAKE-EMPTY-STREAM))
        (T (COMBINE-STREAMS
             (FILTER-ASSERTIONS PATTERN (FIRST-OF-STREAM A-LIST-STREAM))
             (FILTER-A-LIST-STREAM PATTERN (REST-OF-STREAM A-LIST-STREAM)))))))
```

Thus `FILTER-A-LIST-STREAM` is the procedure in charge of feeding association lists to `FILTER-ASSERTIONS`. In its first use, `FILTER-A-LIST-STREAM` works with a stream consisting of one empty association list, feeding that association list to `FILTER-ASSERTIONS`:

```
(FILTER-A-LIST-STREAM '((> ANIMAL) IS A (> TYPE))
                      (ADD-TO-STREAM NIL (MAKE-EMPTY-STREAM)))
  (((ANIMAL SWEEKUMS) (TYPE PENGUIN)) ((ANIMAL BOZO) (TYPE CHEETAH)))
```

In its second use, `FILTER-A-LIST-STREAM` works with a stream of two association lists, feeding them both, in turn, to `FILTER-ASSERTIONS`, combining the results into a new stream:

```
(FILTER-A-LIST-STREAM '((< ANIMAL) IS A PARENT OF (> CHILD))
                      '(((ANIMAL SWEEKUMS) (TYPE PENGUIN))
                        ((ANIMAL BOZO) (TYPE CHEETAH))))
  (((ANIMAL BOZO) (TYPE CHEETAH) (CHILD BILLY))
   ((ANIMAL BOZO) (TYPE CHEETAH) (CHILD SUGAR)))
```

Next, we need a means of using `FILTER-A-LIST-STREAM` once for each antecedent, passing the output of one use to the input of the next. This is done by `CASCADE-THROUGH-PATTERNS`:

```
(DEFUN CASCADE-THROUGH-PATTERNS (PATTERNS A-LIST-STREAM)
  (COND ((NULL PATTERNS) A-LIST-STREAM)
        (T (FILTER-A-LIST-STREAM (CAR PATTERNS)
                                 (CASCADE-THROUGH-PATTERNS (CDR PATTERNS)
                                                           A-LIST-STREAM)))))
```

Here is an example of `CASCADE-THROUGH-PATTERNS` in action:

```
(CASCADE-THROUGH-PATTERNS '(((< ANIMAL) IS A PARENT OF (> CHILD))
                            ((> ANIMAL) IS A (> TYPE)))
                          (ADD-TO-STREAM NIL (MAKE-EMPTY-STREAM)))
  (((ANIMAL BOZO) (TYPE CHEETAH) (CHILD BILLY))
   ((ANIMAL BOZO) (TYPE CHEETAH) (CHILD SUGAR)))
```

The initial list of patterns is extracted from a rule by USE-RULE. Note that USE-RULE also supplies CASCADE-THROUGH-PATTERNS with an empty stream to be fed to the first filter:

```
(DEFUN USE-RULE (RULE)
  (LET* ((RULE-NAME (CADR RULE))
         (IFS (REVERSE (CDR (CADDR RULE))))
         (THENS (CDR (CADDDR RULE)))
         (A-LIST-STREAM (CASCADE-THROUGH-PATTERNS
                            IFS
                            (ADD-TO-STREAM NIL (MAKE-EMPTY-STREAM)))))
    .   . .)))
```

We now have a variable, A-LIST-STREAM, that contains an association list for each way a given rule's antecedents match the data. The hard part is over.

The easy part is using the association-list stream. First we need a procedure that takes a set of actions and an association list, replaces the pattern variables in the action with values, tries to add the resulting assertion to the data, and contributes to a new action stream if successful:

```
(DEFUN SPREAD-THROUGH-ACTIONS (RULE-NAME ACTIONS A-LIST)
  (DO ((ACTIONS ACTIONS (CDR ACTIONS))
       (ACTION-STREAM (MAKE-EMPTY-STREAM)))
      ((NULL ACTIONS) ACTION-STREAM)
    (LET ((ACTION (REPLACE-VARIABLES (CAR ACTIONS) A-LIST)))
      (COND ((REMEMBER ACTION)
             (PRINT `(RULE ,RULE-NAME SAYS ,@ACTION))
             (SETQ ACTION-STREAM (ADD-TO-STREAM ACTION ACTION-STREAM)))))))
```

Here is how SPREAD-THROUGH-ACTIONS handles the association list produced in our example:

```
(SPREAD-THROUGH-ACTIONS 'IDENTIFY16
                        '(((< CHILD) IS A (< TYPE)))
                        '((ANIMAL BOZO) (TYPE CHEETAH) (CHILD BILLY)))
(RULE IDENTIFY16 SAYS BILLY IS A CHEETAH)
  ((BILLY IS A CHEETAH))

(SPREAD-THROUGH-ACTIONS 'IDENTIFY16
                        '(((< CHILD) IS A (< TYPE)))
                        '((ANIMAL BOZO) (TYPE CHEETAH) (CHILD SUGAR)))
(RULE IDENTIFY16 SAYS SUGAR IS A CHEETAH)
  ((SUGAR IS A CHEETAH))
```

Replacing variable names with values is simple:

```
(DEFUN REPLACE-VARIABLES (S A-LIST)
  (COND ((ATOM S) S)
        ((EQUAL (CAR S) '<)
         (CADR (ASSOC (PATTERN-VARIABLE S) A-LIST)))
        (T (CONS (REPLACE-VARIABLES (CAR S) A-LIST)
                 (REPLACE-VARIABLES (CDR S) A-LIST)))))
```

`FEED-TO-ACTIONS` feeds the association-list stream, one association list at a time, to `SPREAD-THROUGH-ACTIONS`. Note that `FEED-TO-ACTIONS` also combines the resulting action streams into a single action stream:

```
(DEFUN FEED-TO-ACTIONS (RULE-NAME ACTIONS A-LIST-STREAM)
  (COND ((EMPTY-STREAM-P A-LIST-STREAM) (MAKE-EMPTY-STREAM))
        (T (COMBINE-STREAMS
            (SPREAD-THROUGH-ACTIONS RULE-NAME
                                    ACTIONS
                                    (FIRST-OF-STREAM A-LIST-STREAM))
            (FEED-TO-ACTIONS RULE-NAME
                             ACTIONS
                             (REST-OF-STREAM A-LIST-STREAM))))))
```

Here then is what `FEED-TO-ACTIONS` does:

```
(FEED-TO-ACTIONS 'IDENTIFY16
                 '(((< CHILD) IS A (< TYPE)))
                 '(((ANIMAL BOZO) (TYPE CHEETAH) (CHILD BILLY))
                   ((ANIMAL BOZO) (TYPE CHEETAH) (CHILD SUGAR))))
(RULE IDENTIFY16 SAYS BILLY IS A CHEETAH)
(RULE IDENTIFY16 SAYS SUGAR IS A CHEETAH)
  ((BILLY IS A CHEETAH) (SUGAR IS A CHEETAH))
```

`USE-RULE` calls `FEED-TO-ACTIONS`, handing over the previously computed association-list stream, taking back the completed action stream. The action stream will be empty and `USE-RULE` will return `NIL` if there are no ways to match the antecedents to the data or if there are some ways but those ways lead to no new assertions.

```
(DEFUN USE-RULE (RULE)
  (LET* ((RULE-NAME (CADR RULE))
         (IFS (REVERSE (CDR (CADDR RULE))))
         (THENS (CDR (CADDDR RULE)))
         (A-LIST-STREAM (CASCADE-THROUGH-PATTERNS
                         IFS
                         (ADD-TO-STREAM NIL (MAKE-EMPTY-STREAM))))
         (ACTION-STREAM (FEED-TO-ACTIONS RULE-NAME THENS A-LIST-STREAM))
    (NOT (EMPTY-STREAM-P ACTION-STREAM))))
```

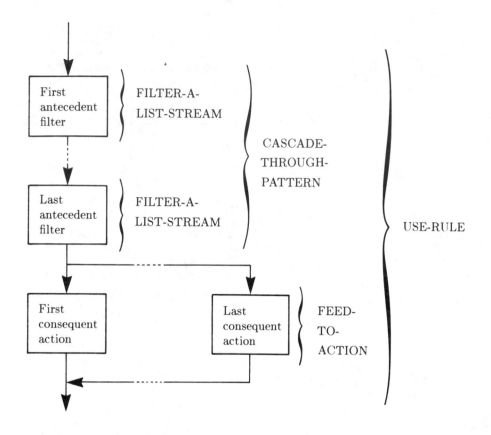

Figure 18-3. The stream-processing procedures involved in implementing a simple rule-based expert system.

So then, consider this:

```
(USE-RULE '(RULE IDENTIFY16
                (IF ((> ANIMAL) IS A (> TYPE))
                    ((< ANIMAL) IS A PARENT OF (> CHILD)))
                (THEN ((< CHILD) IS A (< TYPE)))))
(RULE IDENTIFY16 SAYS BILLY IS A CHEETAH)
(RULE IDENTIFY16 SAYS SUGAR IS A CHEETAH)
  T
```

Figure 18-3 illustrates the relationships between the procedures introduced so far and the steps involved in processing the pattern and action streams.

FORWARD-CHAIN steps through the rule list until it finds a rule that produces a new assertion, whereupon it starts over at the beginning of the rule list. FORWARD-CHAIN stops as soon as it fails to find a new assertion with any rule in the entire list:

```
(DEFUN FORWARD-CHAIN ()
  (DO ((RULES-TO-TRY RULES (CDR RULES-TO-TRY))
       (PROGRESS-MADE NIL))
      ((NULL RULES-TO-TRY) PROGRESS-MADE)
    (COND ((USE-RULE (CAR RULES-TO-TRY))
           (SETQ RULES-TO-TRY RULES)
           (SETQ PROGRESS-MADE T)))))
```

Finally, then, we have this when we start from the beginning, activating
everything with FORWARD-CHAIN, assuming a one-rule system consisting of
IDENTIFY16:

```
(FORWARD-CHAIN)
(RULE IDENTIFY16 SAYS BILLY IS A CHEETAH)
(RULE IDENTIFY16 SAYS SUGAR IS A CHEETAH)
  T
```

Simple Rules Help Identify Animals

If an animal eats meat, it is a carnivore. Alternatively, if it has pointed
teeth, claws, and forward-pointing eyes, it is a carnivore. This knowledge,
represented as if-then rules, looks like this:

```
(RULE IDENTIFY5
      (IF ((> ANIMAL) EATS MEAT))
      (THEN ((< ANIMAL) IS CARNIVORE)))
```

```
(RULE IDENTIFY6
      (IF ((> ANIMAL) HAS POINTED TEETH)
          ((< ANIMAL) HAS CLAWS)
          ((< ANIMAL) HAS FORWARD EYES))
      (THEN ((< ANIMAL) IS CARNIVORE)))
```

IDENTIFY5, IDENTIFY6, and IDENTIFY16 are all drawn from the following rule
list for identification in the animal world:

```
(RULE IDENTIFY1
      (IF ((> ANIMAL) HAS HAIR))
      (THEN ((< ANIMAL) IS MAMMAL)))
```

```
(RULE IDENTIFY2
      (IF ((> ANIMAL) GIVES MILK))
      (THEN ((< ANIMAL) IS MAMMAL)))
```

```
(RULE IDENTIFY3
      (IF ((> ANIMAL) HAS FEATHERS))
      (THEN ((< ANIMAL) IS BIRD)))
```

```
(RULE IDENTIFY4
    (IF ((> ANIMAL) FLIES)
        ((< ANIMAL) LAYS EGGS))
    (THEN ((< ANIMAL) IS BIRD)))

(RULE IDENTIFY5
    (IF ((> ANIMAL) EATS MEAT))
    (THEN ((< ANIMAL) IS CARNIVORE)))

(RULE IDENTIFY6
    (IF ((> ANIMAL) HAS POINTED TEETH)
        ((< ANIMAL) HAS CLAWS)
        ((< ANIMAL) HAS FORWARD EYES))
    (THEN ((< ANIMAL) IS CARNIVORE)))

(RULE IDENTIFY7
    (IF ((> ANIMAL) IS MAMMAL)
        ((< ANIMAL) HAS HOOFS))
    (THEN ((< ANIMAL) IS UNGULATE)))

(RULE IDENTIFY8
    (IF ((> ANIMAL) IS MAMMAL)
        ((< ANIMAL) CHEWS CUD))
    (THEN ((< ANIMAL) IS UNGULATE)
          ((< ANIMAL) IS EVEN TOED)))

(RULE IDENTIFY9
    (IF ((> ANIMAL) IS MAMMAL)
        ((< ANIMAL) IS CARNIVORE)
        ((< ANIMAL) HAS TAWNY COLOR)
        ((< ANIMAL) HAS DARK SPOTS))
    (THEN ((< ANIMAL) IS CHEETAH)))

(RULE IDENTIFY10
    (IF ((> ANIMAL) IS MAMMAL)
        ((< ANIMAL) IS CARNIVORE)
        ((< ANIMAL) HAS TAWNY COLOR)
        ((< ANIMAL) HAS BLACK STRIPES))
    (THEN ((< ANIMAL) IS TIGER)))

(RULE IDENTIFY11
    (IF ((> ANIMAL) IS UNGULATE)
        ((< ANIMAL) HAS LONG NECK)
        ((< ANIMAL) HAS LONG LEGS)
        ((< ANIMAL) HAS DARK SPOTS))
    (THEN ((< ANIMAL) IS GIRAFFE)))

(RULE IDENTIFY12
    (IF ((> ANIMAL) IS UNGULATE)
        ((< ANIMAL) HAS BLACK STRIPES))
    (THEN ((< ANIMAL) IS ZEBRA)))
```

```
(RULE IDENTIFY13
    (IF ((> ANIMAL) IS BIRD)
        ((< ANIMAL) DOES NOT FLY)
        ((< ANIMAL) HAS LONG NECK)
        ((< ANIMAL) HAS LONG LEGS)
        ((< ANIMAL) IS BLACK AND WHITE))
    (THEN ((< ANIMAL) IS OSTRICH)))

(RULE IDENTIFY14
    (IF ((> ANIMAL) IS BIRD)
        ((< ANIMAL) DOES NOT FLY)
        ((< ANIMAL) SWIMS)
        ((< ANIMAL) IS BLACK AND WHITE))
    (THEN ((< ANIMAL) IS PENGUIN)))

(RULE IDENTIFY15
    (IF ((> ANIMAL) IS BIRD)
        ((< ANIMAL) FLIES WELL))
    (THEN ((< ANIMAL) IS ALBATROSS)))

(RULE IDENTIFY16
    (IF ((> ANIMAL) IS A (> TYPE))
        ((< ANIMAL) IS A PARENT OF (> CHILD)))
    (THEN ((< CHILD) IS A (< TYPE))))
```

Problems

Problem 18-2:   Our system adds new elements to the front of streams, not the back. Change it so that the new stream elements go to the back, which is more in keeping with the idea of what a stream is. Note that this is easy because ADD-TO-STREAM has been defined as a mutator.

Problem 18-3:   Determine the action of the animal-identification rules on the following data:

```
(SETQ ASSERTIONS
    '((ROBBIE HAS DARK SPOTS)
      (ROBBIE HAS TAWNY COLOR)
      (ROBBIE EATS MEAT)
      (ROBBIE HAS HAIR)
      (SUZIE HAS FEATHERS)
      (SUZIE FLIES WELL)))
```

Problem 18-4:   Modify USE-RULE so that it maintains a list of rules successfully used, RULES-USED. Each element is to contain the name of the rule, the antecedents, and the conclusion. Then define USEDP, a predicate that answers the question "Have you used rule ...?"

Problem 18-5:   Define a procedure HOW that uses RULES-USED, as described in the previous problem, to answer questions such as "How did you deduce that ...?" HOW is to get an assertion as its argument, it is to print the assertions that allowed its deduction, and it is to return T. If the assertion was not deduced, but was given, HOW should say so. If neither, HOW should return NIL.

Problem 18-6: Define a procedure WHY, similar to HOW, to answer questions such as "Why did you need the assertion ...?" WHY is to get an assertion as its argument, print the assertions that depend on it, and return T. If the assertion was not used, WHY should say so and return NIL.

Project 18-1: The deduction systems described, both forward and backward, say nothing about how certain their consequents are. Read about certainty factors in *Artificial Intelligence (Second Edition)* and extend the system given here to calculate and report on how certain its consequents are.

Summary

- Identification world illustrates how rule-based systems work.
- Assertions and rules can be represented easily.
- Forward chaining means working from antecedents to consequents.
- Our forward-chaining programs use streams.
- Constructors, selectors, and mutators clarify stream use.
- Simple rules help identify animals.

References

Newell and Simon established production systems as a way of looking at human problem solving in their definitive book [1972].

For an excellent treatment of streams, see Abelson and Sussman [1984]. The ideas behind our development are theirs.

For a general introduction to rule-based expert systems, see *Artificial Intelligence (Second Edition)* by Patrick H. Winston [1984]. For information on applications of expert systems, see the chapters by Davis, Kraft, Baker, Pople, and Brown in *The AI Business: The Commercial Uses of Artificial Intelligence* edited by Patrick H. Winston and Karen A. Prendergast [1984].

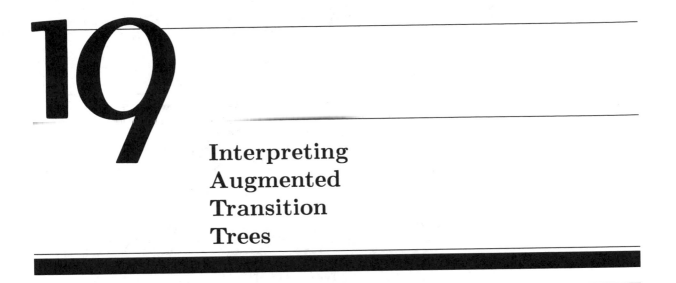

Interpreting Augmented Transition Trees

The purpose of this chapter is to show how LISP can be used to implement other languages via the interpretation process. Specifically, we look at an interpreter for augmented transition trees, showing how to build a simple English data-base interface. In chapter 20, we look at a compiler for augmented transition trees, complementing our study here in this chapter.

Augmented Transition Trees Capture English Syntax

Parsing is the process of determining how the parts of a sentence fit together. One kind of parser is built on descriptions of syntax called ATT diagrams, where ATT is an acronym for augmented transition tree. ATTs facilitate sentence analysis by capturing word-order regularities.[1]

Suppose tool world consists in part of a few screwdrivers lying around on a workbench or hanging on a pegboard. Figure 19-1 exhibits simple ATTs that captures some of the regularities involved in simple questions about tool world.

---

[1] ATTs are special kinds of *augmented transition nets*, or ATNs. An ATN is not an ATT because more than one arc can lead to the same node. Also, ATNs allow backup when motion through a net leads to a dead end. Surprisingly, interesting english interfaces can be implemented using augmented transition trees, in spite of their extra restrictions.

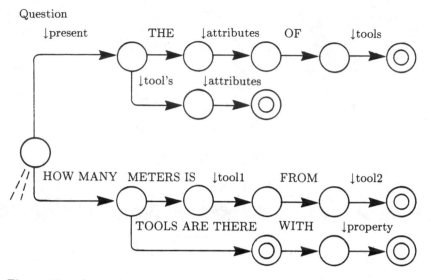

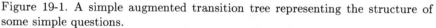

Figure 19-1. A simple augmented transition tree representing the structure of some simple questions.

In particular, the ATTs in figure 19-1 are compatible with sentences like these:

Show me the length of saw3.
Print saw3's color and weight.
How many meters is saw3 from hammer8?

To see how these sentences are handled, note the following rules defining ATTs and how they are used:

- Any given ATT consists of a tree of *nodes* linked by labeled *arcs*. Analysis of a sentence or sentence fragment is accomplished by driving through the network, using the words as directions for choosing which arcs to take. When the words are such that the drive ends up at a *terminal node*, indicated by a double circle, the sentence or sentence fragment is said to be *parsed*.

- Arcs labeled with *uppercase words* are traversed when those words appear at the front of the current word sequence.

Thus the arc labeled SHOW ME in the Present ATT is traversed when the current word sequence starts with *show me*.

- Arcs labeled with *downward-pointing arrows* and *lowercase words* are traversed when the ATT of the same name successfully chews up the words at the front of the word sequence.

Thus the arc labeled ↓present in the Question ATT is traversed when the current word sequence starts with something that goes through the Present ATT successfully, *show me*, for example.

- Legitimate sentences lead to terminal nodes, where a prescribed computation is performed that determines the value returned by the ATT parser.

Thus the value returned by the ATT parser, working with the Present ATT, given a sequence starting with *show me*, evaluates 'PRINT, returning PRINT as the value.

- The value returned by the parser after working through a particular tree is attached to the tree name.

Thus the value of the symbol PRESENT, given the word sequence *show me*, becomes PRINT.

Variable assignment makes it possible to make use of the results of lower-level terminal computations. The ability to compute and to refer to the results of computations is why we say that ATTs are *augmented transition trees*.[2]

An ATT Interpreter Follows an Explicit Description

To make an interpreter for ATTs, we first need a notation that explicitly captures the idea of trees, nodes, and arcs. After inventing such a notation, we will study a program that can analyze sentences by looking at trees one arc at a time:

- An *interpreter* is a program that follows an explicit procedure description incrementally, doing what the procedure description specifies.

To a large extent the notational details are a matter of taste and invention. The PRESENT, ATTRIBUTE, and ATTRIBUTES trees illustrate the notational choices made here.

```
(RECORD PRESENT
        ((BRANCH (SHOW ME (PARSE-RESULT 'PRINT))
                 (WHAT ARE (PARSE-RESULT 'PRINT))
                 (GIVE (PARSE-RESULT 'PRINT))
                 (DISPLAY (PARSE-RESULT 'PRINT))
                 (PRINT (PARSE-RESULT 'PRINT))
                 (PRESENT (PARSE-RESULT 'PRINT)))))
```

---

[2] From a certain point of view, an augmented transition tree is a pattern. In contrast to the patterns used in chapter 17, ATT patterns allow subpatterns to be specified.

```
(RECORD ATTRIBUTES
       ((BRANCH ((PARSE ATTRIBUTE)
                 (PARSE ATTRIBUTES)
                 (PARSE-RESULT (CONS ATTRIBUTE ATTRIBUTES)))
                (AND (PARSE ATTRIBUTE)
                     (PARSE-RESULT (LIST ATTRIBUTE)))
                ((PARSE ATTRIBUTE)
                 (PARSE-RESULT (LIST ATTRIBUTE)))))))

(RECORD ATTRIBUTE
       ((BRANCH (WIDTH (PARSE-RESULT 'WIDTH))
                (BREADTH (PARSE-RESULT 'WIDTH))
                (DEPTH (PARSE-RESULT 'DEPTH))
                (HEIGHT (PARSE-RESULT 'HEIGHT))
                (LENGTH (PARSE-RESULT 'LENGTH))
                (WEIGHT (PARSE-RESULT 'WEIGHT))
                (COLOR (PARSE-RESULT 'COLOR)))))
```

Plainly, the second argument to RECORD is a tree-defining pattern that determines how matching is to be done. BRANCH signals branches. PARSE signals subtree calls.

Each branch is tried in succession until one succeeds or the sequence of branches is exhausted. On success, a two-element list is returned. The first element is the value of the expression heralded by PARSE-RESULT; the second element is a list of the words remaining to be parsed. For example, the result returned by the Attributes tree for the three words *color and weight* is ((COLOR WEIGHT) NIL).

Before we can get to RECORD, we work toward the description of an auxiliary procedure named INTERPRET-ATT, which works by recursively chewing away at the the value of REMAINING-WORDS, which is a list of words, and the value of TREE, which is a pattern. In its most basic form, INTERPRET-ATT handles only patterns consisting entirely of symbols, each of which must match the corresponding word in REMAINING-WORDS exactly, and PARSE-containing elements:

```
(DEFUN INTERPRET-ATT (REMAINING-WORDS TREE)
  (COND ((NULL TREE)
         (LIST T REMAINING-WORDS))
        ((ATOM (CAR TREE))
         (COND ((EQUAL (CAR REMAINING-WORDS) (CAR TREE))
                (INTERPRET-ATT (CDR REMAINING-WORDS) (CDR TREE)))
               (T NIL)))
        ((EQUAL (INSTRUCTION-NAME TREE) 'PARSE)
         (LET ((RESULT (FUNCALL (SUBTREE-NAME TREE) REMAINING-WORDS)))
           (COND (RESULT
                  (SET (SUBTREE-NAME TREE) (CAR RESULT))
                  (INTERPRET-ATT (CADR RESULT) (CDR TREE)))
                 (T NIL))))
        .   .   .))
```

Note that we use two access procedures to avoid the most opaque CAR-CDR combinations:

```
(DEFUN INSTRUCTION-NAME (TREE) (CAAR TREE))

(DEFUN SUBTREE-NAME (TREE) (CADAR TREE))
```

The PARSE handling clause is the complicated one because it implements the variable-assignment feature:

- If a call to a specified program succeeds, the name of the program is treated as a variable.

- The first element in the two-element list returned by the program becomes the value of the variable.

- The second element in the list returned becomes the value of REMAINING-WORDS.

Note that we must use SET, rather than SETQ. Unlike SETQ, SET evaluates its first argument as well as its second. The first argument must evaluate to the name of a dynamic variable, one whose value is to be found dynamically, not lexically. This will be arranged shortly, using PROCLAIM.

Several other COND clauses are useful in INTERPRET-ATT in that they implement other matching features. For example, the following clause implements the branching feature:

```
.
.
.
((EQUAL (INSTRUCTION-NAME TREE) 'BRANCH)
 (INTERPRET-BRANCHES REMAINING-WORDS (CDAR TREE)))
.
.
.
```

INTERPRET-BRANCHES looks like this:

```
(DEFUN INTERPRET-BRANCHES (REMAINING-WORDS BRANCHES)
  (COND ((NULL BRANCHES) NIL)
        ((INTERPRET-ATT REMAINING-WORDS (CAR BRANCHES)))
        (T (INTERPRET-BRANCHES REMAINING-WORDS (CDR BRANCHES)))))
```

Two other clauses allow for explicit return of a value. One, with PARSE-RESULT, works whenever encountered; another, with PARSE-RESULT-IF-END, works only if REMAINING-WORDS is NIL:

```
       .
       .
       .
((EQUAL (INSTRUCTION-NAME TREE) 'PARSE-RESULT)
 (LIST (CAR (LAST (MAPCAR 'EVAL (CDAR TREE))))
       REMAINING-WORDS))
((EQUAL (INSTRUCTION-NAME TREE) 'PARSE-RESULT-IF-END)
 (COND ((NULL REMAINING-WORDS)
        (LIST (CAR (LAST (MAPCAR 'EVAL (CDAR TREE))))
              NIL))
       (T NIL)))
       .
       .
       .
```

Note that both clauses allow for any number of expressions to be evaluated in addition to the one that supplies the value to be returned.

Here then is the complete definition of INTERPRET-ATT:

```
(DEFUN INTERPRET-ATT (REMAINING-WORDS TREE)
  (COND ((NULL TREE)
         (LIST T REMAINING-WORDS))
        ((ATOM (CAR TREE))
         (COND ((EQUAL (CAR REMAINING-WORDS) (CAR TREE))
                (INTERPRET-ATT (CDR REMAINING-WORDS) (CDR TREE)))
               (T NIL)))
        ((EQUAL (INSTRUCTION-NAME TREE) 'PARSE)
         (LET ((RESULT (FUNCALL (SUBTREE-NAME TREE) REMAINING-WORDS)))
           (COND (RESULT
                  (SET (SUBTREE-NAME TREE) (CAR RESULT))
                  (INTERPRET-ATT (CADR RESULT) (CDR TREE)))
                 (T NIL))))
        ((EQUAL (INSTRUCTION-NAME TREE) 'BRANCH)
         (INTERPRET-BRANCHES REMAINING-WORDS (CDAR TREE)))
        ((EQUAL (INSTRUCTION-NAME TREE) 'PARSE-RESULT)
         (LIST (CAR (LAST (MAPCAR 'EVAL (CDAR TREE))))
               REMAINING-WORDS))
        ((EQUAL (INSTRUCTION-NAME TREE) 'PARSE-RESULT-IF-END)
         (COND ((NULL REMAINING-WORDS)
                (LIST (CAR (LAST (MAPCAR 'EVAL (CDAR TREE))))
                      NIL))
               (T NIL)))))
```

Now it is convenient to define RECORD, the procedure that defines pattern-described procedures. It is to create an appropriate DEFUN form, using a given tree name and a given tree. The DEFUN to be produced by RECORD for the ATTRIBUTES procedure is this:

```
(DEFUN ATTRIBUTES (REMAINING-WORDS)
  (PROCLAIM '(SPECIAL ATTRIBUTE ATTRIBUTES)) ;Make them dynamic, not lexical.
  (LET ((ATTRIBUTE NIL)
        (ATTRIBUTES NIL))
    (INTERPRET-ATT REMAINING-WORDS              ;Call interpreter.
                   '((BRANCH ((PARSE ATTRIBUTE)
                              (PARSE ATTRIBUTES)
                              (PARSE-RESULT (CONS ATTRIBUTE
                                                  ATTRIBUTES)))
                             ((AND (PARSE ATTRIBUTE)
                                   (PARSE-RESULT (LIST ATTRIBUTE)))
                              ((PARSE ATTRIBUTE)
                               (PARSE-RESULT (LIST ATTRIBUTE)))))))))
```

Thus, the procedure ATTRIBUTES works by calling the interpreter INTERPRET-ATT on the Attributes tree. For this to happen, the required DEFUN has the following form:

```
(DEFUN <name of tree> (REMAINING-WORDS)
  (PROCLAIM '(SPECIAL <list of dynamic variables derived from the pattern>))
  (LET <list of LET parameter specifications derived from the pattern>
    (INTERPRET-ATT REMAINING-WORDS '<tree description>)))
```

With the backquote mechanism, defining RECORD is mainly a matter of converting the general description of the desired DEFUN into backquote form:

```
(DEFMACRO RECORD (NAME TREE)
  (LET ((VARIABLES (GET-SUBTREE-NAMES TREE)))
    `(DEFUN ,NAME (REMAINING-WORDS)
       (PROCLAIM '(SPECIAL ,@VARIABLES))
       (LET ,(MAPCAR #'(LAMBDA (VARIABLE) (LIST VARIABLE NIL))
                     VARIABLES)
         (INTERPRET-ATT REMAINING-WORDS ',TREE)))))
```

GET-SUBTREE-NAMES is easily defined:

```
(DEFUN GET-SUBTREE-NAMES (X)
  (REMOVE-DUPLICATES (GET-SUBTREE-NAMES1 X)))

(DEFUN GET-SUBTREE-NAMES1 (X)
  (COND ((NULL X) NIL)
        ((ATOM X) NIL)
        ((AND (EQUAL (CAR X) 'PARSE)         ;Detect PARSE expression.
              (CDR X)
              (NOT (CDDR X)))
         (LIST (CADR X)))
        (T (MAPCAN 'GET-SUBTREE-NAMES1 X))))
```

Note that GET-SUBTREE-NAMES uses REMOVE-DUPLICATES, a primitive that removes duplicate entries from lists. REMOVE-DUPLICATES is needed because there may be more than one instance of each variable.

Satisfyingly, the interpreter just described and the compiler of the next chapter are compatible: RECORD, which uses INTERPRET-ATT, and COMPILE-ATT both create definitions that can be freely intermingled. A Question-tree procedure interpreted by INTERPRET-ATT can make use of an Attributes-tree procedure created by COMPILE-ATT or vice versa.

Problems

Problem 19-1:   Modify the interpreter so that if the variable DEBUG is nonNIL, it prints the name of each transition tree entered. In general it is easier to add debugging features to interpreters than to compilers.

Problem 19-2:   Using RECORD, create a Tools ATT to handle tools. Your solution is to handle constructions involving combinations of HAMMER8, SAW3, and WRENCH2.

Problem 19-3:   Using RECORD, create two distinct trees, Tool1 and Tool2, such that a sentence can contain two references to tools. Make use of the already-defined Tool tree.

Problem 19-4:   Translate the ATT required to handle questions into the form required for RECORD. Pattern your answer on the tree shown in figure 19-1. Assume possessives are written as a space followed by an *s* instead of *'s*. Arrange for a suitable printing of the question answers.

Summary

- Augmented transition trees capture English syntax.
- An ATT interpreter follows an explicit description.

References

For a general introduction to natural language understanding, see *Artificial Intelligence (Second Edition)* by Patrick H. Winston [1984]. For early work on ATTs and ATTlike systems, see Bobrow and Fraser [1969], Winograd [1972], Woods [1972], and Kaplan [1972].

Our development of ATTs is based partly on the ideas of Hendrix *et al.* [1978] and partly on the ideas of Harris [1977].

For work on commercial natural-language systems, see Winston and Prendergast [1984]. The chapter by Harris describes INTELLECT and other products marketed by the Artificial Intelligence Corporation, and the chapter by Schank describes products marketed by Cognitive Systems, Incorporated.

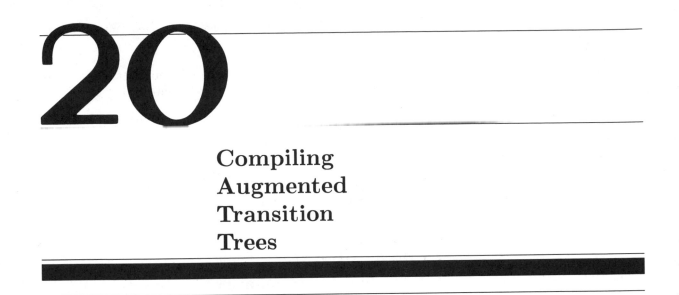

Compiling
Augmented
Transition
Trees

The purpose of this chapter is to take a second look at language interfaces by implementing a compiler for augmented transition trees to complement the interpreter of the previous chapter. Take note that we will be talking about compiling in a general sense meaning translating from one language into another, directly useful one. This is different from the more restricted sense that implies that the translation is into some computer's basic instruction set.

ATTs Can Be Compiled from Transparent Specifications

In a moment, you will see how to translate complete ATTs into LISP procedures. While straightforward, such translation is tedious, and the job should really be done by a program. We shall develop such a translation program. It will be an ATT compiler.

- A *compiler* is a program that translates procedure descriptions from one language into another.

The main job of the ATT compiler is to translate source-language ATT descriptions into deeply nested CONDs, one for each arc in the ATT.

Once our compiler is developed, the entire Attributes and Attribute definitions can be written just as they were for the interpreter:

```
(COMPILE-ATT PRESENT
        ((BRANCH (SHOW ME (PARSE-RESULT 'PRINT))
                 (WHAT ARE (PARSE-RESULT 'PRINT))
                 (GIVE (PARSE-RESULT 'PRINT))
                 (DISPLAY (PARSE-RESULT 'PRINT))
                 (PRINT (PARSE-RESULT 'PRINT))
                 (PRESENT (PARSE-RESULT 'PRINT)))))

(COMPILE-ATT ATTRIBUTES
        ((BRANCH ((PARSE ATTRIBUTE)
                  (PARSE ATTRIBUTES)
                  (PARSE-RESULT (CONS ATTRIBUTE ATTRIBUTES)))
                 (AND (PARSE ATTRIBUTE)
                      (PARSE-RESULT (LIST ATTRIBUTE)))
                 ((PARSE ATTRIBUTE)
                  (PARSE-RESULT (LIST ATTRIBUTE))))))

(COMPILE-ATT ATTRIBUTE
        ((BRANCH (WIDTH (PARSE-RESULT 'WIDTH))
                 (BREADTH (PARSE-RESULT 'WIDTH))
                 (DEPTH (PARSE-RESULT 'DEPTH))
                 (HEIGHT (PARSE-RESULT 'HEIGHT))
                 (LENGTH (PARSE-RESULT 'LENGTH))
                 (WEIGHT (PARSE-RESULT 'WEIGHT))
                 (COLOR (PARSE-RESULT 'COLOR))
                 (SIZE (PARSE-RESULT 'SIZE)))))
```

**Compilers Treat
Programs as Data**

Now the problem is creating COMPILE-ATT, a LISP procedure that converts perspicuous ATT descriptions into descriptions that LISP understands directly. Fortunately, the job involves nothing more than the symbol-manipulating flair so characteristic of LISP.

Much of the work of COMPILE-ATT is to be done by COMPILE-ELEMENTS, a procedure that walks down the defining tree, converting each element of the tree into COND structure. Here is what COMPILE-ELEMENTS is to produce given that the tree looks like ((PARSE <SUBTREE NAME>) ...):

```
(LET* ((PAIR-RETURNED (<subtree name> REMAINING-WORDS))
       (<subtree name> (CAR PAIR-RETURNED))
       (REMAINING-WORDS (CADR PAIR-RETURNED)))
  (COND (PAIR-RETURNED <result of compiling the rest of the tree>)))
```

If the value of REMAINING-WORDS is such that the subtree is successfully traversed, then the new value of REMAINING-WORDS is the old value minus those words consumed by the subtree. Meanwhile the new value of the symbol naming the subtree becomes the value returned from the subtree traversal. Both new values are established in the parameter assignment part of the LET*, and both are available as we dive into the COND.

In general, the result of compiling the rest of the tree will contain more nested instances of LET* and COND. For example, here is what COMPILE-ELEMENTS is to produce when the first element in the remaining part of the ATT is a specific word:

```
(LET* ((CURRENT-WORD (CAR REMAINING-WORDS))
       (REMAINING-WORDS (CDR REMAINING-WORDS)))
  (COND ((EQUAL '<specific word> CURRENT-WORD)
         <result of compiling the rest of the tree>)))
```

Thus, if the tree is ((PARSE <SUBTREE NAME>) <SPECIFIC WORD> ...), then COMPILE-ELEMENTS generates the following:

```
(LET* ((PAIR-RETURNED (<subtree name> REMAINING-WORDS))
       (<subtree name> (CAR PAIR-RETURNED))
       (REMAINING-WORDS (CADR PAIR-RETURNED)))
  (COND (PAIR-RETURNED (LET* ((CURRENT-WORD (CAR REMAINING-WORDS))
                             (REMAINING-WORDS (CDR REMAINING-WORDS)))
                        (COND ((EQUAL '<specific word> CURRENT-WORD)
                               <result of compiling the rest of the tree>))))))
```

Thus only a few arcs can produce extremely wide-looking procedures that would be extremely difficult for us humans to write without erring frequently. Happily, we do not have to, for COMPILE-ELEMENTS does the job for us. In COMPILE-ELEMENTS, we make heavy use of the backquote mechanism to fill in templates with the proper expressions. The following, for example, is the backquote template for trees starting with an element of the form ((PARSE <SUBTREE NAME>) ...):

```
`(LET* ((PAIR-RETURNED (,(SUBTREE-NAME TREE) REMAINING-WORDS))
        (,(SUBTREE-NAME TREE) (CAR PAIR-RETURNED))
        (REMAINING-WORDS (CADR PAIR-RETURNED)))
   (COND (PAIR-RETURNED ,(COMPILE-ELEMENTS (CDR TREE)))))
```

Hence, COMPILE-ELEMENTS contains the following COND clause for handling
PARSE-containing elements:

```
.
.

.

((EQUAL (INSTRUCTION-NAME TREE) 'PARSE)
 `(LET* ((PAIR-RETURNED (,(SUBTREE-NAME TREE) REMAINING-WORDS))
         (,(SUBTREE-NAME TREE) (CAR PAIR-RETURNED))
         (REMAINING-WORDS (CADR PAIR-RETURNED)))
    (COND (PAIR-RETURNED ,(COMPILE-ELEMENTS (CDR TREE))))))

.

.

.
```

The following definition of COMPILE-ELEMENTS is merely a collection of such
COND clauses:

```
(DEFUN COMPILE-ELEMENTS (TREE)
  (COND ((NULL TREE) '(LIST T REMAINING-WORDS))
        ((ATOM (CAR TREE))
         `(LET* ((CURRENT-WORD (CAR REMAINING-WORDS))
                 (REMAINING-WORDS (CDR REMAINING-WORDS)))
            (COND ((EQUAL ',(CAR TREE) CURRENT-WORD)
                   ,(COMPILE-ELEMENTS (CDR TREE))))))
        ((EQUAL (INSTRUCTION-NAME TREE) 'PARSE)
         `(LET* ((PAIR-RETURNED (,(SUBTREE-NAME TREE) REMAINING-WORDS))
                 (,(SUBTREE-NAME TREE) (CAR PAIR-RETURNED))
                 (REMAINING-WORDS (CADR PAIR-RETURNED)))
            (COND (PAIR-RETURNED ,(COMPILE-ELEMENTS (CDR TREE))))))
        ((EQUAL (INSTRUCTION-NAME TREE) 'BRANCH)
         `(OR ,@(MAPCAR #'(LAMBDA (BRANCH) (COMPILE-ELEMENTS BRANCH))
                        (CDAR TREE))))
        ((EQUAL (INSTRUCTION-NAME TREE) 'PARSE-RESULT)
         `(LIST ,(SUBTREE-NAME TREE)
                REMAINING-WORDS))
        ((EQUAL (INSTRUCTION-NAME TREE) 'PARSE-RESULT-IF-END)
         `(COND ((NULL REMAINING-WORDS)
                 (LIST ,(SUBTREE-NAME TREE)
                       NIL))
                (T NIL)))))
```

The first COND clause in COMPILE-ELEMENTS creates a form for trees with no
explicit termination via PARSE-RESULT or PARSE-RESULT-IF-END. The COND
clause for branches fills in a template that looks like this:

```
(COND (<result of using COMPILE-ELEMENTS on first branch>)
      (<result of using COMPILE-ELEMENTS on second branch>)
      .
      .
      .
      (<result of using COMPILE-ELEMENTS on last branch>))
```

The COND clauses for PARSE-RESULT and PARSE-RESULT-IF-END compute as stipulated, returning a list of a value and the remaining words.

Now it is time to define COMPILE-ATT. Here is the simple form for the definitions COMPILE-ATT is to produce:

```
(DEFUN <name of procedure> (REMAINING-WORDS)
  (COMPILE-ELEMENTS <tree>))
```

Using backquote again, it is easy to set up and fill in such a form:

```
(DEFMACRO COMPILE-ATT (NAME TREE)
  `(DEFUN ,NAME (REMAINING-WORDS)
     ,(COMPILE-ELEMENTS TREE)))
```

Of course many improvements and extensions suggest themselves. Error-handling, reporting, and debugging features, for example, are missing.

Compilers Are Usually Harder To Make than Interpreters

Compilers translate programs from a source language to a target language. When the compiled program runs, neither the source-language version nor the compiler is around to help figure things out. Once compiled, a program is on its own. For example, in the compiled ATTs, the tree specifications are present only implicitly in the LISP procedures.

Interpreters follow source-language procedures one step at a time. The source-language procedures are always there to refer to. For example, in working with interpreted ATTs, tree specifications are always explicit, retaining their original form.

Generally, interpreters are easier to write. Generally, compiled programs run faster.

Compilers Are Usually Major Undertakings

In the ATT example, LISP is both the compiler's implementation language and the compilation's target language. Creating the compiler was straightforward because compiling is a symbol-manipulating task for which LISP is eminently suited. Often compilers translate from source languages into languages lying close to the basic instruction set of some computer to achieve high running speed. Working with such compilers is much harder, especially if the compiler itself must be written in a low-level, computer-specific assembler language, again for reasons of speed.

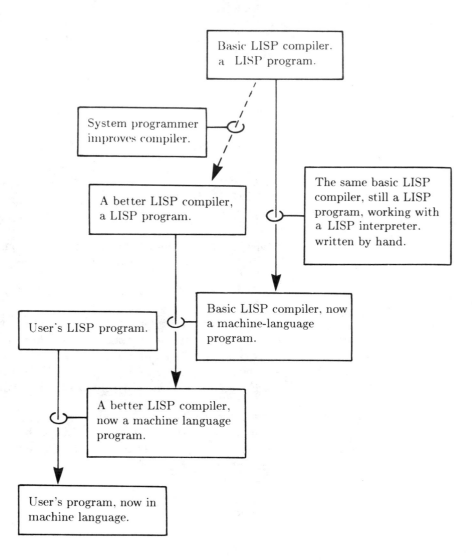

Figure 20-1. Each new version of the LISP compiler is compiled by the previous version. At the very beginning, the original compiler is compiled using an interpreter. User programs are either run by the current version of the interpreter or compiled by the last compiler in the chain. One compiler is better than another if it runs faster or if it produces faster or smaller programs or if it handles more of the language it is compiling.

**LISP Itself Is
Either Compiled or
Interpreted**

First we used a LISP program to interpret ATT descriptions. Then we used another LISP program to compile ATT descriptions into LISP programs.

Of course LISP programs themselves are descriptions of procedures, and as such, they can be interpreted by a program written using the basic machine instructions of a computer or they can be compiled into programs written in those basic instructions.

This makes for the curious set of possibilities shown in figure 20-1. The translation of LISP into basic instructions is a symbol-manipulation job. Hence it is nicely accomplished by a program written in LISP. Said another way, LISP is a good language for writing a LISP compiler. But then the LISP compiler itself is a LISP program that can be compiled. Once compiled, the compiler can compile itself. Indeed the first program a new LISP compiler usually compiles is itself, relying on an interpreter or a previous compiler until the self-compilation is done.

Problems

Problem 20-1: Suppose a LISP compiler is available. Is it possible to gain extra speed improvements by going from ATT descriptions to basic instructions in two steps?

Summary

- ATTs can be compiled from transparent specifications.
- Compilers treat programs as data.
- Compilers are usually harder to make than interpreters.
- Compilers are usually major undertakings.
- LISP itself is either compiled or interpreted.

References

For work on ATT natural language interfaces and commercial natural language systems, see the references at the end of chapter 19.

21

Procedure Writing Programs And English Interfaces

Certainly LISP programs can write programs. We have seen an example of this already because a compiler takes a procedure description as input and produces a procedure as output. The purpose of this chapter is to show that a problem-solving program also may write its own programs and evaluate them in the normal course of problem solving.

The particular program developed here deals again with the tool world, now answering a user's English-stated questions about what tools there are and how many. Instead of just tool names, as in *saw3*, our program must deal with tool descriptions, as in *the large screwdrivers*. The program illustrates some of the ideas behind commercial English data-base interfaces.

Here are some sample sentences of the sort our program handles once activated by the top-level procedure, INTERFACE:

```
(INTERFACE)
> (SHOW ME THE LENGTH OF THE BLUE SCREWDRIVER)
  (S1 LENGTH IS 7)

> (PRINT THE BLUE SCREWDRIVER S COLOR AND WEIGHT)
  (S1 COLOR IS BLUE)
  (S1 WEIGHT IS UNKNOWN)

> (HOW MANY METERS IS THE BLUE SCREWDRIVER FROM THE HAMMER)
  (THE DISTANCE IS 3.14)
```

```
> (IDENTIFY THE LARGE SCREWDRIVERS)
  (THEY ARE S1 S2 S3)

> (IDENTIFY THE LARGE RED SCREWDRIVERS)
  (THEY ARE S2 S3)

> (IDENTIFY A LONG SCREWDRIVER)
  (THERE IS JUST S1)

> (COUNT THE SCREWDRIVERS)
  (THERE ARE 3)

> (COUNT THE LARGE RED SCREWDRIVERS)
  (THERE ARE 2)
```

Answering Requests Is Done in Four Steps

The shape of the request-answering system is illustrated by figure 21-1. Note the following:

- The first step in answering a request is to identify the type of the English question using an ATT.

- Next a construction procedure manufactures a search procedure that can look for the sought-after items in the data base.

- Then the search procedure is evaluated, producing the names of the sought-after items.

- Finally, the items are listed or their number is announced.

The additions to the top-level Question ATT that are required to handle our sample questions are shown in figure 21-2. Let us postpone a detailed study of this ATT until after we have looked at the search procedures to be used.

Simple Procedures Can Count and Enumerate Description-Matching Objects

Translation of a description into a search procedure exploits object property lists. The first step in actually doing the search is to get a list of all the possibilities using the singular form of the tool mentioned in the description. This means that something like (GET 'SCREWDRIVER 'INSTANCE) must appear in the search procedure and therefore must be produced by the translator.

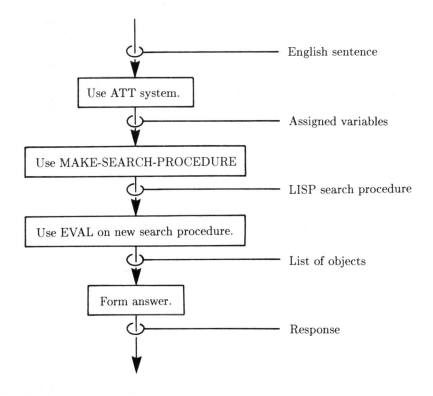

Figure 21-1. The structure of a system that answers English questions about some data base. Note that a program writes a procedure and then executes that procedure.

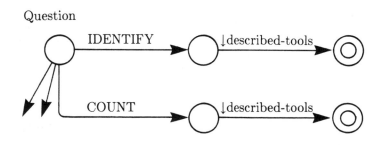

Figure 21-2. The top level of a Question ATT for answering *what* and *how many* questions.

Here are a few of the INSTANCE property values:

Symbol	Property	Value
TOOL	INSTANCE	(HAMMER SCREWDRIVER SAW WRENCH)
HAMMER	INSTANCE	(HAMMER8)
SCREWDRIVER	INSTANCE	(S1 S2 S3 S4 S5)
SAW	INSTANCE	(SAW1)
WRENCH	INSTANCE	(WRENCH1 WRENCH2)

The second step in doing the search is to filter the possibilities generated in the first step, leaving only the ones that fit the descriptive properties.

Property lists supply the needed filter names:

Symbol	Property	Value
LARGE	TEST-PROCEDURE	LARGEP
LONG	TEST-PROCEDURE	LONGP
RED	TEST-PROCEDURE	REDP

```
(DEFUN LARGEP (OBJECT) (EQUAL (GET OBJECT 'SIZE) 'LARGE))

(DEFUN LONGP (OBJECT) (EQUAL (GET OBJECT 'SIZE) 'LONG))

(DEFUN REDP (OBJECT) (EQUAL (GET OBJECT 'COLOR) 'RED))
```

Other representative properties we need are as follows:

Symbol	Property	Value
SCREWDRIVERS	SINGULAR-FORM	SCREWDRIVER
SCREWDRIVER	TYPICAL-LENGTH	8

Now suppose we have the following question:

```
> (IDENTIFY THE LARGE SCREWDRIVERS)
```

Given all the screwdrivers, the large ones can be isolated by using LARGEP along with a REMOVE-IF-NOT that does the required filtered accumulation:

```
(REMOVE-IF-NOT 'LARGEP <a list of all the screwdrivers>)
```

If other properties were present, other filtering steps, using other filters, would handle them. All the filters appear inside a search procedure with two parts: candidate finding and candidate filtering:

```
(LET ((CANDIDATES (GET 'SCREWDRIVER 'INSTANCE)))
  (SETQ CANDIDATES (REMOVE-IF-NOT 'LARGEP CANDIDATES)))
```

Having constructed such a search procedure, the system must evaluate it, producing (S1 S2 S3) as the result, given the following data:

Symbol	Property	Value
S1	SIZE	LARGE
S2	SIZE	LARGE
S3	SIZE	LARGE
S4	SIZE	SMALL
S5	SIZE	SMALL
S1	COLOR	BLUE
S2	COLOR	RED
S3	COLOR	RED
S1	LENGTH	15

Finally the system must report the items in the result:

```
(THEY ARE S1 S2 S3)
```

For further illustration, consider this:

```
> (COUNT THE LARGE RED SCREWDRIVERS)
```

For this example, the search procedure needs two filters:

```
(LET ((CANDIDATES (GET 'SCREWDRIVER 'INSTANCE)))
  (SETQ CANDIDATES (REMOVE-IF-NOT 'REDP CANDIDATES))
  (SETQ CANDIDATES (REMOVE-IF-NOT 'LARGEP CANDIDATES)))
```

The search procedure returns (S2 S3). The answer to be reported is this:

```
(THERE ARE 2)
```

The Question-Answering Program Builds a Procedure and Then Executes It

INTERFACE, the top-level procedure in our program, is straightforward, because most of the interesting work is done inside the Question ATT:

```
(DEFUN INTERFACE ()
  (PRINT '>)
  (DO ((INPUT (READ) (READ)))
      ((NULL INPUT) 'DONE)
    (LET ((ANSWER (QUESTION INPUT)))
      (COND ((OR (NOT ANSWER)              ;Goof, parse failed.
                 (CADR ANSWER))            ;Goof, words remain at end.
             (PRINT '(SORRY - NO PARSE)))))
    (PRINT '>)))
```

The required additions to the Question ATT, shown in figure 21-2, look like this when translated into LISPlike notation:

```
(COMPILE-ATT QUESTION
             ((BRANCH (IDENTIFY (PARSE DESCRIBED-TOOLS)
                           (PARSE-RESULT-IF-END
                              (REPORT-IDENTITY DESCRIBED-TOOLS))))
              (COUNT (PARSE DESCRIBED-TOOLS)
                     (PARSE-RESULT-IF-END
                        (REPORT-NUMBER DESCRIBED-TOOLS)))))))
```

In this ATT, DESCRIBED-TOOLS plays a key role. It constructs a search procedure and then executes it using EVAL.

```
(COMPILE-ATT DESCRIBED-TOOLS
             ((PARSE A-OR-THE)
              (PARSE PROPERTIES)
              (PARSE TOOL-TYPE)
              (PARSE-RESULT-IF-END
                (EVAL (MAKE-SEARCH-PROCEDURE PROPERTIES TOOL-TYPE)))))
```

REPORT-IDENTITY presumes a list of objects as its arguments:

```
(DEFUN REPORT-IDENTITY (OBJECTS)
  (PRINT (COND ((NULL OBJECTS)
                 '(THERE ARE NONE))
               ((NULL (CDR OBJECTS))
                 `(THERE IS JUST ,@OBJECTS))
               (T `(THEY ARE ,@OBJECTS)))))
```

REPORT-NUMBER is similar:

```
(DEFUN REPORT-NUMBER (OBJECTS)
  (PRINT (COND ((NULL OBJECTS)
                 '(THERE ARE NONE))
               ((NULL (CDR OBJECTS))
                 '(THERE IS ONLY 1))
               (T `(THERE ARE ,(LENGTH OBJECTS))))))
```

Now let us see how the key procedure, MAKE-SEARCH-PROCEDURE, arranges to get the objects that REPORT-IDENTITY and REPORT-NUMBER need.

Search Procedures Can Be Written Automatically

Recall that the general form of the search procedures to be built by MAKE-SEARCH-PROCEDURE is as follows:

```
(LET ((CANDIDATES (GET '<singular of tool's name> 'INSTANCE)))
  (SETQ CANDIDATES (REMOVE-IF-NOT <first filter name> CANDIDATES))
  (SETQ CANDIDATES (REMOVE-IF-NOT <second filter name> CANDIDATES))
    .
    .
    .
  (SETQ CANDIDATES (REMOVE-IF-NOT <last filter name> CANDIDATES)))
```

Each SETQ form can be made from a backquote template, given an appropriate value for the symbol FILTER:

```
`(SETQ CANDIDATES (REMOVE-IF-NOT ',FILTER CANDIDATES))
```

The filter names can be obtained from the tool description's properties this way:

```
(MAPCAR #'(LAMBDA (PROPERTY) (GET PROPERTY 'TEST-PROCEDURE))
        <list of properties>)
```

Consequently, we can make a list of all of the necessary SETQ forms like this, using nested MAPCARs:

```
(MAPCAR #'(LAMBDA (FILTER)
            `(SETQ CANDIDATES (REMOVE-IF-NOT ',FILTER CANDIDATES)))
        (MAPCAR #'(LAMBDA (PROPERTY) (GET PROPERTY 'TEST-PROCEDURE))
                PROPERTIES))
```

Putting it all together, with backquote used liberally, we have MAKE-SEARCH-PROCEDURE:

```
(DEFUN MAKE-SEARCH-PROCEDURE (PROPERTIES TOOL)
  `(LET ((CANDIDATES (GET ',(OR (GET TOOL 'SINGULAR-FORM) TOOL)
                          'INSTANCE)))
     ,@(MAPCAR #'(LAMBDA (FILTER)
                   `(SETQ CANDIDATES (REMOVE-IF-NOT ',FILTER CANDIDATES)))
               (MAPCAR #'(LAMBDA (PROPERTY) (GET PROPERTY 'TEST-PROCEDURE))
                       PROPERTIES))))
```

All that remains is to define the remaining ATTs required.

Problems

Problem 21-1: Compose a version of the tool ATT that accepts tool descriptions as well as tool names. This enables desirable generalization of the questions permitted in chapter 19.

Problem 21-2:   Define the remaining ATTs required. That is, define
A-OR-THE, PROPERTIES, and TOOL-TYPE. Use ATTRIBUTES or TOOLS as a model
for PROPERTIES.

Problem 21-3:   Rewrite MAKE-SEARCH-PROCEDURE so that it produces calls
to REMOVE-IF-NOT that are nested rather than sequential. Consider this
example:

```
(MAKE-SEARCH-PROCEDURE '(LARGE RED) 'SCREWDRIVERS)
  (REMOVE-IF-NOT 'LARGEP
                 (REMOVE-IF-NOT 'REDP
                                (GET 'SCREWDRIVER 'INSTANCE)))
```

Write two versions, one using backquote and another not using backquote.

**Properties Are Not
Quite Enough**

The filter REDP uses the COLOR property of the object it is testing:

```
(DEFUN REDP (OBJECT) (EQUAL (GET OBJECT 'COLOR) 'RED))
```

Keeping color information on the property list of each tool is not particularly wasteful because the color of a tool is generally arbitrary and
independent of what it is. A similar procedure could be written for METALP:

```
(DEFUN METALP (OBJECT) (EQUAL (GET OBJECT 'MATERIAL) 'METAL))
```

Now, however, keeping material information on the property list of each
tool is often wastefully redundant; because all screws, for example, are
metallic. In the next chapter, we will see how to identify all screws as
metallic using mechanisms that enable information about specific candidates to be inherited from descriptions that hold for all candidates of the
same type.

Problems

Project 21-1:   Generalize the system to take a wider variety of requests.

Summary

- Answering requests is done in four steps.
- Simple procedures can count and enumerate description-matching ob-
  jects.
- The question-answering program builds a procedure and then executes
  it.
- Search procedures can be written automatically.
- Properties are not quite enough.

References   For work on ATT natural language interfaces and commercial natural lan-
                            guage systems, see the references at the end of chapter 19.

22

Implementing Frames

The purpose of this chapter is to see how to implement fancy data bases that have features beyond those offered by basic LISP. In particular, we will examine a simple frame system featuring defaults, demons, and inheritance. In contrast to flavors, discussed in chapter 16, the inheritance is directed at finding properties rather than at finding methods.

A Frame Is a Generalized Property List

It is easy to say quite a lot about any given symbol by placing information on its property list. For example, in describing some person named Henry, we might do the following:

```
(SETF (GET 'HENRY 'A-KIND-OF) 'MAN)

(SETF (GET 'HENRY 'HEIGHT) 1.78)

(SETF (GET 'HENRY 'WEIGHT) 75)

(SETF (GET 'HENRY 'HOBBIES) '(JOGGING SKIING))
```

These few lines explicitly establish that Henry is a man of a particular height and weight with certain hobbies. Eventually, however, properties and property values are not enough.

There may be a need, for example, for the following information about Paul, about whom little is known:

- A default value. If no one has explicitly given Paul's weight assume it is 57 kilograms by default.

- A procedure activated by placing a value. If Paul's weight ever goes above 60, he should be told to go on a diet.

- A procedure activated to compute a needed value. If no one has explicitly given Paul's weight, or even a default, then multiply his height in meters times 33 because he is a man.

Such information can be conveniently captured if the notion of property list is generalized:

- In part, a *frame* is a generalized property list because there is room in a frame to specify more than property values. In part, a frame is a generalized property list because it is possible for a frame to inherit information from another, related frame.

Frames Can Be Represented as Nested Association Lists

Our implementation of frames uses association lists, in part. Recall that an association list is a list of elements, each of which can be identified and extracted from the list using its key. In the following example, the value of A-LIST becomes a short, two-element association list. The keys are WEIGHT and HOBBIES, and the elements are the lists (WEIGHT 75) and (HOBBIES JOGGING SKIING) that contain both keys and keyed information.

```
(SETQ A-LIST '((WEIGHT 75) (HOBBIES JOGGING SKIING)))
```

The association list is simple to extend using CONS or APPEND:

```
(SETQ A-LIST (CONS '(HEIGHT 1.78) A-LIST))
```

```
(SETQ A-LIST (APPEND '((A-KIND-OF MAN)) A-LIST))
```

One way to represent a frame is as a nested association list. On the highest level, the frame structure looks like this:

```
(<frame name> (<slot name 1> ...)  (<slot name 2> ...)  ...)
```

The CDR of the structure is an A-LIST in which the keys are *slot* names. One level deeper, the slot-keyed elements have the same sort of structure:

```
(<slot name> (<facet name 1> ...)  (<facet name 2> ...)  ...)
```

Now the CDR is again an association list, but the keys are *facet* names. We will look at procedures that use the VALUE, DEFAULT, IF-NEEDED, IF-ADDED, and IF-REMOVED facets.

Finally, the facet-keyed elements look like this:

```
(<facet name> <value 1> <value 2> ...)
```

Thus a frame can have any number of slots. The slots can have any number of facets. And the facets can have any number of *values*. Putting it all together, we have this:

```
(<frame name> (<slot 1> (<facet 1> <value 1>
                                   <value 2>
                                      .
                                      .
                                      . )
                        (<facet 2> <value 1> .   .  .)
                           .
                           .
                        . )
              (<slot 2> (<facet 1> <value 1> .   .  .)  .  .  .)
                 .
                 .
              . )
```

The frame representing the facts known about Henry, previously stored as a set of property values on the property list of Henry or on a plain association list, can be stuck into a frame:

```
(HENRY (A-KIND-OF (VALUE MAN))
       (HEIGHT (VALUE 1.78))
       (WEIGHT (VALUE 75))
       (HOBBIES (VALUE JOGGING SKIING)))
```

This structure has the desirable feature of uniformity at every level. There remains the question of where the structure should be stored. One idea would be to make it the value of HENRY. Another is to make a long list of all the frames and make that list the value of the symbol FRAMES. Still another idea, and the one we use here, is to store the structure on the property list of HENRY under the property FRAME.

Given this structure for frames, we eventually implement the following procedures:

- FGET fetches information. The user supplies an access path consisting of a frame, a slot, and a facet.

- FPUT places information. As with FGET, the user supplies a frame-slot-facet access path.

- FREMOVE removes information. As with FGET and FPUT, the user supplies a frame-slot-facet access path.

- FGET-V-D fetches information. The user supplies an access path consisting only of a frame and a slot. The VALUE facet is inspected first. If nothing is found, then the DEFAULT facet is also inspected.

- FGET-I fetches information. The user supplies a frame-slot access path. If nothing is found in the VALUE facet, then the procedure looks at frames found in the given frame's A-KIND-OF slot under the VALUE facet. This enables a frame to inherit information from frames it is related to by the A-KIND-OF relation.

- FGET-N and FGET-Z fetch information. They use values, defaults, and value-finding procedures, not only as found in the given frame but also in the frames it is related to by the A-KIND-OF relation.

FGET, FPUT, and FREMOVE Are the Basic Frame-handling Procedures

The following simple procedure retrieves information, given a frame-slot-facet access path:

```
(DEFUN FGET (FRAME SLOT FACET)
    (CDR (ASSOC FACET (CDR (ASSOC SLOT (CDR (GET FRAME 'FRAME)))))))
```

It is a pity, but FPUT and FREMOVE will be harder to understand, partly because they do list-structure surgery using RPLACD.

The general strategy for FPUT is this: probe into the frame structure just like FGET does; however, if at any stage a key is not found, add a new element. Thus, if the given frame structure has nothing on its slot list corresponding to a new addition, then the slot list is enlarged. If a slot structure has nothing on its facet list corresponding to a new addition, then the facet list is enlarged. And if the given value is not there, then it too is similarly installed.

Suppose, for example, that the HENRY frame is to be augmented with the following application of FPUT:

```
(FPUT 'HENRY 'OCCUPATION 'VALUE 'TEACHING)
```

Because the HENRY frame has no OCCUPATION slot, the first step is to create one:

```
(HENRY (A-KIND-OF (VALUE MAN))
       (HEIGHT (VALUE 1.78))
       (WEIGHT (VALUE 75))
       (HOBBIES (VALUE JOGGING SKIING))
       (OCCUPATION))
```

Next, because the OCCUPATION slot has no VALUE facet, it is created too:

```
(HENRY (A-KIND-OF (VALUE MAN))
       (HEIGHT (VALUE 1.78))
       (WEIGHT (VALUE 75))
       (HOBBIES (VALUE JOGGING SKIING))
       (OCCUPATION (VALUE)))
```

And finally, the actual value is placed:

```
(HENRY (A-KIND-OF (VALUE MAN))
       (HEIGHT (VALUE 1.78))
       (WEIGHT (VALUE 75))
       (HOBBIES (VALUE JOGGING SKIING))
       (OCCUPATION (VALUE TEACHING)))
```

At this point, the following FPUT application encounters no need to create new structure until it hits the value level:

```
(FPUT 'HENRY 'OCCUPATION 'VALUE 'RESEARCH)
```

The result is this:

```
(HENRY (A-KIND-OF (VALUE MAN))
       (HEIGHT (VALUE 1.78))
       (WEIGHT (VALUE 75))
       (HOBBIES (VALUE JOGGING SKIING))
       (OCCUPATION (VALUE TEACHING RESEARCH)))
```

Because association-list inspection and enlargement are critical to FPUT, we consider it first. EXTEND inspects first, using ASSOC, and if ASSOC fails, EXTEND extends using RPLACD:

```
(DEFUN EXTEND (KEY A-LIST)
  (COND ((ASSOC KEY (CDR A-LIST)))
        (T (CADR (RPLACD (LAST A-LIST) (LIST (LIST KEY)))))))
```

Note that any additions required are done surgically. The RPLACD replaces the CDR of its first argument with its second argument by altering existing list structure, not by building new structure.

Now note that FOLLOW-PATH uses EXTEND to push through frame structure:

```
(DEFUN FOLLOW-PATH (PATH A-LIST)
  (COND ((NULL PATH) A-LIST)
        (T (FOLLOW-PATH (CDR PATH) (EXTEND (CAR PATH) A-LIST)))))
```

Given `FOLLOW-PATH`, the following will do for `FPUT`. Note that `FPUT` returns the value if the value is not already in the value list and `NIL` otherwise.

```
(DEFUN FPUT (FRAME SLOT FACET VALUE)
  (LET ((VALUE-LIST (FOLLOW-PATH (LIST SLOT FACET)
                                 (FGET-FRAME FRAME))))
    (COND ((MEMBER VALUE VALUE-LIST) NIL)
          (T (RPLACD (LAST VALUE-LIST) (LIST VALUE))
             VALUE))))
```

`FPUT` uses `FGET-FRAME` to get an existing frame structure if there is one; if there is none, `FGET-FRAME` makes one.

```
(DEFUN FGET-FRAME (FRAME)
  (COND ((GET FRAME 'FRAME))                              ;Frame already made?
        (T (SETF (GET FRAME 'FRAME) (LIST FRAME)))))      ;If not, make one.
```

To complete the basic frame procedures, we add `FREMOVE` to complement `FGET` and `FPUT`. It works by using `FOLLOW-PATH` to work through frame structure, whereupon `DELETE` attacks, if appropriate:

```
(DEFUN FREMOVE (FRAME SLOT FACET VALUE)
  (LET ((VALUE-LIST (FOLLOW-PATH (LIST SLOT FACET)
                                 (FGET-FRAME FRAME))))
    (COND ((MEMBER VALUE VALUE-LIST)
           (DELETE VALUE VALUE-LIST)
           T)
          (T NIL))))
```

Problems

Problem 22-1:   Define `FCHECK`, a procedure of four arguments:

```
(FCHECK <frame> <slot> <facet> <value>)
```

It is to return `T` if the given value is in the given facet of the given slot of the given frame and `NIL` otherwise.

Problem 22-2:   Define `FCLAMP`, a procedure of three arguments:

```
(FCLAMP <frame 1> <frame 2> <slot>)
```

Its purpose is to tie together the two frames so that anything that goes into the given slot by way of either frame goes automatically into the other. You will need to use a dangerous, list-structure-altering procedure. You may assume that the first frame does not exhibit the given slot at the time `FCLAMP` is used.

Defaults and If-needed Demons Are Easy to Exploit

Using FGET, it is easy to write a procedure that first looks in the VALUE facet of a given slot and then in the DEFAULT facet if nothing is found in the VALUE facet:

```
(DEFUN FGET-V-D (FRAME SLOT)
  (COND ((FGET FRAME SLOT 'VALUE))
        ((FGET FRAME SLOT 'DEFAULT))))
```

Next we add a feature that causes all procedures found in the IF-NEEDED facet to be executed if neither the VALUE nor DEFAULT facets help:

```
(DEFUN FGET-V-D-P (FRAME SLOT)
  (COND ((FGET FRAME SLOT 'VALUE))            ; Try values first.
        ((FGET FRAME SLOT 'DEFAULT))          ; Then try defaults.
        (T (MAPCAN                            ; Combine results, if any.
            #'(LAMBDA (DEMON) (FUNCALL DEMON FRAME SLOT))
            (FGET FRAME SLOT 'IF-NEEDED)))))
```

The if-needed procedures are assumed to take two arguments, the frame name and the slot name. Furthermore, they are to return a list of values, possibly empty.

- Procedures that are activated automatically in response to the need for a value are called *demons*. Procedures that are activated automatically when a value is placed or removed are also called demons. Thus there are if-needed, if-added, and if-removed demons.

The following procedure, ASK, could be a very popular occupant of the IF-NEEDED facet of a slot:

```
(DEFUN ASK (FRAME SLOT)
  (PRINT `(PLEASE SUPPLY A VALUE FOR THE
                  ,SLOT SLOT IN THE
                  ,FRAME FRAME))
  (TERPRI)                                    ; Start new line.
  (LET ((RESPONSE (READ)))                    ; Get user's answer.
    (COND (RESPONSE (LIST RESPONSE))          ; Return list with answer if
          (T NIL))))                          ;  RESPONSE is other than NIL.
```

For calculating Paul's weight, if it is not given explicitly or by default, the following procedure would supply a result if there is a height or default height:

```
(DEFUN CALCULATE-WEIGHT (FRAME SLOT)
  (LET ((HEIGHT (FGET-V-D FRAME 'HEIGHT)))
    (COND (HEIGHT (LIST (FPUT FRAME
                              'WEIGHT
                              'VALUE
                              (* 33 (CAR HEIGHT)))))))))
```

Note that `CALCULATE-WEIGHT` both inserts its conclusion into the frame and returns the conclusion as its value. The procedure would be put in place like this:

```
(FPUT 'PAUL 'WEIGHT 'IF-NEEDED 'CALCULATE-WEIGHT)
```

Now suppose we know Paul's height:

```
(FPUT 'PAUL 'HEIGHT 'VALUE 1.77)
```

With the height known, the `CALCULATE-WEIGHT` if-needed demon can be activated usefully, producing an answer and placing the answer in the weight slot:

```
(FGET-V-D-P 'PAUL 'WEIGHT)
  (58.41)
```

Inheritance Works through the A-KIND-OF Slot

Instead of looking at the `DEFAULT` or `IF-NEEDED` facets of a slot if the `VALUE` facet has nothing, it is possible instead to look for values in frames that the given frame is related to. For this we work through the `A-KIND-OF` slot using a procedure like `FGET-I`, where the `I` is for inherit. `FGET-I` uses `FGET-CLASSES`, a procedure that returns a list of all frames that a given frame is linked to by an `A-KIND-OF` path.

```
(DEFUN FGET-I (FRAME SLOT)
  (FGET-I1 (FGET-CLASSES FRAME) SLOT))

(DEFUN FGET-I1 (FRAMES SLOT)
  (COND ((NULL FRAMES) NIL)                   ;Give up?
        ((FGET (CAR FRAMES) SLOT 'VALUE))     ;Got something?
        (T (FGET-I1 (CDR FRAMES) SLOT))))     ;Climb tree.
```

Other possibilities immediately come to mind to complement `FGET-I`. For example, `FGET-N` does N-inheritance: it first follows `A-KIND-OF` relations looking for values only; finding none, it starts over at the beginning, looking this time for defaults as it moves through the `A-KIND-OF` relations; and finally, if both other possibilities fail, it looks for if-needed procedures. `FGET-Z` is similar in that it looks for values, defaults, and if-needed procedures. It is different in that it exhausts each frame in the `A-KIND-OF` chain before moving up. Note the mnemonic use of the letters `I`, `N`, and `Z`: `FGET-I` makes one trip up the `A-KIND-OF` chain looking only at values; `FGET-N` goes up once, then starts over and goes up again, forming an N if the path is drawn on paper; and `FGET-Z` goes up only once, as does `GET-I`, but it looks at defaults and procedures, as well as values, following a sort of zig-zag pattern.

These new procedures make it possible to put values, defaults, and if-needed procedures in the most general places possible. For example, it is no longer necessary to place the CALCULATE-WEIGHT if-needed procedure in the PAUL frame and in every other man frame. Instead it is placed in the MAN frame where it is accessible whenever any effort is made to find the weight of a man using FGET-N or FGET-Z:

```
(FPUT 'MAN 'WEIGHT 'IF-NEEDED 'CALCULATE-WEIGHT)
```

Problems

Problem 22-3: Define FGET-CLASSES, a procedure that returns a list of all frames that a given frame is linked to by an A-KIND-OF path. Be sure that no frame in the list is returned more than once.
Problem 22-4: Define FGET-Z.
Problem 22-5: Define FGET-N.

**FPUT-P and
FREMOVE-P Activate
Demons**

If-needed procedures are useful when a value is wanted, yet no value or default is explicitly given. If-added and if-removed procedures are useful when the addition or removal of a value should cause some secondary action. Suppose, for example, that Paul's weight should be calculated whenever his height is specified. This could be arranged by way of using CALCULATE-WEIGHT as an if-added procedure. Before it was thought of as an if-needed procedure residing in the IF-NEEDED facet of the WEIGHT slot. Now we can think of it as an if-added procedure residing in the IF-ADDED facet of the HEIGHT slot:

```
(FPUT 'PAUL 'HEIGHT 'IF-ADDED 'CALCULATE-WEIGHT)
```

It would make more sense, however, to put the procedure in the MAN frame, if indeed the calculation makes sense for men in general:

```
(FPUT 'MAN 'HEIGHT 'IF-ADDED 'CALCULATE-WEIGHT)
```

Thus it is reasonable to activate the corresponding procedures found by following A-KIND-OF paths. Hence, the following procedure for using if-added procedures makes sense:

```
(DEFUN FPUT-P (FRAME SLOT FACET VALUE)
  (COND ((FPUT FRAME SLOT FACET VALUE)
         (MAPCAR #'(LAMBDA (E)                              ;Use procedures.
                     (MAPCAR #'(LAMBDA (DEMON) (FUNCALL DEMON FRAME SLOT))
                             (FGET E SLOT 'IF-ADDED)))
                 (FGET-CLASSES FRAME))
         VALUE)))
```

Again assume **FGET-CLASSES** finds all frames that the given frame is linked to by an **A-KIND-OF** path. Needless to say, the definition of **FREMOVE-P** would be very similar.

Problems   **Problem 22-6:**   Define **FREMOVE-P**.

Summary
- A frame is a generalized property list.
- Frames can be represented as nested association lists.
- **FGET, FPUT,** and **FREMOVE** are the basic frame-handling procedures.
- Defaults and if-needed demons are easy to exploit.
- Inheritance works through the **A-KIND-OF** slot.
- **FPUT-P** and **FREMOVE-P** activate demons.

References   For a general introduction to knowledge representation, see *Artificial Intelligence (Second Edition)* by Patrick H. Winston [1984].

The programs in this chapter capture some of the ideas in Marvin Minsky's original paper on frames [1975]. In terms of their function, the programs resemble those in FRL, the frames-representation language designed and first implemented by Ira Goldstein and Bruce Roberts [1977].

23

Lisp
In
Lisp

The best way to describe a procedure often is to give its definition in LISP. Because the evaluation of LISP procedures surely requires a procedure, it is reasonable to conclude that LISP itself might be usefully described in terms of a LISP procedure. The purpose of this chapter is to show how this can be done. In particular, it presents an interpreter for MICRO LISP, a sort of primitive, LISPlike language. To avoid confusion, however, remember that our primitive MICRO LISP differs from LISP in many details.

A Simple Symbol-manipulation Language Can Be Interpreted Easily

To keep things straight, let us begin with some naming conventions:

- All names of built-in primitive procedures in MICRO LISP begin with M-. Thus M-CAR, M-CDR, and M-CONS are the MICRO LISP analogs to CAR, CDR, and CONS in LISP.

- All names of LISP-defined procedures needed to implement MICRO LISP begin with MICRO-. Thus MICRO-EVAL, MICRO-APPLY, and MICRO-READ-EVAL-PRINT are all procedures defined in LISP in order to interpret MICRO LISP expressions.

MICRO-EVAL, MICRO-APPLY, and MICRO-READ-EVAL-PRINT are the key procedures of the interpreter. They will be explained first by a short overview and then by longer explanations accompanied by the complete procedure definitions:

- MICRO-EVAL gets two arguments, a form and an association list of variable values. The job of MICRO-EVAL is to classify forms and to decide how they should be evaluated. If the form is a symbol, MICRO-EVAL retrieves its value from the association list of variable values. Otherwise, MICRO-EVAL assumes the form is a procedure with arguments and evaluates the arguments in the way that is appropriate for the procedure. MICRO-EVAL then gets help from MICRO-APPLY.

- MICRO-APPLY gets three arguments, a procedure name or description, a list of arguments, and an association list of variable values. The job of MICRO-APPLY is to classify procedures and to arrange for their proper application. MICRO-APPLY handles some simple procedures directly. For others, MICRO-APPLY augments the association list of variable values with help from MICRO-EVAL. When procedure definitions are needed, MICRO-APPLY retrieves them from the association list of variable values. Thus both variable values and procedure definitions are stored on the same association list.

- MICRO-READ-EVAL-PRINT reads forms to be evaluated, evaluates them, and prints the results.

Note that the association list of variable values handed back and forth by MICRO-EVAL and MICRO-APPLY is called the *environment*. Soon you will see that the values returned by MICRO LISP forms depend on the details of the environment-handling scheme employed.

Now let us consider MICRO-EVAL in detail. Our first versions will do dynamic variable scoping, in contrast to LISP, which does lexical variable scoping.

MICRO-EVAL's first argument is a form to be evaluated, and its second argument is the environment. If the form given to MICRO-EVAL is a symbol, its value is found in the environment and returned. If the form begins with M-COND or M-SETQ, evaluation is handled by auxiliary procedures, MICRO-EVAL-COND or MICRO-ASSIGN-VALUE. Note that MICRO LISP is much less general than LISP. For example, M-COND clauses all are to have two forms and M-SETQ forms are all to have two arguments.

The test for M-QUOTE in MICRO-EVAL is needed because MICRO LISP needs something equivalent to QUOTE in LISP. M-QUOTE is the answer, because the argument of M-QUOTE is not evaluated. Thus M-QUOTE protects expressions in the same way LISP's QUOTE does.

Otherwise MICRO-EVAL evaluates all of the elements in the form after the first, in left-to-right order, and passes them to MICRO-APPLY along with a procedure name or procedure description and the environment:

```
(DEFUN MICRO-EVAL (FORM ENVIRONMENT)                        ;Preliminary version.
  (COND ((ATOM FORM)                                        ;If atom, then
         (COND ((NUMBERP FORM) FORM)                        ; if number, return;
               (T (MICRO-GET-VALUE FORM ENVIRONMENT))))     ; otherwise, look up.
        ((EQUAL (CAR FORM) 'M-QUOTE) (CADR FORM))           ;If quoted, return.
        ((EQUAL (CAR FORM) 'M-COND)                         ;If conditional,
         (MICRO-EVAL-COND (CDR FORM) ENVIRONMENT))          ; call auxiliary.
        ((EQUAL (CAR FORM) 'M-SETQ)                         ;If assignment,
         (MICRO-ASSIGN-VALUE (CADR FORM)                    ; change
                             (MICRO-EVAL (CADDR FORM)       ; environment.
                                         ENVIRONMENT)
                             ENVIRONMENT))
        (T (MICRO-APPLY (CAR FORM)                          ;Call MICRO-APPLY.
                        (MAPCAR #'(LAMBDA (X) (MICRO-EVAL X ENVIRONMENT))
                                (CDR FORM))
                        ENVIRONMENT))))
```

If MICRO-APPLY is handed a form whose first element is a primitive like M-CAR, M-CDR, or M-CONS, it does the appropriate thing directly. If it is handed a form whose first element is some other procedure name, it fetches a definition from the environment and recurses on itself. Because MICRO LISP definitions and variable values are both stored on the same environment association list, each MICRO LISP symbol can name either a procedure or a variable, but not both, in contrast to real LISP.

If MICRO-APPLY is handed a form whose first element is a procedure description, signaled by the symbol M-LAMBDA, it augments the environment using MICRO-BIND-AND-ASSIGN and hands the body of the m-lambda expression back to MICRO-EVAL:

```
(DEFUN MICRO-APPLY (PROCEDURE ARGS ENVIRONMENT)             ;Preliminary version.
  (COND ((ATOM PROCEDURE)                                   ;Procedure named.
         (COND ((EQUAL PROCEDURE 'M-CAR) (CAAR ARGS))       ;Special cases.
               ((EQUAL PROCEDURE 'M-CDR) (CDAR ARGS))
               ((EQUAL PROCEDURE 'M-CONS) (CONS (CAR ARGS) (CADR ARGS)))
               ((EQUAL PROCEDURE 'M-ATOM) (ATOM (CAR ARGS)))
               ((EQUAL PROCEDURE 'M-NULL) (NULL (CAR ARGS)))
               ((EQUAL PROCEDURE 'M-EQUAL) (EQUAL (CAR ARGS) (CADR ARGS)))
               ((EQUAL PROCEDURE 'M-*) (* (CAR ARGS) (CADR ARGS)))
               (T (MICRO-APPLY (MICRO-EVAL PROCEDURE ENVIRONMENT)
                               ARGS
                               ENVIRONMENT))))
        ((EQUAL (CAR PROCEDURE) 'M-LAMBDA)                  ;Procedure described?
         (MICRO-EVAL (CADDR PROCEDURE)                      ;Extract form.
                     (MICRO-BIND-AND-ASSIGN (CADR PROCEDURE) ;Augment
                                            ARGS              ; environment.
                                            ENVIRONMENT)))))
```

Now let us turn to `READ-EVAL-PRINT`. After it initializes the environment, all it does is read a form, evaluate it using `MICRO-EVAL`, and print the result, over and over:

```
(DEFUN MICRO-READ-EVAL-PRINT ()
  (DO ((ENVIRONMENT (LIST '(T T) '(NIL NIL))))   ;T is T and NIL is NIL
     (NIL)
   (TERPRI)
   (PRINT (MICRO-EVAL (READ) ENVIRONMENT))))      ;Read, evaluate, print.
```

To see how all this fits together, let us walk through an example. To keep things as simple as possible, we start by just using the primitive `M-CAR`, watching how `MICRO-EVAL` and `MICRO-APPLY` cooperate:

```
(MICRO-READ-EVAL-PRINT)
(M-CAR (M-QUOTE (A B C)))
  A
```

This looks simple, and in fact the interaction of `MICRO-EVAL` and `MICRO-APPLY` is simple, as the following trace demonstrates:

```
(MICRO-READ-EVAL-PRINT)
(M-CAR (M-QUOTE (A B C)))
(1 ENTER MICRO-EVAL ((M-CAR (M-QUOTE (A B C)))   ;Form evaluation starts.
                     ((T T) (NIL NIL))))          ;Initial environment.
  (2 ENTER MICRO-EVAL ((M-QUOTE (A B C))          ;Evaluate argument.
                       ((T T) (NIL NIL))))        ;Same environment.
  (2 EXIT MICRO-EVAL (A B C))                     ;Value of argument.
  (1 ENTER MICRO-APPLY (M-CAR ((A B C))           ;Apply procedure.
                        ((T T)                    ;Same environment.
                         (NIL NIL))))
  (1 EXIT MICRO-APPLY A)                          ;Value, procedure application.
(1 EXIT MICRO-EVAL A)                             ;Value, form evaluation.
A
```

Now to take a slightly more difficult example, assume we somehow have managed to get a lambda-style description of a procedure named `M-CADR` onto the environment:

```
((T T) (NIL NIL) (M-CADR (M-LAMBDA (L) (M-CAR (M-CDR L)))))
```

Now we can use `M-CADR`:

```
(M-CADR (M-QUOTE (A B C)))
  B
```

Seeing that `M-CADR` is a name for a procedure, rather than a lambda expression, the appropriate value is retrieved from the environment. This appropriate value is `(M-LAMBDA (L) (M-CAR (M-CDR L)))`. Consequently, the following m-lambda form acts just like `(M-CADR (M-QUOTE (A B C)))` :

```
((M-LAMBDA (L) (M-CAR (M-CDR L))) (M-QUOTE (A B C)))
```

The trace is not so simple, because it is cluttered by things on the environment association list:

```
(MICRO-READ-EVAL-PRINT)
(M-CADR (M-QUOTE (A B C)))
(1 ENTER MICRO-EVAL ((M-CADR (M-QUOTE (A B C)))    ;Form evaluation starts.
                     ((T T)                         ;Environment has definition.
                      (NIL NIL)
                      (M-CADR (M-LAMBDA (L) (M-CAR (M-CDR L)))))))
  (2 ENTER MICRO-EVAL ((M-QUOTE (A B C))            ;Evaluate argument.
                       ((T T)                        ;Same environment.
                        (NIL NIL)
                        (M-CADR (M-LAMBDA (L) (M-CAR (M-CDR L)))))))
  (2 EXIT MICRO-EVAL (A B C))                        ;Value of argument.
(1 ENTER MICRO-APPLY (M-CADR ((A B C))              ;Apply procedure.
                       ((T T)                        ;Same environment.
                        (NIL NIL)
                        (M-CADR (M-LAMBDA (L) (M-CAR (M-CDR L)))))))
  (2 ENTER MICRO-EVAL (M-CADR ((T T)                ;Fetch LAMBDA form.
                              (NIL NIL)
                              (M-CADR (M-LAMBDA (L) (M-CAR (M-CDR L)))))))
  (2 EXIT MICRO-EVAL (M-LAMBDA (L) (M-CAR (M-CDR L))))
  (2 ENTER MICRO-APPLY ((M-LAMBDA (L) (M-CAR (M-CDR L)))  ;Apply LAMBDA form.
                        ((A B C))
                        ((T T)
                         (NIL NIL)
                         (M-CADR (M-LAMBDA (L) (M-CAR (M-CDR L)))))))
    (2 ENTER MICRO-EVAL ((M-CAR (M-CDR L))          ;Evaluate LAMBDA form.
                         ((L (A B C))                ;Addition to environment.
                          (T T)
                          (NIL NIL)
                          (M-CADR (M-LAMBDA (L) (M-CAR (M-CDR L)))))))
      (3 ENTER MICRO-EVAL ((M-CDR L)                ;Evaluate form.
                           ((L (A B C))
                            (T T)
                            (NIL NIL)
                            (M-CADR (M-LAMBDA (L) (M-CAR (M-CDR L)))))))
        (4 ENTER MICRO-EVAL (L ((L (A B C))          ;Evaluate L.
                              (T T)
                              (NIL NIL)
                              (M-CADR (M-LAMBDA (L) (M-CAR (M-CDR L)))))))
        (4 EXIT MICRO-EVAL (A B C))
        (3 ENTER MICRO-APPLY (M-CDR                  ;Apply M-CDR.
                              ((A B C))
                              ((L (A B C))
                               (T T)
                               (NIL NIL)
                               (M-CADR (M-LAMBDA (L) (M-CAR (M-CDR L)))))))
        (3 EXIT MICRO-APPLY (B C))
      (3 EXIT MICRO-EVAL (B C))
```

```
     (3 ENTER MICRO-APPLY (M-CAR ((B C))                    ; Apply M-CAR.
                                  ((L (A B C))
                                   (T T)
                                   (NIL NIL)
                                   (M-CADR (M-LAMBDA (L)
                                                      (M-CAR (M-CDR L)))))))
        (3 EXIT MICRO-APPLY B)
      (2 EXIT MICRO-EVAL B)              ; Value of (M-CDR ...)
     (2 EXIT MICRO-APPLY B)
   (1 EXIT MICRO-APPLY B)
 (1 EXIT MICRO-EVAL B)                   ; Value of (M-CAR ...)
 B
```

Now that we have seen two simple examples, it is time to present the auxiliary procedures. The first pairs parameters with values and augments the environment:

```
(DEFUN MICRO-BIND-AND-ASSIGN (KEY-LIST VALUE-LIST A-LIST)
  (COND ((OR (NULL KEY-LIST) (NULL VALUE-LIST)) A-LIST)
        (T (CONS (LIST (CAR KEY-LIST) (CAR VALUE-LIST))
                 (MICRO-BIND-AND-ASSIGN (CDR KEY-LIST)
                                        (CDR VALUE-LIST)
                                        A-LIST)))))
```

The next auxiliary procedure just retrieves values from the environment, defaulting to NIL if nothing is found:

```
(DEFUN MICRO-GET-VALUE (KEY A-LIST)
  (CADR (ASSOC KEY A-LIST)))
```

The next auxiliary procedure is used when M-SETQ is encountered. The response depends on whether there is already a variable-value pair for the first argument in the environment somewhere. If there already is a variable-value pair, the variable is reassigned; if not, the variable is bound, assigned, and recorded in the back of the environment association list where variables are universally accessible:

```
(DEFUN MICRO-ASSIGN-VALUE (VARIABLE VALUE A-LIST)
  (LET ((ENTRY (ASSOC VARIABLE A-LIST)))
    (COND (ENTRY (RPLACA (CDR ENTRY) VALUE))
          (T (RPLACD (LAST A-LIST)
                     (LIST (LIST VARIABLE VALUE)))))
    VALUE))
```

In our primitive MICRO LISP, we make use of MICRO-ASSIGN-VALUE, via M-SETQ, to place procedure definitions on the environment. Here is how M-CADR is defined, for example:

```
(M-SETQ M-CADR (M-QUOTE (M-LAMBDA (L) (M-CAR (M-CDR L)))))
```

The next auxiliary procedure is used when M-COND is encountered. Although we do not actually follow M-COND in any examples, here is the necessary auxiliary procedure for handling it:

```
(DEFUN MICRO-EVAL-COND (CLAUSES ENVIRONMENT)
  (COND ((NULL CLAUSES) NIL)
        ((MICRO-EVAL (CAAR CLAUSES) ENVIRONMENT)
         (MICRO-EVAL (CADAR CLAUSES) ENVIRONMENT))
        (T (MICRO-EVAL-COND (CDR CLAUSES) ENVIRONMENT))))
```

Note that this definition of MICRO-EVAL-COND permits M-CONDs to have only clauses with exactly two elements.

This concludes the basic development of MICRO LISP. From here, more and more power can be developed by bootstrapping, using MICRO LISP's own procedure-defining mechanism, just as we did when we defined M-CADR. Here is another example, one using M-COND:

```
(M-SETQ M-APPEND
  (M-QUOTE (M-LAMBDA (L1 L2)
                (M-COND ((M-NULL L1) L2)
                        (T (M-CONS (M-CAR L1)
                                   (M-APPEND (M-CDR L1) L2)))))))
```

Both Dynamic and Lexical Variable Binding May Be Arranged

In MICRO LISP, the values of all variables are determined by the environment. Our first versions of MICRO-APPLY and MICRO-EVAL pass environments back and forth such that only dynamic variable scoping is possible. Our next versions pass environments such that both dynamic and lexical variable scoping are possible, with the user determining the choice.

In the body of an m-lambda expression that is inside an M-QUOTE, the values of all free variables will be found by referring to the environment that is current when the m-lambda description *is used* in MICRO-APPLY:

```
(M-QUOTE (M-LAMBDA <parameters> <body, possibly with dynamic variables>))
```

We say that the values of free variables in quoted m-lambda expressions are determined *dynamically*.

Now, however, we introduce a complementary mechanism. We allow m-lambda expressions to appear inside an M-CLOSE:

```
(M-CLOSE (M-LAMBDA <parameters> <body, possibly with lexical variables>))
```

The values of all free variables in the body of an m-lambda expression that is inside an M-CLOSE are found by referring to the environment that was current when the m-lambda description *was first encountered* in MICRO-EVAL. We say that the values of free variables in closed m-lambda expressions are determined *lexically*.

Before introducing the necessary additions to MICRO-EVAL and MICRO-APPLY, let us look at a situation where the difference between dynamic and lexical variables matters. We start by defining a procedure, DO-IT-TWICE, which takes two arguments, the first of which is a procedure. DO-IT-TWICE is to use the procedure given as its first argument on its second argument and then use the procedure again on the result:

```
(M-SETQ DO-IT-TWICE
        (M-QUOTE (M-LAMBDA (P X) (P (P X)))))
```

Now suppose DO-IT-TWICE is used in two situations, one with a quoted m-lambda expression and one with a closed m-lambda expression. In both situations, the m-lambda expression, by accident, uses X as a free variable:

```
(M-SETQ X 3)
  3
(DO-IT-TWICE (M-QUOTE (M-LAMBDA (Y) (M-* X Y))) 2)
  8
(DO-IT-TWICE (M-CLOSE (M-LAMBDA (Y) (M-* X Y))) 2)
  18
```

Note that the results differ because DO-IT-TWICE happens to bind and assign X, the variable that is free in the m-lambda expression. In the situation where the m-lambda expression appears inside M-QUOTE, the free variables are determined by the environment that is current when the m-lambda expression is used by MICRO-APPLY. But by that time, X has been bound and assigned a value of 2 in the process of handling the parameters of DO-IT-TWICE. Consequently, the value used for X is 2 and the result is 8.

On the other hand, in the situation where the m-lambda expression appears inside M-CLOSE, the free variables are determined by the environment that was current when the m-lambda expression was encountered by MICRO-EVAL. At that time, nothing had been done with the parameters of DO-IT-TWICE. Consequently, the value used for X is 3 and the result is 18.

Now let us see how to implement the changes that make M-CLOSE work. The first necessary change has MICRO-EVAL convert m-lambda expressions surrounded by M-CLOSE into m-closure expressions. M-closure expressions have an extra place reserved for the current environment. Consider these:

```
(M-QUOTE (M-LAMBDA (Y) (M-* X Y)))
 (M-LAMBDA (Y) (M-* X Y))

(M-CLOSE (M-LAMBDA (Y) (M-* X Y)))
 (M-CLOSURE (Y) (M-* X Y) <current value of ENVIRONMENT>)
```

The second necessary change has MICRO-APPLY handle m-closure expressions slightly differently from m-lambda expressions. When an m-closure expression is encountered, MICRO-APPLY must dig out the environment that the m-closure expression comes with, instead of using the current environment. Here are the MICRO-APPLY procedure fragments that differ:

```
            '
            .
            .
(MICRO-EVAL (CADDR PROCEDURE)
            (MICRO-BIND-AND-ASSIGN (CADR PROCEDURE) ARGS ENVIRONMENT))
            .
            .

(MICRO-EVAL (CADDR PROCEDURE)
            (MICRO-BIND-AND-ASSIGN (CADR PROCEDURE) ARGS (CADDDR PROCEDURE)))
            .
            .
            .
```

Note that the body of an m-lambda expression is evaluated by adding new parameter-value pairs to the *current environment*, whereas the body of an m-closure expression is evaluated by adding new parameter-value pairs to the *definition environment*, the one that was current when M-CLOSE was encountered.[1]

To summarize, MICRO-EVAL and MICRO-APPLY now look like this:

```
(DEFUN MICRO-EVAL (FORM ENVIRONMENT)
  (COND ((ATOM FORM)
         (COND ((NUMBERP FORM) FORM)
               (T (MICRO-GET-VALUE FORM ENVIRONMENT))))
        ((EQUAL (CAR FORM) 'M-QUOTE) (CADR FORM))
        ((EQUAL (CAR FORM) 'M-COND)
         (MICRO-EVAL-COND (CDR FORM) ENVIRONMENT))
        ((EQUAL (CAR FORM) 'M-CLOSE)                    ;Added to make closures.
         (LIST 'M-CLOSURE
               (CADR (CADR FORM))
               (CADDR (CADR FORM))
               ENVIRONMENT))
        ((EQUAL (CAR FORM) 'M-SETQ)
         (MICRO-ASSIGN-VALUE (CADR FORM)
                             (MICRO-EVAL (CADDR FORM) ENVIRONMENT)
                             ENVIRONMENT))
        (T (MICRO-APPLY (CAR FORM)
                        (MAPCAR #'(LAMBDA (X)
                                    (MICRO-EVAL X ENVIRONMENT))
                                (CDR FORM))
                        ENVIRONMENT))))
```

---

[1] Ensuring that a procedural argument uses the correct environment solves the <u>fun</u>ctional <u>arg</u>ument or *funarg* problem.

```
(DEFUN MICRO-APPLY (PROCEDURE ARGS ENVIRONMENT)
  (COND ((ATOM PROCEDURE)
         (COND ((EQUAL PROCEDURE 'M-CAR) (CAAR ARGS))
               ((EQUAL PROCEDURE 'M-CDR) (CDAR ARGS))
               ((EQUAL PROCEDURE 'M-CONS) (CONS (CAR ARGS) (CADR ARGS)))
               ((EQUAL PROCEDURE 'M-ATOM) (ATOM (CAR ARGS)))
               ((EQUAL PROCEDURE 'M-NULL) (NULL (CAR ARGS)))
               ((EQUAL PROCEDURE 'M-EQUAL) (EQUAL (CAR ARGS) (CADR ARGS)))
               ((EQUAL PROCEDURE 'M-*) (* (CAR ARGS) (CADR ARGS)))
               (T (MICRO-APPLY (MICRO-EVAL PROCEDURE ENVIRONMENT)
                               ARGS
                               ENVIRONMENT))))
        ((EQUAL (CAR PROCEDURE) 'M-LAMBDA)
         (MICRO-EVAL (CADDR PROCEDURE)
                     (MICRO-BIND-AND-ASSIGN (CADR PROCEDURE)
                                            ARGS
                                            ENVIRONMENT)))
        ((EQUAL (CAR PROCEDURE) 'M-CLOSURE)            ;Added to handle closures.
         (MICRO-EVAL (CADDR PROCEDURE)
                     (MICRO-BIND-AND-ASSIGN (CADR PROCEDURE)
                                            ARGS
                                            (CADDDR PROCEDURE))))))
```

Problems

Problem 23-1: Alter MICRO-EVAL so that it will accept procedure definitions in the following form:

```
(M-DEFUN <procedure name> <arguments> <single-expression body>)
```

You may assume that M-DEFUN makes expressions using M-LAMBDA rather than expressions using M-CLOSE, but note what the environment would look like if M-CLOSE expressions were used instead.

Problem 23-2: Programming language aficionados want procedure definitions to be available only in the environment where they are defined. Consequently, it is tempting to add them to the front of the environment association list instead of the back. Unfortunately, adding them to the front has problems: if two procedures are defined in the same environment and m-closures are made for both at the time of definition, then one will not be accessible by the other.

The solution is to generalize the environment association list. Instead of one long association list, the environment is to be a list of association lists. Each time MICRO-BIND-AND-ASSIGN is called, it is to add a new association list to the front of the list of association lists with the new variable assignments. Then, when a new procedure is defined, it can go to the end of the first of the association lists, the one representing the current additions to the environment.

Modify `MICRO-BIND-AND-ASSIGN`, `MICRO-ASSIGN-VALUE`, `MICRO-GET-VALUE`, and `MICRO-READ-EVAL-PRINT` to use environments that are lists of association lists instead of association lists. Then create `MICRO-ASSIGN-DEFINITION`, a procedure that puts a procedure definition in the right place when used as follows:

```
(MICRO-ASSIGN-DEFINITION <procedure name>
                         <parameters>
                         <body>)
```

LISP Is Best Defined in LISP

It may seem weird, but MICRO LISP could be modified and extended to become a language that is more and more like LISP itself. Because we already have described MICRO LISP using LISP, we must conclude that LISP can be described using LISP. To avoid confusion, keep in mind that programs are implementations of algorithms. LISP interpretation requires an algorithm, and LISP itself is a clear, transparent language; therefore, the LISP interpretation algorithm might just as well be implemented as a program in LISP!

- Describing how LISP works using LISP as a tool is similar to the way a dictionary defines words in terms of other, presumably simpler words. LISP can be defined in terms of a small number of primitive procedures.

That this can be done using only `EVAL`, `APPLY`, and a few other simple procedures is suggestive, for it means that a primitive LISP can be created by writing a few procedures in some other implementation language, followed by compiling those procedures into machine language using the implementation language's compiler.

Fancy Control Structures Usually Start Out as Basic LISP Interpreters

Inserting a layer of interpretation is the first step toward implementing fancy control structures. An interpreter interposed between the standard LISP evaluation procedure and a user's program provides the programming-language surgeon with a place to make incisions. There is no need to tamper with the offered version of a LISP interpreter. Instead, it is possible to frolic at will in the more exposed LISP-level implementation. This is the way many very-high-level languages are first implemented and tested.

Summary
- A simple symbol-manipulation language can be interpreted easily.
- Both dynamic and lexical variable binding may be arranged.
- LISP is best defined in LISP.
- Fancy control structures usually start out as basic LISP interpreters.

References   For a sparklingly clear treatment of the funarg problem, see Moses [1970]. For a sparklingly clear treatment of LISP interpretation in LISP, see Abelson and Sussman [1984].

Solutions to
the Problems

**Solutions to Problems
in Chapter 2**

Solution 2-1

ATOM	atom
(THIS IS AN ATOM)	list
(THIS IS AN EXPRESSION)	list
((A B) (C D))	list
3	atom
(3)	list
(LIST 3)	list
(/ (+ 3 1) (- 3 1))	list
)(	malformed expression
((()))	list

```
(()())                          list

((())                           malformed expression

())(                            malformed expression

((ABC                           malformed expression
```

Solution 2-2

```
(/ (+ 3 1) (- 3 1))
  2

(* (MAX 3 4 5) (MIN 3 4 5))
  15

(MIN (MAX 3 1 4) (MAX 2 7 1))
  4
```

Solution 2-3

```
(CAR '(P H W))
  P

(CDR '(B K P H))
  (K P H)

(CAR '((A B) (C D)))
  (A B)

(CDR '((A B) (C D)))
  ((C D))

(CAR (CDR '((A B) (C D))))
  (C D)

(CDR (CAR '((A B) (C D))))
  (B)

(CDR (CAR (CDR '((A B) (C D)))))
  (D)

(CAR (CDR (CAR '((A B) (C D)))))
  B
```

Solution 2-4

```
(CAR (CDR (CAR (CDR '((A B) (C D) (E F))))))
  D

(CAR (CAR (CDR (CDR '((A B) (C D) (E F))))))
  E

(CAR (CAR (CDR '(CDR ((A B) (C D) (E F))))))
  (A B)

(CAR (CAR '(CDR (CDR ((A B) (C D) (E F))))))
  ERROR

(CAR '(CAR (CDR (CDR ((A B) (C D) (E F))))))
  CAR

'(CAR (CAR (CDR (CDR ((A B) (C D) (E F))))))
  (CAR (CAR (CDR (CDR ((A B) (C D) (E F))))))
```

Solution 2-5

```
(CAR (CDR (CDR '(APPLE ORANGE PEAR GRAPEFRUIT))))

(CAR (CAR (CDR '((APPLE ORANGE) (PEAR GRAPEFRUIT)))))

(CAR (CAR (CDR (CDR (CAR '(((APPLE) (ORANGE) (PEAR) (GRAPEFRUIT)))))))))

(CAR (CAR (CAR (CDR (CDR '(APPLE (ORANGE) ((PEAR)) (((GRAPEFRUIT))))))))))

(CAR (CAR (CDR (CDR '((((APPLE))) ((ORANGE)) (PEAR) GRAPEFRUIT)))))

(CAR (CDR (CAR '((((APPLE) ORANGE) PEAR) GRAPEFRUIT))))
```

Solution 2-6

```
(A B C)

((A B C) NIL)

((A B C))
```

Solution 2-7

```
(SETQ TOOLS (LIST 'HAMMER 'SCREWDRIVER))
  (HAMMER SCREWDRIVER)

(CONS 'PLIERS TOOLS)
  (PLIERS HAMMER SCREWDRIVER)

TOOLS
  (HAMMER SCREWDRIVER)

(SETQ TOOLS (CONS 'PLIERS TOOLS))
  (PLIERS HAMMER SCREWDRIVER)

TOOLS
  (PLIERS HAMMER SCREWDRIVER)

(APPEND '(SAW WRENCH) TOOLS)
  (SAW WRENCH PLIERS HAMMER SCREWDRIVER)

TOOLS
  (PLIERS HAMMER SCREWDRIVER)

(SETQ TOOLS (APPEND '(SAW WRENCH) TOOLS))
  (SAW WRENCH PLIERS HAMMER SCREWDRIVER)

TOOLS
  (SAW WRENCH PLIERS HAMMER SCREWDRIVER)
```

Solution 2-8

```
(LENGTH '(PLATO SOCRATES ARISTOTLE))
  3

(LENGTH '((PLATO) (SOCRATES) (ARISTOTLE)))
  3

(LENGTH '((PLATO SOCRATES ARISTOTLE)))
  1

(REVERSE '(PLATO SOCRATES ARISTOTLE))
  (ARISTOTLE SOCRATES PLATO)

(REVERSE '((PLATO) (SOCRATES) (ARISTOTLE)))
  ((ARISTOTLE) (SOCRATES) (PLATO))

(REVERSE '((PLATO SOCRATES ARISTOTLE)))
  ((PLATO SOCRATES ARISTOTLE))
```

Solution 2-9

```
(LENGTH '((CAR CHEVROLET) (DRINK COKE) (CEREAL WHEATIES)))
  3

(REVERSE '((CAR CHEVROLET) (DRINK COKE) (CEREAL WHEATIES)))
  ((CEREAL WHEATIES) (DRINK COKE) (CAR CHEVROLET))

(APPEND '((CAR CHEVROLET) (DRINK COKE))
        (REVERSE '((CAR CHEVROLET) (DRINK COKE))))
  ((CAR CHEVROLET) (DRINK COKE) (DRINK COKE) (CAR CHEVROLET))

(REVERSE '((CAR CHEVROLET) (DRINK COKE))))
  ((DRINK COKE) (CAR CHEVROLET))
```

Solution 2-10

```
(SUBST 'OUT 'IN '(SHORT SKIRTS ARE IN))
  (SHORT SKIRTS ARE OUT)

(SUBST 'IN 'OUT '(SHORT SKIRTS ARE IN))
  (SHORT SKIRTS ARE IN)

(LAST '(SHORT SKIRTS ARE IN))
  (IN)
```

Solution 2-11

```
(SETQ METHOD1 '+)
  +

(SETQ METHOD2 '-)
  -

(SETQ METHOD METHOD1)
  +

METHOD
  +

(EVAL METHOD)
  ERROR

(SETQ METHOD 'METHOD1)
  METHOD1

METHOD
  METHOD1
```

```
(EVAL METHOD)
  +

(EVAL (EVAL '(QUOTE METHOD)))
  METHOD1
```

Solutions to Problems in Chapter 3

Solution 3-1

```
(DEFUN OUR-FIRST (S)
  (CAR S))

(DEFUN OUR-REST (S)
  (CDR S))

(DEFUN CONSTRUCT (ELEMENT S)
  (CONS ELEMENT S))
```

Solution 3-2

```
(DEFUN ROTATE-LEFT (L)
  (APPEND (CDR L)                    ;Append list of all but first element
          (LIST (CAR L))))           ; to list containing the first.
```

Solution 3-3

```
(DEFUN ROTATE-RIGHT (L)
  (APPEND (LAST L)                           ;Append list containing the last element
          (REVERSE (CDR (REVERSE L)))))      ; to list of all but the last.
```

Solution 3-4

```
(DEFUN PALINDROMIZE (L)
  (APPEND L (REVERSE L)))
```

Solution 3-5

```
(DEFUN F-TO-C (TEMPERATURE)
  (- (/ (+ TEMPERATURE 40)
        1.8)
     40))
```

(In some LISP dialects the slash, /, is used to signal an unusual treatment for the next character—it is a way to prevent a space from being interpreted as a separator, for example. As a result, it may be necessary in the above procedure to use // to get the equivalent of a single /.)

```
(DEFUN C-TO-F (TEMPERATURE)
  (- (* (+ TEMPERATURE 40)
        1.8)
     40))
```

Solution 3-6

```
(DEFUN QUADRATIC (A B C)
  (LIST (/ (+ (- B)
              (SQRT (- (* B B) (* 4.0 A C))))
           (+ A A))
        (/ (- (- B)
              (SQRT (- (* B B) (* 4.0 A C))))
           (+ A A))))
```

Solution 3-7

```
(DEFUN OUR-EVENP (N)
  (ZEROP (REM N 2)))
```

Solution 3-8

```
(DEFUN PALINDROMEP (L)
  (EQUAL L (REVERSE L)))
```

Solution 3-9

```
(DEFUN RIGHTP (H A O)
  (< (ABS (- (* H H)
             (+ (* A A)
                (* O O))))
     (* 0.02 H H)))
```

Solution 3-10

```
(DEFUN NOT-REALP (A B C)
  (MINUSP (- (* B B) (* 4.0 A C))))
```

or,

```
(DEFUN NOT-REALP (A B C)
  (< (* B B) (* 4.0 A C)))
```

Solution 3-11

```
(ABS X)    ≡    (COND ((MINUSP X) (- X)) (T X))

(MIN A B)    ≡    (COND ((< A B) A) (T B))

(MAX A B)    ≡    (COND ((> A B) A) (T B))
```

Solution 3-12

```
(NOT U)    ≡    (COND (U NIL) (T T))

(OR X Y Z)    ≡    (COND (X) (Y) (T Z))

(AND A B C)    ≡    (COND ((NOT A) NIL) ((NOT B) NIL) (T C))
```

Solution 3-13

```
(NIL)
```

Note that this is an exception to the equivalence:

```
(CONS (CAR L) (CDR L))    ≡    L
```

Solution 3-14

```
(DEFUN CHECK-TEMPERATURE (X)
  (COND ((> X 100) 'RIDICULOUSLY-HOT)
        ((< X 0) 'RIDICULOUSLY-COLD)
        (T 'OK)))
```

Solution 3-15

```
(DEFUN MEDIAN-OF-THREE (A B C)
   (COND ((< A B)                        ;Are A and B in order?
          (COND ((< B C) B)              ;Are B and C in order? If so B.
                (T (COND ((< A C) C)     ;Are A and C in order? If so C,
                         (T A)))))       ; else A.
         (T (COND ((< A C) A)            ;Are A and C in order? If so A.
                  (T (COND ((< B C) C)   ;Are B and C in order? If so C,
                           (T B)))))))   ; else B.
```

or, somewhat less efficient,

```
(DEFUN MEDIAN-OF-THREE (A B C)
   (MIN (MAX A B) (MAX B C) (MAX C A)))
```

Solution 3-16

```
(DEFUN CIRCLE (RADIUS)
   (LIST (* 2.0 PI RADIUS)
         (* PI RADIUS RADIUS)))
```

Solutions to Problems in Chapter 4

Solution 4-1

```
(DEFUN ADD (X Y)
   (COND ((ZEROP Y) X)
         (T (ADD (+ X 1) (- Y 1)))))
```

Solution 4-2

```
(DEFUN OUR-EXPT (M N)
   (EXPT-AUX M N 1))

(DEFUN EXPT-AUX (M N PRODUCT)
   (COND ((ZEROP N) PRODUCT)             ;n = 0?
         (T (EXPT-AUX M
                      (- N 1)
                      (* M PRODUCT)))))   ;Tail recurse.
```

Solution 4-3

```
(DEFUN OUR-REVERSE (L)  (REVERSE-AUX L NIL))

(DEFUN REVERSE-AUX (L REVER)
  (COND ((NULL L) REVER)                              ;End of list?
        (T (REVERSE-AUX (CDR L)
                        (CONS (CAR L) REVER)))))       ;Tail recurse.
```

Solution 4-4

```
(DEFUN OUR-EXPT (M N)
  (COND ((ZEROP N) 1)
        ((EVENP N) (OUR-EXPT (* M M) (TRUNCATE N 2)))
        (T (* M (OUR-EXPT (* M M) (TRUNCATE N 2))))))
```

or in tail recursive form:

```
(DEFUN OUR-EXPT (M N)
  (OUR-EXPT-AUX M N 1))

(DEFUN OUR-EXPT-AUX (M N RESULT)
  (COND ((ZEROP N) RESULT)
        ((EVENP N) (OUR-EXPT-AUX (* M M) (TRUNCATE M 2) RESULT))
        (T (OUR-EXPT-AUX (* M M) (TRUNCATE N 2) (* RESULT M)))))
```

Solution 4-5

```
(DEFUN COUNT-ATOMS (L)
  (COUNT-ATOMS1 L 0))                   ;Use auxiliary procedure.

(DEFUN COUNT-ATOMS1 (L COUNT)           ;Second argument is count so far.
  (COND ((NULL L) COUNT)                ;Return accumulated count.
        ((ATOM L) (+ COUNT 1))          ;Return count plus one for atom.
        (T (COUNT-ATOMS1 (CDR L)        ;Nothing done to value returned.
                         (COUNT-ATOMS1 (CAR L)    ;Outer count.
                                       COUNT))))) ;Inner count.
```

Note that this procedure is *not* tail recursive, because COUNT-ATOMS1 is invoked a second time, after the inner call to COUNT-ATOMS1 returns. So (CDR L), among other things, has to be remembered while the inner recursive form is evaluated. COUNT-ATOMS1 cannot just hand over control to a copy—it needs to get control back in order to invoke yet another copy, using the result obtained from the first one.

Solution 4-6

It computes the depth to which a given expression is nested.

Solution 4-7

It returns a copy of the expression it is given.

Solution 4-8

```
(DEFUN PRESENTP (ITEM S)
  (COND ((EQUAL S ITEM) T)
        ((ATOM S) NIL)
        (T (OR (PRESENTP ITEM (CAR S))
               (PRESENTP ITEM (CDR S)))))))
```

Solution 4-9

```
(DEFUN SQUASH (S)
  (COND ((NULL S) NIL)
        ((ATOM S) (LIST S))
        (T (APPEND (SQUASH (CAR S))
                   (SQUASH (CDR S)))))))
```

Solution 4-10

```
(DEFUN FIBONACCI (N)
  (FIBONACCI-AUX 1 1 1 N))

(DEFUN FIBONACCI-AUX (FO FN I N)
  (COND ((= I N) FN)                    ;Terminating condition.
        (T (FIBONACCI-AUX FN            ;f(n-1).
                          (+ FO FN)     ;f(n) + f(n-1).
                          (+ I 1)       ;Count up,
                          N))))         ; until i = n.
```

Solution 4-11

```
(DEFUN FIBONACCI (N)
  (ROUND (/ (- (EXPT (/ (+ 1.0 (SQRT 5.0)) 2.0) (+ N 1))
               (EXPT (/ (- 1.0 (SQRT 5.0)) 2.0) (+ N 1)))
            (SQRT 5.0))))
```

The result of the inner computation is a floating-point number. To make this version compatible with the others, we used ROUND to turn the result into an integer. Actually, one of the two terms in the difference is always much smaller than the other and so can be omitted safely if we are going to perform a rounding operation in the end anyway. Also, some efficiency could be gained here by computing the square root of 5 just once. How would you do that?

Solution 4-12

```
(DEFUN OUR-PAIRLIS (A B)                              ;Make list of pairs.
  (COND ((NULL A) NIL)                                ;One list empty?
        ((NULL B) NIL)                                ;Other list empty?
        (T (CONS (LIST (CAR A) (CAR B))               ;Make one sublist, then
                 (OUR-PAIRLIS (CDR A) (CDR B))))))     ; recurse on remainder.
```

We do not, in the above, trap the error that occurs when the lists have different lengths.

Also, the above solution is not tail recursive, because CONS is applied to the result returned by the recursive call to OUR-PAIRLIS. The following version uses an auxiliary procedure with an extra parameter to hold onto the partial result:

```
(DEFUN OUR-PAIRLIS (A B)                              ;Make list of sublists.
  (REVERSE (PAIR-AUX A B NIL)))                        ;Hand off to auxiliary.


(DEFUN PAIR-AUX (A B PARTIAL)
  (COND ((NULL A) PARTIAL)                            ;One list empty?
        ((NULL B) PARTIAL)                            ;Other list empty?
        (T (PAIR-AUX (CDR A)                          ;Recurse on remainder
                     (CDR B)                          ; after making
                     (CONS (LIST (CAR A) (CAR B)) PARTIAL))))) ; a sublist.
```

This version *is* tail recursive, because it does nothing to the value returned by the recursive call to PAIR-AUX. It just passes it upward again as the value *it* returns.

Why do we need REVERSE in the above procedure?

Solution 4-13

```
(DEFUN OUR-UNION (X Y)
  (COND ((NULL X) Y)
        ((MEMBER (CAR X) Y) (OUR-UNION (CDR X) Y))
        (T (CONS (CAR X) (OUR-UNION (CDR X) Y)))))


(DEFUN OUR-INTERSECTION (X Y)
  (COND ((NULL X) NIL)
        ((MEMBER (CAR X) Y)
         (CONS (CAR X) (OUR-INTERSECTION (CDR X) Y)))
        (T (OUR-INTERSECTION (CDR X) Y))))


(DEFUN OUR-SET-DIFFERENCE (IN OUT)
  (COND ((NULL IN) NIL)
        ((MEMBER (CAR IN) OUT) (OUR-SET-DIFFERENCE (CDR IN) OUT))
        (T (CONS (CAR IN) (OUR-SET-DIFFERENCE (CDR IN) OUT)))))
```

Solution 4-14

The procedure INTERSECTION will do the job. The following is a solution that does a little less work:

```
(DEFUN INTERSECTP (A B)
  (COND ((NULL A) NIL)            ;Exhausted A, none found in B.
        ((MEMBER (CAR A) B))      ;Is first element of A in B?
        (T (INTERSECTP (CDR A) B))))  ;Try remaining elements of A.
```

Solution 4-15

Here is a simple solution using SET-DIFFERENCE:

```
(DEFUN SAMESETP (A B)
  (NOT (OR (SET-DIFFERENCE A B) (SET-DIFFERENCE B A))))
```

Next, we show a solution using OUR-SUBSETP, which checks whether one set contains another:

```
(DEFUN SAMESETP (A B) (AND (OUR-SUBSETP A B) (OUR-SUBSETP B A)))

(DEFUN OUR-SUBSETP (A B)
  (COND ((NULL A) T)
        ((MEMBER (CAR A) B) (OUR-SUBSETP (CDR A) B))
        (T NIL)))
```

Note that we could have omitted the last clause in the conditional, exploiting the fact that NIL is returned if COND runs out of clauses to try.

Finally, we have a solution that uses REMOVE to remove elements of one set from the other:

```
(DEFUN SAMESETP (A B)
  (COND ((NULL A) (NULL B))
        ((NULL B) (NULL A))
        (T (SAMESETP (CDR A)
                     (REMOVE (CAR A) B)))))
```

There are, of course, many other ways to solve this problem.

Solution 4-16

```
(DEFUN MOBILEP (M)
  (COND ((ATOM M) M)                          ;Simple case.
        (T (MOBILEP-AUX (CAR M)
                        (MOBILEP (CADR M))
                        (MOBILEP (CADDR M))))))

(DEFUN MOBILEP-AUX (BEAM LEFT RIGHT)
  (AND LEFT                            ;Left submobile must be balanced.
       RIGHT                           ;Right submobile must be balanced.
       (= LEFT RIGHT)                  ;The two must weigh the same.
       (+ BEAM LEFT RIGHT)))           ;Total weight is the sum.
```

Solution 4-17

```
(DEFUN COMPILE-ARITHMETIC (S)
  (COMPILE-ARITHMETIC-AUX 1 S))

(DEFUN COMPILE-ARITHMETIC-AUX (R S)
  (COND ((ATOM S) (LIST (LIST 'MOVE R S)))
        (T (APPEND (COMPILE-ARITHMETIC-AUX R (CADR S))
                   (COMPILE-ARITHMETIC-AUX (+ R 1) (CADDR S))
                   (LIST (LIST (OPCODE (CAR S)) R (+ R 1)))))))

(DEFUN OPCODE (OP)
  (COND ((EQUAL OP '+) 'ADD)
        ((EQUAL OP '-) 'SUB)
        ((EQUAL OP '*) 'MUL)
        ((EQUAL OP '/) 'DIV)
        (T 'ERR)))
```

Solution 4-18

```
(DEFUN TREE-WEIGHT (TREE)
  (COND ((ATOM TREE) 1)                                    ;Easy case.
        (T (WEIGHT-AUX (TREE-WEIGHT (CADR TREE))           ;Left subtree.
                       (TREE-WEIGHT (CADDR TREE))))))       ;Right subtree.

(DEFUN WEIGHT-AUX (A B)
  (COND ((= A B) (+ A 1))                    ;When weights are equal.
        (T (MAX A B))))                      ;When they are unequal.
```

Solution 4-19

```
(DEFUN COMPILE-ARITHMETIC (S)
  (COMPILE-ARITHMETIC-AUX 1 S))


(DEFUN COMPILE-ARITHMETIC-AUX (R S)
  (COND ((ATOM S) (LIST (LIST 'MOVE R S)))
        ((> (TREE-WEIGHT (CADDR S))
            (TREE-WEIGHT (CADR S)))
         (APPEND (COMPILE-ARITHMETIC-AUX R (CADDR S))
                 (COMPILE-ARITHMETIC-AUX (+ R 1) (CADR S))
                 (LIST (LIST (OPCODE (CAR S)) (+ R 1) R))
                 (LIST (LIST 'COPY R (+ R 1)))))
        (T (APPEND (COMPILE-ARITHMETIC-AUX R (CADR S))
                   (COMPILE-ARITHMETIC-AUX (+ R 1) (CADDR S))
                   (LIST (LIST (OPCODE (CAR S)) R (+ R 1)))))))
```

Solution 4-20

```
(DEFUN PLOT-LINE (LENGTH ANGLE)
  (CONNECT-LINE (+ X-OLD (* LENGTH (COS ANGLE)))
                (+ Y-OLD (* LENGTH (SIN ANGLE)))))


(DEFUN CONNECT-LINE (X-NEW Y-NEW)
  (LINE X-OLD Y-OLD X-NEW Y-NEW)
  (SETQ X-OLD X-NEW Y-OLD Y-NEW))
```

Solution 4-21

```
(DEFUN PSEUDO-SIN (N)
  (COND ((MINUSP N) (- (PSEUDO-SIN (- N))))
        ((> N 7) (PSEUDO-SIN (REM N 8)))
        ((> N 3) (- (PSEUDO-SIN (- N 4))))
        ((= N 0) 0.0)
        ((= N 1) SQRT-HALF)
        ((= N 2) 1.0)
        ((= N 3) SQRT-HALF)))
```

Here it is assumed that SQRT-HALF is a free variable whose value is $1/\sqrt{2}$.

Solution 4-22

```
(DEFUN DRAGON-CURVE (LENGTH ANGLE SIGN MIN-LENGTH)
  (COND ((< LENGTH MIN-LENGTH) (PLOT-LINE LENGTH ANGLE))
        (T (DRAGON-CURVE (/ LENGTH (SQRT 2.0))
                         (+ ANGLE (* SIGN (/ PI 4.0)))
                         +1.0
                         MIN-LENGTH)
           (DRAGON-CURVE (/ LENGTH (SQRT 2.0))
                         (- ANGLE (* SIGN (/ PI 4.0)))
                         -1.0
                         MIN-LENGTH))))
```

Solution 4-23

These equivalences apply to LISP forms in general, because NOT always
returns NIL or T.

Solution 4-24

```
(DEFUN REWRITE (L)
  (COND ((ATOM L) L)
        ((EQUAL (CAR L) 'NAND)
         (LIST 'NAND
               (REWRITE (CADR L))
               (REWRITE (CADDR L))))
        ((EQUAL (CAR L) 'NOT)
         (REWRITE (LIST 'NAND (CADR L) T)))
        ((EQUAL (CAR L) 'AND)
         (REWRITE (LIST 'NOT
                        (LIST 'NAND (CADR L) (CADDR L)))))
        ((EQUAL (CAR L) 'OR)
         (REWRITE (LIST 'NAND
                        (LIST 'NOT (CADR L))
                        (LIST 'NOT (CADDR L)))))
        ((EQUAL (CAR L) 'XOR)
         (REWRITE (LIST 'AND
                        (LIST 'OR (CADR L) (CADDR L))
                        (LIST 'OR
                              (LIST 'NOT (CADR L))
                              (LIST 'NOT (CADDR L))))))
        (T (LIST 'ERROR L))))
```

Solution 4-25

```
(DEFUN DYNAMIC-RANGE (NUMBERS)
  (/ (APPLY 'MAX NUMBERS)
     (APPLY 'MIN NUMBERS)))
```

Solution 4-26

```
(DEFUN FACTORIAL (N)
    (DO ((I 1 (+ I 1)) (RESULT 1))          ;Initialize and reset.
        ((> I N) RESULT)                    ;Test and return.
        (SETQ RESULT (* RESULT I))))        ;Update result.
```

or, with an empty DO-body:

```
(DEFUN FACTORIAL (N)
    (DO ((RESULT 1 (* N RESULT))            ;Initialize and reset.
         (N N (- N 1)))                     ;Initialize and reset.
        ((ZEROP N) RESULT)))                ;Test and return.
```

Solution 4-27

```
(DEFUN OUR-MEMBER (ITEM INITIAL)
    (DO ((L INITIAL (CDR L)))               ;Step through all elements.
        ((OR (NULL L)                       ;List exhausted?
             (EQUAL ITEM (CAR L))) L)))      ;First element equal to ITEM?
```

Solution 4-28

```
(DEFUN OUR-REVERSE (INITIAL)
    (DO ((L INITIAL (CDR L))                ;Step through all elements.
         (RESULT NIL (CONS (CAR L) RESULT)))  ;Build result using CONS.
        ((NULL L) RESULT)))                 ;Terminating condition.
```

Solution 4-29

```
(DEFUN COALESCE (PAIRS) (COALESCE-AUX PAIRS NIL))

(DEFUN COALESCE-AUX (PAIRS CLASSES)            ;Remaining pairs and
    (COND ((NULL PAIRS) CLASSES)               ; existing classes.
          (T (COALESCE-AUX (CDR PAIRS)         ;Work on rest after
                           (ABSORB (CAR PAIRS) CLASSES)))))  ; absorbing a pair.

(DEFUN ABSORB (PAIR CLASSES)                   ;Try absorbing a pair.
    (COND ((NULL CLASSES) (LIST PAIR))         ;No match found?
          ((MEMBER (CAR PAIR) (CAR CLASSES))   ;CAR belong here?
           (STICK-IN (CADR PAIR) CLASSES))     ;Yes, stick in CADR.
          ((MEMBER (CADR PAIR) (CAR CLASSES))  ;CADR belong here?
           (STICK-IN (CAR PAIR) CLASSES))      ;Yes, stick in CAR.
          (T (CONS (CAR CLASSES)
                   (ABSORB PAIR (CDR CLASSES)))))) ;Else, try further on.

(DEFUN STICK-IN (NEW CLASSES)                  ;Stick new member in.
    (COND ((MEMBER NEW (CAR CLASSES)) CLASSES) ;Already there?
          (T (CONS (CONS NEW (CAR CLASSES))    ;No, stick it in.
                   (CDR CLASSES)))))
```

Solution 5-1

```
(DEFUN FETCH (KEY A-LIST)
  (COND ((CADR (ASSOC KEY A-LIST)))
        (T '?)))
```

Note that the procedure has only one use of ASSOC for the sake of efficiency. To do this, the procedure exploits the fact that the CAR and CDR of NIL are NIL.

Solution 5-2

```
(DEFUN LIST-KEYS (A-LIST)
  (MAPCAR 'CAR A-LIST))
```

Solution 5-3

```
(DEFUN TREND (OLD NEW)
  (LET ((NEW-TEMP-DIF (ABS (- (FETCH 'TEMPERATURE NEW) 98.6)))
        (OLD-TEMP-DIF (ABS (- (FETCH 'TEMPERATURE OLD) 98.6))))
    (COND ((> NEW-TEMP-DIF OLD-TEMP-DIF) 'SINKING)
          ((< NEW-TEMP-DIF OLD-TEMP-DIF) 'IMPROVING)
          (T 'STABLE))))
```

Solution 5-4

The given procedure will not work correctly if the association list maps X to Y, say, and also maps Y to Z. Depending on the order of substitution, an occurrence of X may be replaced by a Y or a Z. So, for example,

```
(OUR-SUBLIS '((X Y) (Y Z)) '((* X X) (* Y Y)))   ;Buggy version
  ((* Z Z) (* Z Z))                              ; gets surprise.
```

```
(OUR-SUBLIS '((Y Z) (X Y)) '((* X X) (* Y Y)))   ;Buggy version
  ((* Y Y) (* Z Z))                              ; gets it right.
```

The substitutions have to be done in *parallel*, not sequentially. The following works:

```
(DEFUN OUR-SUBLIS (A-LIST L)
  (COND ((NULL L) NIL)                           ;Nothing to do.
        ((ATOM L) (LET ((NEW (ASSOC L A-LIST)))  ;Pick up association
                    (COND (NEW (CADR NEW))        ; if there is one
                          (T L))))                ; else leave as is.
        (T (CONS (OUR-SUBLIS A-LIST (CAR L))     ;Recurse on CAR
                 (OUR-SUBLIS A-LIST (CDR L)))))))  ; and on CDR.
```

Solution 5-5

```
(DEFUN CONNECT (A B)
  (LET ((A-NEIGHBORS (GET A 'NEIGHBORS))
        (B-NEIGHBORS (GET B 'NEIGHBORS)))
    (COND ((NOT (MEMBER B A-NEIGHBORS))
           (SETF (GET A 'NEIGHBORS) (CONS B A-NEIGHBORS))))
    (COND ((NOT (MEMBER A B-NEIGHBORS))
           (SETF (GET B 'NEIGHBORS) (CONS A B-NEIGHBORS))))))
```

Alternatively, you may prefer to use ADJOIN:

```
(DEFUN CONNECT (A B)
  (SETF (GET A 'NEIGHBORS) (ADJOIN B (GET A 'NEIGHBORS)))
  (SETF (GET B 'NEIGHBORS) (ADJOIN A (GET B 'NEIGHBORS))))
```

Solution 5-6

```
(DEFUN DISTANCE (N1 N2)
  (SQRT (+ (SQUARE (- (GET N1 'X) (GET N2 'X)))
           (SQUARE (- (GET N1 'Y) (GET N2 'Y))))))

(DEFUN SQUARE (X) (* X X))
```

By using the procedure SQUARE, we avoid repeating the computation of the arguments that would occur had we simply used *. We could, of course, have used EXPT, with a second argument of 2.

Solution 5-7

```
(DEFUN GRANDFATHER (X)
  (COND ((GET X 'FATHER)
         (GET (GET X 'FATHER) 'FATHER))))
```

Solution 5-8

```
(DEFUN ADAM (X)
  (COND ((GET X 'FATHER)
         (ADAM (GET X 'FATHER)))
        (T X)))
```

Solution 5-9

```
(DEFUN ANCESTORS (X)
  (COND ((NOT X) NIL)
        (T (CONS X (APPEND (ANCESTORS (GET X 'FATHER))
                           (ANCESTORS (GET X 'MOTHER)))))))
```

352

Solutions to Problems in Chapter 6

Solution 6-1

```
(DEFUN PRESENTP (ITEM S)
  (COND ((EQUAL S ITEM) T)
        ((ATOM S) NIL)
        (T (APPLY 'OR (MAPCAR #'(LAMBDA (E) (PRESENT ITEM E))
                             S)))))
```

Solution 6-2

```
(DEFUN SUBSTITUTE-FOR-PARAMETERS (ARGUMENTS LEX)   ;Substitute arguments for
  (SUBLIS (PAIRLIS (CADR LEX) ARGUMENTS)           ; parameters in
          (CADDR LEX)))                            ; body of lambda expression.
```

Solutions to Problems in Chapter 7

Solution 7-1

```
(DEFUN MOVE-DISK (FROM TO)
  (PRINT (LIST 'MOVE (CAR (EVAL FROM))      ;Print out number,
               'FROM FROM                   ; from pin,
               'TO TO))                      ; and to pin.
  (COND ((NULL (EVAL FROM))
         (PRINT (LIST FROM 'EMPTY)))        ;No disks on pin.
        ((OR (NULL (EVAL TO))              ;Either pin is empty
             (> (CAR (EVAL TO))             ; or has larger disk
                (CAR (EVAL FROM))))         ; than one moved.
         (SET TO (CONS (CAR (EVAL FROM))
                       (EVAL TO)))           ;Add to new stack.
         (SET FROM (CDR (EVAL FROM))))       ;Remove from old.
        (T (PRINT (LIST 'CANNOT 'MOVE       ;Illegal move.
                        (CAR (EVAL FROM))
                        'ONTO
                        (CAR (EVAL TO))))))
  (LIST (LIST 'MOVE (CAR (EVAL TO))         ;Number of disk
              'FROM FROM                     ; moved from pin
              'TO TO)))                       ; to this pin.


(DEFUN TOWER-OF-HANOI ()
  (TRANSFER 'A 'B 'C (LENGTH A)))
```

Solution 7-2

```
(DEFUN ECHO1 ()
  (DO ()
      (NIL)
    (PRINT (READ))))

(DEFUN ECHO2 ()
  (DO ()
      (NIL)
    (PRINT (EVAL (READ)))))
```

Solution 7-3

Using SQUASH, as defined in a previous problem, we have:

```
(DEFUN P (MESSAGE)
  (PRINT (SQUASH MESSAGE)))

(DEFUN PC (TRIGGER MESSAGE)
  (COND (TRIGGER (P MESSAGE))))

(DEFUN RQ (MESSAGE)
  (P MESSAGE)
  (EVAL (READ)))
```

Solution 7-4

```
(DEFUN PSENTENCE (MESSAGE)
  (TERPRI)
  (PSENTENCE1 (SQUASH MESSAGE)))

(DEFUN PSENTENCE1 (REMAINDER)
  (COND ((NULL REMAINDER)              ;Just in case MESSAGE is NIL.
         (PRINC '|.|)
         T)
        ((NULL (CDR REMAINDER))        ;The normal termination; no space.
         (PRINC (CAR REMAINDER))
         (PRINC '|.|)
         T)
        (T (PRINC (CAR REMAINDER))     ;Print atom and space and continue.
           (PRINC '| |)
           (PSENTENCE1 (CDR REMAINDER)))))
```

354

Solution 7-5

```
(DEFUN BOOK-PRINT (MESSAGE)
  (TERPRI)
  (PRINC '|   |)
  (PRIN1 MESSAGE))
```

Solution 7-6

```
(DEFUN DATA-ENTRY (FORM)
  (TOP-OF-SCREEN)                                        ;Clear screen.
  (DATA-AUX FORM 0 0))                                   ;Call auxiliary procedure.


(DEFUN DATA-AUX (FORM ROW COLUMN)
  (COND ((NULL FORM))                                    ;See if all done.
        (T (SETQ ROW (DO ((I ROW (+ I 1)))
                         ((= I (CADAR FORM)) I)
                       (TERPRI) (SETQ COLUMN 0)))        ;Go down rows.
           (SETQ COLUMN (DO ((J COLUMN (+ J 1)))
                            ((= J (CADDAR FORM)) J)
                          (PRINC '|   |)))               ;Go across columns.
           (COND ((ATOM (CAAR FORM))                     ;Place to read?
                  (SETQ COLUMN
                        (+ COLUMN (READ-WORD (CAAR FORM) (READ)))))
                 (T (SETQ COLUMN                         ;Place to print.
                          (+ COLUMN (PRINT-WORDS (CAAR FORM))))))
           (DATA-AUX (CDR FORM) ROW COLUMN))))           ;Try next entry.


(DEFUN READ-WORD (NAME INFO)
  (SET NAME INFO)                                        ;Record information
  (+ (LENGTH (SYMBOL-NAME INFO)) 1))                     ; and compute length.


(DEFUN PRINT-WORDS (WORDS)
  (COND ((NULL WORDS) 0)                                 ;End of list of words?
        (T (PRINC (CAR WORDS))                           ;Print word
           (PRINC '|   |)                                ; and a space.
           (+ (+ (LENGTH (SYMBOL-NAME (CAR WORDS))) 1)   ;Add to length
              (PRINT-WORDS (CDR WORDS))))))              ; and do the rest.
```

Note that READ-WORD returns the length of what was read, for use in DATA-
AUX. Similarly, PRINT-WORDS returns the length of what it printed. The
above example is a little tricky because of the use of special variables in
association with SET.

Solution 7-7

```
(DEFUN OUR-PPRINT (L)
  (PPAUX L 0 T)                                          ;Print it nicely.
  (TERPRI)                                               ;Go to new line.
  S)                                                     ;Return S when done.


(DEFUN PPAUX (L COLUMN NEWLINE)                          ;Print one level.
  (COND (NEWLINE (TERPRI)                                ;Need new line?
                 (DO ((I 0 (+ I 1))) ((= I COLUMN))
                     (PRINC '| |))))                     ;Advance to COLUMN.
  (COND ((ATOM L)                                        ;If an atom, print it
         (PRINC L)                                       ; and increase COLUMN.
         (SETQ COLUMN (+ COLUMN (LENGTH (SYMBOL-NAME L)))))
        (T (PRINC '|(|)                                  ;Else, left paren
           (SETQ COLUMN (+ COLUMN 1))                    ; and increment,
           (SETQ COLUMN (PPAUX (CAR L) COLUMN NIL))      ; print first one.
           (COND ((CDR L)                                ;If more,
                  (PRINC '| |)                           ; print a space,
                  (SETQ COLUMN (+ COLUMN 1))             ; increment COLUMN,
                  (PPAUX (CADR L) COLUMN NIL)            ; and print next,
                  (MAPCAR #'(LAMBDA (E)                  ; and then the rest
                              (PPAUX E COLUMN T))
                          (CDDR L))))                    ; on new lines.
           (PRINC '|)|)                                  ;Print right paren
           (SETQ COLUMN (+ COLUMN 1))))                  ; and increment.
  COLUMN)                                                ;Return current column.
```

Note how the value of COLUMN is passed as an argument in calls to PPAUX as well as returned by it. In this fashion we avoid the need for a free variable in this solution. By the way, the above will blow up when we give it something that contains a dotted pair. How can it be modified to catch this and print something reasonable?

Solutions to Problems in Chapter 8

Solution 8-1

```
(DEFMACRO OUR-WHEN (TEST &REST REST)
  `(COND (,TEST ,@REST)))

(DEFMACRO OUR-UNLESS (TEST &REST REST)
  `(COND ((NOT ,TEST) ,@REST)))
```

Solution 8-2

```
(DEFMACRO BACKQUOTE (S)                          ;Macro prevents evaluation.
  (LIST 'BACKQUOTE1 (LIST 'QUOTE S))
  (LIST 'QUOTE (BACKQUOTE1 S)))                  ;Quote cancels exit evaluation.
```

```
(DEFUN BACKQUOTE1 (S)
  (COND ((OR (NULL S) (ATOM S)) S)
        ((EQUAL (CAR S) 'COMMA) (EVAL (CADR S)))
        ((AND (NOT (ATOM (CAR S))) (EQUAL (CAAR S) 'COMMA-AT))
         (APPEND (EVAL (CADAR S)) (BACKQUOTE1 (CDR S))))
        (T (CONS (BACKQUOTE1 (CAR S)) (BACKQUOTE1 (CDR S)))))))
```

Solution 8-3

```
(DEFMACRO DEFINE (NAME-AND-PARAMETERS &REST BODY)
  `(DEFUN ,(CAR NAME-AND-PARAMETERS) ,(CDR NAME-AND-PARAMETERS)
     ,@BODY))
```

Solution 8-4

```
(DEFMACRO OUR-FIRST (S)
  `(CAR ,S))

(DEFMACRO OUR-REST (S)
  `(CDR ,S))

(DEFMACRO CONSTRUCT (A B)
  `(CONS ,A ,B))
```

Solution 8-5

```
(DEFMACRO OUR-DOLIST (VARLIST &REST REST)
  `(DO* ((LST ,(CADR VARLIST) (CDR LST))
         (,(CAR VARLIST) (CAR LST) (CAR LST)))
        ((NULL LST) ,(CADDR VARLIST))
        ,@REST))
```

Solution 8-6

```
(DEFMACRO OUR-DOTIMES (VARCOUNT &REST REST)
  `(DO* ((LIMIT ,(CADDR VARCOUNT))
         (,(CAR VARCOUNT) O (+ ,(CAR VARCOUNT) 1)))
        ((= ,(CAR VARCOUNT) LIMIT) ,(CADDR VARCOUNT))
        ,@REST))
```

Solution 8-7

```
(DEFMACRO OUR-PUSH (ITEM STACK)
  `(SETQ ,STACK (CONS ,ITEM ,STACK)))

(DEFMACRO OUR-POP (STACK)
  `(SETQ ,STACK (CDR ,STACK)))
```

Solution 8-8

```
(DEFMACRO OUR-LET (ARGUMENT-LIST &REST BODY)
  `((LAMBDA ,(MAPCAR 'CAR ARGUMENT-LIST) ,@BODY)
    ,@(MAPCAR 'CADR ARGUMENT-LIST)))
```

Solutions to Problems in Chapter 9

Solution 9-1

```
(DEFUN OUR-NREVERSE (L) (NREVERSE-AUX NIL L))
```

```
(DEFUN NREVERSE-AUX (REV LST)
  (COND ((NULL LST) REV)                    ;End of list?
        (T (LET ((NEW (CDR LST)))           ;Hang on to rest,
             (RPLACD LST REV)               ; while clobbering CDR,
             (NREVERSE-AUX LST NEW)))))      ; and then tail recurse.
```

Solution 9-2

```
(RPLACA X Y)   ≡   (SETF (CAR X) Y)
```

```
(RPLACD X Y)   ≡   (SETF (CDR X) Y)
```

Solution 9-3

```
(DEFMACRO ENQUEUE (ITEM QUEUE)
  `(SETQ ,QUEUE (NCONC ,QUEUE (LIST ,ITEM))))
```

```
(DEFMACRO DEQUEUE (QUEUE)
  `(SETQ ,QUEUE (CDR ,QUEUE)))
```

Solution 9-4

```
(DEFUN N-ATOM (X) (EQUAL (CAR X) 'ATOM))

(DEFUN MARKEDP (X) (CADR X))

(DEFUN MARKIT (X) (RPLACA (CDR X) T))

(DEFUN UNMARK (X) (RPLACA (CDR X) NIL))

(DEFUN N-CAR (X) (CADDR X))

(DEFUN N-CDR (X) (CADDDR X))

(DEFUN N-RPLACA (X Y) (RPLACA (CDDR X) Y))

(DEFUN N-RPLACD (X Y) (RPLACA (CDDDR X) Y))

(DEFUN MAKE-ATOM (X) (LIST 'ATOM NIL X))

(DEFUN N-CONS (X Y) (LIST 'PAIR NIL X Y))
```

Solution 9-5

```
(DEFUN MARK (THIS)
  (COND ((OR (NULL THIS) (ATOM THIS)) THIS)      ;Easy cases.
        (T (DOWNCAR NIL THIS))))                 ;Start down the CAR.

(DEFUN DOWNCAR (OLD THIS)
  (LET ((NEW (N-CAR THIS)))                            ;Pick up new CAR.
    (COND ((OR (NULL NEW) (ATOM NEW) (MARKEDP NEW))    ;If CAR finished,
           (DOWNCDR OLD THIS))                         ; proceed down CDR.
          (T (N-RPLACA THIS OLD) (DOWNCAR THIS NEW))))) ;Reverse & down CAR.

(DEFUN DOWNCDR (OLD THIS)                              ;CAR finished,
  (MARKIT THIS)                                        ; so mark pair.
  (LET ((NEW (N-CDR THIS)))                            ;Pick up new CDR.
    (COND ((OR (NULL NEW) (ATOM NEW) (MARKEDP NEW))    ;If CDR also finished
           (UPCONS THIS OLD))                          ; go back up.
          (T (N-RPLACD THIS OLD) (DOWNCAR THIS NEW))))) ;Reverse & down CAR.

(DEFUN UPCONS (THIS OLD)
  (COND ((NULL OLD) THIS)                          ;Done if back pointer NIL
        (T (COND ((MARKEDP OLD)                    ;Done CAR and CDR yet?
                  (LET ((ANCIENT (N-CDR OLD)))     ;Yes, pick up pointer,
                    (N-RPLACD OLD THIS)            ; unreverse pointers,
                    (UPCONS OLD ANCIENT)))         ; and continue upward
                 (T (MARKIT OLD)                   ;No, mark it,
                    (LET ((ANCIENT (N-CAR OLD)))   ; pick up pointer,
                      (N-RPLACA OLD THIS)          ; unreverse pointers,
                      (DOWNCDR ANCIENT OLD)))))))   ; and continue down CDR.
```

Solutions to Problems in Chapter 10

Solution 10-1

```
(DEFUN PRINT-IMAGE (IMAGE)
  (LET ((N (ARRAY-DIMENSION IMAGE 0))        ;N rows and
        (M (ARRAY-DIMENSION IMAGE 1)))       ; M columns.
    (TERPRI)
    (DO ((I 0 (+ I 1))) ((= I N))            ;Step through rows.
      (DO ((J 0 (+ J 1))) ((= J M) (TERPRI)) ;Step though columns.
        (PRINC (AREF IMAGE I J)) (PRINC '| |)))))   ;Print one element.
```

Solution 10-2

```
(DEFUN STUFF-IMAGE (L)
  (LET ((IMAGE (MAKE-ARRAY (LIST (LENGTH L)
                                 (LENGTH (CAR L))))))  ;Set up array.
    (STUFF-IMAGE-AUX IMAGE 0 L)                        ;Fill it in.
    IMAGE))                                            ;Return as value.
```

Note how this procedure returns the array it created. If it did not do this, there would be no way to access it, and the array would be lost.

```
(DEFUN STUFF-IMAGE-AUX (IMAGE I L)
  (COND ((NULL L))
        (T (STUFF-ROW IMAGE I 0 (CAR L))              ;Go fill one row,
           (STUFF-IMAGE-AUX IMAGE (+ I 1) (CDR L))))) ; then do rest.
```

```
(DEFUN STUFF-ROW (IMAGE I J SL)
  (COND ((NULL SL))
        (T (SETF (AREF IMAGE I J) (CAR SL))           ;Put in one element,
           (STUFF-ROW IMAGE I (+ J 1) (CDR SL)))))    ; then do rest.
```

Note the use of tail recursion.

Solution 10-3

```
(DEFUN ORIENTATION (IMAGE)
  (LET ((N (ARRAY-DIMENSION IMAGE 0))            ;N rows and
        (M (ARRAY-DIMENSION IMAGE 1))            ; M columns.
        (C-0-A (CENTER N M)))                    ;Get center of area.
    (COND ((ATOM C-0-A) C-0-A)                   ;No object found.
          (T (LET ((IO (CAR C-0-A)) (JO (CADR C-0-A))
                   (SUM 0) (A 0) (B 0) (C 0))     ;Accumulators.
               (DO ((I 0 (+ I 1))) ((= I N))      ;Step through rows.
                 (SETQ A (- A (* SUM IO IO))      ;Adjust totals.
                       B (- B (* SUM IO JO))
                       C (- C (* SUM JO JO)))
                 (COND ((AND (ZEROP B) (= A C))   ;Object symmetrical.
                        (APPEND C-0-A '(SYMMETRICAL)))
                       (T (APPEND C-0-A (LIST (/ (ATAN (+ B B) (- A C))
                                                 2.0))))))
               (DO ((J 0 (+ J 1)))
                   ((= J M))                       ;Step through columns.
                 (COND ((ZEROP (AREF IMAGE I J)))  ;Ignore zeros.
                       (T (SETQ SUM (+ (+ SUM 1))
                                A (+ A (* I I))
                                B (+ B (* I J))
                                C (+ C (* J J)))))))))))
```

Note that in this version of ORIENTATION, A, B, and C are integers, up to the point where they are adjusted by the components of the center of area, IO and JO.

Solution 10-4

```
(DEFUN PROJECT (IMAGE)
  (LET ((N (ARRAY-DIMENSION IMAGE 0))            ;N rows and
        (M (ARRAY-DIMENSION IMAGE 1)))           ; M columns.
    (LET ((ROW (MAKE-ARRAY N))                   ;Row sums.
          (COLUMN (MAKE-ARRAY M)))               ;Column sums.
      (DO ((I 0 (+ I 1))) ((= I N))              ;Step through rows.
        (DO ((J 0 (+ J 1))) ((= J M))            ;Step through columns.
          (COND ((ZEROP (AREF IMAGE I J)))       ;Ignore zeros.
                (T (SETF (AREF ROW I)
                         (+ (AREF ROW I) 1))      ;Update row sum.
                   (SETF (AREF COLUMN J)
                         (+ (AREF COLUMN J) 1)))))) ;Update column sums.
      (LIST ROW COLUMN))))                       ;Return the arrays.


(DEFUN CENTER (IMAGE) (CENTER-AUX (PROJECT IMAGE)))   ;Pass sums.
```

```
(DEFUN CENTER-AUX (PROJECTIONS)
  (LET ((N (ARRAY-DIMENSION (CAR PROJECTIONS) 0))        ;N rows and
        (M (ARRAY-DIMENSION (CADR PROJECTIONS) 1))       ; M columns.
        (ROW (CAR PROJECTIONS))
        (COLUMN (CADR PROJECTIONS)))
    (LIST (DO ((I 0 (+ I 1))
               (SUM-R 0 (+ SUM-R (AREF ROW I)))
               (SUM-I 0 (+ SUM-I (* I (AREF ROW I)))))
              ((= I N) (/ (FLOAT SUM-I) (FLOAT SUM-R))))
          (DO ((J 0 (+ J 1))
               (SUM-C 0 (+ SUM-C (AREF COLUMN J0)))
               (SUM-J 0 (+ SUM-J (* J (AREF COLUMN J)))))
              ((= J M) (/ (FLOAT SUM-J) (FLOAT SUM-C)))))))))
```

Solution 10-5

```
(DEFUN ORIENTATION (IMAGE)
  (ORIENTATION-AUX (PROJECT IMAGE)))                     ;Pass sums.


(DEFUN ORIENTATION-AUX (PROJECTIONS)
  (LET ((N (ARRAY-DIMENSION (CAR PROJECTIONS) 0))        ;N rows and
        (M (ARRAY-DIMENSION (CADR PROJECTIONS) 1))       ; M columns.
        (C-O-A (CENTER-AUX PROJECTIONS)))                ;Get center of area.
    (COND ((ATOM C-O-A) C-O-A)                           ;No object found.
          (T (LET ((IO (CAR C-O-A)) (JO (CADR C-O-A))
                   (SUM 0) (A 0) (B 0) (C 0))            ;Accumulators.
               (DO ((I 0 (+ I 1))) ((= I N)              ;Step through rows.
                    (SETQ A (- A (* SUM IO IO)))         ;Adjust totals.
                          B (- B (* SUM IO JO)))
                          C (- C (* SUM JO JO)))
                    (COND ((AND (ZEROP B) (= A C))       ;Object symmetrical.
                           (APPEND C-O-A '(SYMMETRICAL)))
                          (T (APPEND C-O-A
                                (LIST (/ (ATAN (+ B B) (- A C))
                                         2.0)))))
                 (DO ((J 0 (+ J 1))) ((= J M)            ;Step through columns.
                    (COND ((ZEROP (AREF IMAGE I J))      ;Ignore zeros.
                           (T (SETQ SUM (+ (+ SUM 1))
                                    A (+ A (* I I))
                                    B (+ B (* I J))
                                    C (+ C (* J J)))))))))))))
```

First of all, we need a procedure to find row, column, *and* diagonal sums:

```
(DEFUN PROJECT-D (IMAGE)
  (LET ((N (ARRAY-DIMENSION IMAGE 0))           ;N rows and
        (M (ARRAY-DIMENSION IMAGE 1)))          ; M columns.
    (LET ((ROW (MAKE-ARRAY N))                  ;Row sums.
          (COLUMN (MAKE-ARRAY M))               ;Column sums.
          (DIAGONAL (MAKE-ARRAY (- (+ N M) 1))))  ;Diagonal sums.
      (DO ((I 0 (+ I 1))) ((= I N))             ;Step through rows.
        (DO ((J 0 (+ J 1))) ((= J M))           ;Step through columns.
          (COND ((ZEROP (AREF IMAGE I J)))      ;Ignore zeros.
                (T (SETF (AREF ROW I)           ;Update row sum.
                         (+ (AREF ROW I) 1))
                   (SETF (AREF COLUMN J)        ;Update column sums.
                         (+ (AREF COLUMN J) 1))
                   (SETF (AREF DIAGONAL (+ I J))   ;Update diagonal sums.
                         (+ (AREF DIAGONAL (+ I J)) 1))))))
      (LIST ROW COLUMN DIAGONAL))))             ;Return the arrays.
```

Now we can proceed simply as follows:

```
(DEFUN ORIENTATION (IMAGE)
  (ORIENTATION-AUX (PROJECT-D IMAGE)))          ;Pass sums.


(DEFUN ORIENTATION-AUX (PROJECTIONS)
  (LET ((N (ARRAY-DIMENSION (CAR PROJECTIONS) 0))   ;N rows and
        (M (ARRAY-DIMENSION (CADR PROJECTIONS) 1))  ; M columns.
        (C-O-A (CENTER-AUX PROJECTIONS))            ;Center of area.
        (IO (CAR C-O-A)) (JO (CADR C-O-A))
        (ROW (CAR PROJECTIONS))
        (COLUMN (CADR PROJECTIONS))
        (DIAGONAL (CADDR PROJECTIONS)))
    (LET ((SUM-II (DO ((I 0 (+ I 1))
                      (SUM-II 0 (+ SUM-II (* I I (AREF ROW I)))))
                     ((= I N) SUM-II)))
          (SUM-JJ (DO ((J 0 (+ J 1))
                      (SUM-JJ 0 (+ SUM-JJ (* J J (AREF COLUMN J)))))
                     ((= J M) SUM-JJ)))
          (SUM-KK (DO ((K 0 (+ K 1))
                      (SUM-KK 0 (+ SUM-KK (* K K (AREF DIAGONAL K)))))
                     ((= K (- (+ N M) 1)) SUM-KK)))
          (SUM (DO ((I 0 (+ I 1)) (SUM 0 (+ SUM (AREF ROW I))))
                  ((= I N) SUM))))
      (LET ((SUM-IJ (- SUM-KK (+ SUM-II SUM-JJ))))
        (SETQ SUM-II (- SUM-II (* SUM IO IO))
              SUM-JJ (- SUM-JJ (* SUM JO JO)))
        (COND ((AND (ZEROP SUM-IJ) (= SUM-II SUM-JJ))
               (APPEND C-O-A '(SYMMETRICAL)))
              (T (APPEND C-O-A
                   (LIST (/ (ATAN (* 2.0 SUM-IJ) (- SUM-II SUM-JJ))
                            2.0)))))))))
```

Solution 10-6

```
(DEFUN DISTANCE (A B)
  (COND ((AND (NULL A) (NULL D)) 0.0)          ;End of vector.
        ((OR (NULL A) (NULL B)) (PRINT 'ERROR))  ;Mismatch in length.
        (T (+ (SQUARE (- (CAR A) (CAR B)))       ;Sum of product and
              (DISTANCE (CDR A) (CDR B))))))      ; same applied to tail.
```

where SQUARE returns the square of its argument.

Solution 10-7

If the stored feature lists are altered to contain two-element lists of mean and variance, DISTANCE can be easily changed as follows:

```
(DEFUN DISTANCE (A B)
  (COND ((AND (NULL A) (NULL B)) 0.0)
        ((OR (NULL A) (NULL B)) (PRINT 'ERROR))
        (T (+ (/ (SQUARE (- (CAAR A) (CAR B)))
                 (CADAR A))
              (DISTANCE (CDR A) (CDR B))))))
```

Solution 10-8

```
(DEFUN MAKE-TABLE (L)                            ;Next & equivalent.
  (LET ((MAPPING (MAKE-ARRAY (+ (CAR L) 1))))    ;Set up lookup table.
    (FILL-TABLE MAPPING (COALESCE (CADR L)))     ;Fill using equivalences.
    MAPPING))                                    ;Return table.

(DEFUN FILL-TABLE (MAPPING CLASSES)              ;Place result in table.
  (COND ((NULL CLASSES))                         ;Done?
        (T (FILL-CLASS MAPPING (CAAR CLASSES)    ;First is representative.
                       (CAR CLASSES))            ;Rest labeled same.
           (FILL-TABLE MAPPING (CDR CLASSES))))) ;Then do others.

(DEFUN FILL-CLASS (MAPPING N CLASS)              ;Mapping for one class.
  (COND ((NULL CLASS))                           ;Done?
        (T (SETF (MAPPING (CAR CLASS)) N)        ;Put entry in table.
           (FILL-CLASS MAPPING N (CDR CLASS))))) ;Then do others.
```

Note, once again, the use of tail recursion in FILL-TABLE and FILL-CLASS. Actually, the difficult part is making a set of equivalence classes for the labels, using all the pairwise equivalences noted during the labeling process. Fortunately, we already solved that problem with COALESCE, defined in a problem near the end of chapter 4.

364

Solutions to Problems
in Chapter 11

Solution 11-1

```
(DEFUN SIMPLE-SEARCH (TREE GOAL)
  (COND ((EQL TREE GOAL) TREE)
        ((ATOM TREE) NIL)
        (T (CONS (CAR TREE) (OR (SIMPLE-SEARCH (CADR TREE) GOAL)
                                (SIMPLE-SEARCH (CADDR TREE) GOAL))))))
```

Solution 11-2

```
(DEFUN HILL (START FINISH)
  (HILL1 (LIST (LIST START)) FINISH))

(DEFUN HILL1 (QUEUE FINISH)
  (COND ((NULL QUEUE) NIL)
        ((EQUAL FINISH (CAAR QUEUE))
         (REVERSE (CAR QUEUE)))
        (T (HILL1 (APPEND (SORT (EXPAND (CAR QUEUE))
                                #'(LAMBDA (X Y) (CLOSERP X Y FINISH)))
                          (CDR QUEUE))
                  FINISH))))
```

Solution 11-3

```
(DEFUN PATH-LENGTH (CITIES)
  (COND ((NULL (CDR CITIES)) 0)
        (T (+ (DISTANCE (CAR CITIES) (CADR CITIES))
              (PATH-LENGTH (CDR CITIES))))))

(DEFUN SHORTERP (P1 P2)
  (< (PATH-LENGTH P1) (PATH-LENGTH P2)))

(DEFUN BRANCH-AND-BOUND (START FINISH)
  (BRANCH-AND-BOUND1 (LIST (LIST START)) FINISH))

(DEFUN BRANCH-AND-BOUND1 (QUEUE FINISH)
  (COND ((NULL QUEUE) NIL)
        ((EQUAL FINISH (CAAR QUEUE))
         (REVERSE (CAR QUEUE)))
        (T (BRANCH-AND-BOUND1 (SORT (APPEND (EXPAND (CAR QUEUE))
                                            (CDR QUEUE))
                                    'SHORTERP)
                              FINISH))))
```

Solution 11-4

```
(DEFUN BEAM (START FINISH WIDTH)
  (BEAM1 (LIST (LIST START)) FINISH WIDTH))


(DEFUN BEAM1 (QUEUE FINISH WIDTH)
  (COND ((NULL QUEUE) NIL)
        ((EQUAL FINISH (CAAR QUEUE))
         (REVERSE (CAR QUEUE)))
        (T (BEAM1 (SORT (MAPCAN 'EXPAND (FIRST-N QUEUE WIDTH))
                        #'(LAMBDA (X Y) (CLOSERP X Y FINISH)))
                  FINISH
                  WIDTH))))


(DEFUN FIRST-N (L N)
  (COND ((ZEROP N) NIL)
        (T (CONS (CAR L) (FIRST-N (CDR L) (- N 1))))))
```

Solution 11-5

```
(DEFUN RADIX-SORT (TABLE BOTTOM TOP NUM)
  (COND ((ZEROP NUM))                                    ;Terminate after right bit.
        ((= BOTTOM TOP))                                 ;Nothing left to sort here.
        ((= BOTTOM (- TOP 1)))                           ;Sorting one item is easy!
        (T (DO ((BO BOTTOM) (TO TOP))                    ;Up & down scan pointers.
               ((= BO TO)
                (RADIX-SORT TABLE BOTTOM TO (ASH NUM -1))    ;Divide &
                (RADIX-SORT TABLE BO TOP (ASH NUM -1)))      ; conquer!
             (SETQ BO (DO ((BB BO (+ BB 1)))                 ;Up till 1
                          ((OR (= BB TOP)                    ; or top.
                               (LOGTEST (AREF TABLE BB) NUM))
                           BB))
                   TO (DO ((TT TO (- TT 1)))                 ;Down till 0
                          ((OR (= TT BOTTOM)                 ; or bottom.
                               (NOT (LOGTEST (AREF TABLE (- TT 1)) NUM)))
                           TT)))
             (COND ((< BO TO) (LET ((X (AREF TABLE BO))
                                    (Y (AREF TABLE (- TO 1))))
                                (SETF (AREF TABLE (- TO 1)) X)  ;Exchange
                                (SETF (AREF TABLE BO) Y)))))))  ; the two.
```

Solution 11-6

```
(DEFUN SORT-MERGE (L)
  (COND ((NULL (CDR L)) L)                        ;Only one element.
        (T (OUR-MERGE (SORT-MERGE (FIRST-HALF L))  ;Sort first half.
                      (SORT-MERGE (LAST-HALF L)))))) ;Sort second half.


(DEFUN OUR-MERGE (A B)
  (COND ((NULL A) B)                              ;Easy cases first.
        ((NULL B) A)                              ;Easy cases first.
        ((< (CAAR A) (CAAR B))                    ;Pick smaller of the
         (CONS (CAR A) (OUR-MERGE (CDR A) B)))    ; elements at front of
        (T (CONS (CAR B) (OUR-MERGE A (CDR B)))))) ; the two lists.


(DEFUN FIRST-HALF (L) (HEAD L (- (LENGTH L) 1)))  ;Get first half of list.


(DEFUN HEAD (L N)
  (COND ((MINUSP N) NIL)
        (T (CONS (CAR L) (HEAD (CDR L) (- N 2))))))


(DEFUN LAST-HALF (L) (TAIL L (- (LENGTH L) 1)))   ;Get second half of list.


(DEFUN TAIL (L N)
  (COND ((MINUSP N) L)
        (T (TAIL (CDR L) (- N 2)))))
```

Solution 11-7

We use a straight insertion sorting method:

```
(DEFUN SPLICE-IN (ELEMENT S PREDICATE)            ;Insert ELEMENT in sorted S.
  (COND ((NULL S) (LIST ELEMENT))                 ;End of S?
        ((FUNCALL PREDICATE ELEMENT (CAR S))      ;Does ELEMENT belong here?
         (CONS ELEMENT S))                        ;Yes, splice it in.
        (T (CONS (CAR S) (SPLICE-IN ELEMENT       ;No, try further down inside S.
                                    (CDR S)
                                    PREDICATE)))))


(DEFUN OUR-SORT (S PREDICATE)                     ;Peel off one element at a time
  (COND ((NULL S) NIL)                            ; and feed to SPLICE-IN.
        (T (SPLICE-IN (CAR S)
                      (OUR-SORT (CDR S) PREDICATE)
                      PREDICATE))))
```

Solution 11-8

```
(DEFUN WATER-CROCK-OPTIMUM (A B C)
  (WATER-CROCK-AUX (WATER-CROCK A B C)
                   (WATER-CROCK B A C)))


(DEFUN WATER-CROCK-AUX (SEQ-A SEQ-B)
  (COND ((NOT (> (LENGTH SEQ-A) (LENGTH SEQ-B))) SEQ-A)
        (T (SUBST 'B 'TEMP (SUBST 'A 'B (SUBST 'TEMP 'A SEQ-B))))))
```

Solution 11-9

For a board size of 4×4, this can be done using nested DOs:

```
(DEFUN QUEEN ()
  (LET ((BOARD))
    (DO ((MO 0 (+ MO 1))) ((= MO 4))
      (SETQ BOARD (LIST (LIST 0 MO)))
      (DO ((M1 0 (+ M1 1))) ((= M1 4))
        (COND ((CONFLICT 1 M1 BOARD))
              (T (SETQ BOARD (CONS (LIST 1 M1) BOARD))
                 (DO ((M2 0 (+ M2 1))) ((= M2 4))
                   (COND ((CONFLICT 2 M2 BOARD))
                         (T (SETQ BOARD (CONS (LIST 2 M2) BOARD))
                            (DO ((M3 0 (+ M3 0))) ((= M3 4))
                              (COND ((CONFLICT 3 M3 BOARD))
                                    (T (SETQ BOARD (CONS (LIST 3 M3) BOARD))
                                       (PRINT (REVERSE BOARD)))))))))))))))
```

We are essentially doing a search of a (huge) tree, with extensive pruning. This can be written more directly as follows:

```
(DEFUN QUEEN (SIZE) (QUEEN-AUX NIL 0 SIZE))


(DEFUN QUEEN-AUX (BOARD N SIZE)                                ;Start on next row.
  (COND ((= N SIZE) (PRINT (REVERSE BOARD)))                   ;Found a solution.
        (T (QUEEN-SUB BOARD N 0 SIZE))))                       ;Try in this row.


(DEFUN QUEEN-SUB (BOARD N M SIZE)                              ;Try next column.
  (COND ((= M SIZE))                                           ;Hit end of row?
        (T (COND ((CONFLICT N M BOARD))                        ;Conflict?
                 (T (QUEEN-AUX (CONS (LIST N M) BOARD) (+ N 1) SIZE)))  ;No.
           (QUEEN-SUB BOARD N (+ M 1) SIZE))))                 ;Now move right one.
```

Solution 11-10

```
(DEFUN BOARD-PRINT (BOARD) (BOARD-PRINT-AUX BOARD (LENGTH BOARD)))


(DEFUN BOARD-PRINT-AUX (BOARD SIZE)
  (TERPRI)
  (COND ((NULL BOARD))                                    ;Stop if nothing left.
        (T (BOARD-PRINT-SUB (CADAR BOARD) 0 SIZE)         ;Do this row,
           (BOARD-PRINT-AUX (CDR BOARD) SIZE))))          ; then the next row.


(DEFUN BOARD-PRINT-SUB (COLUMN N SIZE)
  (COND ((= N SIZE))                                      ;Enough columns.
        (T (COND ((= COLUMN N) (PRINC 'Q))               ;Place Q here,
                 (T (PRINC '|.|)))                        ; a dot elsewhere and
           (PRINC '| |)                                   ; space in between.
           (BOARD-PRINT-SUB COLUMN (+ N 1) SIZE))))
```

Solution 11-11

```
(DEFUN PERMUTATIONS (SIZE) (PERM-AUX NIL 0 SIZE))


(DEFUN PERM-AUX (PERM N SIZE)                             ;Start on next row.
  (COND ((= N SIZE) (PRINT (REVERSE PERM)))              ;Found a solution.
        (T (PERM-SUB PERM N 0 SIZE))))                   ;Try this row.


(DEFUN PERM-SUB (PERM N M SIZE)                           ;Try next column.
  (COND ((= M SIZE))                                      ;Hit end of row?
        (T (COND ((MEMBER M PERM))                       ;Conflict?
                 (T (PERM-AUX (CONS M PERM) (+ N 1) SIZE)))   ;No.
           (PERM-SUB PERM N (+ M 1) SIZE))))              ;Now move right one.
```

Solutions to Problems
in Chapter 12

Solution 12-1

```
(DEFUN PRE-TO-INF (L)
  (COND ((NULL L) NIL)                          ;Simple case
        ((ATOM L) L)                            ;Simple case.
        (T (LIST (PRE-TO-INF (CADR L))          ;Translate part.
                 (OPSYMBOL (CAR L))             ;Look up symbol.
                 (PRE-TO-INF (CADDR L))))))      ;Translate rest.


(DEFUN OPSYMBOL (X)                             ;Get symbol
  (COND ((EQUAL X 'SETQ) '=)                    ; given LISP primitive.
        ((EQUAL X '+) '+)
        ((EQUAL X '-) '-)
        ((EQUAL X '*) '*)
        ((EQUAL X '/) '/)
        ((EQUAL X 'REM) '\\)
        ((EQUAL X 'EXPT) '^)
        (T X)))
```

Note that in COMMON LISP, the back-slash, \, is used to signal an unusual treatment for the next character—it is a way to prevent a space from being interpreted as a separator, for example. As a result, it is necessary in the above procedure to use \\ to get the equivalent of a single \.

Solution 12-2

```
(DEFUN PRE-TO-INF (L) (PRE-TO-INF-AUX L -1))

(DEFUN PRE-TO-INF-AUX (L WIN)
  (COND ((NULL L) L)                            ;Easy case.
        ((ATOM L) (LIST L))                     ;Easy case.
        (T (LET ((WOUT (PRECEDENCE (CAR L))))   ;Get weight of new.
             (COND ((< WOUT WIN)                ;Compare weights.
                    (LIST (APPEND (PRE-TO-INF-AUX (CADR L) WOUT)
                                  (LIST (OPSYMBOL (CAR L)))      ;Need parens.
                                  (PRE-TO-INF-AUX (CADDR L) WOUT))))
                   (T (APPEND (PRE-TO-INF-AUX (CADR L) WOUT)
                              (LIST (OPSYMBOL (CAR L)))          ;No parens.
                              (PRE-TO-INF-AUX (CADDR L) WOUT)))))))))

(DEFUN PRECEDENCE (X)                           ;Find weight
  (COND ((EQUAL X 'SETQ) 0)                     ; given LISP procedure.
        ((EQUAL X '+) 1)
        ((EQUAL X '-) 1)
        ((EQUAL X '*) 2)
        ((EQUAL X '/) 3)
        ((EQUAL X 'REM) 3)
        ((EQUAL X 'EXPT) 4)
        (T 5)))
```

Solution 12-3

Add the following to INF-AUX,

```
(COND (TRACE-FLAG (PRINT `(AE ,AE))))
(COND (TRACE-FLAG (PRINT `(OPERATORS ,OPERATORS))))
```

and add the following to INF-ITER,

```
(COND (TRACE-FLAG (PRINT `(AE ,AE))))
(COND (TRACE-FLAG (PRINT `(OPERANDS ,OPERANDS))))
```

Solution 12-4

Simply replace (> ...) by (NOT (< ...)).

Solution 12-5

Simply insert after the first clause of the conditional in INF-ITER:

```
((AND AE
      (OR (NOT (ATOM (CAR AE)))
          (= (WEIGHT (CAR AE)) 4)))
 (INF-ITER (CONS '* AE) OPERATORS OPERANDS)))
```

Solution 12-6

```
(SETF (GET '= 'WEIGHT) 0)
(SETF (GET '+ 'WEIGHT) 1)
(SETF (GET '- 'WEIGHT) 1)
(SETF (GET '* 'WEIGHT) 2)
(SETF (GET '/ 'WEIGHT) 2)
(SETF (GET '\\ 'WEIGHT) 2)
(SETF (GET '^ 'WEIGHT) 3)

(SETF (GET '= 'OPCODE) 'SETQ)
(SETF (GET '+ 'OPCODE) '+)
(SETF (GET '- 'OPCODE) '-)
(SETF (GET '* 'OPCODE) '*)
(SETF (GET '/ 'OPCODE) '/)
(SETF (GET '\\ 'OPCODE) REM)
(SETF (GET '^ 'OPCODE) EXPT)


(DEFUN WEIGHT (OPERATOR) (GET OPERATOR 'WEIGHT))

(DEFUN OPCODE (OPERATOR) (GET OPERATOR 'OPCODE))
```

Solution 12-7

In LISP dialects that use | to surround atom names containing break or separator characters one has to use \| as shown below:

```
(SETF (GET '= 'WEIGHT) 0)
(SETF (GET '\| 'WEIGHT) 1)
(SETF (GET '& 'WEIGHT) 2)
(SETF (GET '< 'WEIGHT) 3)
(SETF (GET '> 'WEIGHT) 3)
(SETF (GET '+ 'WEIGHT) 4)
(SETF (GET '- 'WEIGHT) 4)
(SETF (GET '* 'WEIGHT) 5)
(SETF (GET '/ 'WEIGHT) 5)
(SETF (GET '\\ 'WEIGHT) 5)
(SETF (GET '^ 'WEIGHT) 6)

(SETF (GET '= 'OPCODE) 'SETQ)
(SETF (GET '\| 'OPCODE) 'OR)
(SETF (GET '& 'OPCODE) 'AND)
(SETF (GET '< 'OPCODE) '<)
(SETF (GET '> 'OPCODE) '>)
(SETF (GET '+ 'OPCODE) '+)
(SETF (GET '- 'OPCODE) '-)
(SETF (GET '* 'OPCODE) '*)
(SETF (GET '/ 'OPCODE) '/)
(SETF (GET '\\ 'OPCODE) REM)
(SETF (GET '^ 'OPCODE) EXPT)
```

Solution 12-8

```
(DEFUN SPARSE-V-COMPONENT (V N)
  (COND ((NULL V) 0.0)
        ((> (CAAR V) N) 0.0)
        ((< (CAAR V) N) (SPARSE-V-COMPONENT (CDR V) N))
        (T (CADAR V))))
```

Solution 12-9

Simply add the following to the conditional, just before the T-clause:

```
((ZEROP (+ (CADAR A) (CADAR B)))
 (SPARSE-V-PLUS (CDR A) (CDR B)))
```

Solution 12-10

No. They could be negative too. In fact the indices could be floating-point numbers! The only thing that matters is that they are ordered, so that the procedure can tell in which list to proceed when indices at the head of the two lists are not equal.

Solution 12-11

```
(DEFUN SPARSE-M-PRINT (M)
  (COND ((NULL M) (TERPRI))
        (T (PRINT (CAR M))
           (SPARSE-M-PRINT (CDR M))))))
```

Solution 12-12

Because of what may appear to be a superfluous extra layer of parentheses around the vectors representing the rows, it is easy to modify the procedure SPARSE-V-PLUS to add matrices instead of vectors. Simply change all calls to SPARSE-V-PLUS to SPARSE-M-PLUS, and all calls to + to SPARSE-V-PLUS:

```
(DEFUN SPARSE-M-PLUS (A B)
  (COND ((NULL A) B)
        ((NULL B) A)
        ((< (CAAR A) (CAAR B))
         (CONS (CAR A) (SPARSE-M-PLUS (CDR A) B)))
        ((< (CAAR B) (CAAR A))
         (CONS (CAR B) (SPARSE-M-PLUS (CDR B) A)))
        (T (CONS (LIST (CAAR A) (SPARSE-V-PLUS (CADAR A) (CADAR B)))
                 (SPARSE-M-PLUS (CDR A) (CDR B))))))
```

Solution 12-13

```
(DEFUN SPARSE-M-TIMES-V (M V)
  (COND ((NULL M) NIL)
        (T (CONS (LIST (CAAR M)
                       (SPARSE-DOT-PRODUCT (CADAR M) V))
                 (SPARSE-M-TIMES-V (CDR M) V)))))
```

For example:

```
(SETQ MATRIX-A '((1 ((1 2.0) (3 4.0)))
                 (3 ((2 1.0) (3 4.0) (4 -5.0) (5 7.0)))
                 (5 ((1 0.5) (2 3.0) (4 9.0)))))

(SETQ VECTOR-A '((1 3.0) (3 -1.0) (4 2.0)))

(SPARSE-M-TIMES-V MATRIX-A VECTOR-A)
  ((1 2.0) (3 -14.0) (5 19.5))
```

Note, however, that this straightforward solution may lead to the inclusion of zero elements when the dot-product is zero.

Solution 12-14

One way to find the transpose is to first expand the list representing the matrix into one that is more symmetrical in the row and column indices:

```
(M-EXPAND '((1 ((2 1.2) (4 1.4)))
            (3 ((1 3.1) (5 3.5) (6 3.6)))
            (4 ((2 4.2) (3 4.3)))))
 ((1 2 1.2) (1 4 1.4) (3 1 3.1) (3 5 3.5) (3 6 3.6) (4 2 4.2) (4 3 4.3))
```

This can be accomplished using:

```
(DEFUN M-EXPAND (L)
  (COND ((NULL L) NIL)
        (T (APPEND (M-EXPAND-AUX (CAAR L) (CADAR L))
                   (M-EXPAND (CDR L))))))

(DEFUN M-EXPAND-AUX (I L)
  (COND ((NULL L) NIL)
        (T (CONS (LIST I (CAAR L) (CADAR L))
                 (M-EXPAND-AUX I (CDR L))))))
```

The procedure M-COMPRESS performs the inverse operation:

```
(DEFUN M-COMPRESS (MAT)  (M-ASSEMBLE (CAAR MAT) NIL MAT))

(DEFUN M-ASSEMBLE (N NEW OLD)
  (COND ((NULL OLD) (LIST (CONS N (LIST (REVERSE NEW)))))        ; Assemble last
        ((= N (CAAR OLD))                                        ; Same row?
         (M-ASSEMBLE N (CONS (CDAR OLD) NEW) (CDR OLD)))         ; Collect more.
        (T (CONS (CONS N (LIST (REVERSE NEW)))                   ; Assemble row
                 (M-ASSEMBLE (CAAR OLD) NIL OLD)))))             ;  and do rest.
```

The row and column indices can be switched around using M-ALTER-FLIP:

```
(DEFUN M-ALTER-FLIP (L)
  (COND ((NULL L) NIL)
        (T (CONS (LIST (CADAR L) (CAAR L) (CADDAR L))
                 (M-ALTER-FLIP (CDR L))))))
```

Next, it is necessary to sort on the new row indices:

```
(DEFUN M-ALTER-SORT (MAT) (M-ALTER-AUX MAT NIL))

(DEFUN M-ALTER-AUX (OLD NEW)
  (COND ((NULL OLD) NEW)
        (T (M-ALTER-AUX (CDR OLD) (INSERT (CAR OLD) NEW)))))

(DEFUN LESS (X Y)
  (OR (< (CAR X) (CAR Y)) (AND (= (CAR X) (CAR Y))
                              (< (CADR X) (CADR Y)))))
```

```
(DEFUN INSERT (X SORTED)
  (COND ((NULL SORTED) (LIST X))
        ((LESS X (CAR SORTED)) (CONS X SORTED))
        (T (CONS (CAR SORTED) (INSERT X (CDR SORTED))))))
```

Finally, all of this can be put together:

```
(DEFUN SPARSE-M-TRANSPOSE (L)
  (M-COMPRESS (M-ALTER-SORT (M-ALTER-FLIP (M-EXPAND L)))))
```

Solution 12-15

```
(DEFUN SPARSE-M-TIMES (A B)
  (SPARSE-M-TRANSPOSE (SPARSE-M-TIMES-AUX A (SPARSE-M-TRANSPOSE B))))
```

```
(DEFUN SPARSE-M-TIMES-AUX (A B)
  (COND ((NULL B) NIL)
        ((CONS (LIST (CAAR B)
                     (SPARSE-M-TIMES-V A (CADAR B)))
               (SPARSE-M-TIMES-AUX A (CDR B))))))
```

Solution 12-16

The solution shown uses y as an initial estimate, instead of 1, as did ISQRT.

```
(DEFUN ICURT (Y)
  (COND ((ZEROP Y) Y)
        (T (ICURT-AUX Y
                      Y
                      (TRUNCATE (+ Y Y (TRUNCATE 1 Y)) 3)))))
```

```
(DEFUN ICURT-AUX (Y XN XN1)
  (COND ((EQUAL XN1 XN) XN1)
        ((EQUAL XN1 (TRUNCATE Y (* XN XN))) XN1)
        (T (ICURT-AUX Y
                      XN1
                      (TRUNCATE (+ XN1 XN1 (TRUNCATE Y (* XN1 XN1))) 3)))))
```

Solution 12-17

```
(DEFUN OUR-+ (X Y)                                              ;Add two numbers.
  (COND ((AND (NUMBERP X) (NUMBERP Y)) (+ X Y))                 ;Real simple.
        ((NUMBERP X) (OUR-+ (FORCE-COMPLEX X 0.0) Y))           ;Complex contagion.
        ((NUMBERP Y) (OUR-+ X (FORCE-COMPLEX Y 0.0)))           ;Complex contagion.
        (T (OUR-COMPLEX (+ (OUR-REALPART X) (OUR-REALPART Y))        ;Add real
                        (+ (OUR-IMAGPART X) (OUR-IMAGPART Y)))))))   ; & image.


(DEFUN OUR-- (X Y)
  (COND ((AND (NUMBERP X) (NUMBERP Y)) (- X Y))
        ((NUMBERP X) (OUR-- (FORCE-COMPLEX X 0.0) Y))
        ((NUMBERP Y) (OUR-- X (FORCE-COMPLEX Y 0.0)))
        (T (OUR-COMPLEX (- (OUR-REALPART X) (OUR-REALPART Y))
                        (- (OUR-IMAGPART X) (OUR-IMAGPART Y))))))


(DEFUN OUR-* (X Y)                                              ;Multiply two numbers.
  (COND ((AND (NUMBERP X) (NUMBERP Y)) (* X Y))                 ;Real simple.
        ((NUMBERP X) (OUR-* (FORCE-COMPLEX X 0.0) Y))           ;Complex contagion.
        ((NUMBERP Y) (OUR-* X (FORCE-COMPLEX Y 0.0)))           ;Complex contagion.
        (T (LET ((A (OUR-REALPART X)) (B (OUR-IMAGPART X))           ;Grab real and
                 (C (OUR-REALPART Y)) (D (OUR-IMAGPART Y)))          ; image parts.
             (OUR-COMPLEX (- (* A C) (* B D))
                          (+ (* B C) (* A D)))))))


(DEFUN OUR-/ (X Y)
  (COND ((AND (NUMBERP X) (NUMBERP Y)) (/ X Y))
        ((NUMBERP X) (OUR-/ (FORCE-COMPLEX X 0.0) Y))
        ((NUMBERP Y) (OUR-/ X (FORCE-COMPLEX Y 0.0)))
        (T (LET* ((A (OUR-REALPART X)) (B (OUR-IMAGPART X))
                  (C (OUR-REALPART Y)) (D (OUR-IMAGPART Y))
                  (RS (+ (* C C) (* D D))))
             (OUR-COMPLEX (/ (+ (* A C) (* B D)) RS)
                          (/ (- (* B C) (* A D)) RS))))))
```

Here we have used a very simple way of dealing with complex contagion. The assumption is that this conversion does not happen that often, and so it is not worth writing a more complex procedure that takes care of the special cases explicitly. Similarly, the conditional is easy to understand but not as efficient as it could be, because some testing is repeated unnecessarily. How would you improve the above procedures to take care of these deficiencies?

Solution 12-18

```
(DEFUN NEGATE (X)                           ;Compute negative of complex number.
  (COND ((NUMBERP X) (- X))
        (T (OUR-COMPLEX (- (OUR-REALPART X)) (- (OUR-IMAGPART X))))))

(DEFUN OUR-CONJUGATE (X)                     ;Compute conjugate of complex number.
  (COND ((NUMBERP X) X)
        (T (OUR-COMPLEX (OUR-REALPART X) (- (OUR-IMAGPART X))))))

(DEFUN RECIPROCAL (X)                        ;Compute reciprocal of complex number.
  (COND ((NUMBERP X) (/ 1.0 X))
        (T (LET* ((A (OUR-REALPART X)) (B (OUR-IMAGPART X))
                  (RS (+ (* A A) (* B B))))
             (OUR-COMPLEX (/ A RS) (/ (- B) RS))))))
```

Solution 12-19

```
(DEFUN OUR-ABS (X)                           ;Compute modulus of complex number.
  (COND ((NUMBERP X) (ABS X))
        (T (SQRT (+ (SQUARE (OUR-REALPART X))
                    (SQUARE (OUR-IMAGPART X)))))))

(DEFUN OUR-PHASE (X)                          ;Compute argument of complex number.
  (COND ((NUMBERP X) (COND ((MINUSP X) PI)
                           (T 0.0)))
        (T (ATAN (OUR-IMAGPART X)
                 (OUR-REALPART X)))))
```

We could also have computed the modulus as follows:

```
(DEFUN OUR-ABS (X) (SQRT (OUR-REALPART (OUR-* X (OUR-CONJUGATE X)))))
```

Solution 12-20

```
(DEFUN OUR-SQRT (X)                                        ;Complex SQRT.
  (COND ((NUMBERP X) (COND ((NOT (MINUSP X)) (SQRT X))     ;Easy case.
                           (T (OUR-COMPLEX 0.0 (SQRT (- X))))))
        (T (LET ((A (OUR-REALPART X)) (B (OUR-IMAGPART X)))
             (SQRT-PUNT A                                  ;Real part.
                        B                                  ;Imaginary part.
                        (SQRT (+ (* A A) (* B B))))))))     ;Modulus.

(DEFUN SQRT-PUNT (C D R)
  (COND ((MINUSP D)
         (OUR-COMPLEX (SQRT (/ (+ R C) 2.0))               ;Real part.
                      (- (SQRT (/ (- R C) 2.0)))))         ;Imaginary.
        (T (OUR-COMPLEX (SQRT (/ (+ R C) 2.0))             ;Real part.
                        (SQRT (/ (- R C) 2.0))))))         ;Imaginary.
```

Solution 12-21

```
(DEFUN ADMITTANCE (CIRCUIT OMEGA)
  (RECIPROCAL (IMPEDANCE CIRCUIT OMEGA)))
```

Solution 12-22

```
(DEFUN CURT (X)
  (CURT-ITER (COND ((MINUSP X) (- (EXP (/ (LOG (- X)) 3.0))))
                   ((ZEROP X) 0.0)
                   (T (EXP (/ (LOG X) 3.0))))
             X))
```

```
(DEFUN CURT-ITER (X Y)  (/ (+ X X (/ Y (* X X))) 3.0))
```

Solution 12-23

```
(DEFUN MAKE-POLY (ROOTS)                      ;List of roots is given.
  (POLY-AUX (LIST 1.0                         ;Linear seed polynomial
                  (NEGATE (CAR ROOTS)))       ; using first root.
            (CDR ROOTS)))                     ;Rest of the roots.
```

The next procedure multiplies a polynomial represented by its coefficients by the linear term $(x - r)$, where the list of coefficients is represented by COEFF and r is the first root in the list ROOTS. The result is a new, larger list of coefficients.

```
(DEFUN POLY-AUX (COEFF ROOTS)                 ;Multiply a polynomial by
  (COND ((NULL ROOTS) COEFF)                  ; many linear polynomials.
        (T (POLY-AUX (CONS (CAR COEFF)
                           (POLY-IT COEFF
                                    (CAR ROOTS)))
                     (CDR ROOTS)))))
```

In the above, a polynomial is multiplied by a single linear term. Finally, we get to the procedure that does all the work:

```
(DEFUN POLY-IT (COEFF ROOT)                   ;Multiply through by one
  (COND ((NULL (CDR COEFF))                   ; linear polynomial.
         (LIST (OUR-* (CAR COEFF) (NEGATE ROOT))))
        (T (CONS (OUR-- (CADR COEFF)
                        (OUR-* (CAR COEFF) ROOT))
                 (POLY-IT (CDR COEFF) ROOT)))))
```

Note the use of tail recursion in POLY-AUX and POLY-IT.

Here we have used the procedures introduced earlier to do complex arithmetic. If we use MAKE-POLY to check the roots, we expect to get back the coefficients of the polynomial. In practice, because of limited precision of floating-point representation of real numbers, we may get slightly different values. These may even have a small imaginary component.

Solution 12-24

```
(DEFUN POLY-VALUE (COEFF X) (POLY-VALUE-AUX (CDR COEFF) (CAR COEFF) X))


(DEFUN POLY-VALUE-AUX (COEFF VAL X)
  (COND ((NULL COEFF) VAL)
        (T (POLY-VALUE-AUX (CDR COEFF)
                           (OUR-+ (OUR-* VAL X) (CAR COEFF)) X))))
```

Note, once again, the use of tail recursion here in implementing Horner's method for computing the value of a polynomial.

Here we have used the procedures introduced earlier to do complex arithmetic. If we use POLY-VALUE to check a root of a polynomial, we expect zero as the answer. In practice, of course, because of limited precision of floating-point representation of real numbers, we may get some small (possibly complex) but nonzero value.

Solution 12-25

```
(DEFUN INSERT-ROOT (NEW ROOTS)                          ;Keep real roots ordered.
  (COND ((NULL ROOTS) (LIST NEW))                       ;Easy case, last one.
        ((NOT (NUMBERP (CAR ROOTS))) (CONS NEW ROOTS))   ;Real before complex.
        ((NOT (NUMBERP NEW))                            ;NEW is complex.
         (CONS (CAR ROOTS) (INSERT-ROOT NEW (CDR ROOTS))))
        ((> (CAR ROOTS) NEW)                            ;NEW not highest.
         (CONS (CAR ROOTS) (INSERT-ROOT NEW (CDR ROOTS))))
        (T (CONS NEW ROOTS))))                          ;NEW most positive.
```

Strictly speaking, the (second) recursive call to INSERT-ROOT is not needed if all we want to do is ensure that the most positive root is first in the list. But why not keep all the real roots sorted while we are at it? It costs little extra.

Solution 12-26

Simply replace the two APPENDs with APPEND-ROOTS, where

```
(DEFUN APPEND-ROOTS (RA RB)
  (COND ((NULL RA) RB)
        (T (APPEND-ROOTS (CDR RA) (INSERT-ROOT (CAR RA) RB)))))
```

Solutions to Problems in Chapter 14

Solution 14-1

If OUR-BREAK were a procedure, the environment would be the global environment, rather than the local environment. This means there would be no way to find parameter values. Making OUR-BREAK a macro works because the expanded macro is spliced into the place where the macro call appears, so the environment is the local environment. Here is a simple version:

```
(DEFMACRO OUR-BREAK (&OPTIONAL MESSAGE)
  `(PROGN
    (PRINT (CONS 'BREAK: ,MESSAGE))        ;Print message.
    (PRINT '>)                             ;Prompt user.
    (DO ((QUERY (READ) (READ)))            ;Read user's expression.
        ((EQUAL QUERY 'CONTINUE) NIL)      ;Stop if indicated.
      (PRINT (EVAL QUERY))                 ;Print appropriate value.
      (PRINT '>))))                        ;Prompt user again.
```

Solution 14-2

```
(DEFUN PUT-ON (OBJECT SUPPORT)
    (COND ((EQUAL OBJECT SUPPORT)
           (OUR-BREAK '(PUT-ON CANNOT PUT SOMETHING ON ITSELF))))
    (PUT-AT OBJECT (GET-SPACE OBJECT SUPPORT))   ;Put object at place.
    (REVERSE PLAN)))
```

Solutions to Problems in Chapter 15

Solution 15-1

```
(DEFUN TELL-HOW (SITUATION)              ;Modified from DEPTH.
  (HOW1 (LIST 'HISTORY) SITUATION))
```

```
(DEFUN HOW1 (QUEUE SITUATION)            ;Modified from DEPTH1.
  (COND ((NULL QUEUE) NIL)
        ((EQUAL SITUATION
                (GET (CAR QUEUE) 'SITUATION))
         (MAPCAR #'(LAMBDA (E) (PRINT (GET E 'SITUATION)))
                 (GET (CAR QUEUE) 'CHILDREN))
         T)
        (T (HOW1
            (APPEND (GET (CAR QUEUE) 'CHILDREN)
                    (CDR QUEUE))
            SITUATION))))
```

Solution 15-2

```
(DEFUN TELL-WHY (SITUATION)                    ;Modified from DEPTH.
  (WHY1 (LIST 'HISTORY) SITUATION))

(DEFUN WHY1 (QUEUE SITUATION)                  ;Modified from DEPTH1.
  (COND ((NULL QUEUE) NIL)
        ((EQUAL SITUATION
                (GET (CAR QUEUE) 'SITUATION))
         (PRINT (GET (GET (CAR QUEUE) 'PARENT) 'SITUATION))
         T)
        (T (WHY1
            (APPEND (GET (CAR QUEUE) 'CHILDREN)
                    (CDR QUEUE))
            SITUATION))))
```

Solution 15-3

```
(DEFUN TELL-WHEN (SITUATION)                   ;Modified from DEPTH.
  (WHEN1 (LIST 'HISTORY) SITUATION))

(DEFUN WHEN1 (QUEUE SITUATION)                 ;Modified from DEPTH1.
  (COND ((NULL QUEUE) NIL)
        ((EQUAL SITUATION
                (GET (CAR QUEUE) 'SITUATION))
         (PRINT (GET (CLIMB-TO-TOP (CAR QUEUE))
                     'SITUATION))
         T)
        (T (WHEN1
            (APPEND (GET (CAR QUEUE) 'CHILDREN)
                    (CDR QUEUE))
            SITUATION))))

(DEFUN CLIMB-TO-TOP (NODE)                      ;Modified from DEPTH1.
  (LET ((PARENT (GET NODE 'PARENT)))
    (COND ((EQUAL PARENT 'HISTORY) NODE)
          (T (CLIMB-TO-TOP PARENT)))))
```

Solution 15-4

```
(DEFSTRUCT (NODE)
  (PARENT NIL)
  (CHILD NIL)
  (SITUATION NIL))

(DEFUN ATTACH (C P)
  (SETF (NODE-PARENT C) P)                      ;Attach parent to child.
  (SETF (NODE-CHILDREN P)                       ;Attach child to parent.
        (APPEND (NODE-CHILDREN P) (LIST C))))
```

```
(DEFMACRO DEFUN-WITH-HISTORY (NAME PARAMETERS &REST BODY)
  `(DEFUN ,NAME ,PARAMETERS
     (LET ((PARENT CHILD)
           (CHILD (MAKE-NODE :SITUATION (LIST ',NAME ,@PARAMETERS))))
       (ATTACH CHILD PARENT)
       ,@BODY)))
```

Solution 15-5

```
(DEFMACRO DEFUN-WITH-HISTORY (NAME PARAMETERS &REST BODY)
  (LIST 'DEFUN
        NAME
        PARAMETERS
        (CONS 'LET
              (CONS '((PARENT CHILD)
                      (CHILD (GENSYM)))
                    (CONS '(ATTACH CHILD PARENT)
                          (CONS (LIST 'SETF
                                      (LIST 'GET 'CHILD ''SITUATION)
                                      (CONS 'LIST
                                            (CONS (LIST 'QUOTE NAME)
                                                  PARAMETERS)))
                                BODY))))))
```

Solution 15-6

```
(DEFMACRO DEFUN-WITH-HISTORY (NAME PARAMETERS &REST BODY)
  `(DEFUN ,NAME ,PARAMETERS                              ;Substitute in skeleton.
     (LET ((PARENT (COND ((BOUNDP 'CHILD) CHILD)
                         (T 'HISTORY)))
           (CHILD (GENSYM)))
       (ATTACH CHILD PARENT)
       (SETF (GET CHILD 'SITUATION)
             (LIST ',NAME ,@PARAMETERS))
       ,@BODY)))
```

Solution 15-7

```
(DEFMACRO TRACE1 (NAME)
  (LET* ((LAMBDA-EXPRESSION (SYMBOL-FUNCTION NAME))
         (PARAMETERS (CADR LAMBDA-EXPRESSION)))
    `(PROGN
       (SETF (GET ',NAME 'TRACED-FUNCTION) ',LAMBDA-EXPRESSION)
       (DEFUN ,NAME ,PARAMETERS
         (LET ((TRACE-RESULT)
               (TRACE-DEPTH (COND ((BOUNDP 'TRACE-DEPTH)
                                   (+ TRACE-DEPTH 1))
                                  (T 0))))
           (INDENT-PRINT TRACE-DEPTH
                         (LIST 'ENTERING ',NAME ,@PARAMETERS))
           (SETQ TRACE-RESULT (FUNCALL (GET ',NAME 'TRACED-FUNCTION)
                                       ,@PARAMETERS))
           (INDENT-PRINT TRACE-DEPTH
                         (LIST 'EXITING ',NAME TRACE-RESULT))
           TRACE-RESULT)))))
```

Solution 15-8

```
(DEFMACRO UNTRACE1 (NAME)
  (LET* ((LAMBDA-EXPRESSION (GET NAME 'TRACED-FUNCTION))
         (PARAMETERS (CADR LAMBDA-EXPRESSION))
         (BODY (CDDR LAMBDA-EXPRESSION)))
    `(PROGN
       (SETF (GET ',NAME 'TRACED-FUNCTION) NIL)
       (DEFUN ,NAME ,PARAMETERS ,@BODY))))
```

Solution 15-9

```
(DEFUN INDENT-PRINT (N MESSAGE)
  (TERPRI)
  (INDENT-PRINT1 N MESSAGE))


(DEFUN INDENT-PRINT1 (N MESSAGE)
  (COND ((ZEROP N) (PRINC MESSAGE) T)
        (T (PRINC '| |)
           (INDENT-PRINT1 (- N 1) MESSAGE))))
```

Solution 15-10

In the following definition, note that (TRACE1 E) and (FUNCALL 'TRACE1 E) would not work. We need (EVAL (LIST 'TRACE1 E)) to get the macro's argument evaluated before the macro is evaluated.

```
(DEFMACRO OUR-TRACE (&REST FUNCTIONS)
  (COND ((NULL FUNCTIONS) 'TRACED-FUNCTIONS)
        (T `(REMOVE-IF-NOT #'(LAMBDA (E)
                               (COND ((MEMBER E TRACED-FUNCTIONS) NIL)
                                     (T (EVAL (LIST 'TRACE1 E))
                                        (SETQ TRACED-FUNCTIONS
                                              (CONS E TRACED-FUNCTIONS))
                                        T)))
                            ',FUNCTIONS))))

(DEFMACRO OUR-UNTRACE (&REST FUNCTIONS)
  `(REMOVE-IF-NOT #'(LAMBDA (E)
                      (COND ((MEMBER E TRACED-FUNCTIONS)
                             (EVAL (LIST 'UNTRACE1 E))
                             (SETQ TRACED-FUNCTIONS
                                   (REMOVE E TRACED-FUNCTIONS))
                             T)
                            (T NIL)))
                   (COND ((NULL ',FUNCTIONS) TRACED-FUNCTIONS)
                         (T ',FUNCTIONS))))
```

Solutions to Problems in Chapter 16

Solution 16-1

```
(DEFUN AREA (OBJECT)
  (FUNCALL (GET (GET OBJECT 'A-KIND-OF) 'AREA)
           OBJECT))

(DEFUN PERIMETER (OBJECT)
  (FUNCALL (GET (GET OBJECT 'A-KIND-OF) 'PERIMETER)
           OBJECT))

(SETF (GET 'CIRCLE 'AREA)
  #'(LAMBDA (OBJECT) (* PI (EXPT (GET OBJECT 'RADIUS) 2))))

(SETF (GET 'CIRCLE 'PERIMETER)
  #'(LAMBDA (OBJECT) (* PI 2.0 (GET OBJECT 'RADIUS))))

(SETF (GET 'SQUARE 'AREA)
  #'(LAMBDA (OBJECT) (EXPT (GET OBJECT 'LENGTH) 2)))

(SETF (GET 'SQUARE 'PERIMETER)
  #'(LAMBDA (OBJECT) (* (GET OBJECT 'LENGTH) 4.0)))
```

Solution 16-2

```
(DEFUN OPERATOR (LIST) (CAR LIST))


(DEFUN ARG1 (LIST) (CADR LIST))


(DEFUN ARG2 (LIST) (CADDR LIST))


(DEFUN DIFFERENTIATE (E X)
  (COND ((ATOM E) (COND ((EQUAL E X) 1)
                        (T 0)))
        (T (FUNCALL (GET (OPERATOR E)
                         'DIFFERENTIATE)
                    E X))))


(SETF (GET '+ 'DIFFERENTIATE)
  (LAMBDA (E X) `(+ ,(DIFFERENTIATE (ARG1 E) X)
                    ,(DIFFERENTIATE (ARG2 E) X))))


(SETF (GET '* 'DIFFERENTIATE)
  (LAMBDA (E X) `(+ (* ,(ARG1 E) ,(DIFFERENTIATE (ARG2 E) X))
                    (* ,(ARG2 E) ,(DIFFERENTIATE (ARG1 E) X)))))
```

Solution 16-3

```
(DEFMACRO DEFMETHOD (OBJECT KEY METHOD PARAMETERS &REST BODY)
  (SETF (GET OBJECT METHOD)
        (CONS (LIST KEY `(LAMBDA ,PARAMETERS ,@BODY))
              (GET OBJECT METHOD)))
  `',METHOD)
```

**Solutions to Problems
in Chapter 17**

Solution 17-1

Add the following clause to MATCH's conditional, changing COND to APPEND:

```
(DEFUN MATCH (P D ASSIGNMENTS)
  (COND .
        .
        .
        ((EQUAL (PATTERN-INDICATOR (CAR P)) '<+)
         (MATCH (APPEND (PULL-VALUE (PATTERN-VARIABLE (CAR P))
                                    ASSIGNMENTS)
                        (CDR P))
                D
                ASSIGNMENTS))
        .
        .
        .))
```

Note that PULL-VALUE works with both < and <+ variable values.

Solution 17-2

Here is a version using backquote; you may prefer a version without.

```
(DEFUN TRANSLATE (E)
  (LET (A-LIST NIL)
    (COND ((SETQ A-LIST (MATCH '((+ L) IS (+ R)) E NIL))
           `(= ,(TRANSLATE (MATCH-VALUE 'L A-LIST))
               ,(TRANSLATE (MATCH-VALUE 'R A-LIST))))
          ((SETQ A-LIST (MATCH '(THE DIFFERENCE BETWEEN (+ L)
                                     AND (+ R)) E NIL))
           `(- ,(TRANSLATE (MATCH-VALUE 'L A-LIST))
               ,(TRANSLATE (MATCH-VALUE 'R A-LIST))))
          ((SETQ A-LIST (MATCH '(THE SUM OF (+ L) AND (+ R)) E NIL))
           `(+ ,(TRANSLATE (MATCH-VALUE 'L A-LIST))
               ,(TRANSLATE (MATCH-VALUE 'R A-LIST))))
          ((SETQ A-LIST (MATCH '((+ L) TIMES (+ R)) E NIL))
           `(* ,(TRANSLATE (MATCH-VALUE 'L A-LIST))
               ,(TRANSLATE (MATCH-VALUE 'R A-LIST))))
          ((SETQ A-LIST (MATCH '(TWICE (+ R)) E NIL))
           `(* 2 ,(TRANSLATE (MATCH-VALUE 'R A-LIST))))
          ((SETQ A-LIST (MATCH '(THE SQUARE OF (+ R)) E NIL))
           `(EXPT ,(TRANSLATE (MATCH-VALUE 'R A-LIST)) 2))
          ((SETQ A-LIST (MATCH '((+ L) SQUARED) E NIL))
           `(EXPT ,(TRANSLATE (MATCH-VALUE 'L A-LIST)) 2))
          ((SETQ A-LIST (MATCH '((RESTRICT (> V) NUMBERP)) E NIL))
           (MATCH-VALUE 'V A-LIST))
          (T E))))
```

Solution 17-3

```
(DEFUN INF-TO-PRE (E)
  (LET (A-LIST NIL)
    (COND ((ATOM E) E)
          ((SETQ A-LIST (MATCH '((> V)) E NIL))
           (INF-TO-PRE (MATCH-VALUE 'V A-LIST)))
          ((SETQ A-LIST (MATCH '((+ L) (RESTRICT? ONEPLUS) (+ R)) E NIL))
           `(+ ,(INF-TO-PRE (MATCH-VALUE 'L A-LIST))
               ,(INF-TO-PRE (MATCH-VALUE 'R A-LIST))))
          ((SETQ A-LIST (MATCH '((+ L) - (+ R)) E NIL))
           `(- ,(INF-TO-PRE (MATCH-VALUE 'L A-LIST))
               ,(INF-TO-PRE (MATCH-VALUE 'R A-LIST))))
          ((SETQ A-LIST (MATCH '((+ L) * (+ R)) E NIL))
           `(* ,(INF-TO-PRE (MATCH-VALUE 'L A-LIST))
               ,(INF-TO-PRE (MATCH-VALUE 'R A-LIST))))
          ((SETQ A-LIST (MATCH '((+ L) / (+ R)) E NIL))
           `(/ ,(INF-TO-PRE (MATCH-VALUE 'L A-LIST))
               ,(INF-TO-PRE (MATCH-VALUE 'R A-LIST))))
          ((SETQ A-LIST (MATCH '((+ L) ^ (+ R)) E NIL))
           `(EXPT ,(INF-TO-PRE (MATCH-VALUE 'L A-LIST))
                  ,(INF-TO-PRE (MATCH-VALUE 'R A-LIST))))
          ((SETQ A-LIST (MATCH '(- (+ R)) E NIL))
           `(- ,(INF-TO-PRE (MATCH-VALUE 'R A-LIST))))
          (T E))))
```

ONEPLUS and the restriction are needed because the + for plus would be confused with the match-any-string symbol recognized by MATCH.

Solution 17-4

```
(DEFUN DOCTOR ()
  (PRINT '(SPEAK UP!))
  (TERPRI)
  (DO ((S (READ) (READ)) (A-LIST NIL NIL) (MOTHER))
      (NIL)
    (COND ((SETQ A-LIST (MATCH '(I AM WORRIED (+ L)) S NIL))
           (PRINT `(HOW LONG HAVE YOU BEEN WORRIED
                         ,@(MATCH-VALUE 'L A-LIST))))

          ((MATCH '(+ MOTHER +) S NIL)
           (SETQ MOTHER T)
           (PRINT '(TELL ME MORE ABOUT YOUR FAMILY)))

          ((MATCH '(+ COMPUTERS +) S NIL)
           (PRINT '(DO MACHINES FRIGHTEN YOU)))

          ((OR (MATCH '(NO) S NIL)
               (MATCH '(YES) S NIL))
           (PRINT '(PLEASE DO NOT BE SO SHORT WITH ME)))
```

```
((MATCH '(+ (RESTRICT > BADWORDP) +) S NIL)
 (PRINT '(PLEASE DO NOT USE WORDS LIKE THAT)))

(MOTHER (SETQ MOTHER NIL)
        (PRINT '(EARLIER YOU SPOKE OF YOUR MOTHER)))
(T (PRINT '(I AM SORRY OUR TIME IS UP))
   (RETURN 'GOODBYE)))
(TERPRI)))
```

Note that READ and PRINT establish communication with the user. Note also that if a sentence containing MOTHER is encountered, the variable MOTHER is set to T. Then later on, if nothing else in the conditional is triggered, the response of (EARLIER YOU SPOKE OF YOUR MOTHER) seems very judicious.

Solutions to Problems in Chapter 18

Solution 18-1

```
(DEFUN RECALL (PATTERN)
  (RECALL1 PATTERN ASSERTIONS))                    ;ASSERTIONS is free.


(DEFUN RECALL1 (PATTERN ASSERTIONS)
  (COND ((NULL ASSERTIONS) NIL)
        ((MATCH PATTERN (CAR ASSERTIONS) NIL)  ;Ignore association list, if any.
         (CONS (CAR ASSERTIONS)                ;Keep matching assertion, if any.
               (RECALL1 PATTERN (CDR ASSERTIONS))))
        (T (RECALL1 PATTERN (CDR ASSERTIONS)))))
```

Solution 18-2

```
(DEFUN ADD-TO-STREAM (E S) (APPEND S (LIST E)))
```

Solution 18-3

```
(RULE IDENTIFY1 SAYS ROBBIE IS A MAMMAL)
(RULE IDENTIFY3 SAYS SUZIE IS A BIRD)
(RULE IDENTIFY5 SAYS ROBBIE IS A CARNIVORE)
(RULE IDENTIFY9 SAYS ROBBIE IS A CHEETAH)
(RULE IDENTIFY15 SAYS SUZIE IS A ALBATROSS)
```

388

Solution 18-4

If something happens, the new USE-RULE calls FEED-TO-RULES-USED:

```
(DEFUN USE-RULE (RULE)
  (LET* ((RULE-NAME (CADR RULE))
         (IF-LIST (REVERSE (CDR (CADDR RULE))))
         (THEN-LIST (CDR (CADDDR RULE)))
         (A-LIST-STREAM (CASCADE-THROUGH-PATTERNS
                          IF-LIST
                          (LIST (MAKE-EMPTY-STREAM))))
         (ACTION-STREAM (FEED-TO-ACTIONS RULE-NAME
                                         THEN-LIST
                                         A-LIST-STREAM)))
    (COND ((NOT (EMPTY-STREAM-P ACTION-STREAM))     ;Something happened?
           (FEED-TO-RULES-USED RULE-NAME IF-LIST THEN-LIST A-LIST-STREAM)
           T))))
```

For each way of matching the rule to the data base, FEED-TO-RULES-USED makes a list of the rule's name, together with the antecedents and consequents, with variables replaced:

```
(DEFUN FEED-TO-RULES-USED (RULE-NAME IF-LIST THEN-LIST A-LIST-STREAM)
  (COND ((EMPTY-STREAM-P A-LIST-STREAM) T)
        (T (SETQ RULES-USED
                 (CONS (LIST RULE-NAME
                             (REPLACE-<-AND->
                              IF-LIST
                              (FIRST-OF-STREAM A-LIST-STREAM))
                             (REPLACE-<-AND->
                              THEN-LIST
                              (REST-OF-STREAM A-LIST-STREAM)))
                       RULES-USED))
           (FEED-TO-RULES-USED RULE-NAME
                               IF-LIST
                               THEN-LIST
                               (REST-OF-STREAM A-LIST-STREAM)))))
```

FEED-TO-RULES-USED needs a more vigorous replacement procedure, however:

```
(DEFUN REPLACE-<-AND-> (S A-LIST)
  (COND ((NULL S) NIL)
        ((AND (ATOM S) (OR (EQUAL (PATTERN-INDICATOR S) '<)
                           (EQUAL (PATTERN-INDICATOR S) '>)))   ;New line.
         (CADR (ASSOC (PATTERN-VARIABLE S) A-LIST)))
        ((ATOM S) S)
        (T (CONS (REPLACE-<-AND-> (CAR S) A-LIST)
                 (REPLACE-<-AND-> (CDR S) A-LIST)))))
```

The required test predicate is simple:

```
(DEFUN USEDP (RULE)
  (COND ((ASSOC RULE RULES-USED) T)
        (T NIL)))
```

Solution 18-5

Note in HOW1 that SUCCESS-SWITCH keeps track of whether there were any
rules that used the fact so that the end test can do the right thing.

```
(DEFUN HOW (FACT)
  (HOW1 FACT RULES-USED NIL))
```

```
(DEFUN HOW1 (FACT POSSIBILITIES SUCCESS-SWITCH)
  (COND ((NULL POSSIBILITIES)
         (COND (SUCCESS-SWITCH T)
               ((RECALL FACT) (PRINT `(,@FACT WAS GIVEN)) T)
               (T (PRINT `(,@FACT IS NOT ESTABLISHED)) NIL)))
        ((MEMBER FACT (CADDR (CAR POSSIBILITIES)) :TEST 'EQUAL)
         (PRINT `(,@FACT DEMONSTRATED BY))
         (MAPCAR #'(LAMBDA (A) (PRINT A))
                 (CADR (CAR POSSIBILITIES)))
         (HOW1 FACT (CDR POSSIBILITIES) T))
        (T (HOW1 FACT (CDR POSSIBILITIES) SUCCESS-SWITCH))))
```

Solution 18-6

```
(DEFUN WHY (FACT)
  (WHY1 FACT RULES-USED NIL))
```

```
(DEFUN WHY1 (FACT POSSIBILITIES SUCCESS-SWITCH)
  (COND ((NULL POSSIBILITIES)
         (COND (SUCCESS-SWITCH T)
               (T (PRINT `(,@FACT WAS NOT USED)) NIL)))
        ((MEMBER FACT (CADR (CAR POSSIBILITIES)) :TEST 'EQUAL)
         (PRINT `(,@FACT IS NEEDED TO SHOW))
         (MAPCAR #'(LAMBDA (A) (PRINT A))
                 (CADDR (CAR POSSIBILITIES)))
         (WHY1 FACT (CDR POSSIBILITIES) T))
        (T (WHY1 FACT (CDR POSSIBILITIES) SUCCESS-SWITCH))))
```

**Solutions to Problems
in Chapter 19**

Solution 19-1

In front of the main COND clause in INTERPRET-ATT, add the following:

```
(COND (DEBUG (PRINT `(ENTERING THE ,TREE TREE))))
```

Solution 19-2

The solution is easily adapted from the attributes and attribute trees:

```
(RECORD TOOLS
        ((BRANCH ((PARSE TOOL)
                  (PARSE TOOLS)
                  (PARSE-RESULT (CONS TOOL TOOLS)))
                 (AND (PARSE TOOL)
                      (PARSE-RESULT (LIST TOOL)))
                 ((PARSE TOOL)
                  (PARSE-RESULT (LIST TOOL))))))


(RECORD TOOL
        ((BRANCH (HAMMER8 (PARSE-RESULT 'HAMMER8))
                 (SAW3 (PARSE-RESULT 'SAW3))
                 (WRENCH2 (PARSE-RESULT 'WRENCH2)))))
```

Solution 19-3

```
(RECORD TOOL1 ((PARSE TOOL) (PARSE-RESULT TOOL)))


(RECORD TOOL2 ((PARSE TOOL) (PARSE-RESULT TOOL)))
```

Solution 19-4

```
(RECORD QUESTION
        ((BRANCH ((PARSE PRESENT)
                  (BRANCH (THE (PARSE ATTRIBUTES) OF (PARSE TOOLS)
                           (PARSE-RESULT-IF-END
                            (REPORT-ATTRIBUTES ATTRIBUTES TOOLS)))
                          ((PARSE TOOL) S (PARSE ATTRIBUTES)
                           (PARSE-RESULT-IF-END
                            (REPORT-ATTRIBUTES ATTRIBUTES TOOLS)))))
                 (HOW MANY METERS IS (PARSE TOOL1) FROM (PARSE TOOL2)
                  (PARSE-RESULT-IF-END
                   (REPORT-DISTANCE TOOL1 TOOL2))))))


(DEFUN REPORT-ATTRIBUTES (ATTRIBUTES TOOLS)
  (MAPCAR #'(LAMBDA (TOOL)
              (MAPCAR '(LAMBDA (ATTRIBUTE) (PRINT `(,TOOL
                                                   S
                                                   ,ATTRIBUTE
                                                   IS
                                                   ,(GET TOOL ATTRIBUTE))))
                      ATTRIBUTES))
          TOOLS))


(DEFUN REPORT-DISTANCE (X Y)
  (PRINT `(THE DISTANCE IS
               (SQRT (+ (SQUARE (- (GET X 'X-COORDINATE)
                                   (GET Y 'X-COORDINATE)))
                        (SQUARE (- (GET X 'Y-COORDINATE)
                                   (GET Y 'Y-COORDINATE)))
                        (SQUARE (- (GET X 'Z-COORDINATE)
                                   (GET Y 'Z-COORDINATE)))))))))
```

Solutions to Problems in Chapter 20

Solution 20-1

Yes, but only if COMPILE-ATT is available. INTERPRET-ATT does not help because it never translates ATT descriptions into LISP, and LISP programs are the only things the LISP compiler knows how to work with.

392

Solutions to Problems in Chapter 21

Solution 21-1

Only a simple addition is required to the tools ATT worked out in a problem in chapter 19:

```
(RECORD TOOLS
        ((BRANCH ((PARSE DESCRIBED-TOOLS)
                  (PARSE-RESULT DESCRIBED-TOOLS)
                 ((PARSE TOOL)
                  (PARSE TOOLS)
                  (PARSE-RESULT (CONS TOOL TOOLS)))
                 (AND (PARSE TOOL)
                      (PARSE-RESULT (LIST TOOL)))
                 ((PARSE TOOL)
                  (PARSE-RESULT (LIST TOOL)))))))
```

Solution 21-2

```
(COMPILE-ATT A-OR-THE
        ((BRANCH (A (PARSE-RESULT 'INDEFINITE))
                 (THE (PARSE-RESULT 'DEFINITE)))))

(COMPILE-ATT PROPERTIES
        ((BRANCH ((PARSE PROPERTY)
                  (PARSE PROPERTIES)
                  (PARSE-RESULT (CONS PROPERTY PROPERTIES)))
                 (AND (PARSE PROPERTY)
                      (PARSE-RESULT (LIST PROPERTY)))
                 ((PARSE PROPERTY)
                  (PARSE-RESULT (LIST PROPERTY))))))

(COMPILE-ATT PROPERTY
        ((BRANCH (LARGE (PARSE-RESULT 'LARGE))
                 (SMALL (PARSE-RESULT 'SMALL))
                 (RED (PARSE-RESULT 'RED))
                 (BLUE (PARSE-RESULT 'BLUE))
                 (LONG (PARSE-RESULT 'LONG))
                 (SHORT (PARSE-RESULT 'SHORT)))))

(COMPILE-ATT TOOL-TYPE
        ((BRANCH (HAMMERS (PARSE-RESULT 'HAMMERS))
                 (SCREWDRIVERS (PARSE-RESULT 'SCREWDRIVERS))
                 (SAWS (PARSE-RESULT 'SAWS))
                 (WRENCHES (PARSE-RESULT 'WRENCHS))
                 (HAMMER (PARSE-RESULT 'HAMMER))
                 (SCREWDRIVER (PARSE-RESULT 'SCREWDRIVER))
                 (SAW (PARSE-RESULT 'SAW))
                 (WRENCH (PARSE-RESULT 'WRENCH)))))
```

Solution 21-3

Even in this simple situation, the backquote version is easier to write and
less likely to have bugs because it is easier to get the quoting right:

```
(DEFUN MAKE-SEARCH-PROCEDURE (PROPERTIES TOOL)
  (COND ((NULL PROPERTIES)
           `(GET ',(OR (GET TOOL 'SINGULAR-FORM) TOOL)
                 'INSTANCE))
          (T `(REMOVE-IF-NOT ',(GET (CAR PROPERTIES)
                                    'TEST-PROCEDURE)
                             ,(MAKE-SEARCH-PROCEDURE (CDR PROPERTIES)
                                                     TOOL)))))
```

```
(DEFUN MAKE-SEARCH-PROCEDURE (PROPERTIES TOOL)
  (COND ((NULL PROPERTIES)
          (LIST 'GET
                (LIST 'QUOTE (OR (GET TOOL 'SINGULAR-FORM) TOOL))
                (LIST 'QUOTE 'INSTANCE)))
          (T (LIST 'REMOVE-IF-NOT
                   (LIST 'QUOTE (GET (CAR PROPERTIES) 'TEST-PROCEDURE))
                   (MAKE-SEARCH-PROCEDURE (CDR PROPERTIES)
                                          TOOL)))))
```

Solutions to Problems in Chapter 22

Solution 22-1

```
(DEFUN FCHECK (FRAME SLOT FACET VALUE)
      (COND ((MEMBER VALUE (FGET FRAME SLOT FACET)) T)
            (T NIL)))
```

Solution 22-2

```
(DEFUN FCLAMP (FRAME1 FRAME2 SLOT)
  (RPLACD (FGET-FRAME FRAME1)
          (LIST (FOLLOW-PATH (LIST SLOT) (FGET-FRAME FRAME2))))
  SLOT)
```

Solution 22-3

```
(DEFUN FGET-CLASSES (START)
  (REVERSE (FGET-CLASSES1 (LIST START) NIL)))


(DEFUN FGET-CLASSES1 (QUEUE CLASSES)
  (COND ((NULL QUEUE) CLASSES)                          ;Return when queue empty.
        (T (FGET-CLASSES1                               ;Try again with new queue.
           (APPEND (FGET (CAR QUEUE) 'A-KIND-OF 'VALUE)  ;New nodes in front.
                   (CDR QUEUE))                         ;Rest of queue.
           (COND ((MEMBER (CAR QUEUE) CLASSES)          ;Accumulate class, if new.
                  CLASSES)
                 (T (CONS (CAR QUEUE) CLASSES))))))))
```

Solution 22-4

```
(DEFUN FGET-Z (FRAME SLOT)
  (FGET-Z1 SLOT (FGET-CLASSES FRAME)))


(DEFUN FGET-Z1 (SLOT CLASSES)
  (COND ((NULL CLASSES) NIL)
        ((FGET-V-D-P (CAR CLASSES) SLOT))               ;Got something?
        (T (FGET-Z1 SLOT (CDR CLASSES)))))
```

Solution 22-5

```
(DEFUN FGET-N (FRAME SLOT)
  (LET ((CLASSES (FGET-CLASSES FRAME)))
    (COND ((FGET-N1 SLOT CLASSES 'VALUE))
          ((FGET-N1 SLOT CLASSES 'DEFAULT))
          ((FGET-N2 SLOT CLASSES 'IF-NEEDED))
          (T NIL))))


(DEFUN FGET-N1 (SLOT CLASSES KEY)
  (COND ((NULL CLASSES) NIL)
        ((FGET (CAR CLASSES) SLOT KEY))
        (T (FGET-N1 SLOT (CDR CLASSES) KEY))))


(DEFUN FGET-N2 (SLOT CLASSES KEY)
  (COND ((NULL CLASSES) NIL)
        ((MAPCAN #'(LAMBDA (E) (APPLY E NIL))
                 (FGET (CAR CLASSES) SLOT KEY)))
        (T (FGET-N2 SLOT (CDR CLASSES) KEY))))
```

Solution 22-6

```
(DEFUN FREMOVE-P (FRAME SLOT FACET VALUE)
  (COND ((FREMOVE FRAME SLOT FACET VALUE)
         (MAPCAR #'(LAMBDA (E)
                     (MAPCAR #'(LAMBDA (F) (APPLY F NIL))
                             (FGET E SLOT 'IF-REMOVED)))
                 (FGET-CLASSES FRAME))
         VALUE)))
```

Solutions to Problems in Chapter 23

Solution 23-1

Add these lines:

```
((EQUAL (CAR FORM) 'M-DEFUN)
 (MICRO-ASSIGN-VALUE (CADR FORM)
                     (CONS 'M-LAMBDA (CDDR FORM))))
```

If M-CLOSE expressions were used, the environment would be part of the M-CLOSE expression and the M-CLOSE expression would be part of the environment. The result would be a circular list structure that would cause PRINT to collapse.

Solution 23-2

```
(DEFUN MICRO-BIND-AND-ASSIGN (KEY-LIST VALUE-LIST A-LISTS)
  (CONS (MICRO-PAIR-UP KEY-LIST VALUE-LIST) A-LISTS))

(DEFUN MICRO-PAIR-UP (KEY-LIST VALUE-LIST)
  (COND ((OR (NULL KEY-LIST) (NULL VALUE-LIST)) NIL)
        (T (CONS (LIST (CAR KEY-LIST) (CAR VALUE-LIST))
                 (MICRO-PAIR-UP (CDR KEY-LIST)
                               (CDR VALUE-LIST))))))

(DEFUN MICRO-ASSIGN-VALUE (VARIABLE VALUE A-LISTS)
  (LET ((ENTRY (ASSOC VARIABLE (CAR A-LISTS))))
    (COND (ENTRY (RPLACA (CDR ENTRY) VALUE))
          ((CDR A-LISTS) (MICRO-ASSIGN-VALUE VARIABLE VALUE (CDR A-LISTS)))
          (T (RPLACD (LAST (CAR A-LISTS))
                     (LIST (LIST VARIABLE VALUE)))))
    VALUE))

(DEFUN MICRO-GET-VALUE (KEY A-LISTS)
  (LET ((PAIR (ASSOC KEY (CAR A-LISTS))))
    (COND (PAIR (CADR PAIR))
          (T (MICRO-GET-VALUE KEY (CDR A-LISTS))))))
```

```
(DEFUN MICRO-READ-EVAL-PRINT ()
  (DO ((ENVIRONMENT (LIST (LIST '(T T) '(NIL NIL)))))
      (NIL)
    (TERPRI)
    (PRINT (MICRO-EVAL (READ) ENVIRONMENT))))

(DEFUN MICRO-ASSIGN-DEFINITION (NAME CLOSURE A-LISTS)
  (LET ((ENTRY (ASSOC NAME (CAR A-LISTS))))
    (COND (ENTRY (RPLACA (CDR ENTRY) CLOSURE))
          (T (RPLACD (LAST (CAR A-LISTS))
                     (LIST (LIST NAME CLOSURE)))))
    NAME))
```

Bibliography

Abelson, Harold and Gerald Jay Sussman (1984), *Structure and Interpretation of Computer Programs*, MIT Press, Cambridge, Massachusetts, to be published.

Abramowitz, M. and I. A. Stegan (editors) (1964), *Handbook of Mathematical Functions with Formulas, Graphs, and Mathematical Tables*, National Bureau of Standards, United States Department of Commerce.

Aho, Alfred V., John E. Hopcroft, and Jeffrey D. Ullman (1974), *The Design and Analysis of Computer Algorithms*, Addison-Wesley, Reading, Massachusetts. Reprinted 1976.

Allen, John (1978), *Anatomy of* LISP, McGraw-Hill, New York.

Allen, John (1979), "An Overview of LISP," *Byte*, Vol. 4, No. 8.

Association for Computing Machinery (Sponsor) (1982), *Proceedings of the 1982 ACM Symposium on* LISP *and Functional Programming*, Association for Computing Machinery, New York.

Auslander, M. A. and H. R. Strong (1976), "Systematic Recursion Removal," Report RC 5841, IBM Research Center, Yorktown Heights, New York.

Backus, John (1978), "Can Programming be Liberated from the Von Neumann Style? A Functional Style and Its Algebra of Programs," *Communications of the ACM*, Vol. 21, No. 8.

Baird, Michael (1978), "SIGHT-I: A Computer Vision System for Automated IC Chip Manufacture," *IEEE Transactions on Systems, Man and Cybernetics*, Vol. SMC-8, No. 2.

Baker, Henry G., Jr. (1978a), "List Processing in Real Time on a Serial Computer," *Communications of the ACM*, Vol. 21, No. 4.

Baker, Henry G., Jr. (1978b), "Shallow Binding in LISP 1.5," *Communications of the ACM*, Vol. 21, No. 7. Also in *Artificial Intelligence: An MIT Perspective*, Volume 2, edited by Patrick H. Winston and Richard H. Brown, 1979.

Baker, Henry G., Jr. (1979), "Optimizing Allocation and Garbage Collection of Spaces," in *Artificial Intelligence: An MIT Perspective*, Volume 2, edited by Patrick H. Winston and Richard H. Brown.

Baker, Henry G., Jr. and Carl Hewitt (1977), "The Incremental Garbage Collection of Processes," Memo No. 454, Artificial Intelligence Laboratory, MIT, Cambridge, Massachusetts.

Ballard, D. H. and Christopher M. Brown (1982), *Computer Vision*, Prentice-Hall, Englewood Cliffs, New Jersey.

Barth, Jeffrey M. (1977), "Shifting Garbage Collection Overhead to Compile Time," *University of California at Berkeley*.

Bawden, Alan, Richard Greenblatt, John Holloway, Tom Knight, David Moon, and Daniel Weinreb (1977), "LISP Machine Progress Report," Memo No. 444, Artificial Intelligence Laboratory, MIT, Cambridge, Massachusetts. Also in *Artificial Intelligence: An MIT Perspective*, Volume 2, edited by Patrick H. Winston and Richard H. Brown, 1979.

Berkeley, E. C. and Daniel G. Bobrow (editors) (1964), *The Programming Language* LISP: *Its Operation and Applications*, Information International Incorporated, Cambridge, Massachusetts. Also, Second Edition, The MIT Press, Cambridge, Massachusetts.

Berliner, Hans J. (1979), "The B* Tree-search Algorithm: A Best-first Proof Procedure," *Artificial Intelligence*, Vol. 12, No. 1.

Black, F. (1964), "A Deductive Question-Answering System," Ph. D. Thesis, Harvard University. Also in *Semantic Information Processing*, edited by Marvin Minsky, 1968.

Blair, Fred W. (1979), "LISP/370 Concepts and Facilities," Report RC 7771, IBM Research Center, Yorktown Heights, New York.

Blair, Fred W. and R. D. Jenks (1970), "LPL—LISP Programming Language," Report RC 3062, IBM Research Center, Yorktown Heights, New York.

Bobrow, Daniel G. (1962), "A Question-Answerer for Algebra Word Problems," Memo No. 45, Artificial Intelligence Project, Computation Center and Research Laboratory of Electronics, MIT, Cambridge, Massachusetts.

Bobrow, Daniel G. (1963), "METEOR: A LISP Interpreter for String Transformations," Memo No. 51, Artificial Intelligence Project, Computation Center and Research Laboratory of Electronics, MIT, Cambridge, Massachusetts.

Bobrow, Daniel G. (1964), "Natural Language Input for a Computer Problem-Solving System," Memo No. 66, Artificial Intelligence Project, Computation Center and Research Laboratory of Electronics, MIT, Cambridge, Massachusetts, 1964. Also in *Semantic Information Processing*, edited by Marvin Minsky, 1968.

Bobrow, Daniel G. (1972), "Requirements for Advanced Programming Systems for List Processing," *Communications of the ACM*, Vol. 15, No. 7.

Bobrow, Daniel G. and Douglas W. Clark (1979), "Compact Encoding of List Structure," *ACM TOPLAS*, Vol. 1, No. 2.

Bobrow, Daniel G., and Bruce Fraser (1969), *Proceedings of the 1st International Joint Conference on Artificial Intelligence*, Washington, D. C.

Bobrow, Daniel G. and D. Murphy (1967), "The Structure of a LISP System Using Two-level Storage," *Communications of the ACM*, Vol. 10, No. 3.

Bobrow, Daniel G. and Bertram Raphael (1964), "A Comparison of List-Processing Languages," *Communications of the ACM*, Vol. 7, No. 4.

Bobrow, Daniel G. and Bertram Raphael (1974), "New Programming Languages for Artificial Intelligence Research," *ACM Computing Surveys*, Vol. 6, No. 3.

Bobrow, Daniel G. and Ben Wegbreit (1973), "A Model and Stack Implementation of Multiple Environments," *Communications of the ACM*, Vol. 16, No. 10.

Bobrow, R. J., R. R. Burton, J. M. Jacobs, and D. Lewis (1973), "UCI LISP Manual," Technical Report 21, Department of Information and Computer Science, University of California, Irvine, California.

Bobrow, Daniel G., L. D. Darley, D. L. Murphy, C. Solomon, and W. Teitelman (1966), "The BBN-LISP System," AFCRL-66-180, Bolt, Beranek and Newman, Cambridge, Massachusetts.

Bolce, J. F. (1968), "LISP/360: A Description of the University of Waterloo LISP 1.5 Interpreter for the IBM/360," University of Waterloo, Waterloo, Ontario, Canada.

Boley, Harold (1983), "Artificial Intelligence Languages and Machines," *Technology and Science of Informatics*, Vol. 2, No. 3.

Boyer, R. S. and J. S. Moore (1975), "Proving Theorems about LISP Functions," *Journal of the ACM*, Vol. 22, No. 1.

Braffort, P. and D. Hirshberg (editors) (1963), *Computer Programming and Formal Systems*, North Holland, Amsterdam.

Briabrin, Victor (1978), "How to Run and Maintain DILOS-INTERLISP System," *Linkoeping University*.

Brown, W. S. (1971), "On Euclid's Algorithm and the Computation of Polynomial Greatest Common Divisors," *Journal of the ACM*, Vol. 18, No. 4.

Burge, W. H. (1975), *Recursive Programming Techniques*, Addison-Wesley, Reading, Massachusetts.

Burington, R. S. (1973), *Handbook of Mathematical Tables and Formulas*, Fifth Edition, McGraw-Hill, New York.

Burke, Glenn S., George J. Carrette and Christopher R. Eliot (1984), *NIL Reference Manual*, MIT/LCS/TR-311, Laboratory for Computer Science, MIT, Cambridge, Massachusetts.

Burstall R. M. and John Darlington (1977), "A Transformation System for Developing Recursive Programs," *Journal of the ACM*, Vol. 24, No. 1.

Burstall R. M., J. S. Collins, and R. J. Popplestone (1971), *Programming in POP-2*, Edinburgh University Press, Edinburgh, Scotland.

Cannon, Howard I. (1982), "A Non-hierarchical Approach to Object-oriented Programming," unpublished paper, Artificial Intelligence Laboratory, MIT, Cambridge, Massachusetts.

Chailloux, Jérôme (1983), "Le LISP de l'INRIA," Institut National De Recherche en Informatique et en Automatique, Domaine de Voluceau, Rocquencourt, 78153 Le Chesmay Cédex.

Chaitin, Gregory J. (1976), "A Toy Version of the LISP Language," Report RC 5924, IBM Research Center, Yorktown Heights, New York.

Charniak, Eugene (1978), "On the Use of Framed Knowledge in Language Comprehension," *Artificial Intelligence*, Vol. 11, No. 3.

Charniak, Eugene, C. Riesbeck and D. McDermott (1980), *Artificial Intelligence Programming*, Lawrence Erlbaum Associates, Hillsdale, New Jersey.

Cheney, C. J. (1970), "A Nonrecursive List Compacting Algorithm," *Communications of the ACM*, Vol. 13, No. 11.

Chikayama, Takashi (1981), "UTI LISP Manual," METR 81-6, Department of Mathematical Engineering and Instrumentation Physics, University of Tokyo.

Church, Alonzo (1941), "The Calculi of Lambda-Conversion," *Annals of Mathematical Studies*, Vol. 6, Princeton University Press, Princeton, New Jersey. Reprinted by Klaus Reprints, New York, 1965.

Ciccarelli, E. (1977), "An Introduction to the EMACS Editor," Memo No. 447, Artificial Intelligence Laboratory, MIT, Cambridge, Massachusetts.

Cody, William J. Jr. and William Waite (1980), *Software Manual for Elementary Functions*, Prentice Hall, Englewood Cliffs, N.J.

Cohen, Donald and G. Levitt (1965), "Sort by Exchange on Linked Lists," Report P-3122, Rand Corporation.

Conrad, William R. (1974), "A Compactifying Garbage Collector for ECL's Non-Homogeneous Heap," Technical Report 2-74, Center for Research in Computing Technology, Harvard University, Cambridge, Massachusetts.

Conte, S. D. and C. de Boor (1972), *Elementary Numerical Analysis—an Algorithmic Approach*, Second Edition, McGraw-Hill, New York.

Darlington, J. and R. M. Burstall (1976), "A System Which Automatically Improves Programs," *Acta Informatica*, Vol. 6.

Davenport, James H. and Richard D. Jenks (1980), "MODLISP," Mathematics Sciences Department, IBM Thomas J. Watson Research Center, Yorktown Heights, New York.

Davis, C. F. and D. E. Knuth (1970), "Number Representations and Dragon Curves," *Journal of Recreational Mathematics*, Vol. 3.

Davis, Randall and Douglas Lenat (1980), *Knowledge-Based Systems in Artificial Intelligence*, McGraw-Hill, New York.

Deutsch, E. S. (1972), "Thinning Algorithms on Rectangular, Hexagonal, and Triangular Arrays," *Communications of the ACM*, Vol. 15, No. 9.

Deutsch, L. P. (1973), "A LISP Machine With Very Compact Programs," *Proceedings of the 3rd International Joint Conference on Artificial Intelligence*, Stanford, California. Available from Stanford Research Institute, Menlo Park, California.

Deutsch, L. P. and E. Berkeley (1964), "The LISP Implementation for the PDP-1 Computer," in *The Programming Language* LISP: *Its Operation and Applications*, edited by E. C. Berkeley and Daniel G. Bobrow.

Deutsch, Peter L. and Daniel G. Bobrow (1976), "An Efficient, Incremental, Automatic Garbarge Collector," *Communication of the ACM*, Vol. 19, No. 9.

Deutsch, L. P. and B. W. Lampson (1965), "Reference Manual, 930 LISP," University of California, Berkeley, California.

Deutsch, P. (1979), "Experience with a Microprogrammed INTERLISP System," *IEEE Transactions on Computers*, Vol. C-28, No. 10.

Dijkstra, Edsger W. (1978), "On-the-Fly Garbage Collection: An Exercise in Cooperation," *Communications of the ACM*, Vol. 21, No. 11.

Dodd, George, D., and Lothar Rossol (editors) (1979), *Computer Vision and Sensor-Based Robotics*, Plenum Press, New York.

Duda, Richard O. and Peter E. Hart (1973), *Pattern Recognition and Scene Analysis*, Wiley, New York.

Duda, Richard O., Peter E. Hart, P. Barrett, John G. Gaschnig, K. Konolige, R. Reboh, and J. Slocum (1978), "Development of the Prospector Consultation System for Mineral Exploration," Final Report, SRI Projects 5821 and 6415, SRI International, Menlo Park, California.

Eastlake, Donald (1972), "ITS Status Report," Memo No. 238, Artificial Intelligence Laboratory, MIT, Cambridge, Massachusetts.

Eastlake, Donald, Richard Greenblatt, Jack Holloway, Thomas Knight and Stewart Nelson (1969), "ITS 1.5 Reference Manual," Memo No. 161A, Artificial Intelligence Laboratory, MIT, Cambridge, Massachusetts.

Ejiri, Masakazu, Tekeshi Uno, Michihiro Mese, and Sadahiro Ikeda (1973), "A Process for Detecting Defects in Complicated Patterns," *Computer Graphics and Image Processing*, Vol. 2, No. 3.

Ernst, G. W. and A. Newell (1967), *Generality and GPS*, Carnegie Institue of Technology, Pittsburgh, Pennsylvania.

Ernst, G. W. and A. Newell (1969), *GPS: A Case Study in Generality and Problem Solving*, Academic Press, New York.

Evans, A. Jr. (1972), "The Lambda Calculus and its Relation to Programming Languages," *Proceedings of the ACM Annual Conference*, Association for Computing Machinery, New York.

Feigenbaum, Edward, A. and Julian Feldman (editors) (1963), *Computers and Thought*, McGraw-Hill, New York.

Fenichel, R. R. (1970), "A New List-Tracing Algorithm," Technical Report 19, Project MAC, MIT, Cambridge, Massachusetts.

Fenichel, R. R. and J. C. Yochelson (1969), "A LISP Garbage-Collector for Virtual-Memory Computer Systems," *Communications of the ACM*, Vol. 12, No. 11.

Firestone, Roger M. (1980), "An Experimental LISP System for the Sperry Univac 1100 Series," *ACM SIGPLAN Notices*, Vol. 15, No. 1.

Foderaro, John K., Keith L. Skowler and Kevin Layer (1983), *The* FRANZ LISP *Manual*, University of California, Berkeley, California.

Forsythe, G. E., M. A. Malcomb and C. B. Moler (1977), *Computer Methods for Mathematical Computations*, Second Edition, Addison-Wesley, Reading, Massachusetts.

Foster, J. M. (1967), *List Processing*, American Elsevier, New York.

Friedman, D. (1974), *The Little* LISP*er*, Science Research Associates, Palo Alto, California.

Gabriel, P. Richard, Rodney Brooks and Guy L. Steele (1982), "S-1B COMMON LISP Implementation," *Proceedings of the 1982 ACM Symposium on* LISP *And Functional Programming*, Association for Computing Machinery, New York.

Galley, S. W. and Greg Pfister (1975), *The MDL Language*, Document SYS.11.01, Laboratory for Computer Science, MIT, Cambridge, Massachusetts.

Gelernter, H. (1963), "Realization of a Geometry Theorem-Proving Machine," *Proceedings Internatinal Conference Information Processing* UNESCO House, Paris, Also in *Computers and Thought*, edited by Edward A. Feigenbaum and Julian Feldman.

Gilmore, P. C. (1963), "An Abstract Computer with a LISP-like Machine Language without a LABEL Operator," in *Computer Programming and Formal Systems*, edited by P. Braffort and D. Hirshberg.

Gleason, Gerald J. and Gerald J. Agin (1979), "A Modular Vision System for Sensor-Controlled Manipulation and Inspection," Technical Note 178, Artificial Intelligence Center, SRI International, Menlo Park, California.

Golay, M. J. E. (1969), "Hexagonal Parallel Pattern Transformations," *IEEE Transactions on Computers*, Vol. C-18, No. 8.

Goldberg, Adele and David Robson (1984), *Smalltalk-80; the Language and its Implementation*, Addison-Wesley, Reading, Massachusetts.

Golden, Jeffrey P. (1970), "A User's Guide to the A.I. Group LISCOM LISP Compiler: Interim Report," Memo No. 210, Artificial Intelligence Laboratory, MIT, Cambridge, Massachusetts.

Goldstein, Ira P. (1973), "Pretty-Printing—Converting List to Linear Structure,", Memo No. 279, Artificial Intelligence Laboratory, MIT, Cambridge, Massachusetts.

Goto, Eiichi (1974), "Monocopy and Associative Algorithms in an Extended LISP," Information Science Laboratory, University of Tokyo.

Gray, S. B. (1971), "Local Properties of Binary Images in Two Dimensions," *IEEE Transactions on Computers*, Vol. C-20, No. 5.

Greenberg, Bernard S. (1976), *Notes on the Programming Language* LISP, Student Information Processing Board, MIT, Cambridge, Massachusetts.

Greenberg, Bernard S. (1977), "The Multics MACLISP Compiler—the Basic Hackery," unpublished paper, Honeywell Information Systems, Cambridge, Massachusetts.

Greenberg, Bernard S. (1980), "MULTICS EMACS—An Experiment in Computer Interaction," Honeywell Information Systems, Inc. Cambridge Information Systems, Laboratory, MSD/LIS.

Greenberg, Bernard S. and Katie Kissel (1979), *EMACS Text Editor Users' Guide*, Order Number CH27-00, Honeywell, Waltham, Massachusetts.

Greenblatt, Richard (1974), "The LISP Machine," Working Paper 79, Artificial Intelligence Laboratory, MIT, Cambridge, Massachusetts.

Greenblatt, Richard, Tom Knight, John Holloway, and David Moon (1979), *The* LISP *Machine*, Artificial Intelligence Laboratory, MIT, Cambridge, Massachusetts.

Greussay, P. (1976), "Iterative Interpretation of Tail-Recursive LISP Procedures," Technical Report 20-76, University of Vincennes, Paris.

Griss, M. L. and B. Morrison (1981), "The Portable Standard LISP Users Manual," Utah Symbolic Computations Group TR-10, Department of Computer Science, University of Utah, Salt Lake City.

Griss, M. L. and M. R. Swanson (1977), "MBALM/1700: A Microprogrammed LISP-Machine for the Burroughs B1726," UUCS-77-109, Computer Science, Utah University, Salt Lake City, Utah.

Guzman, Adolfo. (1981), "A Heterarchical Multi-Microprocessor LISP Machine," *IEEE Computer Workshop on Architecture for Pattern Analysis and Image Database Management*, Technical Report AHR-81-17, Hot Springs, Virginia.

Hamming, R. W. (1962), *Numerical Methods for Scientists and Engineers*, McGraw-Hill, New York.

Hansen, Wilfred J. (1969), "Compact List Representation: Definition, Garbage Collection, and System Implementation," *Communications of the ACM*, Vol. 12, No. 9.

Harris, Larry R. (1977), "A High Performance Natural Language Processor for Data Base Query," *ACM SIGART Newsletter 61*.

Harrison, M. C. (1970), "BALM—An Extensible List-Processing Language," *Proceedings of AFIPS Spring Joint Computer Conference*, Vol. 36.

Hart, T. P. (1963), "MACRO Definitions in LISP," Memo No. 57, Artificial Intelligence Project, Computation Center and Research Laboratory of Electronics, MIT, Cambridge, Massachusetts.

Hart, T. P. and T. G. Evans (1964), "Notes on Implementing LISP for the M-460 Computer," *The Programming Language* LISP*: Its Operation and Applications*, edited by E. C. Berkeley and Daniel G. Bobrow.

Hayashi, H., A. Hattori and H. Akimoto (1983), "ALPHA: A High-Performance LISP Machine," Fujitsu Laboratories Limited, Kawasaki, Japan.

Hayes-Roth, Frederick, and Victor R. Lesser (1977), "Focus of Attention in the Hearsay-II Speech Understanding System," *Proceedings of the 5th International Joint Conference on Artificial Intelligence*, Cambridge, Massachusetts, 22–25 August 1977. Available from Department of Computer Science, Carnegie-Mellon University, Pittsburgh, Pennsylvania.

Hearn, Anthony C. (1966), "Standard LISP," *ACM SIGPLAN Notices*, Vol. 4, No. 9.

Hearn, Anthony C. (1969), "Standard LISP," AIM-90, Artificial Intelligence Project, Stanford University, Stanford, California.

Hearn, Anthony C. and Arthur C. Norman (1979), "A One-pass Prettyprinter," *ACM SIGPLAN Notices*, Vol. 14, No. 12.

Henderson, Peter (1980), *Functional Programming*, Prentice Hall, Englewood Cliffs, New Jersey.

Hendrix, Gary G., Earl D. Sacerdoti, Daniel Sagalowicz, and Jonathan Slocum (1978), "Developing a Natural Language Interface to Complex Data," *ACM Transactions on Database Systems*, Vol. 3, No. 2.

Hewitt, Carl (1977), "Viewing Control Structures as Patterns of Passing Messages," *Artificial Intelligence*, Vol. 8, No. 3.

Hildebrand, F. B. (1974), *Introduction to Numerical Analysis*, Second Edition, McGraw-Hill, New York.

Hoare, C. A. R. (1962), "Quicksort," *Computer Journal*, Vol. 5, No. 1.

Holland, S. W., L. Rossol and M. R. Ward (1979), "CONSIGHT-1: A Vision-controlled Robot System for Transferring Parts From Belt Conveyors," in *Computer Vision and Sensor-Based Robotics*, edited by George D. Dodd and Lothar Rossol.

Holloway, Jack, Guy L. Steele Jr., Gerald J. Sussman and Alan Bell (1980), "The SCHEME-79 Chip," A.I. Memo. 559 Artificial Intelligence Laboratory, MIT, Cambridge, Massachusetts.

Hood, Robert and Robert Melville (1980), "Real Time Queue Operations in Pure LISP," TR80-433, Department of Computer Science, Cornell University, Ithaca, New York.

Horn, Berthold K. P. (1970), "Shape-from-Shading: A Method for Obtaining the Shape of a Smooth Opaque Object from One View," Technical Report 79, Project MAC, MIT, Cambridge, Massachusetts, November 1970. Also in *The Psychology of Computer Vision*, edited by Patrick H. Winston, April 1975.

Horn, Berthold K. P. (1974), "Determining Lightness from an Image," *Computer Graphics and Image Processing*, Vol. 3, No. 1.

Horn, Berthold K. P. (1977), "Understanding Image Intensities," *Artificial Intelligence*, Vol. 8, No. 2.

Horn, Berthold K. P. (1979), "Artificial Intelligence and the Science of Image Understanding," in *Computer Vision and Sensor-Based Robots*, edited by George G. Dodd and Lothar Rossol.

Horn, Berthold K. P. (1980), "Derivation of Invariant Scene Characteristics from Images," *Proceedings of AFIPS National Computer Conference*, Vol. 49.

Horn, Berthold K. P. (1985), *Robot Vision*, MIT Press, Cambridge, Massachusetts, to be published.

Horn, Berthold K. P. and Patrick H. Winston (1975), "Personal Computers," *Datamation*.

Hu, T. C. (1982), *Combinatorial Algorithms*, Addison-Wesley, Reading, Massachusetts.

IBM (1978), "LISP/370 Program Description/Operations Manual," Program Number: 5796-PKL, Manual Number: SN20-2076-0, IBM, Detroit.

Iyanga, S. and Y. Kawada (editors) (1977), *Encyclopedic Dictionary of Mathematics*, (English tranlation), The MIT Press, Cambridge, Massachusetts.

Johnson, E. S. and R. F. Rosin (1965), "SLIP: A Symmetric List Processor," Computing Center, Yale University, New Haven, Connecticut.

Kameny, S. L. (1965), LISP *1.5 Reference Manual for Q-32*, TM-2337/101/0, System Development Corporation.

Kaplan, R. M. (1972), "Augmented Transition Networks as Psychological Models of Sentence Comprehension," *Artificial Intelligence*, Vol. 3, No. 4.

Kent, J. (1966), "LISP 3600: User's Manual," Norwegian Defense Research Establishment, Catalogue L2 KCIN LISP, Kjeller, Norway.

Kleene, Stephen Cole (1950), *Introduction to Metamathematics*, Von Nostrand, Princeton.

Klimbie, J. W. and K. I. Koffeman (editors) (1974), *Data Base Management*, North-Holland, Amsterdam.

Knight, Thomas (1974), "The CONS Microprocessor," Working Paper 80, Artificial Intelligence Laboratory, MIT, Cambridge, Massachusetts.

Knight, Tom, David Moon, John Holloway, and Guy Steele (1979), "CADR," Memo No. 528, Artificial Intelligence Laboratory, MIT, Cambridge, Massachusetts.

Knuth, Donald E. (1968), *The Art of Computer Programming, Volume 1, Fundamental Algorithms*, Addison-Wesley, Reading, Massachusetts.

Knuth, Donald E. (1975), *The Art of Computer Programming, Volume 3, Sorting and Searching*, Second Printing, Addison-Wesley, Reading, Massachusetts.

Knuth, Donald E. (1981), *The Art of Computer Programming, Volume 2, Seminumerical Algorithms*, Second Edition, Addison-Wesley, Reading, Massachusetts.

Knuth, Donald E. (1974), "Structured Programming with GO-TO Statements," *ACM Computing Surveys*, Vol. 6, No. 4.

Knuth, D. E. and J. C. Knuth (1973), "Mathematics and Art: The Dragon Curve in Ceramic Tile," *Journal of Recreational Mathematics*, Vol. 6, No. 3.

Kornfeld, William A. (1979), "Pattern-directed Invocation Languages," *Byte*, Vol. 4, No. 8.

Kung, H. T. and S. W. Song (1977), "An Efficient, Parallel Garbage Collection System and its Correctness Proof," Department of Computer Science, Carnegie-Mellon University, Pittsburgh, Pennsylvania.

Landin, P. (1964), "The Mechanical Evaluation of Expressions," *Computer Journal*, Vol. 6, No. 4.

Landin, P. (1965), "A Correspondence between ALGOL 60 and Church's LAMBDA-Notation," *Communications of the ACM*, Vol. 8, No. 2, February 1965, and Vol. 8, No. 3.

LeFaivre, R. (1978), *Rutgers/UCI* LISP *Manual*, Rutgers University.

Levialdi, S. (1972), "On Shrinking Binary Picture Patterns," *Communications of the ACM*, Vol. 15, No. 1.

Lieberman, Henry and Carl Hewitt (1980), "A Real Time Garbage Collector that can Recover Temporary Storage Quickly," Memo No. 569, Artificial Intelligence Laboratory, MIT, Cambridge, Massachusetts.

Lozano-Perez, Tomas (1980), "Spatial Planning with Polyhedral Model," Ph. D. Thesis, MIT, Cambridge, Massachusetts.

Maekilae, K. and T. Risch (1975), "PL360-LISP—A LISP 1.5 Interpreter Written in PL360," FOA Report C10041-M3(E5), Foervarets Forskninganstalt, Stockholm, Sweden.

Marti, J., A. C. Hearn, M. L. Griss, and C. Griss (1979), "Standard LISP Report," *ACM SIGPLAN Notices*, Vol. 14, No. 10.

Martin, William A. and Tim Hart (1963), "Revised User's Version, Time Sharing LISP for CTSS," Memo No. 67, Artificial Intelligence Project, Computation Center and Research Laboratory of Electronics, MIT, Cambridge, Massachusetts.

Maurer, W. D. (1973), *A Programmer's Introduction to* LISP, American Elsevier, New York.

McCarthy, John (1958), "Programs with Common Sense," *Mechanisation of Thought Processes, Proceedings Symposium National Physics Laboratory*, Vol. 1, Her Majesty's Stationary Office, London. Also in *Semantic Information Processing*, edited by Marvin Minsky, 1968.

McCarthy, John (1960), "Recursive Functions of Symbolic Expressions and their Computation by Machine, Part I," *Communications of the ACM*, Vol. 3, No. 4.

McCarthy, John (1961a), "A Basis for a Mathematical Theory of Computation," *Proceedings of the Western Joint Computer Conference*, Vol. 19. Corrected version in *Computer Programming and Formal Systems*, edited by P. Braffort and D. Hirshberg, 1963.

McCarthy, John (1961b), "Computer Program for Checking Mathematical Proofs," *Proceedings of the American Mathematical Society on Recursive Function Theory*, New York.

McCarthy, John (1978), "A Micromanual for LISP—Not the Whole Truth," *ACM SIGPLAN Notices*, Vol. 13, No. 8.

McCarthy, John (1978), "History of LISP," *ACM SIGPLAN Notices*, Vol. 13, No. 8. Also in *History of Programming Languages* Wexelblat, Richard L. (Ed.), Academic Press, New York.

McCarthy, John, P. W. Abrahams, D. J. Edwards, T. P. Hart, and M. I. Levin (1962), LISP *1.5 Programmer's Manual*, The MIT Press, Cambridge, Massachusetts.

McCarthy, John, R. Brayton, D. Edwards, P. A. Fox, L. Hodes, D. Luckham, K. Maling, D. Park, and S. Russell (1960), "LISP 1 Programmer's Manual," Artifical Intelligence Group, Computation Center and Research Laboratory of Electronics, MIT, Cambridge, Massachusetts.

McDermott, Drew V. (1975), "Very Large PLANNER-type Data Bases," Memo No. 339, Artificial Intelligence Laboratory, MIT, Cambridge, Massachusetts.

McDermott, Drew V. and Gerald Jay Sussman (1974), "The CONNIVER Reference Manual," Memo No. 259A, Artificial Intelligence Laboratory, MIT, Cambridge, Massachusetts.

Meehan, J. R. (1979), *New UCI* LISP *Manual*, Lawrence Erlbaum Associates, Hillsdale, New Jersey.

Metcalfe, R. M. and D. R. Boggs (1976), "ETHERNET: Distributed Packet Switching for Local Computer Networks," *Communications of the ACM*, Vol. 19, No. 7.

Mikelsons, Martin. (1981), "Prettyprinting in an Interactive Programming Environment," RC 8756 (37459), Computer Science Department, IBM Thomas J. Watson Research Center, Yorktown Heights, New York, March 1981.

Minsky, Marvin (editor) (1968), *Semantic Information Processing*, The MIT Press, Cambridge, Massachusetts.

Minsky, Marvin (1963), "A LISP Garbage Collector Using Serial Secondary Storage," Memo No. 58, Artificial Intelligence Laboratory, MIT, Cambridge, Massachusetts.

Minsky, Marvin (1975), "A Framework for Representing Knowledge," in *The Psychology of Computer Vision*, edited by Patrick H. Winston.

Minsky, Marvin and Seymour Papert (1969), *An Introduction to Computational Geometry*, The MIT Press, Cambridge, Massachusetts.

Moon, David (1974), MACLISP *Reference Manual, Version 0*, Laboratory for Computer Science, MIT, Cambridge, Massachusetts. Parts 1,2, and 3 revised 1978.

Moon, David A. (1981), "Operating the LISP Machine," Working Paper 209, Artificial Intelligence Laboratory, MIT, Cambridge, Massachusetts.

Moon, David, Richard Stallman and Daniel Weinreb (1983), LISP *Machine Manual*, Fifth Edition, MIT Artificial Intelligence Laboratory.

Moore, J. Strother (1976), "The INTERLISP Virtual Machine Specification," CSL-76-6, Xerox Corporation, Palo Alto Research Center, Palo Alto, California.

Morris, F. Lockwood (1978), "A Time- and Space-Efficient Garbage Compaction Algorithm," *Communications of the ACM*, Vol. 21, No. 8.

Morris, James H. (1981), "Real Programming in Functional Languages," CSL-81-11, Xerox Palo Alto Research Center, Palo Alto, California.

Moses, Joel (1970), "The Function of FUNCTION in LISP," *ACM SIGSAM Bulletin*.

Moses, Joel and Robert Fenichel (1966), "A New Version of CTSS LISP," Memo No. 93, Artifical Intelligence Group, Computation Center and Research Laboratory of Electronics, MIT, Cambridge, Massachusetts.

Nagy, George (1969), "Feature Extraction on Binary Patterns," *IEEE Transactions on Systems Science and Cybernetics*, Vol. SSC-5, No. 4.

Newell, Allen (editor) (1961), *Information Processing Language V Manual*, Prentice Hall, Englewood Cliffs, New Jersey.

Newell, Allen and Herbert A. Simon (1972), *Human Problem Solving*, Prentice Hall, Englewood Cliffs, New Jersey.

Nilsson, Nils J. (1980), *Principles of Artificial Intelligence*, Tioga Publishing Company, Palo Alto, California.

Nordstroem, Mats, Erik Sandewall, and Diz Breslow (1975), "LISP F1: A FORTRAN Implementation of LISP 1.5," Department of Computer Science, Uppsala University. Uppsala, Sweden.

Norman, Eric (1978), LISP *Reference Manual for the UNIVAC 1108*, Computing Center, University of Wisconsin.

Novak, Gordon S. Jr. (1982), "GLISP Users' Manual," Report No. STAN-CS-82-895, Department of Computer Science, Stanford University, Stanford, California.

Oppen, Derek C. (1979), "Pretty Printing," STAN-CS-79-770, Department of Computer Science, Stanford University, Stanford, California.

Organick, E. I., A. I. Forsythe, and R. D. Plummer (1978), *Programming Language Structures*, Chapter 7, Academic Press, New York.

Osman, E. (1971), "DDT Reference Manual," Memo No. 147A, Artificial Intelligence Laboratory, MIT, Cambridge, Massachusetts.

Pitman, Kent M. (1983), *The Revised* MACLISP *Manual*, MIT/LCS/TR-295, Laboratory for Computer Science, MIT, Cambridge, Massachusetts.

Pitman, Kent M. (1980) , "Special Forms in LISP," *Conference Record of the 1980* LISP *Conference*, Stanford University.

Postma, Stefan Willem (1979), "A Critical Evaluation of the Programming Language LISP with Suggestions for Possible Improvements," M. Sc. Dissertation, Computer Science, Randse Afrikaanse Universiteit, Johannesburg.

Pratt, T. W. (1975), *Programming Languages: Design and Implementation*, Chapters 7 and 14, Prentice Hall, Englewood Cliffs, New Jersey.

Pratt, Vaughan R. (1976), "CGOL—An Alternative External Respresentation for LISP Users," Working Paper 121, Artificial Intelligence Laboratory, MIT, Cambridge, Massachusetts.

Pratt, Vaughan R. (1979), "A Mathematician's View of LISP," *Byte*, Vol. 4, No. 8.

Preston, K. (1971), "Feature Extraction by Golay Hexagonal Pattern Transforms," *IEEE Transaction on Computers*, Vol. C-20, No. 9.

Quam, L. and W. Diffie (1972), *Stanford* LISP *1.6 Manual*, Operating Note 28.7, Artificial Intelligence Laboratory, Stanford University, Stanford, California.

Ramshaw, Lyle (1983), "Deftly Replacing GO-TO Statements with EXITs," CSL-83-10, Xerox Palo Alto Reserach Center, Palo Alto, California.

Reboh, R. and Earl Sacerdoti (1973), "A Preliminary QLISP Manual," Technical Note 81, Artificial Intelligence Center, Stanford Research Institute, Menlo Park, California.

Reddy, Raj (1976), "Speech Recognition by Machine: a Review" *Proceedings of the IEEE*, Vol. 64, No. 4.

Rees, Jonathan A. and Norman I. Adams IV (1982), "T: a Dialect of LISP, or, Lambda: the Ultimate Software Tool," *Proceedings of the 1982 ACM Symposium on* LISP *and Functional Programming*, Association for Computing Machinery, New York.

Rees, Jonathan A., Norman I. Adams and James R. Meehan (1984), *The T Manual*, Fourth Edition, Computer Science Department, Yale University, New Haven Connecticut.

Ribbens, D. (1970), *Programmation Non Numerique*, LISP *1.5*, Dunod, Paris.

Roberts, R. Bruce and Ira P. Goldstein (1977a), "The FRL Primer," Memo No. 408, Artificial Intelligence Laboratory, MIT, Cambridge, Massachusetts.

Roberts, R. Bruce and Ira P. Goldstein (1977b), "The FRL Manual," Memo No. 409, Artificial Intelligence Laboratory, MIT, Cambridge, Massachusetts.

Rogers, Hartley, Jr. (1967), *Theory of Recursive Functions and Effective Computability*, McGraw-Hill, New York.

Rulifson, J. F., J. A. Derksen, and R. J. Waldinger (1972), "QA4: A Procedural Calculus for Intuitive Reasoning," Technical Note 73, Artificial Intelligence Center, Stanford Research Institute, Menlo Park, California.

Sacerdoti, Earl D. (1976), "QLISP—A Language for the Interactive Development of Complex Systems," *Proceedings of AFIPS National Computer Conference.*

Samuel, A. L. (1959), "Some Studies in Machine Learning Using the Game of Checkers," *IBM Journal of Research and Development*, Vol. 3, Also in *Computers and Thought*, edited by Edward A. Feigenbaum and Julian Feldman, 1963.

Samson, Peter (1966), "PDP-6 LISP," Memo No. 98, Artifical Intelligence Group, Computation Center and Research Laboratory of Electronics, MIT, Cambridge, Massachusetts.

Sandewall, Erik (1971), "A Proposed Solution to the FUNARG Problem," *ACM SIGSAM Bulletin*, Vol. 17.

Sandewall, Erik (1975), "Ideas About Management of LISP Data Bases," *Advance Papers of the 4th International Conference on Artificial Intelligence*, Artificial Intelligence Laboratory, MIT, Cambridge, Massachusetts.

Sandewall, Erik (1978), "Programming in the Interactive Environment: The LISP Experience," *ACM Computing Surveys*, Vol. 10, No. 1.

Saunders, Robert A. (1964), "The LISP System for the Q-32 Computer," in *The Programming Language* LISP: *Its Operation and Applications*, edited by E. C. Berkeley and Daniel G. Bobrow.

Schank, Roger C., and Robert P. Abelson (1977), *Scripts, Plans, Goals, and Understanding*, Lawrence Erlbaum Associates, Hillsdale, New Jersey, distributed by Halstead Press, a division of John Wiley, New York.

Schorr, H. and W. M. Waite (1967), "An Efficient Machine-Independent Procedure for Garbage Collection in Various List Structures," *Communications of the ACM*, Vol. 10, No. 8,

Sedgewick, Robert (1983), *Algorithms*, Addison-Wesley.

Shannon, C. E. (1950), "Programming a Computer for Playing Chess," *Philosophical Magazine*. Series 7, Vol. 41.

Shapiro, Stuart C. (1979), *Techniques of Artificial Intelligence*, Van Nostrand, New York.

Siklóssy, Laurent (1976), *Let's Talk* LISP, Prentice-Hall, Englewood Cliffs, New Jersey.

Siklóssy, Laurent, A. Rich, and V. Marinov (1973), "Breadth-first Search: Some Surprising Results," *Artificial Intelligence*, Vol. 4, No. 1.

Siemens (Company) (1976), "Siemens INTERLISP 4004 Users Manual," Siemens Datenverarbeitung, Munich, Germany.

Smith, David C. (1970), "MLISP," AIM-135, Artificial Intelligence Project, Stanford University, Stanford, California.

Smith, David C. and H. J. Enea (1973), "MLISP2," AIM-195, Artificial Intelligence Project, Stanford University, Stanford, California.

Stanford University (Sponsor) (1980), *Conference Record of the 1980* LISP *Conference*, Stanford University, Stanford, California.

Stallman, Richard, M. (1979), "EMACS—The Extensible, Customizable, Self-Documenting Display Editor," Memo No. 519, Artificial Intelligence Laboratory, MIT, Cambridge, Massachusetts.

Steele, Guy L. Jr. (1984), COMMON LISP *Reference, Manual*, Digital Press, Bedford, Massachusetts.

Steele, Guy Lewis, Jr. (1975), "Multiprocessing Compactifying Garbage Collection," *Communications of the ACM*, Vol. 18, No. 9. ;September 1975.

Steele, Guy Lewis, Jr. (1976), "LAMBDA—The Ultimate Imperative," Memo No. 353, Artificial Intelligence Laboratory, MIT, Cambridge, Massachusetts.

Steele, Guy Lewis, Jr. (1977a), "Data Representation in LISP," Memo No. 420, Artificial Intelligence Laboratory, MIT, Cambridge, Massachusetts. Also in *Proceedings of the MACSYMA User's Conference*, NASA, Berkeley, California, 1977.

Steele, Guy Lewis, Jr. (1977b), "Fast Arithmetic in MACLISP," Memo No. 421, Artificial Intelligence Laboratory, MIT, Cambridge, Massachusetts. Also in *Proceedings of the MACSYMA User's Conference*, NASA, Berkeley, California, 1977.

Steele, Guy Lewis, Jr. (1977c), "Debunking the 'Expensive Procedure Call' Myth," *Proceedings ACM National Conference*, Seattle, Washington, 1977. Revised as Memo No. 443, Artificial Intelligence Laboratory, MIT, Cambridge, Massachusetts.

Steele, Guy Lewis, Jr. (1979), "Compiler Optimization Based on Viewing LAMBDA as RENAME plus GOTO," *Artificial Intelligence: An MIT Perspective*, Volume 2, edited by Patrick H. Winston and Richard H. Brown.

Steele, Guy L, Jr. (1981), *Spice* LISP *Reference Manual*, Department of Computer Science, Carnegie Mellon University, Pittsburgh.

Steele, Guy Lewis, Jr. and Gerald Jay Sussman (1978a), "The Revised Report on SCHEME: A Dialect of LISP," Memo No. 452, Artificial Intelligence Laboratory, MIT, Cambridge, Massachusetts.

Steele, Guy Lewis, Jr. and Gerald Jay Sussman (1978b), "The Art of the Interpreter, or, The Modularity Complex," Memo No. 453, Artificial Intelligence Laboratory, MIT, Cambridge, Massachusetts.

Steele, Guy Lewis, Jr. and Gerald Jay Sussman (1979), "Design of LISP-Based Processors," Memo No. 514, Artificial Intelligence Laboratory, MIT, Cambridge, Massachusetts.

Steele, Guy L. Jr. and Gerald Jay Sussman (1980), "The Dream of a Lifetime: A Lazy Variable Extent Mechanism,' *Conference Record of the 1980* LISP *Conference*, Computer Science Department, Stanford University.

Stefanelli, R. and A. Rosenfeld (1971), "Some Parallel Thinning Algorithms for Digital Pictures," *Journal of the ACM*, Vol. 18, No. 2.

Sussman, Gerald Jay and Drew V. McDermott (1972), "Why Conniving is Better than Planning," Memo No. 255A, Artificial Intelligence Laboratory, MIT, Cambridge, Massachusetts.

Sussman, Gerald Jay and Guy Lewis Steele, Jr. (1975), "SCHEME: An Interpreter for Extended Lambda Calculus," Memo No. 349, Artificial Intelligence Laboratory, MIT, Cambridge, Massachusetts.

Sussman, Gerald, Terry Winograd, and Eugene Charniak (1971), "MICRO-PLANNER Reference Manual," Memo No. 203A, The Artificial Intelligence Laboratory, MIT, Cambridge, Massachusetts.

Teitelman, Warren (1974), INTERLISP *Reference Manual*, Xerox Corporation, Palo Alto Research Center, Palo Alto, California, and Bolt, Beranek and Newman, Cambridge, Massachusetts, revised 1978.

Thacker, C. P., E. M. McCreight, B. W. Lampson, R. F. Sproull, and D. R. Boggs (1979), "ALTO: A Personal Computer," CSL-79-11 Xerox Corporation, Palo Alto Research Center, Palo Alto, California.

Touretzky, David S. (1984), LISP—*A Gentle Introduction to Symbolic Computation*, Harper and Row, New York.

Touretzky, David S. (1979), *A Summary of* MACLISP *Functions and Flags*, Department of Computer Science, Carnegie-Mellon University, Pittsburgh, Pennsylvania.

University of Texas at Austin (Sponsor) (1984), *Proceedings of the 1984 conference on* LISP *And Functional Programming*.

Ullman, J. D. (1982), *Principles of Data Base Systems*, Computer Science Press, Rockville, Maryland.

Urmi, Jaak (1976a), "INTERLISP/370 Reference Manual," Department of Mathematics, Linkoeping University, Linkoeping, Sweden.

414

Urmi, Jaak (1976b), "A Shallow Binding Scheme for Fast Environment Changing in a 'Spaghetti Stack' LISP System," Report 76-18, Department of Mathematics, Linkoeping University, Linkoeping, Sweden.

Urmi, Jaak (1978), "A Machine Independent LISP Compiler and its Implications for Ideal Hardware," Report 78-22, Department of Mathematics, Linkoeping University, Linkoeping, Sweden.

Wadler, Philip L. (1976), "Analysis of an Algorithm for Real Time Garbage Collection," *Communications of the ACM*, Vol. 19, No. 9.

Wang, Hao (1960), "Towards Mechanical Mathematics," *IBM Journal of Research and Development*, Vol. 4.

Warren, David H. D. and Luis Pereira (1977), "PROLOG: The Language and Its Implementation Compared with LISP," *Proceedings of the Symposium on Artificial Intelligence and Programming Languages*, Rochester, New York, *ACM SIGPLAN Notices* Vol. 12, No. 8.

Waterman D. A. and F. Hayes-Roth (editors) (1978), *Pattern Directed Inference Systems*, Academic Press, New York.

Waters, Richard C. (1981), "GPRINT: A LISP Pretty Printer Providing Extensive User Format-Control, Mechanisms," AI Memo No. 611, Artificial Intelligence Laboratory, MIT, Cambridge, Massachusetts.

Waters, Richard C. (1982), "LetS: An Expressional Loop Notation," AI Memo No. 680, Artificial Intelligence Laboratory, MIT, Cambridge, Massachusetts. Revised February 1983.

Weinreb, Daniel L. (1979), "A Real-Time Display-Oriented Editor for the LISP Machine," S. B. Thesis, Department of Electrical Engineering and Computer Science, MIT.

Weinreb, Daniel and David Moon (1978), LISP *Machine Manual*, Artificial Intelligence Laboratory, MIT, Cambridge, Massachusetts. Revised 1979 and 1981.

Weissman, Clark (1967), LISP *1.5 Primer*, Dickenson Publishing Company, Belmont, California.

Weizenbaum, Joseph (1962), "Knotted List Structures," *Communications of the ACM*, Vol. 5, No. 3.

Weizenbaum, Joseph (1963), "Symmetric List Processor," *Communications of the ACM*, Vol. 6, No. 10.

Weizenbaum, Joseph (1965), "ELIZA—A Computer Program for the Study of Natural Language Communication between Man and Machine," *Communications of the ACM*, Vol. 9, No. 1.

White, John L. (1967), "PDP-6 LISP (LISP 1.6) Revised," Memo No. 116A, Artificial Intelligence Laboratory, MIT, Cambridge, Massachusetts.

White, John L. (1970), "An Interim LISP User's Guide," Memo No. 190, Artificial Intelligence Laboratory, MIT, Cambridge, Massachusetts.

White, Jon L. (1977a), "LISP: Program is Data—A Historical Perspective on MACLISP," *Proceedings of the MACSYMA User's Conference*, NASA, Berkeley, California.

White, Jon L. (1977b), "LISP: Data is Program—A Tutorial in LISP," *Proceedings of the MACSYMA User's Conference*, NASA, Berkeley, California.

White, Jon L. (1978), "LISP/370: A Short Technical Description of the Implementation," *ACM SIGSAM Bulletin*, Vol. 48.

White, Jon L. (1979), "NIL—A Perspective," *Proceedings of the MACSYMA User's Conference*, Washington, D. C., 20 June 1979. Available from Laboratory for Computer Science, MIT, Cambridge, Massachusetts.

Wiederhold, Gio (1981), "Binding in Information Processing," Report No. STAN-CS-81-851, Department of Computer Science, Stanford University, Stanford, California.

Wilber, B. M. (1976), "A QLISP Reference Manual," Technical Note 118, Artificial Intelligence Center, Stanford Research Institute, Menlo Park, California.

Winograd, Terry (1972), *Understanding Natural Language*, Academic Press, New York.

Winston, Patrick Henry (1984), *Artificial Intelligence (Second Edition)* Addison-Wesley, Reading, Massachusetts.

Winston, Patrick Henry (editor) (1975), *The Psychology of Computer Vision*, McGraw-Hill, New York.

Winston, Patrick H. and Richard H. Brown (editors) (1979a), *Artificial Intelligence: An MIT Perspective*, Volume 1, (Expert Problem Solving, Natural Language Understanding and Intelligent Computer Coaches, Representation and Learning), The MIT Press, Cambridge, Massachusetts.

Winston, Patrick H. and Richard H. Brown (editors) (1979b), *Artificial Intelligence: An MIT Perspective*, Volume 2, (Understanding Vision, Manipulation and Productivity Technology, Computer Design and Symbol Manipulation), The MIT Press, Cambridge, Massachusetts.

Winston, Patrick H. and Karen A. Prendergast (editors) (1984), *The AI Business: The Commercial Uses of Artificial Intelligence* The MIT Press, Cambridge, Massachusetts.

Wood, Richard J. (1980), "The Direct LISP Approach To Function Environment Manipulation," TR-907, Department of Computer Science, University of Maryland, College Park, Maryland.

Woods, William A. and R. M. Kaplan, and B. Nash-Webber (1972), "The Lunar Sciences Natural Language Information System: Final Report," BBN Report No. 2378, Bolt Beranek and Newman, Cambridge, Massachusetts.

Yasuhara, A. (1971), *Recursive Function Theory and Logic*, Academic Press, New York.

Appendix:
Using Common Lisp

The way one interacts with COMMON LISP at a terminal depends to some extend on the version. We therefore must be content to give a short scenario to give the feel of what can happen.

The following would be typical for users doing ordinary things using GOLDEN COMMON LISP, a version of COMMON LISP developed by Gold Hill Computers, of Cambridge, Massachusetts. Text typed by the system is in uppercase, while the users input is shown in lowercase so that you may distinguish between them easily.

Note that *control characters* are typed by holding down the control key while pressing another key. If the character z is typed in this fashion, this will be shown as ⟨CONTROL Z⟩. Similarly, the return key is shown as ⟨NL⟩, for new line, while the escape and alternate-mode keys are indicated using ⟨ESC⟩ and ⟨ALT⟩.

```
A>                                      ;PC DOS operating system prompt.
GCLISP                                  ;User has placed GCLISP diskette in drive
                                        ;A — user then types GCLISP to load the
                                        ;GCLISP interpreter.
Golden Common LISP (U), Version x.xx    ;GCLISP responds,
(c) Copyright Gold Hill Computers, Inc 1984   ;lights blink, disks
                                        ;whirl, more messages.
```

417

```
*
(+ 3.14 2.71)
5.85
```
;Finally, GCLISP types its own prompt.
;The user requests a simple addition.
;GCLISP responds with the result.

```
(car '(simple list))
SIMPLE
```
;The user tries another example.
;GCLISP evaluates the expression and prints
;the result.

```
(ed "demo")
```
;More serious work requires that a file be
;created containing a few procedures and
;some data for them to work on. This is
;conveniently done using the system's
;editing program. (ed "demo") calls up the GMACS
;editing program, asking it to get the file
;named DEMO.LSP — if there is no such
;file, one will be created.

```
(defun sum-squares (a b)
  (+ (* a a (* b b))))
<alt>z
```
;User enters a procedure definition.

;Typing ⟨alt⟩z causes the definition form to
;be evaluated. This works with any
;top-level form lying against the left margin,
;not just definitions. The cursor may be
;anywhere inside the form.

```
SUM-SQUARES
```
;Value is typed in GMACS's echo window.

```
<control z>
```
;When defining new procedures and editing
;old ones is complete, it is time to go
;back to GCLISP. A new version of DEMO.LSP is
;written on mass storage.

```
*
(sum-squares 2 3)
36
```
;GCLISP's prompt character again.
;User tries the new procedure.
;GCLISP returns result – not what the
;user expected!
;Bugs will occur. TRACE and BREAK will
;probably help find them. But for now,
;let us suppose we want to just go back to
;the editor.

```
<control e>
<control s> (* a a
<esc>
```
;One way to get back to the editor.
;The user searches for place to fix the problem.
;The user stops search, enters missing
;parenthesis, and deletes the extra one at
;the end of the definition.

```
<alt>z
SUM-SQUARES
<control z>
```
;The new definition is evaluated as before.
;Value is typed in GMACS's echo window as before.
;Now return to GCLISP from editor.

```
*                            ; GCLISP's prompt character.
(sum-squares 2 3)            ; The user tries the new version.
13                           ; GCLISP returns result.
                             ; The GCLISP ... GMACS ... GCLISP ... loop
                             ; will no doubt be repeated many times.
                             ; Finally, it is time to get off the system.

(exit)                       ; The way to get back to the PC DOS
                             ; operating system.  Once this is done,
                             ; there is no going back to the same
                             ; GCLISP.  (To get to PC DOS, with a view
                             ; toward getting back into the same GCLISP,
                             ; (dos) is typed instead.  Later, EXIT is
                             ; typed to PC DOS to get back to GCLISP.)
<click>                      ; User turns off power.
```

Next time the system is used, the user can type the following to GCLISP so that GCLISP will read all of the definitions previously prepared in the file DEMO.LSP:

```
(load "demo")
```

References   GMACS is a version of the powerful EMACS editor developed by Richard M. Stallman [1979]. See also Ciccarelli [1977] and Stallman [1979]. Interestingly, GMACS is written in GCLISP. For a discussion of an earlier version of EMACS written in MACLISP for the Honeywell MULTICS system, see Greenberg [1979].

Index of
Defined Procedures

Index of
Common Lisp Primitives
Used in this Book

427

General Index